THE
CAPTAINS

THE
CAPTAINS

THE STORY BEHIND AUSTRALIA'S
SECOND MOST IMPORTANT JOB

MALCOLM KNOX

hardie grant books

MELBOURNE · LONDON

Published in 2010 by Hardie Grant Books

Hardie Grant Books (Australia)
85 High Street
Prahran, Victoria 3181
www.hardiegrant.com.au

Hardie Grant Books (UK)
Dudley House, North Suite
34–35 Southampton Street
London WC2E 7HF
www.hardiegrant.co.uk

Front cover images, from left: Don Bradman (Rick Smith private collection);
baggy green, Adam Gilchrist with Shane Warne, Greg Chappell (Getty Images).
Back cover images, from left: Hugh Trumble (MCC Library Collection);
Steve Waugh, Ricky Ponting (Getty Images); Richie Benaud (Rick Smith
private collection).
Inside back flap, from left: Kim Hughes, Herbie Collins, Monty Noble
(Rick Smith private collection).
Images in the text: pp. 85 (Bob Thomas), 163, 173, 200, 223, 254 (L. Blandford),
259, 270, 277, 285, 286 (Dennis Oulds), 291 (Dennis Oulds), 308, 321, 328, 335
(Adrian Murrell), 342, 352 (Adrian Murrell/Allsport), 360 (Adrian Murrell),
390 (Mark Dadswell), 395, 407 (Shaun Botterill), 411 (Shaun Botterill/
Allsport), 414 (Greg Wood/AFP), 416 (Hamish Blair) courtesy Getty Images;
p. 79 courtesy State Library Victoria; pp. 96 and 111 courtesy Melbourne
Cricket Club Library Collection; p. 348 courtesy Newspix. All other images
kindly provided by Rick Smith from his private collection.

National Library of Australia Cataloguing-in-Publication Data:

Knox, Malcolm, 1966–
The captains/Malcolm Knox.
ISBN 9781740669566 (hbk.)
Includes index.
Cricket captain—Australia.
Cricket players—Australia.
Cricket—Australia—History.
796.3580994

Cover design by Luisa Laino Design
Text design by Design by Committee/Patrick Cannon
Typeset in Minion 10.5/14pt by Cannon Typesetting
Printed in Australia by Ligare Printing and Publishing
10 9 8 7 6 5 4 3 2 1

CONTENTS

INTRODUCTION

I N 1975, Ray Robinson published the definitive portrait of Australia's cricket captains. *On Top Down Under*, updated by Gideon Haigh in 1996, set the standard in the art of portraiture of that club of what was then 39 men.

This book is not an attempt to reheat Robinson, which has in any case been done by Roland Perry, in his 2000 book *Captain Australia*. For the early captains, reliance on similar sources has produced similar profiles; with recent captains, an over-abundance of sources has, paradoxically, resulted in a similar narrowing effect.

Though it was peerless in composing pictures by the use of the telling anecdote, what *On Top Down Under* never did was knit the pen-portraits into a narrative of the game in Australia. Robinson depicted each captain in isolation, with the significant events of cricket history as their background. There is also, in Robinson's approach, an unavoidable chronological toing and froing. When Bill Lawry was sacked in 1971, the book left the cliffhanger behind, to tell the life story of Barry Jarman – Lawry's replacement for one Test in 1968 – before returning to 1971 and Ian Chappell. The format forced the story to a jarring halt.

The object of this book is to put the story of Australian cricket first, and tell it through the prism of the captaincy: the office and the men who have occupied it. This approach tries to enjoin Sir Donald Bradman's words that the captains, like all players, have been stewards of a greater history.

Some vital themes will carry us through the 42 Australian Test captains from Dave Gregory to Ricky Ponting. One is the strain the job has placed on each incumbent, capping their terms, with rare exceptions, at a four-year maximum. Another theme is player power, and the captains' evolution from managing director and shop steward through to their opposite, and back again. Yet another theme is the perception of the office's prestige, which has ebbed and flowed with that of the game itself.

In 1975, there was no need for Ray Robinson to further define our *Test* cricket captains. Since then, Australia has had a number of captains in the limited-overs game and in minor tour matches, who have not also been Test cricket captains. Shane Warne, Michael Clarke, David Boon, Geoff Marsh and Ian Healy are among those to have led Australia in the past 20 years, but are not a part of this study because they have not led in Test cricket.

Of the 42 Test captains, 14 have been stand-ins, deputising for the permanent captain or standing in when he was unavailable. Tom Horan, Hugh Massie, George Giffen, Hugh Trumble, Syd Gregory, Warren Bardsley, Victor Richardson, Bill Brown, Arthur Morris, Ray Lindwall, Neil Harvey, Brian Booth, Barry Jarman and Adam Gilchrist occupy some place in this narrative, but more for their influence as players than as Australian captains. They did, however, hold the post for as few Tests as Jarman's one or as many as Syd Gregory's six, so the narrative would be incomplete without them.

E.L. Doctorow's 2005 novel *The March* describes, unforgettably, the union army in the last days of the American Civil War. Doctorow embodies the marching thousands as a single organism, like a snake, which is nonetheless comprised of individual, wilful, rebellious, unpredictable parts. It moves through space and time as a singular thing, yet within it is the disparate chaos of human wills in conflict.

The Australian cricket team can be seen the same way: a single organism snaking through our history, personifying the hopes and disappointments of a nation in constant metamorphosis. Within that organism are the bowlers, batsmen and wicketkeepers, each with their own hopes and fears and performances both great and ignominious. The most singular individual in that body is the captain, himself a human being full of ideals and frustrations and quarrels and triumphs, yet also the steward of an office, which would become, in many eyes, the second most important in the land.

1

DAVE GREGORY'S DREAM

IF the DNA of a species is contained in its seed, the first holder of the Australian Test cricket captaincy promised a fiery future.

Photographs of David William Gregory are as was typical in the dawn of photography, deceptive. In team arrangements he sits centrally, behind an authoritative black beard. His dark glare and calm forehead befit 'Handsome Dave', the born leader if only for the look in his eye.

But Gregory was a man of many parts and contradictions. An accused chucker, he had given up bowling amid a ferocious inter-colonial dispute. As a batsman his record was modest, even by the era's unprepossessing standards. Yet despite this, and not being captain of either New South Wales nor Victoria, his acclamation as leader of a combined colonial team was one of the few matters on which the members agreed.

Gregory was a self-made man, an orphan's son who rose to the top of the New South Wales public service, yet his petulance also sparked the worst riot in Australia's cricket history. He had the financial brilliance to form the first white cricket tour of England as a joint stock company and make a splendid profit, but sullied that tour with over-aggression, unwillingness to accept umpires' decisions, and a brawl with the hosts over one of his players. At the same time,

Handsome, headstrong Dave

he raised a large donation for the surviving English relatives of those lost in a shipping disaster.

So, Gregory: no great player, but respected by his team; a financial genius but no diplomat; a lion-heart and a spoilt brat; a colonial establishment figure but a rebel. The captaincy, since Gregory, has asked its occupants to assume many personalities. Gregory took this demand to an extreme.

Before 1877 three England teams had toured Australia to play cricket. The second of those, led by George Parr in 1863–64, included William Caffyn, a high-octane all-rounder known, depending on the mood, as either 'The Surrey Pet' or 'Terrible Billy'. On that undefeated tour, the lob bowler 'Spider' Tinley took 171 wickets at 3.65, and the Englishmen's superior skills were acknowledged by the colonials. The humble directors of the Melbourne Cricket Club offered to make Caffyn the highest-paid English cricketer, with an annual wage of £300, as long as he stayed to teach the locals how to overcome the degradations of their convict origins.

In New South Wales, Caffyn came across an ambitious round-arm bowler who made his first-class debut before 5,000 spectators on The Domain, behind Sydney's Parliament House, on Boxing Day 1866. David Gregory was a 22-year-old mathematics whiz who worked for the audit office and played for the National Cricket Club. His father Edward had been brought to Sydney as a nine-year-old on the *Broxbornebury* in 1814, to be dumped in the Male Orphanage with two brothers when their mother died and their father returned to England. Having been trained as a shoemaker, Edward Gregory became a schoolteacher, and married Mary Anne Smith, the daughter of a Melbourne parliamentarian and grand-daughter of a woman transported for forgery.

As well as teaching, Edward played cricket for the Australian Club at Sydney's Hyde Park, in single-wicket matches with under-arm bowling. To interest spectators, betting was encouraged: the first Marylebone Cricket Club laws, published by the *Sydney Morning Herald* in 1842, included guidelines for wagering.

Edward and Mary Anne had 13 children, including four sons who would play cricket for New South Wales. David, born while Edward was posted to a school at Fairy Meadow, near Wollongong, was the second.

David attended the St James Model School in central Sydney and excelled in mathematics, receiving a medal from Governor Sir William Denison. The governor urged the children to aim for a good job, and the story, possibly apocryphal, goes that when Gregory graduated some years later he walked to Government House and told Denison: 'I've come about that job.'

He was working in the auditor-general's office by the time his club bowling, against teams mustered from hotels and the military garrison, earnt him selection for NSW in the biggest game on the calendar, its Christmas fixture against Victoria.

Gregory slung his round-armers unchanged, taking 3/36 off 24.1 four-ball overs as Victoria tumbled for 74. He was bowled for a duck in NSW's 145, but sent down another 23 overs, taking 4/31 as Victoria fell for 58. In 16 years of top cricket, Gregory would never improve on those figures.

Tutored by Caffyn, Gregory continued as a bowler until 1871 when, promoted from the tail to the top against Victoria, he scored 51. The same summer, he and his brothers Ned and Charles delighted 5,000 at The Domain by beating a powerful Victorian trio of John Conway, Tom Wills and Sam Cosstick in a single-wicket game. It was a good thing that Dave's batting was improving because his bowling days were numbered.

For the March 1872 intercolonial match in Melbourne, Victoria's captain was Wills, redoubtable cricketer, founder of Australian Rules football and future suicide. In his first and second overs, Wills was no-balled for throwing by NSW's travelling umpire Sellars. In the transitional years between underarm and round-arm to overarm, bowling actions were wildly diverse, Gregory's among them. When Sellars did not no-ball him the Victorians cried foul, the *Argus* protesting that Gregory was allowed 'to indulge in a deliberate throw' while Wills, their champion, was rubbed out.

Nine months later the Victorians got square. Representing a NSW/Tasmania/South Australia selection at the Melbourne Cricket Ground, Gregory was twice called and stopped after three overs. Rarely would he bowl, or throw, again. The next year, even when offered the NSW captaincy, he boycotted the Melbourne match 'for work reasons'.

While assertive and intelligent, Gregory did not lead NSW. Opening bowler Edwin 'Ted' Evans was captain while Gregory developed his batting. At the Albert Ground in Waterloo, Gregory played three notable innings: a top score of 32 against W.G. Grace's Englishmen in 1874, 74 in a win over Victoria in February 1876, and a draw-saving 53 not out against James Lillywhite's Englishmen in January 1877.

Lillywhite's group, lacking Grace, had been a popular outfit in odds games against Victoria and NSW. John Conway, Victoria's manager, persuaded Lillywhite to stage an 11-a-side match in Melbourne against a combined colonial team. In the meantime, the English sailed to New Zealand, with mixed results. They won games but wicketkeeper Ted Pooley ended up in jail in Christchurch. In a pub on the eve of a match between the English XI and a local XVIII, Pooley declared he could predict each batsman's score. He offered a shilling for each wrong answer but would take a pound for each correct one. Four locals took him on, but were slow to realise that Pooley's potential liability, 58 shillings, was less than £3. They understood his scam when he forecast that every man would make a duck. The hapless locals realised that only three batsmen out of 58 in the match would have to make ducks before Pooley started making a profit.

There were 11 ducks, putting Pooley £8 ahead. The New Zealanders refused to pay, and in the ensuing brawl Pooley hit a retired surveyor named Ralph Donkin over the head with a walking stick.

With their wicketkeeper facing charges in a Christchurch lock-up, Lillywhite's men arrived in Melbourne after a rough Tasman crossing on 14 March 1877. Conway had scheduled the fixture against an 'All Australia' or 'United Australia' XI for the next day.

The English weren't the only ones in disarray. Victoria and NSW had agreed that five from the former and six from the latter would comprise the team. But Ted Evans would not travel, and Victorian speedster Frank Allan attended an agricultural show in his home town of Warrnambool, where his family were local notables. The non-appearance of Evans and Allan says less about their motivations than it does about the status of the fixture. At the time, the Melbourne game was seen as more of a 'pick-up' match than the most important cricket encounter yet played.

In Evans's absence, Gregory was elected captain. He selected a team from what was left, choosing his elder brother Ned as a batsman and Victoria's Jack Blackham ahead of Sydney's Billy Murdoch as wicketkeeper, which left Gregory in an almighty row with his best remaining bowler, Fred Spofforth.

Spofforth was the most dangerous bowler in the colonies. Tall and stringy, he had a sharp faster ball but a more lethal slower one, deceiving batsmen with an unchanged action. His nickname, 'The Demon', while yet to be coined, referred more to his pugnacity and his Mephistophelean appearance than his pace. In Gregory, though, the irresistible force was meeting an immovable object.

Two weeks before the game, Spofforth wrote a 'Dear Dave' letter. He attacked Blackham's wicketkeeping and said only Murdoch could handle him; more hurtfully, he wrote: 'How you ever came to select Ned I cannot understand.' Ned Gregory, six years Dave's senior, had been a better player than his younger brother in the 1860s, but by 1877 he was 38, and reaching his end. Spofforth also resented the number of Victorian bowlers, and concluded: 'I beg to withdraw my name from the number as I cannot stand Melbourne doing all the work.'

Spofforth had picked the wrong man to threaten. Gregory sided with the Victorians, retaining Blackham as keeper and a southern-dominated bowling attack. It was a rare act of cross-border loyalty, a sign that Gregory deserved his election as a unifier.

What can he have seen in Blackham, 22, who had only played thrice for Victoria in three years? Conway, Blackham's club captain, had a lot to do with it. Born in North Fitzroy, Blackham played his first cricket as a batsman for Carlton. His father, Frederick, was a newsagent who turned out for the Press Cricket Club, and in one game, fielding against a country team, young Jack began to edge closer and closer to the wicketkeeper until he took over. Seeing Blackham keeping with bare hands, Conway recruited him to South Melbourne.

Blackham had caught Gregory's eye in 1874, dismissing four New South Welshmen and scoring 32 against Spofforth. What was most discussed about Blackham's wicketkeeping was his discarding the long-stop, a position thought as essential as slip or cover. A South Melbourne teammate had complained of having nothing to do at long-stop behind Blackham, and moved to fine leg. 'At first,' Blackham said modestly, 'I did not like being deprived of the safety valve.' But soon he would be roaring at captains who positioned a long-stop: 'Get him somewhere he can be of use!'

By 1877, Blackham grew the spade-shaped beard from behind which he glowers in team photos. He seems, more than any other of those characters, to have grown into his very name.

Nobody knew, of course, what Test cricket was to become. The match itself would only be recognised as cricket's first Test, and Gregory thereby Australia's first captain, in 1894, when London's *Cricket* magazine published Clarence P. Moody's 'Record of Test Matches', initialising the 1877 Test.

The game started at 1.05 pm on 15 March, Alfred Shaw bowling a round-arm dot ball to the NSW right-hander Charles Bannerman. A new five-bay grandstand held 1,500 spectators. The stand was reversible, to take advantage of football matches in Yarra Park behind. Bannerman cut the second ball for a single, and the crowd grew to 4,500 in three-and-a-half hours during the afternoon.

Nat Thompson, bowled for 1, was the first Test dismissal a few minutes into the match. Bannerman was joined by Tom Horan, a young Irish-born Victorian who was only in the team because of the quota of five southerners. Stumpy and thickset with a plate-like face and broad jowls, Horan was a capable batting all-rounder, preferring fast bowling and hitting through the on-side. In the manly fashion of the time, he batted without protective gloves. Having played with Blackham at Bell Street School in Fitzroy,

Horan represented Carlton and South Melbourne before switching to East Melbourne. As a teenager in 1874–75, he had played in the inaugural match between Victoria and an 18-man South Australia at Adelaide, taking 11/29 in the visitors' second innings.

Seeing how cleanly Bannerman was hitting the ball, Horan defended his end. In a stand of 38, Horan played anchor, a role he repeated with a top-scoring and ultimately decisive 20 in Australia's second innings.

Bannerman made plenty more; his 165 out of Australia's 245 would be the difference between the teams and more. His innings comprised 67.3 per cent of his side's total, still a Test record. By the time he retired hurt with a split finger, he had seen off all his partners including number four Dave Gregory, who by one run avoided the distinction of the first Test duck. That honour went to Ned, who would not play another Test. Ned's legacy would, however, arguably outlast Dave's. As curator of the Sydney Cricket Ground in 1894, Ned would lay the first Bulli soil wicket, and devise the first Australian-style scoreboard, which would supersede the more cryptic English model. Ned, who lived in a cottage between the Number One and Number Two SCGs, would also sire four state representatives: daughters Nellie and Lily, plus Charles, and Syd, who would play 58 Tests and be Australian captain himself.

Australia's 45-run win in the first Test match was widely attributed to Bannerman's batting and Gregory's selections. Gregory had insisted on 18-year-old Sydney University law student Tom Garrett, who made a crucial unbeaten 18. Praised for sticking with Blackham, Gregory also gave most of the bowling to the Victorians. The Victorian Cricketers' Association, thrilled by the receipts (about 20,000 watched the four days), struck gold medals for the winning Australians, moulding a larger one for the captain.

Gregory would be, uniquely, Australian captain for his entire Test career. The Second Test, 12 days after the first, was a benefit game for Lillywhite's team, which won by four wickets, notwithstanding Gregory's stubborn 43 as an opener in the second innings.

This time, Spofforth and Murdoch played. That Spofforth had stood up for Murdoch to his own detriment said much for the fast bowler's loyalty, for Murdoch, 22, was not even the regular keeper for NSW. Nor had his batting shown much. In three first-class matches since 1875, Murdoch's scores, down the order, were 6, 9, 1, 7 not out and 5. On this flimsy basis, the greatest bowler of the era had sacrificed his place in the inaugural Test match.

But Spofforth knew Murdoch from boyhood scraps on an earthen pitch at King Street, Balmain. The Tasmanian Murdochs had moved to Sydney via Victoria, where Billy had been born in 1854. Billy's elder brother Gilbert was also a handy cricketer who played with Spofforth in Balmain, and the three would join the Albert Club. The chunky Billy Murdoch showed his nimbleness keeping to Spofforth, and was soon racking up scores at the top of the order.

Following Gilbert into Sydney University's law faculty, Murdoch struggled to carry his club form into intercolonial matches. Spofforth was such a champion of his, however, that in March 1877 Gregory relented and picked them as a job lot for the Second Test. But Blackham would keep, and bat, ahead of the callow Murdoch.

Batting number eight, Murdoch couldn't have had a worse start to his Test career. He was run out for 3, then Blackham defied commonsense by standing up to the stumps to Spofforth. With feet spread wide and ramrod back, the 5'9" (175.2cm) Blackham was taking Spofforth's zingers with leather gloves so weak they would barely blunt the jolt of an orange pip and so stiff that they had to be moistened with water. Not only was Blackham's keeping watertight to Spofforth's bowling, but he pulled off a feat of magical skill and courage. In Spofforth's third over, a ball to Alfred Shaw spat off a length. Shaw fell forward, his back foot lifting. Blackham gloved the ball and whisked off the bails. Not only was Spofforth convinced, but Murdoch too.

The calamity of Murdoch's first Test was completed with 8 in a second-innings collapse. His first-class average was now 6.50 from seven innings. Spofforth's four wickets also had limited impact. By April 1877, the two men from Balmain were wondering if they had any place in this kind of cricket.

A year after the successful Melbourne Tests, Lillywhite invited Conway and Gregory to bring a team to England. Apart from the Aboriginal side of 1868, no Australian team had gone 'home' to play the counties. Lillywhite promised to help fund the tour and arrange fixtures.

Conway and Gregory met resistance from the NSW and Victorian associations, who objected to players organising tours. Conway and Gregory decided to go anyway under the sky blue and white colours of Conway's East Melbourne Cricket Club.

Gregory's financial acumen was his power base. He set up the tour as a joint-stock company, the 12 selected players contributing £50 apiece as shareholders. They drew lots to decide who would be porter each day, lugging the canvas kit bag they called The Caravan, on which Gregory had the words 'Australian Eleven' painted.

The 1878 tour was Gregory's greatest cricketing achievement, and arguably the most important tour undertaken by an Australian team. Yet they would play no 'Tests'. They left as a team of six New South Welshmen – including Spofforth and Murdoch – four Victorians, one Tasmanian (George Bailey), and Conway as manager. They played some fundraisers before setting sail. Gregory, known to enjoy a drink and a smoke but seldom seen affected, omitted Tom Kendall from the squad because of the player's reputation for drunkenness. The 12th man, Billy Midwinter, who had represented Australia in the 1877 series but was now turning out for Grace's Gloucestershire, would join them on arrival. Or at least, that was the plan.

One of Gregory's priorities was to soften intercolonial animosity. When the team's ship hit a storm off New Zealand, Spofforth asked Charles Bannerman, an expert swimmer, what he would do if the ship was wrecked.

'First,' Bannerman said, 'I'll save [his brother] Alick, then Murdoch, then yourself.'

'Well, what about the Victorians?' Spofforth asked.

'Let them drown!' was Bannerman's reply. Interesting, too, that Bannerman had not offered to save his captain, even though Gregory was from NSW.

The 1878 team, in East Melbourne colours, with four of the first five captains: Murdoch, Horan and Gregory alongside each other in the middle row, and Blackham by Gregory's left knee.

The outward journey took 46 days, by steamship to San Francisco, train to New York and steamship to Liverpool. Gregory's men arrived to cancelled county fixtures and no match against a combined England. After a heavy loss in icy winds to Nottinghamshire, the tour was almost stillborn. 'What on earth induced us to come all this way?' Gregory asked his teammates. 'I wish I was back in Sydney with the sun on my back.' The sole highlight was Horan's bowling. He would take only eight wickets on the tour, but in the atrocious defeat at Nottingham, when the Australians were scrambling for their silk shirts and thickest sweaters, he took five wickets for 30.

Horan was an interesting tourist. Working for the Victorian audit office at the time – which met with Gregory's approval – he was a certain selection. Horan was young, almost baby-faced, with his smooth upper lip among all those moustaches and commanding beards. Horan was a contented, robust, humorous touring mate, and under his pen name of 'Felix' his missives for *The Australasian* would shape opinions back home.

The watershed came early in the tour, on 27 May 1878 at Lord's. The Marylebone Cricket Club had eventually offered a team led by Dr Grace, the dominant all-rounder and personality of cricket for 40 years, who was commissioned to put the Australians firmly in their place. When Grace opened the batting, Gregory showed his knack for placing a field. Grace usually got going by whipping the ball square through the on-side. Ostentatiously, Gregory left square leg vacant for the first ball, bowled by Frank Allan. Grace chipped it to the rope. Then, as Allan ran in again, Gregory sneaked Midwinter into the area. Allan bowled a similar ball and Grace repeated the shot – this time straight into Midwinter's hands.

In front of 4,742 spectators, including some 400 Australians, a historic day unfolded. The MCC were 2/25 when Gregory made his only bowling change: Spofforth for Allan. In his first 23 balls at Lord's, Spofforth took six wickets for 4 runs including a hat-trick. The MCC's innings, begun at 12.03 pm, was over by 1.08, and amounted to 33 runs. Spofforth and Victoria's Harry Boyle were mobbed as they returned to the pavilion.

By 3.57 pm, the English were back in, Australia having fallen for 41. Spofforth took his second new ball in four hours. He went straight through Grace, and the English, described by *Wisden* as 'one of the strongest MCC elevens that had ever played for the famous old club', lasted 69 balls and made 19 runs. By 6.20 pm the game, which had been expected to go for three days, was over, Australia winning by nine wickets.

The significance of the win did not escape the press on either side of the world. In *The Australasian,* Horan (who had hit the winning runs) said: 'The win over the MCC shows that any fear which may ever have been entertained about the possible physical degeneration of the English race in the bright Australian climate is hitherto wanting in any support of evidence.'

The English *Review of Reviews* commented on the 'unfilial yearning on the part of young Australia to triumphantly thrash the mother country'. It remains scandalous that this history-changing encounter is not recognised as a Test match.

Gregory's tour was ignited by that day, which netted the Australians a gate of £120. His competitive drive overrode his financial one when the MCC offered a rematch the next day. Gregory, who had made one of 16 ducks in the match, demurred, saying his men needed rest. They would have earnt more by playing again, but he could see the longer-term benefit in letting word spread of the Lord's win.

The 1878 team played 41 times. At Clifton they beat Grace's Gloucestershire, previously undefeated on the ground. Playing Surrey at The Oval, they entertained a record crowd of 30,000 which broke through the fences. Unrecognised in April, Gregory's tourists were celebrities by June; when their train came to a station, crowds asked to see Spofforth (who took 357 wickets at 7.49 in England). Some, remembering the 1868 tourists, were astounded that the Australians were white-skinned. Against Elland, Boyle took seven wickets in eight balls. Charles Bannerman regularly showed why his batting was regarded second only to Grace's. *The Times* observed that whereas English teams had used to go to Australia to compete with 11 men against sides of 22, now the balance was reversed, and the Australians were often playing sides of 18 and 22 men.

The 1878 tour, a venture that inspires the imagination like no other, did not just set a course for outstanding cricket. It was one of the signal moments in the transition towards Australian Federation, where a club team had collected cricketers from around the continent who would have liked to call themselves not 'East Melbourne' but 'Australia'. But also, under Gregory's captaincy, the darker side of Australian competitiveness would show itself.

Gregory played 38 of the 41 games, 15 of which are now regarded as first-class, but scored lightly. He was a competitive man who expected much of himself. With each cheap dismissal, he grew querulous. His generalship received steady praise. He pioneered the first slip position for himself and silly mid-on for others, while dispensing with orthodoxies such as long-stop and fly slip. He tailored his field for each batsman and had his fieldsmen move in quickly and throw for run-outs. When returning the ball, the Australians kept it dry, rather than bouncing it in. Gregory was praised by the *London Standard* for trying to get opposition teams out 'and not to prolong innings by a series of useless maiden overs which, while they gratify the bowler's vanity, weary the field and spectators'. The impact on English cricket would be immeasurable, sparking improvements in wickets, bowling (higher arm actions to imitate Spofforth and Boyle), and better payment for professionals. Formerly, composite 'England' sides had toured the counties, but now nothing less than an Australian team would do.

But Gregory was frustrated by his batting failures. His team's onfield behaviour declined. When Lord Hawke called the tour 'the commencement of the modern era of cricket', he meant it in more ways than one. Gregory set an example of complaint, as Chris Harte wrote in the *Penguin History of Australian Cricket*: 'In truth the 1878 Australians were a rough side, rough in their behaviour and rough in their attitudes. They became over-fond of criticising English umpires and … left behind a poor impression.'

Nothing epitomised this as much as the Midwinter Affair.

Midwinter joined Gregory's team for the first nine matches including the famous win at Lord's. As well as being a handy all-rounder, Midwinter was a quarter-mile runner, a rifle shooter and a billiards player. Grace valued him highly, however, and wanted him for Gloucestershire, citing his birth in the county, ignoring the fact that Midwinter had lived in Australia from the age of nine.

On 20 June, Midwinter was practising in the Lord's nets for Australia's 10th game, against Middlesex. Grace's Gloucestershire were at The Oval preparing to play Surrey. Hearing that Midwinter was across town, Grace summoned Conway, who took a carriage to The Oval and told Grace that Midwinter considered himself an Australian. Grace accused Conway of bribing Midwinter. Conway left in high dudgeon in a hansom cab. Grace followed him to Lord's, where there was more arguing, now involving Gregory. Midwinter was by now padded up to open the Australians' batting against Middlesex. Grace burst into the dressing room, wrestled Midwinter into a cab and raced to The Oval. Conway, Gregory and Boyle gave chase in another carriage. Grace, who knew something about bribes, offered Midwinter £10, five times the going rate, to play for Gloucestershire, plus an end-of-season benefit match worth £500. By the time they arrived at The Oval, Midwinter was a Gloucestershire player and Grace called the pursuing Australians 'a damn lot of sneaks'.

Midwinter would later represent England, then again play for Australia. *The Sydney Mail* described him as 'this very slippery cricketer'.

Having secured Midwinter for the rest of the 1878 season, Grace apologised to the Australians for his 'unparliamentary language'. Australia then thrashed Gloucestershire at Bristol by 10 wickets, a game for which Midwinter was 'rested'.

Outwitted, or outbid, by Grace, Gregory's mood swung harder the longer the tour went on. In September, when a steamship collided with the pleasure boat 'Princess Alice' on the Thames and 700 died, Gregory organised a donation of £100. The *Times* farewelled his team as 'hard to beat and impossible to despise. They have accrued the habit of working together, of seconding each other's play.'

But a month later, the ugly side resurfaced. Among homeward fundraisers in North America was a game against Philadelphia at Nicetown, Pennsylvania. Disagreeing with umpiring decisions, Gregory led his men off, disappointing 10,000 spectators. It was only after being told his team's pay cheque would be dishonoured that Gregory changed his mind.

The 15 months of the tour, and its success, only heightened Gregory's feistiness when he got home. His attitude would increasingly prefigure that of his distant successor, Ian Chappell: a tactical innovator on the field, a tough shop steward off it, fortified by the loyalty of his men.

On 30 November 1878 the team arrived to a cheering crowd in Sydney. The joint-stock company yielded £750 per player, a massive profit equal to $36,000 in today's money but enough to buy several houses per man. That sum would generate the biggest controversies in the game for the next 35 years. Not for a century would Australian players touring England get the same pay-off as the teams of 1878 to 1884. Never again, in purchasing power, would Australian cricketers earn as much.

Yet for Gregory it wasn't enough. He pressured the NSW premier, Henry Parkes, to pay him, Garrett and Charles Bannerman their full public-service salaries for the 15 months they had been away. For Gregory, this would come to £400. Parkes refused, but Gregory organised 32 members of parliament, led by Richard Driver, his friend who was president of the NSW Cricket Association, to petition Parkes. Gregory received half of his demand, Bannerman and Garrett nothing: more evidence of Gregory's blend of shop-floor representation and free-market individualism.

Gregory's truculence grew. An English group of mostly amateur players led by Lord Harris had already arrived for a two-Test series. At the Melbourne Cricket Ground, Gregory's Australia won by 10 wickets. A week later Gregory was dropped from the NSW team to play Harris's men, for not explaining a missed practice session.

After 15 months touring, then exhibition matches around Australia, and now Tests against England, without having contributed much as a batsman, Gregory was at boiling point. There was a public outcry at his omission, but it was his behind-the-scenes manoeuvring that earnt him reinstatement for NSW's next match against England in February.

Betting, as has been noted, was an integral part of cricket. Not just match results but individual scores were the subject of gambling, which generated more cash than gate receipts. At the SCG match between England and NSW in February 1879, as was customary, the members' pavilion was well patronised by bookmakers and punters.

England scored 267, then Murdoch carried his bat in a superlative unbeaten 82 in NSW's 177. England travelled with an umpire of their choice, George Coulthard, a Melbourne Cricket Club bowler who would, two years later, play a Test for Australia. Coulthard was unpopular with the New South Welshmen (with their wildlife too, it seemed, as he had been attacked by a shark in Sydney Harbour in 1877). His decisions in the first innings raised Gregory's temper before it erupted in the second, when Coulthard gave Murdoch run-out.

The gamblers and bookmakers led the heckling, crying 'Not out!' as Murdoch left the field. The Englishmen waited for the next batsman. Harris walked to the boundary to ask Gregory what had happened. Gregory strode down to the fence. Harris asked if another batsman was coming out. Gregory replied that no batsman would come until Harris replaced Coulthard.

'On what grounds?' Harris asked.

'General incompetence.'

As the crowd booed, Harris asked his team if they would consent to changing the umpire. They refused. Harris walked back to the fence to tell Gregory, who replied:

'Then the game is at an end.'

Harris went back to the other umpire, who happened to be Edmund Barton, who in 22 years would be the first prime minister of the federated Australian nation. This day he was a cricket umpire who happened to agree with Coulthard on the Murdoch run-out and advised Harris to call Gregory's bluff. If Gregory didn't send a batsman out, Barton said, the match would be England's.

What followed was the most infamous episode in Australian cricket. As the Englishmen tried to leave, several were hit and A.N. Hornby had his shirt torn. Some rioters had allegedly heard an Englishman call them 'sons of convicts'. The English denied it. If it had happened, the reaction seems to validate the description.

Two attempts were made to restart play, without Murdoch, but the crowd rioted again, overcoming a small police squad, and the day was abandoned. After rain on a rest day, Gregory backed down and NSW were swiftly bowled out, losing their last five wickets with the score on 49. The game was England's and the shame was Australia's, the *Sydney Morning Herald* reporting on the 'most disgraceful scene we ever remember to have witnessed on any cricket ground in the metropolis … The English team soon found themselves in the middle of a surging, gesticulating and shouting mob, and one rowdy struck Lord Harris across the body with a stick or whip.' Two thousand participated in the riot. That weekend Ned Kelly's gang raided a bank at Jerilderie, but the front pages were consumed by the cricket.

As for Gregory's role, explanations vary from dire to sinister. His declining sportsmanship, surfacing in England and Philadelphia, escaped any restraint on his home turf. Gregory felt victimised by umpires, and, after so long on the road, was taking a stand. The darker speculation was that he was in league with the gamblers. *The Sydney Mail* said Gregory had been 'coerced by certain persons in the pavilion not to send another man in when Murdoch was given out.' English player Charles Absolom insinuated that Gregory, senior NSWCA officials and the bookmakers were in cahoots.

The incident ended Gregory's Test career. The Second Test was called off, and Harris wrote a letter to the NSWCA stating how 'I implored Gregory as a friend, for the sake of the NSWCA … not to raise the objection, but he refused to take my view'. Although two rioters were charged and prosecuted (by Gregory's friend Richard Driver), the belief grew that they were scapegoats and the person whose obstinacy was most responsible was Dave Gregory.

Gregory was invited to lead the 1880 tour of England but declined. He turned out for NSW until 1882–83, occasionally contributing a score and sometimes even bowling. In 1883 he became Inspector of Public Accounts, and was sole selector for NSW in 1888. As honorary secretary of the NSWCA from 1883 to 1889, he proposed the formation of a unifying Australasian Cricket Council. When Australia was federated in 1901, Gregory declined a knighthood and the position of head of the Commonwealth Treasury. After so many bruising public battles, he had settled into life as a family man, married three times and the father of 16. He walked, fished, played the flute, gardened and bred red setters in the leafy northern Sydney suburb of Turramurra.

Yet there is something still mysterious about Dave Gregory, the natural leader who got himself into so many fights and often behaved like a spoilt child. When he died of heart disease at 74 in 1919, Gregory went out, in Jack Pollard's summation, 'with all his teeth intact, never having worn glasses in his life, carriage upright to the last'. His captaincy's great strengths – his solidity, his decisiveness – became so strong that they turned into its great weaknesses. The first of a kind, Gregory remains the most intriguing of Australia's cricket leaders.

2

KING BILLY

IN 1879, after just three Tests, international cricket was dead. When an Australian team proposed touring England in 1880, Lord Harris refused to play them. Most counties fell into line and only five matches were scheduled.

Gregory's successor would have to be a more emollient figure, a diplomat who could rescue the game.

After his unfortunate first Test in 1877, Billy Murdoch had again relied on Spofforth to get him onto Gregory's 1878 tour. In 25 first-class innings, Murdoch finished fourth in the batting aggregates behind Charles Bannerman, Horan and Spofforth. As wicketkeeper in the Lord's epic, Murdoch managed to stump the last two of Spofforth's hat-trick victims; otherwise his tour was one of development rather than accomplishment.

The investment began to pay off at home. He scored 70 and 49 for NSW against Harris's team, then, a week later, became the first player to carry his bat in Australian first-class cricket with his unbeaten 82. It was his second-innings run-out that sparked the riot.

Murdoch was an innocent bystander, but his life was hardly running smoothly. The law firm he had set up with his brother Gilbert was declared bankrupt with debts of £775, and by the middle of 1879 Billy's only assets were £10 in clothing.

When the 1880 touring team was chosen, this time backed by colonial associations desperate to mend fences with England, Murdoch was not captain. Harry Boyle, the black-bearded 'Very Devil', Spofforth's fast-bowling foil, had the job. But when the SS *Garonne* reached the Suez Canal, a team meeting voted to replace Boyle with Murdoch. Boyle was a determined man and a fearless catcher – he invented silly mid-on, then called 'Boyle's mid-on'. But although he would become a national selector and an influential personality, he did not relish captaincy and gladly handed over to the convivial Murdoch. The team's average age was 24, and Murdoch, at 25, was closer to them than the 32-year-old Boyle.

Boyle thought he was handing over a poisoned chalice. The tourists had to advertise in English newspapers for opponents, and were confined initially to club games. Even a Canadian team was awarded fixtures ahead of Australia. Murdoch proposed an Australia–England game at Lord's to reprise the wonderful 1878 match, proceeds going to a cricketers' benevolent fund, but not even the support of Grace, with whom Murdoch enjoyed a growing friendship, was enough. The MCC rejected the proposal. Lord Harris, still unreconciled, said the MCC would play Australia only if Murdoch issued a public statement agreeing that the colonials would play as amateurs, 'for the pleasure of the game'. The financially embattled Murdoch, remembering the £750-a-man bounty the last team had taken home, refused. Only after the Australians had beaten Yorkshire and Gloucestershire did Harris, under pressure from Grace, relent, and in late August a Test was arranged at The Oval.

The first Test match on English soil was a showcase for the captains. *Wisden* said that 'in the history of the game no contest has created such world-wide interest'. Before 20,814 spectators on a fine Monday, 6 September, Grace creamed 152 off an Australian attack lacking Spofforth, who had pulled out with a broken finger. England's 420 was colossal, and Australia's 149 (Murdoch, opening, making a duck) made it even more so. Australia was drifting towards a humiliating defeat until, in front of 19,863, Murdoch played the innings that made his name, the first of the performances that prompted Grace to name him the greatest Australian batsman.

With light feet and the eye for angles that made him a feared billiards shark, Murdoch did not give a chance. Australia was 8/187 early on the third day, but Murdoch hauled them up to 327, at least setting England a target. The home team would win, but Murdoch's 153 not out, one better than Grace, was the talking point. Grace gave Murdoch a gold sovereign which he wore on his watch chain until his death.

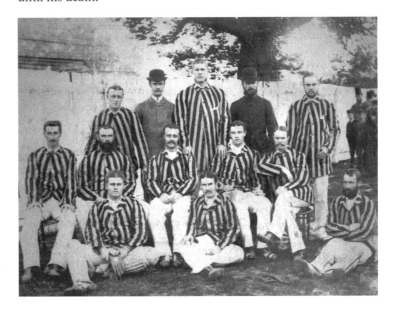

In this photo of the 1880 tourists, George Bonnor has a hand on two Australian captains' shoulders: Murdoch, with the moustache, and the youthful McDonnell.

The other batting star of the 1880 tour was Percy Stanislaus McDonnell. Born in London in 1858, McDonnell had been brought to Australia in 1862 when his barrister father, the Honourable Morgan Augustine McDonnell, emigrated, eventually to be a minister in the Victorian government. Percy was Catholic-educated at St Patrick's and Xavier Colleges, studied Greek and mathematics, and toyed with medicine before becoming a teacher with the Victorian Education Department. His cricketing talent flowered early, and he was on Murdoch's tour at the age of 21 on the strength of a top-scoring 48 opening against NSW at the SCG. If he could do that against Spofforth, Murdoch reasoned, he might be able to handle the English.

In the first Test on English soil, the teenager was undaunted by Grace and The Oval, making 27 in the first innings and 43 in the second. More stylish than Murdoch, McDonnell drove crisply and was an even bigger hitter than Hugh Massie and George Bonnor, when he put his mind to it, which was not often because, unlike those Goliaths, he put a high price on his wicket and a low trajectory on his shots. At a time when no Australian batsman was known for aesthetics – Murdoch was described as 'scientific' rather than 'pretty' – McDonnell stood out for his debonair strokeplay.

The Australians received £1,110 from the Oval gate, and the trip would be regarded as a success, with 21 wins and four losses from 37 games, nine of which were first-class. Peace had been restored and a year later an England team would return to the colonies. Never again would Canada be given precedence over Australia.

While the 1880 tour made Murdoch's reputation as a batsman and captain, his business affairs had been pounded and he would never again live in Sydney. Unmarried, he moved to Cootamundra to practise law, enjoy social billiards, rugby and pigeon shooting, and play cricket against the likes of Yass and Grenfell.

In England he had become well known for his 'dog-leg' shot, a glance played under a raised front leg. But now, in the bush, Murdoch worked to make his batting more disciplined. He showed the benefits in the first matches of the 1881–82 summer, with several good scores preceding an unheard-of 321 against Victoria on the SCG.

To put his innings into perspective, it is still the highest score by an Australian wicketkeeper, and nobody topped it on the SCG until Don Bradman 40 years later. It was compiled under pressure: on the fourth day, Murdoch had to jump on a train to Cootamundra to represent a client in court. On the fifth, he returned to keep wicket in NSW's innings win. He was rewarded with a collection of £200, a gold watch and a gold trophy in the shape of a Maltese Cross.

Murdoch led Australia against Alfred Shaw's all-professional English team on its fence-mending tour of 1881–82. The home side won 2–0, their cricket increasingly resembling our idea of the modern game. More regular playing hours were established, fielding was fast and aggressive, bowling actions were higher and straighter, and the batting, influenced by Murdoch, Horan and McDonnell, had a more methodical look. The scores took a modern shape, the drawn first Test in Melbourne being the first time a Test aggregate passed 1,000.

Horan, with 124, was the star. He had not gone on the 1880 tour, partly due to his loyalty to Dave Gregory and partly because he was switching careers from the audit office to full-time journalism. George Giffen would say of Horan, 'He could talk cricket as gracefully as he wrote about it.' His 'Cricket Chatter' column, under the pseudonym 'Felix', started in September 1879, running weekly for 37 years.

'Felix' was not above blowing Horan's trumpet. In the Boxing Day match, Horan had scored 95 against NSW. 'Felix' wrote that Horan hit two unrecorded fours, one mistakenly recorded as byes and the other missed by the scorers. He had Horan down for 103!

A week later there was no need to gild the lily. Chasing England's 294 under great pressure, Horan came in at number five and hit his sole Test hundred in a chanceless 250 minutes. With South Australia's Test debutant Giffen, Horan added 107 for the fifth wicket, Australia's first century partnership.

It was apt that the partners were the two finest player-writers of their era. Yet while Horan was at the peak of his career, Giffen was just beginning two decades that would ensconce him as one of the all-time greats.

The third son of a carpenter, Giffen was five years younger than the generation of Murdoch, Spofforth, Horan and Blackham, which left him outside the team's ruling clique. He was also an outsider because he walked in from the desert, a prodigy from faraway Adelaide, where he worked in the General Post Office as a letter sorter. His deep-rooted South Australianness marked him out at a time when intercolonial distinctions meant as much as national ones would later.

Giffen was a cricket fanatic. In 1874, aged 15, he had bowled in the nets to W.G. Grace in Adelaide. Three summers later he was last-chosen in a South Australian XXII against Lillywhite's Englishmen. For Norwood, he was taking wickets at 3.88 apiece. But South Australia's isolation and his youth stood between him and the attention of Gregory, Murdoch and company, and he would have to impose himself personally. He would also have to choose between cricket and Australian Rules football. He chose the former of course, even after being the first man to kick a goal for Norwood in the South Australian Football Association, featuring in two premiership sides and representing South Australia.

Selected to play cricket for South Australia four days after his 18th birthday and top-scoring in both innings, Giffen found his destiny. He played in SA's first match against another colony (Tasmania in 1877), and for 25 years *was* South Australian cricket.

South Australia were still not playing 11-a-side cricket when word of the Giffen phenomenon reached Murdoch in Sydney. The 22-year-old had scored 95 against Shaw's Englishmen, so Murdoch decided to give him a run in the First Test. Giffen, picked on a rumour, made an immediate splash. His contribution to the partnership with Horan was nervous, taking 50 minutes to notch his first run, but his eventual 30, alongside Horan's 124, was a memorable debut.

Murdoch batted consistently through the 1881–82 series, Giffen observing his 'thorough mastery of the science of the game, rare coolness and the patience of Job'. As captain, Murdoch was still capable of some prehistoric turns, however, bowling George Palmer and Ted Evans unchanged for 115 four-ball overs in the Second Test on a customarily dreadful Sydney wicket.

Percy McDonnell's maiden first-class century came there in the next Test. Giffen would dub him 'Greatheart', his technique and determination carrying him through the worst conditions. Coming in after Massie, Murdoch and Horan had all failed, McDonnell survived four chances in a 250-minute 147, including a five that landed near the caretaker's cottage on what are now the turf practice nets. His stand of 191 with Alick Bannerman (70) was easily an Australian record; the next highest Australian score was 7. Australia won and McDonnell outshone even Murdoch in the series. Giffen wrote of McDonnell: 'If I live to be a hundred I shall not see more elegant, graceful and effective batting. If "hit" was the game, he would blaze away like fury, but if he were not under orders and the wicket was good, he would settle down and bat as pretty as a Palairet', a reference to Somerset's Lionel, the English stylist.

A series in the 1880s could never pass without controversy. Halfway through the English tour George Ulyett and John Selby were alleged to have taken bookmakers' money to fix a result against Victoria. The allegation came 'from Cootamundra' – shorthand for Murdoch. The English hunted down the accuser, Billy Midwinter, now playing for England but still a friend of Murdoch. Ulyett and Selby cornered Midwinter and gave him a beating. Before long, Midwinter would be again playing for Australia in the strangest of Test careers.

The Fourth Test in Sydney ended after four days when the English had to play two matches in country Victoria. It was the last drawn Test in Australia until the introduction of fixed-length Tests in 1946–47. Within days both teams were bound for England, to resume hostilities in a series all the more anticipated because of Australia's home win. So desperate was McDonnell to join Murdoch's tourists that, after an attack of sunstroke, he had himself carried aboard on a stretcher.

For young Australian cricketers, an invitation to tour under Murdoch was the chance of a lifetime. After his first Test, Giffen's form had tailed off, but Murdoch was impressed by his dedication, his strong physique – nearly six foot, thirteen stone (177cm and 79kg) of pure muscle, and hands like grappling hooks – and asked if Giffen would like to join the tour.

'Had a thunderbolt struck me,' Giffen wrote, 'I would not have been more astonished, although I had so often built castles in the air about a trip to the Old Country … I found my tongue at last, and it was of course to signify assent.'

Giffen's greatness still lay ahead; this tour was his apprenticeship in more than cricket. He wrote of the voyage, 'sailing on the bosom of the mighty deep and practising the art of elocution', and developed the literary skills that would eventually result in his 1898 memoir, *With Bat and Ball*, a classic of Australian cricket writing and a priceless first-hand record of the early Test years.

Despite the horrors of seasickness – the meaty Horan was reduced to a diet of apples – Murdoch was his usual jolly self on the eight-week voyage, leading the team in song and dance, and starring in onboard black-and-white minstrel shows. He had every reason to feel buoyant. This Australian team was the strongest in the first 15 years of Test cricket. Murdoch and McDonnell were the most gifted batsmen of the time, experience and solidity came in Horan and Alick Bannerman, big-hitting potential lay with George Bonnor, while Blackham was the game's best keeper. Bowling had already established itself as Australia's strong suit, and the quartet of Spofforth, Boyle, Garrett and Palmer was its best for a generation.

The last man chosen was Hugh Hamon Massie. In a ritual that seems cruel from our perspective and can't have seemed much otherwise then, the team ran a poll during their voyage to predict the squad member least likely to succeed. Massie has been described, by Jack Pollard, as 'a genial, companionable character'. His geniality must have been stretched when he won the poll almost unanimously.

They were wrong, and how. Massie was a young man of ambition. The eldest of seven children, he was born on a property known as 'The Swamp' on the Eumeralla River, 50 kilometres from Belfast (now Port Fairy) in western Victoria. The property was owned by Thomas Browne, who under the pseudonym of Rolf Boldrewood wrote the great bushranging novel *Robbery under Arms*. Massie's parents were desperate to improve their social standing. They moved to Goulburn when Hugh was a child, then sent him to The King's School in Parramatta. As a teenager he played for East Sydney but moved to the more powerful Albert Club, where he was spotted by Dave Gregory and selected for NSW in 1874.

Massie declined. He had just started a career in banking, and could not get – or did not want – leave to play a cricket match, no matter how important. A few months later, he was again chosen, as 12th man, but didn't attend. He started as he meant to go on. No selector would be under any illusion about Massie, for whom cricket came a distant second behind banking.

He again put his career first when Murdoch invited him to join the 1880 peacemaking tour. Good form for NSW in late 1881 led to his Test selection, but, opening the batting, Massie charged Billy Midwinter and was stumped. For the rest of the 1881–82 series, Massie did just enough to get on the boat. This time the bank let him go. When he stepped out to open the batting in the first match of the tour, against Oxford University, the wind was cold and the pitch soft. Massie had shown discomfort as far from home as Melbourne. He never fired outside Sydney. But by lunch in Oxford, Australia was 145 and Massie was 100. Not until Michael Slater did it 111 years later would an Australian opener score a century before lunch at Oxford. Massie didn't stop. Before tea, he scored another century, taking his score to 206 while his partners combined for 12. Topped up by his second-innings 46, Massie's 252 runs remain the most by an Australian on debut overseas.

It is impossible to overstate the significance of Massie's innings. Financially, the tour hung by a thread. Fixtures were tentative. For a touring team to be a viable enterprise, it had to be taken seriously and be entertaining to watch. With that innings – Massie's one and only first-class century – he won Murdoch's gratitude. It set the tour up, as contest and spectacle.

Massie was a large man, at six foot one and 12 and a half stone (183cm and 70kg). Bowlers feared his charges down the pitch to drive them straight. No back-foot dabs or glances for Massie; he seldom cut, preferring to slam short off-side balls off the front foot. Bonnor, cut from similar cloth, struck 66 in half an hour against Cambridge University, and Murdoch's 286 not out against Sussex was not only a record but prompted the county to seek his services, a request to which he would accede several years later.

Though this was a smoother tour than 1878 and 1880, there were remnants of bitterness. When Australia played Nottinghamshire, the county's secretary Jack 'Hellfire' Holden refused them lunch in the pavilion, as they were professionals. He directed them to the refreshment tent for 'beer and a sandwich'. Murdoch's Australians left the game with their professional status confirmed – they collected £328 in gate profits – a win, and, later, an apology from the Notts committee.

England were careful to choose their best XI for the stand-alone Test at The Oval. The most famous of Tests started terribly for Australia. Murdoch won the toss, but in a miserable 80 overs they were all out for 63. Spofforth was revved up, however, and by stumps England were out for 103, the Demon taking 7/46.

Showers interrupted the second morning, but this was when the only batting of substance occurred. Throughout the tour, Massie's power hitting had combined successfully with 'Barndoor' Bannerman's defence – faced with one batsman who was the slowest scorer of his generation and a partner who was the fastest, bowlers didn't know which way was up.

Massie and Bannerman went in at 12.10 pm, trailing by 38. Massie decided that as the wicket dried out it would take more spin. Not wanting to wait, he launched at the new ball. By 12.45 pm, the deficit was gone. Grace changed the bowlers twice. Bannerman kept them out, and Massie belted them to all corners.

Dropped on 38, by 1 pm Massie was 50. Five minutes later he was 55, with nine fours, at a run a minute. English complacency had been rocked. A cheer of relief broke out when Massie lost his leg stump. Murdoch came in at first drop, but as the pitch dried wickets began to tumble.

In mid-afternoon, Australia led by 76 when Murdoch's partner, Sammy Jones, left his ground to garden the wicket. Grace moved up to the stumps and knocked off the bails. The English appealed, and the umpire gave Jones out.

Murdoch, fighting on the most treacherous wicket imaginable, lost his temper with Grace. The friends argued and their teammates joined in. Although furious, Murdoch managed to calm down and accept the umpire's decision. A good thing, perhaps, that Dave Gregory wasn't still Australian captain. But Australia only made another 8 runs, Murdoch 29, and the match was as good as lost.

In their changing room the Australians were still boiling over Grace's act. 'This thing can be done,' fumed Spofforth, more in hope than expectation.

Grace and Hornby started their innings at 3.45 pm. The afternoon has inspired endless prose, poetry, song and apocrypha, but a narration of the cricket facts is inspiring enough.

In nine overs, Grace and Hornby added 15, bringing the target down to 70. The wicket was dry and playing at its easiest. Spofforth took Hornby's off-stump, then bowled Barlow first ball. Two for 15, but all thoughts of a collapse were staved off by England's best, Grace and George Ulyett, who took the score to 51. Then Murdoch pulled one of those moves by which captains earn a reputation for the uncanny. With the match seeming lost, he switched Spofforth to the pavilion end and put on Boyle.

Bowling against a darker background, Spofforth had Ulyett caught behind brilliantly by a diving Blackham. Grace then scooped Boyle to Bannerman at mid-off, and England were 4/53, still firm favourites, but the Australians were ecstatic at removing Grace, whose 32 was the second-highest of the match behind Massie's 55.

Lyttelton joined Lucas, and scoring halted. 'Suddenly a new phase came over the innings,' wrote Clarence Moody. 'The batsmen could not get the ball past fieldsmen. Spofforth was bowling the most remarkable break-backs at tremendous pace; Boyle, from the other end, maintained a perfect length.' Spofforth and Boyle sent down an astonishing 12 straight maidens. 'Something of the spirit of the struggle pervaded the thousands of spectators, and their oppressive silence was punctuated by a mighty shout when Lyttelton broke the spell with a single,' Moody wrote. Another four maidens followed before Spofforth bowled Lyttelton.

England were half out, with 19 to win. Lucas struck a boundary off Boyle but Alan Steel, one of the batsmen of the decade, chipped a return catch to Spofforth, who then bowled Maurice Read. Billy Barnes hit a two, then three byes brought the target down to 10.

Thousands crowded into Kennington. In John Masefield's poem '85 to Win' he writes of a spectator dropping dead. Horan wrote that Epsom stockbroker Arthur Courcy chewed the handle of his brother-in-law's umbrella down to a stub, and that the scorer was so nervous that he wrote down Ted Peate's name as 'Geese'. Horan observed of each incoming England batsman: 'They had ashen faces and parched lips.'

Even allowing for poetic and journalistic license, there is no reason to think the closing overs were any less tense than they would be today. Lucas, after scoring 5 in an hour, chopped Spofforth onto his wicket: 8/75. Spofforth had taken six wickets for 2 runs in 20 balls, a greater feat even than his exploits at Lord's four years earlier. Giffen wrote that Spofforth's bowling was so accurate that 'every one of [his] balls would have hit the stumps had a bat not intervened'.

The last rites were left to Boyle, who dismissed Barnes and Peate. There was a stunned silence followed by an outbreak of cheering. Spofforth, with 7/44 to pair with his first-innings 7/46, was chaired from The Oval. Manager Charlie Beal's mother raced out of her seat and embraced the first player she could find, the broad-chested Giffen.

Australia had won by 7 runs. Peate would face criticism for not giving more strike to his partner, the soon-to-be missionary C.T. Studd, who had scored two centuries against Australia that summer. Peate responded: 'Mr Studd was so nervous I did not feel I could trust him to score the runs.' The Surrey secretary, C.W. Alcock, wrote: 'Men who were noted for their coolness at critical moments were trembling like a leaf, some were shivering as if with cold, some even fainted.'

Reginald Brooks wrote a mock obituary for English cricket in the *Sporting Times*. The coverage was fair and respectful. *Bell's Life* magazine wrote: 'We were beaten by a magnificent eleven, before whose prowess it was no disgrace to fall.' In *Punch*, the magazine edited by Brooks's father, was a poem:

> *Well done Cornstalks! Whipped us fair and square*
> *Was it luck that tript us? Or was it scare?*
> *Kangaroo land's Demon or our own*
> *Want of devil, coolness, nerve, backbone.*

The two giants whose friendship rescued Test cricket in the 1880s: Murdoch and Grace.

The worthiest tribute came from Grace. He had intended to retire from international cricket to concentrate on his medical practice. Now, he would play on until he had revenge.

Murdoch became the most popular of Australian captains. In 1880 he had rebuilt the bridges burnt by Gregory, and in 1882 he affirmed the Australians' name as entertainers and competitors. Ray Robinson wrote that 'Whenever frictions occurred in a touring side, [Murdoch] settled them at once and never referred to them again.' An example can be found in his treatment of Bonnor, the big-talking big hitter who had averaged 9 on the previous tour. Whenever Bonnor needed gingering up, Murdoch would drop him down the order and say he would give the run-scoring job to better-qualified players. Bonnor, none too bright and easily riled, would go out and smash the bowling.

Murdoch's diplomacy can be heard in a speech at London's Crichton Hotel on 28 September, thanking his hosts for their hospitality through the 38-match tour. While mentioning the 'daring enterprise to beard the lion in his den', Murdoch did not gloat. 'Since landing in May,' he said, 'we have been constantly engaged in playing matches, and on all occasions very simply did our best to play up to the true letter and spirit of the game. I can assure you that on the few occasions we lost there were not fourteen more grieved men in the world …

'Personally I have attained the height of my ambition, having captained a team which has beaten a representative eleven of England. Having done this, I do not wish to any more play cricket.'

To this there were cries of 'No! No!'

'But if,' Murdoch continued, 'I am called upon to occupy the position of commanding such a team again, I shall only be too proud to do so, and shall do my very best to win. If we have attained any position as cricketers, you in England have yourselves to thank for it, for you have been our instructors.'

Giffen recorded the excitement of the team's return home: 'We were heroes. Everyone joined in honouring us. Personally, when I reached Adelaide again, I was made the recipient of a chronograph watch and chain valued at 100 guineas.'

Murdoch's 1882 tour was a high-water mark. Within two years he would descend through aggravation and bitterness towards a disgusted self-imposed exile. His good cheer and high reputation would never shine brighter than in 1882.

With Ivo Bligh's English team coming for a three-Test series, Murdoch's power and popularity were at an unprecedented high. The 1882 Oval Test had achieved the status of myth, Brooks's joke obituary sparking antipodean talk of possessing the 'ashes' of English cricket, the term that was to become synonymous with these contests 20 years later.

The popularity of Murdoch's team was confirmed by the attendances for the First Test of 1882–83 in Melbourne. The three days drew 15,000, 23,000 and 16,000. Australia – the 1882 team retained as a whole – won by nine wickets, thanks to some power hitting from Bonnor, two good innings from Murdoch, and 'Joey' Palmer's 10 wickets. England's top fast bowler, Fred Morley, had fallen over and cracked a rib when, off Colombo, their ship had collided with another. He soldiered on but would be dead, from dropsy, within six months. Nor had Bligh escaped the trip unscathed, injuring a hand during a deck game and missing the first six matches of the tour.

Murdoch was in his prime. But with popularity came scrutiny, and his tolerant, player-friendly style was always going to be praised only as long as the team was winning. As it happened, Billy Bates (13/100) undid Australia in the Second Test; in the Third, Murdoch's men, chasing 153, collapsed for 83. A group of Australian ladies, one of whom, Florence Morphy, would become Bligh's wife, completed the second half of the 'ashes' story by burning a bail and presenting the English captain with the cremains.

The press and public turned on Murdoch, accusing him of laziness and over-indulging his players. An article criticised him for preferring 'shooting, picnics and social parties' to the serious business of beating England. Murdoch's competitive fire was undimmed, however – during that Sydney Test, he had confronted

Bligh over Barlow's spikes marking up the pitch – and he was scalded by how quickly praise had turned to pillory.

A fourth Test was added in Sydney, and Murdoch showed his mettle. Pressured to change the 1882 team, he brought in Midwinter, now an Australian again, for the out-of-form Massie, and dropped Percy McDonnell, whose Third Test pair capped a mystifying loss of form. The Test was an experimental one, different pitches being used for each innings. Before chasing 199 in the fourth innings, Murdoch tried his pacemen at each end on the various strips, trying to guess which was the flattest. He chose correctly: Blackham's unbeaten 58 steered Australia home thrillingly.

While Murdoch is often portrayed as a jolly, smiling fellow with his round face and drooping moustache, the experience of bankruptcy and the criticism in early 1883 scarred him. Now that he was leading a commercially attractive operation, he was determined to enrich himself and his men. There was no central Australian cricket authority to employ or control them. Murdoch was a very different man from Gregory, but the office of captaincy overrode those differences. Like Gregory, Murdoch was the boss, the managing director, the chief entrepreneur, and the shop steward. Whatever the captain's personality, his power base within the team was unquestioned as long as he ran a profitable tour.

Murdoch also transformed the captaincy by being his team's champion batsman. He set a mould that would be followed all the way through Don Bradman to Ricky Ponting, the ideal of captain and champion being one and the same man. In 1883–84, he amassed 567 runs at 113.4, a scarcely believable average on uncovered wickets. He scored 158 against Victoria and 279 not out for Australia against a Combined XI. Horan, who witnessed the 279 as the despairing fielding side's captain, called it 'an exhibition of true, scientific cricket, elegant and vigorous in attack, graceful and impregnable in defence'.

The team Murdoch took to England in 1884 was virtually unchanged from 1882, even though many were past their best. The up-and-coming batsman Henry Scott and Midwinter came in, while Massie and Horan were occupied with work, but the substantial parts were unchanged. Murdoch was loyal to veterans, for whom this would be a last chance to cash in.

Now that Murdoch's men had proven themselves, the English were less likely to treat them as an amusing distraction. This was the tour when cricket got serious about standardising its laws. Grace produced a measuring gauge to ensure Australian bats fell within the now-regulation four-and-a-half-inch width. They did – while Grace's own bat didn't! It was the first tour when Australia played only 11-a-side matches – 32 of them, of which they would win 18 and lose 7.

Giffen wrote admiringly of Spofforth, who took 14 wickets for 37 runs in a rage triggered by bad umpiring at Birmingham: 'He looked the Demon every inch of him' and 'the batsman had to look out for squalls'. Of his captain, Giffen wrote: 'No matter how tight the hole we were in, Billy, with a smile of assurance and a cheering word, would go in himself and often master the bowling with his

The 1884 Australian team. Back row, l to r: PS McDonnell, G Alexander, G Giffen, GE Palmer; middle: FR Spofforth, JM Blackham, WL Murdoch (c), GJ Bonnor, WE Midwinter, AC Bannerman, HF Boyle; front: WH Cooper, HJH Scott.

splendid defence … It was an education to watch how he drove or cut the ball along the sward, seldom mistiming his stroke one iota.'

Conscious of not having shown his best in England in 1882, Giffen responded by working harder. On the steamers he shovelled coal, for the pure pleasure of building his physique. Against Lancashire at Old Trafford, Giffen scored 113 and backed up with six wickets including a hat-trick. No other player has ever recorded a century and a hat-trick in the one match, but Giffen was just getting started on a run of stupendous, even superhuman, cricketing feats. He had already taken 10 wickets in an innings in Australia. His tour of England was successful by any measure – third in the batting aggregates behind Murdoch and McDonnell, third in the bowling behind Spofforth and Palmer – but in the Tests he grew frustrated that he wasn't showing his best in the Old Country.

Australia drew the First Test and lost the Second. Murdoch's most notable contribution in the first was to catch Scott for 75 while fielding as a substitute for England – a foretaste of his appearance in an English cap nearly a decade later. A slightly built five-foot-nine (175cm), the medical student Scott stroked the Englishmen around Lord's in his first appearance there. His 69-run partnership with Boyle was the highest for the 10th wicket for Australia at Lord's until Dennis Lillee and Ashley Mallett equalled it 91 years later. Scott was Melbourne establishment to his roots: his grandfather Charles had been a Royal Marines officer, and his father John was secretary of the Melbourne Gas and Coke Company. Harry, along with two brothers, attended Wesley College and studied engineering at the University of Melbourne before switching to medicine in his third year. Two years after this tour, he would be Murdoch's unexpected and unfortunate successor as leader of an Australian tour to England.

When, after two golden ducks, Murdoch finally found form in the Third Test at The Oval, Scott was by his side. Dropped on 60, the Victorian student made his only Test century. But his 102 paled next to Murdoch's effort. In the seventh year of Test cricket Murdoch scored its first double-century, 211 in the first Test innings in which every player bowled. Lord Harris tried, literally, everything.

His trump card in the end was the wicketkeeper, Alfred Lyttelton, who took 4/19 with underarm lobs. The laws prevented Australia from declaring, and their 551 soaked up too much time to force a result.

Murdoch topped the aggregates and averages again, with 1,377 runs at 31.29 in 49 innings. But this tour, more than the previous ones, would be overshadowed by what was seen as Murdoch's overly 'commercial' attitude.

After the First Test at Lord's, which drew 15,000 each day, the Australians claimed £1,334 from gate takings. The English professionals, who were being paid a set rate of £10 per man, were furious that the Australians had broken with convention and not given them a share. Murdoch said, cheekily, that the Australians were only imitating the accounting methods that awarded Grace steep personal appearance fees, and needed all the money to 'cover costs'.

But the Australians would make £900 per man in profits, and tensions broke into the open during their 1 August match against the Players at The Oval. Murdoch was already feeling hostile towards some of the hosts, notably their top batsman, Arthur Shrewsbury, who had boycotted a Players' match against Australia at Sheffield. Then, at The Oval, when Australia needed just 11 runs to win with nine wickets in hand, Murdoch requested an unscheduled lunch break. There was a theory that Murdoch did so to give the pitch more time to dry, but with such a small target that is unlikely. At the ground, it was alleged that Murdoch, with an eye on gate takings, had called for the lunch break to allow more paying spectators to be lured in.

Those in the ground already were understandably peeved. In protest, they occupied the pitch and the game was nearly abandoned. Murdoch relented and played it out, but his reputation for avarice was growing.

By the end of 1884, Murdoch was weary and stressed after four tours in six and a half years. On the SS *Mirzapore*, on the return voyage, he met Jemima Watson, the heiress to a Victorian goldfields fortune. Within a month of their return they had married, and Murdoch was missing practices for NSW and Australia.

When not courting, Murdoch was fighting. England sent a fully professional group under the sponsorship of Shaw and Lillywhite, with Murdoch's bête noire, Shrewsbury, as co-organiser, captain and opening batsman. Murdoch was blindsided when John Conway, the Australian team manager from 1877–78, took up a position as England's financial adviser. Murdoch was personally offended by what he saw as Conway's betrayal.

Murdoch and his 1884 tourists boycotted England's lead-up matches. The NSW, Victorian and South Australian associations lined up with the English and prepared a public relations offensive, the *Age* reporting on 22 November that the Australian players 'were amazed at statements being made to the effect that public opinion could and would be aroused to force them to play on the English manager's terms'.

If their commitment to playing cricket was slipping, so was the fitness of a tired team. The First Test would be the inaugural international fixture in Adelaide, starting four days after Murdoch's wedding. Spofforth didn't play because of a family bereavement, Midwinter was injured, Giffen was suffering from rheumatism and Bannerman would split his finger fielding in the first innings.

Percy 'Greatheart' McDonnell, opening, carried the Australian batting, with a peerless 124 in 195 minutes. He scored more than half of Australia's 243. England replied with 369, the belligerent Barnes denting the short square boundaries with 134. In the second innings, McDonnell appeared certain to be the first man to score twin Test centuries. Despite Murdoch's second failure for the match, Australia cruised to 2/125, one run from erasing the deficit. McDonnell was 83, having added 69 with Giffen. But the local hero was struggling. Bowling 56.2 overs had piled lumbago on top of his rheumatism. McDonnell forced a ball through the off-side, called for an easy run and set off. But Giffen did not respond and McDonnell was stranded. Sixty-six runs later the Australians were all out, and the game was gone.

The real story was off the field. Murdoch had demanded half of the gate takings from the South Australian Cricket Association, which offered him 30 per cent. Murdoch refused. Eventually the

SACA offered a flat fee of £450 per team, which Murdoch accepted. The English, who had seen the Australian tourists take the lions' share of receipts in 1884, were incensed at a half-half split. But the real losers were the SACA, who had overestimated the gate takings and ended up taking a heavy hit.

Murdoch was also losing sympathy by objecting to Lillywhite standing as England's umpire. Lillywhite had always been a popular and industrious promoter of Anglo-Australian cricket, and his place in history was assured by his captaincy in the first Test series. But Murdoch felt Lillywhite would be biased. His intransigence angered the English and turned the Australian public, finally, against him.

After the first Test, Murdoch batted himself back into form against Victoria, scoring 97 and 11. This would, however, be his last top-level game in Australia for more than five years.

Murdoch's brinkmanship was his undoing for the Second Test in Melbourne, when he again demanded half the gate. This time the VCA, which was in a stronger position than the SACA, refused point-blank. Murdoch modified his demand, asking that after the Englishmen were paid a set fee, the excess go to the Australian players. Rather than negotiate itself into a loss, as the SACA had, the VCA staged a coup: it took over the selection of the Australian team and announced a new XII, containing none of Murdoch's band. Further, it banned the six Victorian members of Murdoch's team from any game which the VCA controlled.

Amid international shock, the Test at Melbourne proceeded farcically, England crushing a team of nine Australian debutants, six of them playing their one-and-only Test match. Tom Horan was the new captain, and Murdoch retired from top cricket in disgust, stewing over the VCA's coup. The press accused him of 'putting money before nation', a charge that cut deeply. He was perceived as the ringleader of a greedy group. For five years he would remain Australian cricket's king in exile.

3

THE SUMMER
OF FARCE

LIKE Achilles, Murdoch brooded on the sidelines as Australian cricket began a plunge into years of disarray and defeat. Even though Murdoch's men returned to the Australian team, without him Test cricket almost perished. He refused approaches from Boyle, Blackham and Horan to play for Victoria, and lost half a decade smouldering in Cootamundra.

Tom Horan, born in County Cork, was no natural or willing leader, but he became, in the Second and Fifth Tests of 1884–85, Australia's only Irish-born cricket captain. He was plucked out of semi-retirement, having sat out the 1884 tour. It could never be said that Horan wanted, or angled for, the captaincy of any team. His Victorian leader was Blackham, but the Prince of Wicketkeepers, one of Murdoch's staunchest teammates, was among those banned in 1884–85.

In the tumult of December 1884, the captaincy was foisted upon Horan. Although he led what was effectively a Scab XI, in print he had not toed the authorities' line. In fact, 'Felix' had been a vocal supporter of Murdoch on finances. When the English press attacked Murdoch's supposed avarice, 'Felix' called them 'narrow-minded' and 'insulting'. As a protégé of Gregory and Blackham, and a financial beneficiary of three England tours, Horan had no problem with Murdoch's policy on gate takings.

In December 1884, 'Felix' again lined up behind Murdoch, writing that the Adelaide Test was played 'under a deep and lasting shadow, which cast a universal gloom upon our manly game'. The villains, in 'Felix's view, were Shrewsbury and the confrontational English.

Yet when the Victorian Cricketers' Association sacked Murdoch's XI for Melbourne, Horan was the logical replacement as captain, if only because he was the sole available player with much Test experience.

It says a lot about Horan that his acceptance of the captaincy enhanced his standing among his peers. His oldest cricket friend and mentor Blackham did not hold it against Horan. Australia was in the deepest crisis and someone had to lead the novices, so it might as well be the popular Irishman.

Tom Horan, aka Felix

Horan led the weakest team Australia has fielded. Only he and Sammy Jones had played Tests. Among nine debutants, five would only play this one Test. Sam Morris, a Tasmanian of West Indian parentage, opened the batting and scored 14 runs in two digs. In the middle order were Roland 'The Doc' Pope, who was to become a trusted medical adviser on future tours to England; 22-year-old Alfred Marr, who would record a century for Arncliffe Juniors in Sydney at the age of 67 but only made a handful in his Test; and Harry Musgrove, who would be tour manager to England in 1896. A year later Musgrove managed a disastrous Australian baseball tour of the USA which left him embroiled in allegations of fraud and theft. William 'Digger' Robertson batted eleven, made 0 and 2, and took no wickets with his leg-breaks. He subsequently lived for a decade in California where he was so successful in local cricket that he was known as 'Champion of the Pacific Slope'.

England scored 401. Sammy Morris, who for decades was the only black man to play for Australia, dismissed Shrewsbury and Barnes and was the best of Horan's threadbare attack.

Horan's 63 at number three in Australia's reply was the innings of his career. He had good support from 'Billy' Trumble, replacement wicketkeeper Affie Jarvis and Jack Worrall, but they could not prevent a 10-wicket loss.

Seven weeks would lapse before the Third Test, in Sydney. England would spend that time in New Zealand. The NSWCA, breaking ranks with the VCA, said it would select a Test match team from the 1884 tourists, picking Spofforth, Alick Bannerman, Garrett, Massie and Evans. Murdoch, sacrificed to keep the English happy, remained in Cootamundra.

Meanwhile, the VCA maintained its ban on Blackham, Bonnor, Boyle, McDonnell, Palmer and Scott. Horan felt the recriminations had gone far enough, and his dismal few days as Test captain persuaded him that the cream of Australian cricket had to be forgiven. But the VCA was immovable. Consequently, Horan declared himself unavailable for Victoria. He had crossed the picket, from appeaser to striker.

The mayhem worsened over the next month. Bonnor, sick of the VCA's punitive attitude, went north over the Murray to his home state. 'Felix' complained, saying there should be a residential qualification before a player could switch colonies. His alter-ego Horan, meanwhile, was restored by the VCA to play NSW, along with Henry Scott, but Blackham, Boyle, Palmer and McDonnell remained under the VCA's ban.

By the time the Englishmen came back from New Zealand to play the Third, Fourth and Fifth Tests, Australia had patched together a motley crew. Horan, Jones, Trumble and Jarvis survived from the Second Test. The restored rebels were Bannerman, Scott, Bonnor, Massie, Spofforth and Garrett. Still banned were Blackham, Boyle, Palmer, McDonnell and Murdoch. Ted Evans, the leader of NSW in Dave Gregory's time, was called up for the third of his six Tests spaced over nearly a decade. Horan had been stood down as captain in favour of Massie.

Massie had never exceeded his 206 not out at Oxford and 55 at The Oval in 1882. Since then, he had concentrated on banking again, rising in the Commercial Banking Company of Sydney and finding little time for cricket. He would marry the boss's daughter, live prosperously in North Sydney and Point Piper, and die leaving the largest estate of any Test captain before Bradman. For the Third Test of 1884–85, he was wheeled out as the compromise leader.

Having played only five first-class matches in two years, Massie was in no batting shape. He won the toss, but appeared cursed by bad luck when a lunchtime hailstorm blanketed the SCG. After the hail melted the innings was a rout, Australia losing eight wickets and Massie making 2.

The next morning, though, Garrett and Evans fought back marvellously, adding 80 for the last wicket. Garrett's unbeaten 51 was a record for a number ten, and Evans, who was not a true number eleven (he had batted number three in his previous Test), hit 33.

Being relieved of the captaincy lightened Horan's step and brought out the best in his cricket. He took six for 40 in England's first innings, making the most of the rough chopped up by Spofforth's spikes, and Australia led by 50. Massie then produced a masterstroke by promoting Bonnor, and the giant's quick 29 inspired Horan to hoist Wilfred Flowers into the Showboat Pavilion.

Massie supplying a useful 21 at number seven, Australia's 165 left England 214 to win. Matters proceeded satisfactorily as Spofforth and Billy Trumble removed the England top order. But the pitch dried out further overnight, and Flowers and Maurice Read, coming together at 6/92, whittled down the target. Massie switched Spofforth to the Randwick End, but the Demon received some uncustomarily rough treatment. Massie switched him back to the Paddington End, but nothing was working. Like many an Australian captain, Massie kept throwing the ball to his spearhead. He had no Plan B.

At 194, needing 20 for a remarkable win, Bates played around Spofforth and was bowled for 56. When two more wickets fell, Australia seemed to have turned the game on its head. But wicket-keeper Joe Hunter stayed with Flowers, who was having a tremendous all-round match. Seven short of victory, he cut Spofforth hard. Evans, the Sydney veteran, took a diving catch at gully. Australia had won by six, one run fewer than the spine-tingler at The Oval.

Hugh Massie, the big-hitting banker

Massie – one from one as captain – was summarily dropped. He had been commissioned to stop a gap, and had done so quietly and successfully. He would only represent NSW twice more. Dave Gregory, the sole NSW selector, would refuse to pick him because of his lack of commitment. The breach was telling for the future of the captaincy. The two men were both financial heavyweights, but Gregory, the scrapper, set the tone, while Massie, whose interests in life went far beyond cricket, who had no taste for a brawl, passed into history almost unnoticed. The only Australian captains to match his 100 per cent record would be Hugh Trumble, Bill Brown and Neil Harvey, all of them gentlemen in the Massie style.

The fourth Australian captain in four Tests was Jack Blackham, whom the NSWCA reinstated, along with McDonnell and Giffen, in the interest of strengthening the team.

Since his debut in 1877, Blackham had been Australia's only Test wicketkeeper aside from Murdoch's brief adventure with the gloves in 1877. Along with Murdoch, Spofforth and Giffen, Blackham was one of the four pillars of early Australian Test cricket, who could hold places in any all-time Australian team.

Blackham had toured England in 1878, 1880, 1882 and 1884. We know that the ball from the famous first 'Ashes' Test in 1882 did not end up in the urn, because Blackham pocketed it, only relinquishing it 34 years later in an auction to aid Australia's war effort. It fetched £617.

As the Australians' competitiveness was being recognised, so were Blackham's skills. *Cricket* magazine noted in 1882: 'He stands up without the slightest fear, no matter how fast the bowling. There is no pretence or show about his keeping, but he takes every kind of ball with the greatest ease, and on the leg side he is surer than anyone we have ever seen.' At a time when keepers had short active lives, their fingers piecemeal with fractures, Blackham's hands were so sure that Lord Harris said that on retirement 'his hands were as free from enlargements as a young lady's'. Not so pretty were his teeth, mostly knocked out by 1880. But missing teeth never meant missing a match, and nor did the permanent dent in his chest from a Spofforth kicker.

Blackham's standing up to the wicket added menace to the bowling of Spofforth and Boyle. Against a Stockport XVIII in 1878, he caught six and stumped four in the match. In 1884, when Australia beat the Gentlemen at The Oval, he stumped the last three batsmen. Not all of the English approved. As English keepers started to copy Blackham, the local clergy complained that long-stop was the vicar's position in village cricket and Blackham was leading nothing less than a revolt against the church.

Blackham was a fair appealer, raising one arm to ask the question and limiting his demands to when he thought the batsman was out. Once he seemed to have stumped Grace but did not appeal, informing the batsman and the umpire that he had taken the ball fractionally in front of the stumps. The unlikelihood of such a sportsmanlike admission coming from his victim only elevated Blackham's standing.

Yet he also toured with Australian teams noted for the hardness of their play. In the game between Australia and a Combined XI at the SCG in March 1881, the game slipping humiliatingly from Australia, Jack Edwards played and missed at George Alexander. According to the *Town and Country Journal*, 'Blackham appealed for a catch … The batsman thinking he was out stepped out of his crease, and the bails were whipped off in an instant.'

Victoria made Blackham captain in 1882–83. As a batsman he strolled out with his free hand in his pocket and scored half-centuries from every position in the order, including a 96 in an intercolonial match in Sydney and 57 and 58 not out in Australia's tight Sydney Test win of 1882–83, making him the first to pass 50 twice in a Test. In 1884–85, he followed a 66 in the First Test with 109 for Victoria. Prior to going out, Blackham had been admonishing his younger teammates for chasing off-side balls. When they questioned him about the number of balls he had been chasing, he said: 'From now on I hope you'll know *how* to do it.' It was his only first-class century in 21 seasons, and he was bowled by Harry Moses – *his* only wicket in 14 seasons.

The Prince of Wicketkeepers showing off his miraculously straight fingers

The musical chairs of the 1884–85 summer brought Blackham out of disgrace and into the captaincy for the Fourth Test. Next to Murdoch, he was the senior man among the 1884 rebels, and took the brunt of the VCA's vindictive attitude. But the NSWCA was more conciliatory.

This would be his only Test as captain between 1877 and 1891, but he did at least lead a winning side. In another innovation to combat poor pitches, it was agreed that two strips would be used for the Test. The captains could choose which they wanted to bat on first, but had to bat on the other later.

Losing the toss turned out to be a win for Blackham. One pitch was considerably better than the other. England batted on the good one first, making 269, limited by Giffen's seven wickets. Blackham tried to 'reverse' the batting order, sending out Palmer, Garrett and Billy Trumble at the top and holding back Bannerman, McDonnell, Giffen, Horan and Bonnor, believing the pitch would flatten out further with time. Although Palmer and Trumble failed, the move worked, Australia making 309 thanks to Bannerman's 51 and a career-best 128, in 115 minutes, from Bonnor at number eight.

Going in on the 'bad' pitch, England collapsed for 77 to the unchanged Spofforth (5/30) and Palmer (4/32). Australia only had to bat for an hour on the inferior wicket, hunting down 38. Levelling the series 2–2 was an astonishing coup. But the 1884–85 summer was like no other, and four days between the Fourth and Fifth Tests were long enough for a new spate of madness.

The deciding Test would be in Melbourne and run by the VCA. Despite his tactical triumph in Sydney, Blackham was still unacceptable to the VCA along with McDonnell and Palmer. Bonnor, though by birth a New South Welshman, was considered not only a Victorian by the VCA but a traitorous one. Notwithstanding his blistering century on 16 March, Bonnor was out of the team by 21 March.

Almost laughably, Horan was reinstated as captain. The team he led was not as callow as that of the Second Test, but it still included a Melbourne ironmonger playing his only Test, Frank Walters, and Patrick McShane, who in the Fourth Test had been one of the umpires.

Speaking of umpires, the build-up to the Fifth Test would take a sad turn. The original umpires appointed for the match were James Lillywhite and Ned Elliott. The Australian umpire, however, had been in ill health. During the Fourth Test he had been sick one morning, Hugh Massie umpiring in his place. Days later, on 19 March, he died. His place was taken by George Hodges.

Lillywhite, whose umpiring had sparked Murdoch's objection at the beginning of the summer – seemingly aeons ago – stood down on the morning of the Fifth Test, replaced by 'Dimboola Jim' Phillips. Phillips was one of the most extraordinary characters involved with Australian cricket. He had been a high-quality player who was mostly overlooked for colonial or national selection due to his residence in remote western Victoria. At 35 he moved to Melbourne to become a ground bowler at the Melbourne Cricket Club and later became an umpire as well as playing for Victoria, and then, for nine seasons in the 1890s, for Middlesex. His most important contribution would come at the turn of the century, when he staged a one-man crusade against chuckers. Inimitably, he would succeed in having the rules on chucking both changed and enforced.

But that was all ahead of Dimboola Jim. In the Fifth Test of 1884–85, Horan won the toss and surprised everyone by electing to bat on a wet wicket. Australia slumped to 9/99 until Spofforth blasted 50, the first half-century by a number eleven in 34 years of first-class cricket in Australia.

England restored normal service in their innings, Shrewsbury making an unbeaten 105 and Barnes 74. Horan opted against using the roller for Australia's second innings and they only made 125. The series was lost 3–2.

Australia's heavy loss was again overshadowed by bizarre developments with the umpiring. The Englishmen were constantly complaining about Hodges's decisions over the first two days. On the third, he walked out. No other umpires were available, so for the last session of the third day, Phillips was joined by Tom Garrett, who became the first to umpire and play in the same Test. On day four, Lillywhite took over from Garrett, but Phillips didn't turn up at all. News came through that he was ill, and a Melbourne player, J.C. Allen, took his place for the last day.

This ludicrous decider of 1884–85 would be Horan's last Test. He would represent Victoria until 1891, but had had enough of playing for Australia. Selected for the 1886 tour of England, he declined. Still capable of defiant batting, he would score an unbeaten 117 against England in December 1886, withstanding the fire and guile of George Lohmann, and four more first-class half-centuries. Horan was picked for Australia to play in the sole Test of 1887–88, only to refuse (alongside Giffen, Bruce and Jarvis) because they were not being offered enough money.

As 'Felix', Horan would build a reputation for putting principle above parochialism. He often took the sword to his former team-mates, criticising Giffen's captaincy for South Australia and Alick Bannerman's habit of disputing umpires' decisions. 'Some men require to be told half a dozen times that they are out before they will move away,' 'Felix' thundered in 1890. He was acknowledged as the foremost commentator through the Golden Age and up to the First World War, always praising entertaining cricket. His popular annual 'Round the Ground' pieces were not only read but collected. Horan was lucky enough never to retire from writing. 'Felix' filed his last piece for *The Australasian* on 25 March 1916, and died from dropsy at his home in Malvern a fortnight later.

4

THE RESTLESS YEARS

THE summer of 1884–85 was when things fell apart for Australian cricket. The dumping of Murdoch and the players' strike would leave a 10-year legacy. Up to the start of the 1884–85 series, Australia had an overall Test record against England of seven wins, five losses and four draws from 16 matches. For the next decade, they played 24, won five, lost 17 and drew two. Murdoch's exile and Spofforth's decline had a lot to do with it, as did the emergence of some fine English talent. But there was a malaise within the Australian team that would take fully a decade to heal.

The Australian captains immediately after Murdoch were fall guys. Harry Scott was captain for one disastrous tour. When the colonial associations were resisting players' demands for payment, the nearest local approximation for an amateur gentleman was the Toorak-born Victorian. Scott was, in a sense, what we have come to think of as an 'English'-style captain: diplomatic, well heeled and courteous, but not quite up to the job as a player. In a dry land Scott was, in a word, wet. While his life outside cricket would unveil heroic qualities that a mere game could not bring out, Scott's brief engagement as captain was an unmitigated failure.

Dr Harry Scott, a success at everything in life, bar captaincy

His club cricket was with St Kilda and East Melbourne, and it was as a bowler that he made his first dent for Victoria. He took a third of his career wickets – 6/33 – in his first game, against NSW in the first-ever colonial match played at the Association Ground, or SCG, in February 1878.

Indifferent form and the return of national players limited Scott's Victorian appearances and he gave up bowling for a sound, defensive batting technique. In December 1883 he scored 114 not out against NSW in Melbourne, adding a record 161 with Horan. Murdoch, who scored 158 for the visitors, was impressed enough to invite Scott to join the 1884 tour after Evans, Garrett and Horan had declared themselves unavailable. That tour was Scott's high point as a player. With nothing to lose, a junior man in a team of stars, Scott batted 51 times and finished third in the averages behind Murdoch and McDonnell. His teammates enjoyed his quiet company, though he was never one of the Murdoch late-night clique. Instead he took solitary excursions around London in buses which cost twopence. Amused teammates dubbed him 'Tup'.

His batting was a revelation, as we have seen, with his 75 at Lord's and 102 at The Oval. He topped the averages in the Test series and came home as one of Murdoch's well-paid, highly lauded XI.

Just when he was ready to show his England form to home crowds, Scott was one of the VCA-banned Murdoch men. No rebel, he was restored for the Third Test under Massie, failed twice and was dropped again.

Bad blood coursed through Australian cricket in the 1885–86 season as the colonial associations continued their push to wind back the players' professional aspirations. When the Melbourne Cricket Club was organising a party to tour England in 1886, Scott had two recommendations for the captaincy: he was batting well, and was a pliable fellow who might, under the wing of the tour manager, Melbourne CC secretary Major Ben Wardill, be able to quell the players' perceived avarice.

Scott's captaincy was doomed before it began. He was a man for whom cricket was a hobby. His medical career, backed by a wealthy family, was his real life. But although hardened professionals such as Bannerman, Boyle, Horan and Murdoch were unavailable, the squad still included many for whom cricket was life. Giffen, Palmer, Bonnor, Blackham, Garrett and Spofforth had jobs outside the game but their achievements in cricket had won them fame on both sides of the globe and the income to go with it. They agreed to join Scott, but if they drew crowds in England, how long would it be before they asked for their usual slice?

The team left Australia on two separate boats, only coming together in Naples. Ted Evans, after two previous refusals, had agreed to tour. But Evans was 37, while Palmer, Bonnor, Garrett and, most significantly, Spofforth were one tour past their best. Spofforth dislocated his right middle finger and was not a force. Bonnor would total 9 runs in four Test innings. Injuries were so prevalent that Wardill played two games and 'Doc' Rowley Pope four. George Lohmann, Dick Barlow and Johnny Briggs destroyed Australia with the ball in the three Tests, and Grace was dropped four times on his way to 170 at The Oval. The only success of the tour was Giffen, who topped both batting and bowling averages. On the first tour which was unsuccessful overall, he came to the fore as an individual.

Despite, or because of, Australia's heavy losses, the tour was hugely popular. At Lord's, 33,000 attended the three days of the Test. Most of the 40 matches were sold out. Hardheads like Blackham, Giffen, Spofforth and Palmer expected a share, but tensions arose when Wardill reminded them that the tour was not designed to enrich them. Fistfights ensued, and Scott was called upon to mediate between the factions and even pull two quarrellers apart.

Giffen would write that Scott was 'overweighted' by the cares of captaincy, and *Wisden* concluded that he 'led the team with the best of intentions and greatest sincerity, but he was no Murdoch. It is exceedingly doubtful whether even an ideal captain would have pulled the team through its engagements unless, indeed, he had been backed by that confidence and energy which we so seldom see in any team.'

Dealt a bad hand, Scott was never going to be able to put off the inevitable. He was the nominal leader of players with far more experience, who expected better reward from the tour, and who had built their lives around the game.

But he tried. Although Arthur Haygarth, the outstanding English cricket writer of the day, wrote that 'the cares of leadership affected his run-getting, for quarrels among the players were many, and he did not have sufficient strength of character to cope with the situation', the records show that Scott, personally, did everything possible. He played in all but four of the 40 games, took on the responsibility of opening the batting in the Manchester and Lord's Tests, and was third in the averages and aggregates, making 1,278 runs at 22.03. His batting highlight came against Yorkshire at Sheffield, where he hit a record, matchwinning 22 runs off the last four-ball over. So dizzying was Scott's hitting that the fieldsmen changed ends in confusion after three balls and had to be recalled by the umpire.

The 1886 Australian Team led by Harry Scott. Back row, l to r: G Giffen, FR Spofforth, Major B Wardill (manager); middle: Farrand (umpire), Bates (scorer), W Bruce, J McIlwraith, TW Garrett, E Evans, JW Trumble, Salter (scorer), R Thoms (umpire); seated: GJ Bonnor, JM Blackham, HJH Scott (c), SP Jones, GE Palmer; front: AH Jarvis.

But that was a dollop of cream. The tour was a disaster. When the team returned to Australia *The Bulletin* lampooned them in a cartoon showing them disembarking from their ship wearing slings, walking on crutches, and covered in bruises and bandages. Scott was not among them. He had stayed in England to complete his medical studies, and would play neither Test nor first-class cricket again. He returned to Australia to practise medicine around the gold mines at Bathurst, then at Scone after having married Mary Minnie Mickle, a Warrnambool grazier's daughter, and settled down to the life, in Ray Robinson's words, of 'a saddle-sore Samaritan'. He would be chief magistrate and mayor of Scone, which named its hospital after him. At his funeral in 1910, after he died of typhoid contracted while working, he would be mourned by his close friend Banjo Paterson. Cricket was not Scott's life, and his unsuccessful Australian captaincy represents a turning point. From here on, the guiding spirit of the job would be not amateur but professional.

One of the reasons Scott's 1886 team failed was the absence of Australia's two premier batsmen. Murdoch was in Cootamundra and Percy McDonnell, Murdoch's heir as the champion, had started a new life in Sydney.

McDonnell had been the unluckiest man in the fall-out of 1884–85. His 124 and 83 in the inaugural Adelaide Test stamped him as the next great Australian batsman. But he did not play the Second and Third Tests, made 20 and 3 in the Fourth, and was banned again for the Fifth. He might have been a government minister's son, but McDonnell's loyalties were with Murdoch. The Victorian Education Department had rejected his request for leave to tour England in 1884, so disenchantment already bubbled. Unhappy with the VCA and Victoria, he left for NSW in the winter of 1885 and took a job with the Australian Joint Stock Bank. Refusing to play cricket for peanuts, he had made himself unavailable for Scott's 1886 tour.

For the 1886–87 Australian summer, the Marylebone Cricket Club tried to organise a tour of English professionals, who were themselves at loggerheads with their administrators. Offered £10 per man per match, Lillywhite, Shrewsbury and Shaw declined and organised their own 29-match tour.

The public had caught on, and for the first time an English tour would lose money. Substandard cricket and a disillusionment with the bickering would, after a decade of growth, produce a sudden reversal, with falling attendances and receipts, which in turn aggravated the player–administrator brawl over a now-shrinking pie.

With Scott having remained in England, Australia needed a new captain. McDonnell, now a New South Welshman, reminded

Percy Greatheart McDonnell, looking every part the Greek scholar

everyone of his skills by travelling to the MCG for the Boxing Day match and cracking 239 against his erstwhile teammates, among 310 scored while he was at the crease. Horan wrote that the bowlers 'knew not where to pitch the ball to avoid his resolute and powerful strokes … and [he] never once played in a faltering or hesitating style'. Again, McDonnell was producing his best in the worst conditions. The next-highest scorer, Harry Moses, made 29.

The English-born, privately educated son of a Victorian attorney-general, McDonnell might have fit the establishment's model when it was trying to screw down the players. Yet he was a pugnacious type, no pet of the associations. In desperation, they made him captain for the 1886–87 series, setting a course for what would become known as the 'Australian way': pick your best batsman as captain, and build a team around him.

At the SCG on 28 January 1887, Shrewsbury called wrongly and McDonnell became the first Test captain to put an opponent into bat. Orthodoxy decreed that winning the toss meant batting, but circumstances were unusual to say the least.

That morning, the SCG had been double-booked, as NSW and Victoria were still finishing their clash. Lest it be thought that this match had run over-time, the scores were: Victoria 61, NSW 89, Victoria 68, NSW 4/42. It was simply an administrative cock-up. The state of the pitch can only be imagined, but at 1.45 pm that afternoon, a Test was commenced on the same pitch.

Spofforth, salivating, did not get a bowl. Instead, McDonnell exposed England to the NSW right–left pairing of Charles Turner and Jack Ferris. Within 36 overs England were out for 45. This was their second encounter with Turner and Ferris: a month earlier, under McDonnell's NSW captaincy, Turner (13/54) and Ferris (7/49) had taken all 20 English wickets. Turner had dismissed the great Shrewsbury for a pair, following which the publican of the Oxford Hotel presented the England captain with a pair of gold spectacles. Now Turner and Ferris were repeating the prescription at Test level, on debut.

'Terror' Turner, from Bathurst, had honed his bowling during his free hours after morning shifts with Cobb & Co. He had played for NSW since 1882–83 but took four years to refine his front-on, round-arm action. Today we might call such a bowler a fast off-spinner or a slow-medium off-cut exponent. Turner's pace, accuracy and ability to break the ball back made him Spofforth's successor. Like Spofforth, he would excel on grippy English wickets. Turner was also a genuine all-rounder, scoring nearly 4,000 first-class runs and holding 85 catches in hands which, Arthur Mailey later observed, could crush the pips out of oranges.

Jack 'The Tricky' Ferris, like Turner a bank worker, was five years younger and bowled left-arm swing, changing to spin as the ball aged. That 1886–87 season was Ferris's first in top-level cricket, and Turner might have needed Ferris's arrival to reach his own peak. Throughout their careers, Turner would overshadow Ferris, who would only play for Australia for four years before qualifying for Gloucestershire and representing England. His skills deserted him utterly in the 1890s and he would die in the Boer War.

That January 1887 afternoon in Sydney, Terror and The Tricky delivered what should have been a matchwinning performance. But the pitch was truly awful – this was the first Test in which nobody scored 50. Bannerman took nearly an hour to score his first single, McDonnell made 14 and 0, and Australia managed to lose by 13 runs even after Turner and Ferris rumbled England a second time for 184.

As if to prove that bad pitches produce bad cricket and bad tempers, McDonnell had an altercation with Billy Barnes after the game. Barnes was known for his singing, but the Australians found him a truculent figure. Dismissed on the second day, Barnes stayed on the pitch to pat down the spot where the ball had bounced. The *Sydney Morning Herald* chided his 'impertinence'. Lillywhite wrote to the paper saying Barnes was repairing damaged turf. The *Herald* replied: 'That is precisely what cricketers do not think of doing.'

It was a bad-tempered tour all round, but never worse than after the First Test. McDonnell, dismissed by Barnes in both innings, got into a heated discussion with the Englishman in a pub. 'History is silent,' wrote Robinson, 'on what led to the telegraphed punch that failed to find its addressee.' Barnes took a swing at the Australian captain and connected so firmly with a brick wall as to put himself out of the rest of the tour. Alfred Shaw, who was in the pub, wrote: 'Personally, I think both were to blame, in that they both lost their tempers, and therefore their sense of self-respect.'

'Felix' was adamant that Greatheart would never have lowered himself to be involved in a punch-up. In 1919, Charlie Beal told J.C. Davis of *The Referee* that the blow had actually been aimed at Hugh Hiddilston, a NSW cricketer and accomplished boxer who had poked his nose into the heated discussion between Barnes and McDonnell. In 1890 Hiddilston was sacked from the NSW Attorney-General's Department for dodgy dealings. He was sentenced to 10 years imprisonment for fraud, and disappeared to WA after his release in the mid-1890s.

As if things weren't bad enough for McDonnell (though they could have been worse if Barnes had better aim), he lost five of his best players to a pay dispute before the Second Test. Giffen, Blackham, Billy Bruce, Joey Palmer and Billy Trumble – the experienced core of the Australian team – declined to play. Blackham, moreover, refused to play any more that season. Incredibly, he had only allowed 11 byes in 171 overs in Sydney. But he did not believe cricket should be played until the standard of pitch preparation caught up with his professionalism. He spent most of the summer fishing.

Bannerman and Spofforth were dropped, the Demon for the first and last time, clearly superseded by Turner and Ferris. The greatest bowler of the era would quit Australia for England, where he played with his old comrade Murdoch and died a wealthy man through his management of a tea-trading company.

In another low-scoring match, Australia were again routed. England's new spearhead George Lohmann, who learned during the Test that his mother had died, took 8/35 in the first innings and had McDonnell caught in the second just as Greatheart was turning the match around. Turner and Ferris starred again, taking 18 wickets, but their heroics would be rewarded, not for the first or last time, by defeat.

McDonnell led Australia for another year and a half, winning only one Test out of six, before he retired in disillusionment.

The 1887–88 summer was a low point, with two English teams coming out, an amateur one led by George Vernon and the professional outfit of Shaw and Shrewsbury. The amateurs were invited by the Melbourne Cricket Club, which was in open warfare with the VCA over the scheduling of Victoria's games, and the professionals were the guests of the NSWCA. Lord Hawke, who played with Vernon's amateurs, wrote: 'There was never such a prominent case of folly' as the two tours. Crowds agreed, flocking from the cricket grounds.

By February 1888, after Australian and colonial XIs had played both England teams ad nauseum, it was agreed that a 'best of' England would face Australia in an official Test in Sydney. Giffen and Horan were among five late Australian withdrawals. Yet again, McDonnell was playing without a full deck.

These games were bowlers' picnics. Turner and Ferris dismissed England for 113, but Lohmann and Bobby Peel had Australia out for a farcical 42. Turner and Ferris bowled England out for 137, but McDonnell was again ineffective as Lohmann and Peel sent Australia packing for 82.

More than the 1879 riot, more than Bodyline, more than World Series Cricket, this was the nadir for England–Australia cricket. Pitches, administration and playing standards were abysmal. The crowd for the Sydney Test, around 2,000 spread over three rainy days, remains the lowest for a Test in Australia. All the work done during the previous decade to bring in crowds and money had been undone by squabbling. Newspaper cartoons showed the game being drowned by an octopus of greed. Between the three colonies and the English, one point was resolved after 1887–88: that no England tours of Australia take place until professionalism and intercolonial rivalries had been sorted out. For the foreseeable future, there would be no Test cricket in Australia. Shrewsbury's English team went home, cancelling their planned tour of New Zealand due to lack of interest.

There remained interest in Australian teams touring England, however, and McDonnell would take his last tour in 1888. Giffen stayed home, in protest at the non-selection of his brother Walter.

Arriving in London, Sammy Jones was found to have smallpox. Charlie Beal, the manager, sequestered Jones in a hotel and did not let the secret out, fearing the team would be sent home. While the news of Jones's smallpox never got out (and Jones would live until 90), Sammy Woods was recruited from Cambridge. Woods did little on tour, averaging 5.40 with the bat and 27.09 with the ball, but did manage to utter the line of the season when he bowled W.G. Grace. As Grace walked, Woods said, 'I shouldn't go, Doctor, there's still one stump standing.'

Thanks to Turner and Ferris, the tour was not a complete disaster. Turner took 283 wickets at 11.68, Ferris 199 at 14.74. So reliant was McDonnell on them that Turner bowled 9,710 balls on the tour and Ferris 8,321. The 11 other bowlers managed 123 wickets between them.The English took Turner and Ferris for testing to divine their secrets. Nothing was forthcoming except, at Woolwich Arsenal, Turner's bowling was timed at 55 miles per hour (88km/hr), no doubt by primitive equipment unable to measure his true speed.

Under McDonnell, the 1888 team played better than the sum of its parts. *Wisden* wrote: 'There can be no doubt that the team that sailed from Adelaide last March did not deserve a quarter of the contemptuous things said about them by newspapers of their own colonies.' But the series, due to poor batting, was lost. They won at Lord's, but lost by an innings at The Oval and Manchester. McDonnell topped the tour averages and aggregates (1,331 runs at a low 23.35), and, in one hour's batting against the North of England at Old Trafford, revived his glory years by scoring 82 runs.

After such a struggle, McDonnell had little to look forward to, cricket-wise, at home. No English teams were coming. Victorian cricket was being torn apart between the MCC and VCA. McDonnell led the returning 1888 tourists to Adelaide for a game against Giffen's South Australia, but more people (2,000) attended the pre-match cocktail party than the game, which South Australia won easily.

Through these restless years, Giffen was the undisputed champion of domestic cricket. For South Australia, he was a one-man team, dominating the batting, opening the bowling, leading the third colony to success exceeding its resources. No Australian cricketer before Bradman would produce such a sequence of eye-popping feats.

A Murdoch loyalist, Giffen had missed the guts of the 1884–85 home series but returned for the Fourth Test to take 7/117, setting up Australia's win. That was under Blackham, who gave him 52 overs. He had stamina and accuracy that dwarfed that of any other man, Australian or English. The original Mr Cricket, he was without question the fittest player of the 19th century.

Unlike most modern all-rounders, who have tended to swashbuckle with the bat, Giffen took himself as seriously as his top-order position warranted. He was a defensive batsman, stooping with prodigious concentration for lengthy innings, outconcentrating even Murdoch. As a bowler, he decanted his energy over the longest spells. Coming in off an eight-step run, he wound up by swinging his arms behind his back, loped in with his bowling arm concealed behind his right flank, and delivered mostly off-spinners, but with variations in flight, pace and spin that ground batsmen down before getting them out. He bowled top-spinners and skidders with greater accuracy than any other Australian slow-medium. His high frequency of caught-and-bowled dismissals attests to a poisonously deceptive slower ball.

Another marker of how the dispute of 1884–85 and the Murdoch exile gutted Australian cricket was that in the seven years after that inaugural Adelaide Test, such a stirring moment for Giffen, he played just five Tests. In five and a half years between winter 1886, when he was 27, and January 1892, when he was 32, Giffen played no Test cricket. Little wonder that his most stupendous performances were delivered under the red cap of his colony.

Stupendous they were. He only played one first-class match in 1885–86, against Victoria at the Adelaide Oval, but did enough in it to be second in the season's national bowling aggregates: he took

The mighty George Giffen

9/91 and 8/110, and scored 20 and 82. Nobody before him had achieved 100 runs/10 wickets match figures in Australia, the first of nine such doubles for the strongman.

Typically of Giffen, the calamitous 1886 tour under Harry Scott was his best. He topped the batting and bowling averages, with 1,424 runs at 26.86 and 154 wickets at 17.36. In five successive innings, Giffen piled up 40 wickets at 5.50 apiece, starting with 7/41 and 9/60 against Derbyshire, followed two matches later by 8/23 and 9/60 against Lancashire. But in the lost Test series, he was distinctly ordinary, scoring 3, 1, 3, 1, 5 and 47, and taking four wickets. When it really mattered on English soil, Australia's Grace was no Grace at all.

On sunbaked home pitches, Giffen was the greatest Australian cricketer of the 19th century and arguably the greatest before Bradman. He would not tour England again until 1893, so the best years of his career went untested – unverified? – by Test cricket on English turf.

He became South Australian captain at the MCG in February 1887. Argumentatively, he refused the Victorian suggestion of bowling six- rather than four-ball overs. He knew the way he wanted things: having sorted out the rules, he took 8/83 and 4/104, bowling himself virtually unchanged

His brother Walter, four years younger, was scoring heavily for Mitcham in Adelaide and George wanted him for South Australia. Walter would later lose two fingers in a gasworks accident, but in his early twenties seemed destined to follow in George's bootprints. George's blindly loyal patronage of Walter, which would cost him heavily, was apparent from the start. In 1887–88, playing against Vernon's English amateurs, Giffen ensured Walter was picked. George went out to toss with Lord Hawke, who called 'Woman' for tails. Giffen insisted on a re-toss with Hawke calling tails. Hawke declared: 'Not at any price. In all my life I never called anything but "Woman".'

Giffen acquiesced, but was less yielding when, on the fourth day, he and Walter formed a staunch partnership. At 2/121 chasing 278, there was a mix-up, and the bails were removed at the end to which Walter was running. He quickly walked off, but the English protested, saying the Giffens had not crossed and therefore it was the more dangerous George who should go. Play was held up for half an hour while George and the English argued. This time it was the English who gave in. George scored 81 to go with the hat-trick he had taken earlier in the match, but it was not enough to win the game.

It was inevitable that such a forceful personality who played so much cricket would be followed by controversy. Giffen was no provocateur, but he took the game seriously. Two months after the run-out incident with Walter, Vernon's team returned to Adelaide and received a sound thrashing from George, who took five wickets in the first innings. With South Australia well behind in the match, the pitch was vandalised overnight: a spiked roller run over it and water poured into the holes. Vernon, alerted by curator Charlie Checkett at dawn on the third day, refused Giffen's request that the game restart on a new wicket. Giffen, justifiably, felt disadvantaged by the damage. Vernon, perhaps also justifiably, suspected a set-up by South Australian team sympathisers seeking some way to turn the match around.

Vernon won the point, but not the argument: Giffen accepted that he had to bat on the disfigured pitch. In a fit of pique, he struck 203. His feistiness won support from *The Bulletin*, which wrote: 'The Australians, whether amateur or professional, will never consent to be spat upon by dirty little cads whose soap-boiling or nigger-murdering grandfathers left enough money to get the cads' fathers "ennobled" and to enable the cad himself to live without working.' If a cricketer could not say what he really thought – and Giffen had a genuine respect for his opponents – a nationalistic press operated under no such constraints.

Giffen's feats were starting to take on a mythic quality. Later that summer, against Victoria in Adelaide, he bowled unchanged in the first innings to take 8/65, then scored 166 runs in six hours, then bowled unchanged again to take 6/60. South Australia won by an innings and 113. Without Giffen they would probably have lost by just as many. His achievement of scoring a century and taking

10 wickets in a match was something he would repeat five times before anyone else in Australia did it once.

But the onfield amazements would be punctuated by off-field impasses. Giffen refused to play in the 1887–88 Test. His grievance was simple. He was trying to hold down a job that was not well paid, and every time he travelled to play cricket he was testing his employer's patience. When first picked for Australia, back in 1881–82, he had been scared to ask his boss for unpaid leave. Giffen's demand was not greedy: all he wanted was £10 a week, the equivalent of his foregone salary. He was not alone: Blackham, Bruce, Palmer and Trumble also asked for 'loss of time payments' to play against the English. All were refused.

Giffen was invited on McDonnell's 1888 England tour, but declined when Walter was not selected. The truth was that George did not really want to tour, as he did not believe the team could generate enough interest to draw crowds, raise money, and make the tour financially worthwhile. In short, Giffen could not afford to risk his livelihood on a weakened tour, though he was so essential to the Australian team that his absence fulfilled his own prophecy.

On its return, McDonnell's 1888 Australians played each of the colonies. In Adelaide, Giffen captured 5/54 and 4/72 as the South Australians – as *Giffen* – humbled the national XI. Then, against Victoria at the MCG, he scored 135 and 19 and took 6/82 and 7/77. By the end of the 1880s, there was no Australian cricketer to match Giffen. But the king was about to emerge from his exile.

5

MURDOCH REDUX

ALTHOUGH no England teams were touring Australia, the prospect of Australia not touring England was unthinkable. Scott's 1886 and McDonnell's 1888 tours, while unable to regain the Ashes, had produced windfalls for the English counties, and there remained an appetite to invite Australian teams.

When the Marylebone Cricket Club invited Melbourne to send an Australian team in 1890, Harry Boyle, the Very Devil, was sole selector and team manager. Looking for a captain, Boyle could see only wreckage. Scott had left cricket to become a country doctor. McDonnell, who had married in 1888, had not played for two years and was dedicating himself to teaching. The remaining pillars of Australian cricket, Blackham and Giffen, once firm friends, were at loggerheads.

It had been Giffen who, purloining a nickname bestowed on England's Dick Pilling, called Blackham 'the Prince of Wicket-keepers'. Giffen would write: 'Australia has had two heroes each of them the populace have frequently called "Old Jack". One is Carbine, the equine champion … the other is Jack Blackham.' It is through Giffen's vivid writing that Blackham survives:

> With eyes as keen as a hawk, and regardless of knocks, he would take the fastest bowling with marvellous dexterity, and woe betide the batsman who so much as lifted a heel of his back foot as he played forward and missed the ball.

Yet Giffen and Blackham were too combative to always be friends. In the Victoria–South Australia match of 1889–90, Giffen, on 9, refused to walk when the Victorians appealed for hit-wicket. He wrote:

> In making the stroke I slipped down, and in the act of rising again was said to have knocked the wicket with my foot, and a bail fell off … I knew I had not touched the wicket and moreover, had got into my head the idea that the ball was dead and that a second appeal could not be made, so I declined to leave the crease.

Blackham threatened to take his team off. Both stood their ground, until Blackham, as the visitor, backed down, continuing under protest. Giffen made 85, but Victoria won.

After the game, the Victorians passed a motion: 'If any cricketer refuses to obey the rules, and to concede to the judgement of the umpire, he must be disqualified for a particular term.'

The controversy flared, VCA members writing to Lord's and an outraged SACA refusing to play Victoria until a process was resolved for the pre-approval of umpires.

Giffen later described his refusal to walk as his greatest regret, and the SACA backed down from its threats of boycott. 'Of course,' Giffen wrote, 'afterwards I realised I had acted wrongly and I was not sorry when our last wicket fell at the end of the match with the Victorians 18 runs to the good.'

On the heels of the Giffen incident, Boyle asked Blackham to help him select the 1890 team. Giffen said he would only tour if Turner and Ferris were picked, which, in his view, ensured a degree of success. Terror and The Tricky were, of course, chosen, and Giffen was ready to tour until he discovered that his brother Walter wasn't on the list. So George spent another the winter in the Adelaide post office.

Boyle and Blackham sent another desperate plea to Cootamundra. At several points during Murdoch's exile, they had asked him to play for Victoria. He had come close only once, in 1887, but had backed down at the last minute.

Now Boyle was able to flatter Murdoch into one last tour with a mission as big as the man himself. The stakes? To save Anglo-Australian cricket, no less. The great man would be granted the financial and personnel control that he had wielded in 1880, 1882 and 1884.

After more than five years in exile, Murdoch came back for one pre-tour game, in February 1890. He scored 13. Aged 36, he could not expect his mastery to return quickly, so he needed support. But the selected touring team was full of holes: McDonnell and Giffen were out, as were the veteran Bannerman and younger players Billy Bruce and Harry Moses.

The worst selection blooper was when the last spot, Blackham's wicketkeeping back-up, was awarded to E.J.K. Burn of Tasmania. Horan wrote in *The Australasian*: 'The last notion of sending for Kenny Burn I like very well.' But neither Horan nor Boyle knew what they were talking about. When the team assembled in Adelaide, Kenny Burn confessed that he had never kept wicket and had no appetite to learn on the job. 'Felix' Horan, tail between his legs, explained: 'Blackham had seen in print that "Burn" had stumped men in Tasmania – but that Burn was Kenny's brother, and quite an inferior player.'

By 1890, Murdoch had added a few pounds but lost none of his style.

Such was the method of Australian team selection in 1890. Kenny 'The Scotsman' Burn, though he could not keep wicket, was still put on the boat. On the tour he would score 344 runs at 10.42 and become the second Tasmanian, after George Bailey, to play a Test for Australia.

Murdoch's team was further depleted during the voyage on the SS *Liguria*. Big-hitting South Australian opener Jack Lyons fell onto the deck from a trapeze exercise, and was incapacitated. Then the ship collided with two others off Gibraltar and nearly sank. When they arrived in England, Murdoch and Boyle called on Sammy Woods, an expat who had filled in usefully for Australia on previous tours, but Woods declined to play.

The 1890 team lost the Tests 2–0 and became the first Australian tourists to finish with a losing record. Of 34 matches, they won 10, lost 16 and drew 8. The bowling, headed by Turner and Ferris, was strong enough, but the batting was timid and Murdoch's day was past. He topped the batting figures, but his average of 24.45 was his lowest on four tours as a captain.

Just below Murdoch in the averages was the 24-year-old Harry Trott, the one young player whose tour was a success. Born in Collingwood, the third of eight children, Trott had played for the Capulet Cricket Club until South Melbourne recruited him after seeing how strongly he hit down the ground. A post office worker, he had caught his fellow postman Giffen's eye with an unbeaten 54 in Adelaide. Giffen took 9/91 in the innings, but not Trott, who astounded him by 'plunking me over the chains'.

In his early career, Trott's looping leg-spin was his stronger suit. In 1887–88 he took 26 first-class wickets, often opening the bowling. When Giffen slaughtered the Victorians with 166 in Adelaide, Trott stood alone, taking 7/216 off 62 overs.

While never of Giffen's quality, Trott emerged as a genuine all-rounder on the 1890 tour. His bowling was useful and sporadically unplayable. In the tour lead-up games against Tasmania in January 1890, he took 6/10 and 6/81, the latter including a burst of four wickets for no runs in six balls. In England Trott hit a career-best 186 against Cambridge University, and more than 1,000 runs all up. In the two-day Oval Test, when Australia were rolled for 92 and 102 on a sticky, Trott top-scored in both innings with 39 and 25, reputation-building innings that led to Giffen's pronouncement: 'The greater the match, the better he plays.'

Trott's fielding and catching at point were so sure that the position was named 'strong point' when he stood there, closer to the bat than convention dictated. But he was not infallible: in the second innings of that Test at The Oval, with England chasing 95 and Grace on a pair, Trott dropped him, the doctor made 16 and England won by two wickets.

The tour degenerated into the most poorly disciplined cricket venture to England so far. Murdoch's fondness for a party had bonded his men in 1880, 1882 and 1884. In 1890, his tolerance produced factions and hangovers unredeemed by victory. Boyle and Lyons reportedly had a fistfight, and *The Bulletin* mocked the team:

> The Australian cricketer in England, batting a day after a banquet, sees at least two balls approaching. One is dead on the wicket. He smites at the other and sees four bails flying about, two wicket-keepers looking the other way, two prostrate and two erect stumps. Then he retires to two pavilions, makes 22 excuses, and another cable about bad luck and wet wickets is dispatched. The Australians always bat on a wet wicket after a banquet.

Murdoch, who had only come back to lead the tour after Boyle's pleading, felt betrayed, again, by his country. He was doing it a favour, he thought, and when a weakened team had been unable to deliver, he was copping the blame again.

He did not return to Australia: a clear signal of his feelings. Like many Australian cricketers since, he felt more loved in England. He decided to play again, as a professional for Sussex, who had been chasing him since his fabled unbeaten 286 eight years earlier. He went on to represent them 137 times and renewed his friendship with Grace, among others.

As a new Englishman, approaching 40, Murdoch's cricket enjoyed an Indian summer. The majestic off-side strokeplay re-emerged, and he kept wickets so well that he was selected for England against South Africa in Cape Town in 1892. Only four others have played for both England and Australia, and Murdoch is the only Australian captain to have done so.

Although he would return to Australia in 1893–94 to play three matches for NSW (his highest score 64 not out against Victoria), Murdoch's home was now Sussex. His breach with Australia never fully healed. When he was not chosen for Australia on its 1893 Ashes tour, *Wisden* lamented his absence, saying his 'judgement, tact and strong will would have been invaluable in the management of the team despite, or perhaps because of, his residence in England'.

Charles Fry extolled his off-field bonhomie, noting how he was 'a man who would enjoy a Klondyke or a Mansion House dinner … his spirit would refuse to be unfortunate, his body scorn incapacity for meat and drink … He walks, talks, eats, drinks, smokes and wears a hat distinctively.' Fry loved Murdoch's 'cheerful, well-fed voice [and] his kind, cheery face, tanned and determined,' but nor could he forget 'that brilliant half-cut, half-drive, that marvellous crack past cover-point'.

Murdoch, who had lost six prime years, would play to 49. He joined London County alongside Grace. In his last match, for Gentlemen against Players at The Oval in 1904, Murdoch scored 140.

Seven years later, he was the guest of the Melbourne Cricket Club to watch Australia play South Africa. At lunch, the 56-year-old made an outlandish prediction of a South African collapse. When it eventuated, he declared that he had brought bad luck on 'those poor boys' and would never forecast again. He was right. Eating in the MCC committee room, he put a hand to his forehead. Asked what was wrong, he said, 'Neuralgia, I think … I have a pain here.' Within moments he had suffered a stroke and fallen into a coma. Two hours later, at a private hospital near the MCG, he died. In accordance with his wishes, Australia's first great batsman was not buried in his home country. Instead, he was embalmed and shipped to his adopted one, where, in honour of his funeral, all first-class games were suspended. His last act, posthumously, was to turn his back on the country that, he believed, had turned its back on him.

6

BLACK JACK

THE humiliated 1890 Australians returned, without Murdoch, to another Giffen-dominated home season. Improved pitch preparation was about to usher in an era of higher batting scores. Giffen would not only exceed all others in the hugeness of his innings, but his patient off-spin was so effective on drier, better-rolled wickets that he was one of the only bowlers whose figures did not suffer correspondingly.

That summer, he topped the national batting with 275 at 91.66, and was third in the bowling with 19 at 18.52. Against NSW, he bowled unchanged for a herculean 83.3 overs, taking 6/150. But he reserved his greatest punishment for the Victorians. In January 1891, at the MCG, he scored 237 in 445 minutes. When Victoria replied, Giffen bowled unchanged for 51.2 overs and took 5/89. He made Victoria, out for 220, follow on. This time they totalled 190. Except for a single over, Giffen bowled unchanged again, taking 7/103.

Giffen returned home to a mayoral reception in Adelaide Town Hall and, in his recollection, 'a purse of sovereigns'.

In more than 115 years since, the achievement of a double century and 10 wickets in a game has only been rivalled once: by the same man, the next time his state met Victoria.

The opening match of 1891–92 saw South Australia hosting Victoria. Giffen won the toss and batted … and batted … Of South Australia's 562, he scored 271 in a touch over seven hours. Blackham's Victorians, in despair, tried everything and more. John Harry, the unlucky wicketkeeper left out of the 1890 tour for Kenny Burn, ran in to bowl to Giffen right-handed but switched the ball, without warning, to his left. Such a deceit was within the rules, but it did not dislodge Giffen. Harry McLean pulled a similar trick, switching mid-stride to underarm. Blackham himself took the ball for two underarm overs.

Only brother Walter could disrupt George. The pair added 161 for the fifth wicket, a South Australian record, concluding when George smote a straight drive down the wicket and crushed Walter's fingers against the handle of his bat.

Another double-century didn't sate Giffen's appetite for destroying Victoria. After his seven hours' batting, he bowled 50.1 overs and took 9/96. Victoria made 36 runs fewer than he had. Following on, they had to face him unchanged for yet another 25.5 overs. He took seven more wickets for 70. That match, with 271 runs and 16/166, is so much greater than anything Bradman put together in one game, or anyone else for that matter, that it alone elevates Giffen to the highest rank of Australian cricketers. The fact that he did it in his first outing after scoring 237 and taking 12/192 is one of those things that needs to be read over and over again before it will sink in. Only Bradman has had Giffen's ability to invite such disbelief.

The historian Harry Altham said Giffen's Adelaide match was 'surely the greatest all-round performance in recorded history of any class' of cricket. Grace declared that 'you have the best all-round man in the world'.

Grace, that month, arrived in Australia for the first time since 1874, when a 15-year-old Giffen had bowled to him in the Adelaide nets. Now, at 43, Grace was playing his only overseas Test series, the first English tour for four years and the precursor to cricket's first Golden Age.

In Murdoch's wake, the Australian captaincy fell to Old Faithful. Never the most imaginative, willing or inspiring captain, Blackham was the Allan Border of his time. If he had been made captain in 1885, he might have held the role for a decade and Australia might have emerged sooner from its drought. Blackham was the one constant in the Australian team, home and away. Since 1877 his position had never been questioned. Asked who was the best wicketkeeper he had seen, Grace exclaimed: 'Don't be silly, there has been only one – Jack Blackham.'

Among the four pillars, only Blackham revolutionised technique. Adam Gilchrist is said to have done this recently, because of the dynamism of his batting. But Blackham invented the way glove-men would position themselves, take the ball, and effect catches and stumpings for the next 130 years. On keeping wicket, he wrote the book. He was universally popular with crowds, a dark and unyielding folk hero. Dick Lilley, who would become England's best gloveman of the turn of the century, said he was first inspired to keep wicket by watching Blackham play for Australia against Warwickshire in 1888.

Financially, for Blackham, the failure of the 1890 tour had been hard. He had made a number of poor investments in Australia and needed cricket to live. But no tour would return as much as the £750 he had earned back in 1878 as one of Dave Gregory's stockholders and the £900 he had lugged home in 1880 and 1884.

It is salutary that when, at 37, Blackham was finally made permanent Australian captain, the team's performances began to improve.

Grace's 1891–92 team to Australia was sponsored by Lord Sheffield, whose monetary gift to the colonies would partly pay for the shield bearing his name. Grace and Blackham led their teams from behind a bearded ferocity. In Melbourne, Blackham tossed his lucky Victorian coin and batted. It would be the first Test to adopt six-ball overs and the first to go into a fifth day. Australia scored 240, Giffen notoriously given out lbw for 2 when Grace appealed from square of the wicket. In England's reply, Grace opened and Blackham stationed a man at silly mid-off. Grace wheeled on Blackham and shouted, 'Do you want a funeral in your team?'

Grace made 50, England 264. Australia set them 213 in the fourth innings, and the only funeral was for England's hopes. Turner's pace and Harry Trott's leg-breaks, Blackham daringly throwing the Victorian spinner the new ball against Grace, broke their resistance.

For the Second Test, Grace objected to Blackham's lucky penny but still called incorrectly. Blackham batted first on a suspect pitch and when Harry Moses started limping, Grace told Blackham he should 'expect no sympathy' and refused a runner. Australia trailed by 162 on the first innings but staged one of the great fightbacks. Bannerman made 91 in what can only be assumed was an excruciating 420 minutes, underlined by the fact that medium-pacer 'Dick' Attewell bowled 204 balls to him from which he extracted five scoring shots. Keeping the crowds awake, Jack Lyons belted 134 in 185 minutes and Billy Bruce 72, putting the hosts ahead by 219. Giffen and Turner ran through the Englishmen, and Australia won a series for the first time since 1882–83. A loss in the Third Test at Adelaide could not dim Blackham's pent-up satisfaction.

Grace, like Giffen, was as much Blackham's admirer as his nemesis. The doctor wrote how Blackham 'was marvellously quick, taking shooters and yorkers between the wicket and the pads with comparative ease'. Knowing the difficulty of the task, even the toughest opponents marvelled at Blackham's skills.

After years of faulty administration, at Dave Gregory's instigation the Australasian Cricket Council was formed at a meeting at the Oxford Hotel in Sydney's Darlinghurst on 13 September 1892. One of its first moves was to appoint six selectors for the 1893 tour of England. The six would be the nucleus of the team itself: Blackham as captain, Alick Bannerman, George Giffen, Jack Lyons, Harry Trott and Charles Turner.

The meeting's other key decision was to convert Lord Sheffield's gift into a shield for the winner of the colonial competition. In the inaugural Sheffield Shield game, between South Australia and New South Wales in Adelaide in December 1892, Giffen took three balls to claim the inaugural dismissal, that of Sammy Jones, his first of 12 in the match.

South Australia could not win the Shield that first year, despite Giffen's best efforts. He topped the national batting and bowling averages, with 468 runs at 58.50 and 33 wickets at 23.00. In the Sydney fixture, he personally swept the wicket before the South Australian innings but could not prevent defeat. In the home game against Victoria, he was again their menace, scoring 43 and 181 and taking 11 wickets. Giffen got the highest score of the season, to go with the first wicket, but Victoria took the Shield.

Blackham, fresh from an unbeaten 64 for Victoria which set up a win in the decisive Shield match, got the touring side he wanted, with one exception. George Giffen insisted on Walter's selection. No Walter, no George. George argued that Walter had played in the last two Tests of 1891–92. Other selectors argued that Walter, in those Tests, had scored 1, 3, 3 and 2 as a tail-ender and had not bowled. Yet such was George's sway, his threat prevailed.

Another questionable choice was Arthur Coningham, a Queenslander whose name for pranks outlasted his contributions as a cricketer. Against Blackpool on the tour, Coningham gathered sticks and lit a fire in the outfield to keep himself warm. A spectator offered him hot potatoes to put in his pockets.

A century from Melbourne's Harry Graham, 'The Little Dasher', saved a draw in the First Test, but the Second was lost by an innings in tropical heat at The Oval. Blackham's personality and experience, assets in so many ways, were not leavened by any of the glad-handing knack that could douse anxieties on a long hard tour. He often seemed overwhelmed by worry. Giffen nicknamed him 'the Caged Lion' for the way he paced around changing rooms bemoaning poor luck or fretting about bad omens. He was 'far from an ideal captain', Giffen wrote, 'on account of his tendency to worry and magnify temporary misfortunes'. When his younger players needed his steadiness, Blackham would bury his face in his towel. In tense games, rather than watch Blackham would hire a hansom cab and ride around the ground in circles until the crisis had passed. He lost one stone in weight between the First and Third Tests. It was said that he did not sleep during Test matches and would stay in the one place in changing rooms – enforcing the rule on others – if things were going well. Superstition did not start with Jack Blackham, but he set a pattern for many of his successors.

After their Second Test loss, the Australians took a so-called 'pleasure ride' on a train to the Sussex coast. As on the 1890 tour, there were feuds between the drinkers and non-drinkers, as well as the usual cross-colonial rivalries. Whatever the cause, and the exact personalities involved never became publicly known, the train trip descended into a fistfight that left the carriage spattered in blood. Blackham, while not one of the fighters, lacked the skills to bring his men together. *The Bulletin* said the team was failing because it couldn't 'find an effective pick-me-up the morning after a binge'. *The Sydney Mail* said the teetotallers had simply grown tired of 'doing too much of the drinkers' work'.

The Third Test was drawn, thanks to a time-soaking partnership between Blackham and Turner, and an acrimonious tour came to a bad end when Blackham led the first Australian team to lose to Philadelphia, by an innings and 68 runs. While Graham, Lyons, Trott and Turner had performed sturdily, Blackham was criticised, having let through 72 byes in three Tests and not using his bowlers as intelligently as he might have.

Giffen captured 118 wickets on the tour, behind only Turner, but was not as penetrative as in 1886 and was seventh in the batting averages. He put on a show against Grace's Gloucestershire, hitting 180 and taking 7/11, and captured 7/128 in Australia's loss at The Oval, but in all it was another underwhelming tour by his standards. Nor had he and Blackham been able to leave their old friction behind. In one tour game, Giffen objected to Blackham not giving him a bowl, and the two had to be separated by teammates.

A rare bright spot was the emerging leadership of Harry Trott. Trott is often portrayed as a lovable bon vivant, looking drolly from drooping eyelids. He allegedly put on a stone a year and was known as the type of joker who would smoke a cigar with Prince Edward rather than keep it as a souvenir, then offer numerous butts to keepsake-hunters with the claim that this was the one that the heir to the throne had sucked on. When Spofforth came to commiserate with Trott after another collapse at The Oval, Trott famously replied: 'Things could hardly be worse. But tell me, Spoff, are there any decent leg shows in the theatres?' So fond of the power of alcohol was Trott that when NSW's Frank Iredale, a teetotaller, lost confidence on the next England tour Trott offered him a potion of brandy and water. Iredale, not knowing why he was feeling so blissful, went out and rediscovered his freedom.

Trott didn't win respect by being a good drinker, however. He had gone on strike from the Boxing Day match in 1891 when two South Melbourne players were not chosen alongside him. He was hard-nosed when necessary, even to the point of cynicism. When Victoria didn't want South Australia to follow on in a Sheffield Shield match (follow-ons were compulsory), Trott ordered Hugh Trumble to bowl three intentional no-balls so that South Australia would pass the target. When the Victorian players were asked to nominate a player-delegate to the Australasian Cricket Council and a selector of the 1893 tour, Trott was their choice, even though Blackham was still the Victorian and Australian captain and the leader of the colony. Trott, as Blackham's lieutenant, was also his foil: unflappable when Blackham succumbed to nerves, rosily cheerful when Blackham sank into depression. Scoring another thousand runs on the 1893 tour, Trott supported Blackham amid the tensions over money and drinking, and struck 92 in the second innings of the Second Test, again coming to the fore when all others failed.

Money was the usual subtext for disharmony on England tours, and 1893 was worse than most. When the Australasian Cricket Council set up the tour, it had not been able to wrest control of finances and profits from the players. But the ACC did appoint the tour accountant, NSWCA manager Vic Cohen. In November 1893, as the team sailed home, Cohen told the squad that the tour dividend would be £50–80 per man. There was uproar. Blackham and others stormed Cohen's cabin to see the books. A vigorous discussion resulted in each player's share being raised to £190. It was a lose–lose result. The infant ACC lost its planned profits, and the players realised they were a pale financial shadow of their predecessors.

Nearly 40, Blackham became involved increasingly in onfield spats. In the January 1894 intercolonial game in Sydney, Blackham said the umpire, Jack Tooher, was favouring NSW by delaying a start on the fourth day. An outraged Tooher said he would never again umpire a match in which Blackham played. The NSWCA president George Reid – also the NSW premier and a future prime minister – said Blackham was 'blue mouldy for a fight'. Blackham eventually backed down and apologised to Tooher.

Blackham wanted to retire but couldn't find the right moment. Cricket was his life. He had been a permanent fixture – *the* permanent fixture – in the Australian team since 1877. So when he led Australia onto the SCG in December 1894 against a glamorous and talented England team led by Andrew Stoddart, the 40-year-old was not thinking of retirement. His captaincy had survived 1893 and his status in the game was unimpeachable. He also saw the size of the crowd – 62,213 for that Sydney Test – and figured he couldn't quit the game just when it was threatening to pay decent money again.

The decision was made for him, by circumstances and his characteristically obstinate response to them.

Surveying a perfect dry pitch at the toss, Stoddart said to Blackham, 'Someone will be swearing directly, Jack. I hope it's you!' It was Stoddart. Blackham won the toss and batted.

Alongside Alick Bannerman and Giffen, the eternal Blackham was the only survivor of the grand early 1880s. Murdoch and Spofforth were living in England, Boyle was running a sportsgoods empire, Horan was spinning out columns in *The Australasian*, Massie was in the bank, Scott was riding around tending to the sick in the Hunter Valley, and McDonnell was living in Queensland, battling the heart disease that would kill him, still a young man, within two years.

Blackham was lining up with a new generation: Dave Gregory's nephew Syd, Giffen's South Australian protégés Joe Darling, Jack Lyons and Ernie Jones, the emerging Frank Iredale and Harry Trott. The all-star English, who had pummelled Australia in 1893, boasted Archie MacLaren, Stoddart, Bobby Peel, John Brown, Johnny Briggs, and the black-haired 'Surrey Express' Tom Richardson.

A mouth-watering series started with one of the great Tests. Giffen, 13 years after his debut, finally recorded a Test century. He came in at 1/10 and was joined by Iredale at 3/21, Richardson having devoured the top order. Unusually aggressive, Giffen took the long handle to Richardson, Briggs and Peel, racking up 161 in 254 minutes. Iredale (81) and Gregory, on his way to 201, took Australia towards a record score. Blackham, batting at ten, joined Gregory at 8/409, and some blistering hitting set one of the longest-standing records, 154 in 76 minutes for the ninth wicket. Blackham's thumb was split open by a snorter, but pain never registered with the gloveman, who had his eye on a maiden century to match Giffen's.

Although Blackham was bowled by Richardson for 74, Australia made 586, its highest score and the first to exceed 500 since the Murdoch-led innings at The Oval in 1884.

Blackham would not rest his thumb, and during England's 325 he knocked it again. His agony compounded as England, following on, scored 437, building a lead of 186 despite Giffen's eight wickets for the match.

Blackham spent the last night pacing the corridors of the Coogee team hotel, putting everyone on edge. Set 187 to win, Australia had cruised to 2/113, Giffen leading a stand with the debutant Darling, whose 53 was an improvement on his first-ball duck, skittled by Richardson, four days earlier. But Blackham heard the rain falling, and the next morning his worst fears were realized. On a sticky wicket that turned stickier as the sun dried it, Peel and Briggs went to work. When Briggs trapped Giffen the Australian middle-order lost their nerve. Peel, freshened by a cold shower to help him over the effects of a night's carousing, took six wickets and Australia fell 420 short of their first innings, 20 shy of the target.

Blackham, caught by Archie MacLaren for 1, was part of the collapse. Not for 87 years would Australia again lose after enforcing a follow-on.

Blackham, never one to spare himself, tried to play in the Second Test but his thumb swelled up and he was replaced by Giffen as captain and Affie Jarvis as keeper. Coming back in the Sheffield Shield in January, Blackham split his thumb again, and that was the end.

Blackham's modern-day heirs are Boon and Border: moody, silent, pared-down players of epic durability. Blackham's humour came, appropriately, in black. Asked his advice on keeping wicket, he said: 'Give it up and take on bowling.'

7

TOWARDS THE GOLDEN AGE

THE Second Test started 20 minutes late. The Australians were in their changing room electing a new captain. When the winner of the vote emerged onto the MCG to toss with Stoddart, it was Giffen.

In his mid-thirties, a 17-year first-class cricketer, Giffen was finally ready to rule the English. His 202 runs and eight wickets in Sydney were a Test best. In the earlier tour match in Adelaide, Giffen became the first to score half-centuries and take at least five wickets in all four innings of a first-class match with 64 and 58 not out, and 5/175 and 6/49. South Australia won. Then, in December, he scored 94 not out and took 12/147 in a routine crushing of the Victorians. If ever he was ready to deliver against England, it was now.

He was not a natural Test captain, with his unwillingness to delegate and his bloodyminded pursuit of principle over common-sense. But he was the leader of an inexperienced group, traumatised by Sydney and bereft of Blackham. Four were South Australians. The eccentric Coningham made his Test debut, while Billy Trumble's younger brother Hugh, destined to be Australia's next great bowler and, briefly, its captain, made his first Test appearance in Australia.

Giffen, 35 and at the long peak of his powers, won the toss and sent Stoddart in. Coningham opened the bowling and took a wicket – the magisterial MacLaren – with his first Test delivery, cut to 'strong point' Harry Trott. Coningham, Turner and Hugh Trumble rolled the tourists for 75 but Australia, notwithstanding Giffen's 32, could not capitalise and led by just 48.

England dug in on the now-dry wicket, Stoddart making 173. Giffen led Australia as he had South Australia: he bowled, and kept on bowling. He sent down 78.2 overs, taking 6/155. Trumble begged for a bowl. Giffen responded by taking himself off and resuming at the other end. Chasing 428, Giffen tried to do it all with the bat, but his 43, and half-centuries to Iredale, Bruce and the splendid Trott could not stop another amazing English turnaround.

Giffen needed no rest. In his next game, for South Australia against NSW, he took 8/77 and 8/109, to this day the best haul in the Sheffield Shield.

For the original Mr Cricket, the fitness freak who was up each dawn to run through Adelaide's parks and perform callisthenics so that he could bat and bowl all day, we can only imagine 11 January 1895 with a lump in the throat. George Giffen led an Australian Test team onto his Adelaide Oval. He lacked the unavailable Turner and Moses, and the omitted Lyons and Graham, but Giffen had himself.

In gathering heat, he won the toss and batted. Giffen, in early at three, stitched together the innings despite running out Trott. Like Bradman and Steve Waugh, Giffen rarely let himself get run out.

After Giffen was out for 58, Australia slumped. But his three-hour vigil had worn down the England bowlers, and they were vulnerable to some last-wicket hitting from newcomers Syd Callaway and Albert Trott, who added 81.

'Alberto' Trott, seven years the younger, was like Harry but more so. Albert was a colossal talent, one of the shining talents of the Golden Age, but also the most wasted. He bowled faster than Harry and hit further. He shared Harry's love of a tipple but turned it into a compulsion. Both brothers would die young, but only Harry fulfilled his cricketing promise.

If you were an Australian bowler from the 1870s to the 1900s,
this was a familiar sight: Giffen, immovable.

When England batted, Giffen gave the younger Trott three overs before taking control. His off-spin and Callaway's fast-mediums went unchanged for 52 overs, dismissing England for 124. Feeling the heat, Giffen used a newly written law and declined to enforce the follow-on. Helped by Iredale's century and Albert Trott's unbeaten 72 at number ten, Australia got ahead by 525.

Giffen was ready to give 'Alberto' his head now. Trott took 8/43 and Giffen 2/74 as Australia wrapped up their largest-yet win, by 382 runs.

Trott's wondrous debut would become an albatross. Nineteen years later he would be putting a loaded gun to his head in a squalid London flat. But this day, as a 21-year-old, he would be chaired from the Adelaide Oval. As he looked across the heads of the crowd he would see his captain also aloft.

Giffen would be criticised for overbowling himself, but not a word was spoken in Adelaide. This was the way Giffen operated: if you can do it all yourself, don't leave it to anybody else. When it worked, it worked spectacularly.

In Sydney a fortnight later, Giffen won the toss, batted, but failed. Harry Graham came back with a counter-punching century and Albert Trott, promoted to number nine, blasted 85 not out. He had now scored 195 vital runs in three innings without being dismissed.

Australia's 284 was remarkable on a pitch where Stoddart had predicted 20 wickets a day. On the second day, his forecast came true: England scored 65 and 72. Giffen took three wickets in the first innings and five in the second. He bowled unchanged with Turner, who took 4/33. Nobody was complaining about him over-bowling now. In the same innings Giffen and Turner became the first two Australians to take 100 Test wickets.

Under Giffen, Australia had rebounded from 0–2 to 2–2. The decider, at Melbourne, would be one of the best-ever matches to cap one of the best-ever Ashes series. 'The match of the century', as the press dubbed it, would also be the first Test to raise 100,000 spectators and receipts beyond £4,000.

Giffen, a lucky tosser, batted again and scored 57 in Australia's 414. He must, when Harry Trott took a wicket in the second over of England's reply, have felt the the series was in the bag. But MacLaren, Stoddart and Peel got on top of the Australian bowlers and England made 385. One reason was that Turner, the most prolific Australian Test bowler, had been voted out by Giffen and Blackham in favour of Tom McKibbin, who they thought would turn the ball dangerously in Melbourne.

McKibbin failed to penetrate and Giffen, always ready – too ready? – to assume responsibility, bowled 45 overs and took four wickets in a late burst. Having hurt his right little finger batting, he dropped two return chances from MacLaren. They would, as much as his omission of Turner, prove disastrous.

Giffen top-scored with 51 out of Australia's 267, Harry Trott his main ally. Giffen was full of praise: 'On a good wicket, I have seen Harry Trott adopt forcing tactics worthy of the big hitter, and in the very next match play keeps on a difficult pitch with wonderful skill.'

A lead of 296 should have been ample, especially when England quickly lost two wickets. Enter Yorkshire's John Brown, a stocky smoker and drinker. Coming in at 2/28, with a thunderstorm on the horizon, Brown massacred the Australian bowlers with 50 in 28 minutes. Unlike most sloggers, he took a breath and paced himself to 140 in 145 minutes. By the time Giffen caught him off McKibbin, the match and the series were England's.

Giffen's series was an overdue personal triumph. He had taken 34 wickets and scored 450 runs, a five-Test achievement yet to be equalled. His Australian summer of 93 first-class wickets and 902 runs was the nearest anyone has come to the 100–1000 double. But Australia had failed to win the Ashes, and Giffen received widespread blame. Pelham Warner said, simply, 'He bowled himself too much.' There were days when Giffen's teammates begged him to rest. He ignored them. The *Sydney Morning Herald* accused him of having a big head. But this was how he played, and he had taken the weakest colony to the top. Why change a winning formula?

His four Tests in 1894–95 would comprise his full tenure as captain. There was a mood for generational change, and Giffen was the last of the 1870s veterans. As a measure of the man, he acquiesced to the change and went to England on the 1896 tour, playing under Harry Trott and mentoring his rising South Australian stars Darling and Clem Hill. The next five captains of Australia would benefit from playing with Giffen.

With Queensland cricket better organised in the 1890s, Percy McDonnell came out of retirement against Stoddart's Englishmen at Brisbane's Exhibition Ground, scoring 21 and 22. He led them in two more games but could not control Coningham, the all-rounder who had moved north to be the marquee player. Against England, Coningham lost his temper at being called for chucking by Charles Bannerman. Next ball, instead of bowling, Coningham stood behind Bannerman and pelted it at Stoddart. The England captain demanded an apology. Bannerman threatened to have Coningham thrown off the field. McDonnell was powerless. Coningham apologised to Stoddart. Next ball, he ran in and, with a straight arm, clean-bowled the English captain.

Coningham must have been the toughest test for any captain's ticker. Against NSW, he refused to play for less than £10. The opposition paid his wage and soon regretted it: Coningham rattled off 151, Queensland's first-ever century. McDonnell, with 65, helped him add 107, Queensland's first century partnership. It was a fitting sign-off, though McDonnell was hoping for a few more years' cricket. He led The Rest against an Australian XI in March 1896, but by September of that year was dead from heart failure, the first Australian Test captain to pass away.

As the first Catholic and the only English-born man to captain Australia (Horan the only overseas-born captain), McDonnell has a certain symbolic resonance. His appointment showed that nationalist and sectarian biases were no exclusion in the 19th century. At the time of his death, he was still the only Australian to have scored three Test centuries. But when McDonnell stopped playing Tests in 1888, the national team was crying out for leadership. It found its leaders had been there all along: it was not a champion batsman but the old-timers Giffen and Blackham who carried Australia from chaos into the Golden Age.

8

THE COMING MEN

HARRY Trott, elected captain by the group touring England in 1896, represented a clear break. He had been 10 years old when Dave Gregory, Murdoch, Horan and Blackham had played the first Test series. Trott was almost a decade younger than Giffen.

Paid £10 for home Tests, a cricketer knew his best chance for compensation was to tour England. The captain, responsible for the tour's profitability, carried a direct and onerous weight. So for all his cheeriness, Harry Trott came into the job with mixed feelings; he was charged with making his teammates some money, and he had to do so without his right-hand man and star attraction.

The good-time Trott brothers had led Victoria with every expectation of joining the tour to England. Albert, in three Tests, had a batting average of 102.5. But a strange thing happened when Giffen, Billy Bruce and Tom Garrett sat down to select the team. They picked five Victorians, including Harry, as captain, but excluded Albert. Victoria's Jack Harry was selected, then dropped for an Adelaide teenager chosen at Giffen's insistence, Clem Hill.

Nobody was as predestined for Test greatness as Clement Hill. He was born during the inaugural Test match. When he was eight months old, his father John, who ran stage coaches, scored the first century on the Adelaide Oval, for North Adelaide against Kent. John Hill fathered 16 children, eight boys and eight girls. Among such a population a few cricketers can be predicted, but the Hills surpassed all probabilities. Two older than Clem – Percival ('Peter') and Arthur ('Farmer') – and three younger – Henry ('Harry'), Les and Stanley ('Solly') – represented South Australia. Three, including Clem, played Australian football for South Australia.

Nuggety Clem was the only left-hander, a precocious youngster who retained the air of a child prodigy for much of his career. Nine days after his 16th birthday, his batting for Prince Alfred College got him called up for South Australia. As a wicketkeeper-batsman, the boy was a failure, with a golden duck and a missed catch in Ernie Jones's first over. He gave up wicketkeeping, fearing that Jones's thunderbolts would damage his hands.

The next summer, even though he didn't play a first-class game, Hill scored 360 in a school match. His coach threatened to drop him, not for hogging the bowling but for continually hooking the ball from outside off-stump. Others, including Giffen, would later counsel Hill to moderate his hooking. He moderated it, but only moderately; the shot would score too many thousands for him to kick the habit.

When the English toured in 1894–95 and Giffen finally led Australia, Hill had still been too underripe to represent his country. He took 20, batting number ten, off the English in November, but when Stoddart's team returned to Adelaide four months later they found a different teenager. South Australia collapsed to Richardson, Peel, Briggs and Lockwood, but Hill counter-attacked from number eight and reached 63 by stumps. The next morning, knowing that he would be keeping wicket for the rest of the game – Jarvis had crashed his carriage on his way home – Hill whipped the cream of England for an unbeaten 150. He was 18 years and 11 days old. Giffen, sensing a tough mind to go with the talent, wrote that Hill was 'a boy who would not spoil himself'.

Hill enrolled in engineering and batted consistently for South Australia but not well enough to win selection in Harry Trott's initial touring squad until, at the SCG, he hit 206 not out in five hours, passing Giffen's Shield record, against a NSW bowling attack including the great Turner and, more strategically, Tom Garrett, one of the selectors for the Ashes tour. Elevated to bat in a trial between the designated Test team and a Rest XI, Hill made 74. The selectors called him up, risking a public lynching by leaving out Trott's charismatic younger brother. Time would prove them spot-on.

Clem Hill might have stood on the wrong side of the bat for the purists, but there was no better player in the Golden Age.

Tom Horan led the public outcry at Albert's omission, calling him 'one of the finest young cricketers Australia has ever produced', notwithstanding the fact that Albert's home season had yielded an anticlimactic 134 runs at 13.40 and 15 wickets at 26.66. Albert cut his brother, the Australian captain, stone cold when he saw him in the street. Then Albert announced that he was going to England anyway, to play *against* Australia for Middlesex. He would eventually reconcile with Harry, but in his short and sad life 'Alberto' had played his last Test for Australia.

Now breaching 100 kilograms, Harry led another apparently weak Australian team. Instead, they outdid every tour since Murdoch's men of 1884 and formed a conduit from the depressed second decade of Test cricket to the golden third.

Trott's great weapon was 'Jonah' Jones, an ex-miner and bricklayer from Broken Hill and unquestionably the fastest Australian bowler. In the tour opener against Lord Sheffield's XI in Sussex, Jones hit Grace on the body and sent another whistling through the great man's beard.

'Whatever are ye at?' Grace roared.

Trott stepped in and calmed the temperamental Jones. But Jonah had a sense of humour. 'Sorry Doctor,' he said. 'She slipped.'

More than 15,000 watched that day, and 30,000 came to the first day of the Test series at Lord's. On both occasions Australia fought back from horrendous batting collapses. Against the MCC they fell for 18. Against England they mustered 53 against Richardson (6/39) and Lohmann (3/13). Lord's was not what it would become: grazing sheep, maintained to mow the grass, had left it bumpy. But the Englishmen suffered no unevenness, replying with 292. Grace's 66 included his thousandth Test run.

In his first Test as captain, Trott's head was on the block. His decision to bat now looked 'brave', in the sense of 'stupid'. In the second innings Australia were 2/3 when the captain came in. They were three for 62 when he was joined by Syd Gregory. Australia had lost thirteen for 115 in the match and were still 177 behind. If Giffen was right, this was a situation tailor-made for Harry Trott. If Giffen was wrong, his captaincy might be over as soon as it started.

The counter-attack, given the quality of the bowling, was simply astounding. In three hours Richardson and Lohmann were smashed up hill and down ridge. The Trott–Gregory partnership was 221, putting Australia dangerously in front. But when Gregory fell for 103, the last seven wickets evaporated for 64 and Australia lost by six wickets. Trott's 143, his only Test century, came at the most crucial time. It did not win the match but it stalled England's momentum. No Australian captain would score another Test century in England until Bill Woodfull in 1930.

The team's confidence feeding upon their captain's, Australia charged back at Old Trafford, taming Richardson (who still took 7/168 from 68 overs) and totalling 412. Trott was out, cheaply and notably, to wicketkeeper Dick Lilley, whom a desperate Grace had given five overs. Lilley's second-last ball was a wide one, which Trott nicked. Grace took Lilley off. He couldn't believe the gloveman had removed Australia's captain. 'He must have been bowling with the wrong arm,' Grace concluded.

Australia, leading by 179, looked set, but England had their own secret weapon. His Highness the Jam Sahib of Nawanagar, Kumar Shri Ranjitsinhji, had been chosen for England because his native India did not have Test-playing status. No less a personage than Lord Harris opposed the selection of Ranji, known to his teammates as 'Smith'. But Trott and the Australian manager, the ex-player and theatre impresario Harry Musgrove, allowed Ranji to play, because they liked his style and wanted to see how he would fare. They did not show a moment's regret for their magnanimity in the second innings, as Ranji stroked a silken 154 not out in three hours, including 113 before lunch on the third day, the first of his numerous adornments to the Golden Age.

Richardson tried to defend 125, but Trott's tourists won by three wickets. For the first time since 1884, an Australian touring team had England on the back foot. Trott was held responsible, *Wisden* writing: 'Blessed with a humour that nothing could ruffle, Harry Trott was always master both of himself and his team, whatever the position of the game.'

Rain, and politics, ruined the Third Test at The Oval. Several England professionals threatened to strike unless they received better pay and treatment (they were still not allowed to dress in the same rooms as the amateurs). Lohmann and Billy Gunn didn't play, and Richardson, Bobby Abel and Tom Hayward took the field under protest. The game was a personal triumph for Hugh Trumble, who took 6/59 and 6/30, but in a few hours all four innings were completed and England had won the series.

Australia's discovery of the tour was the South Australian left-hander Joe Darling, whom Trott, in another instinctive move, had promoted to opener. Darling duly scored 1,555 runs, a record for a first-time tourist. The English gave back-handed recognition, *Wisden* remarking that he had 'as orthodox a game as a right-handed man'. In his preparation, Darling had been diligent in the extreme. This was, after all, a student of Giffen. Before leaving Adelaide, Darling had ordered practice pitches watered so that he could bat while they were drying, just like an English 'sticky dog'.

Darling, not Hill, promised to be the wonder batsman of his generation. The sixth son of John Darling, a wealthy Presbyterian wheat exporter and member of the South Australian Legislative Assembly, Joe had attended Prince Alfred College seven years ahead of Hill. On his last day as a 14-year-old, he batted for six hours against the Collegiate School of St Peter, scoring 252 with bare blistered hands and passing the mighty Giffen's schools record of 209 not out. The innings earnt him a place in a South Australian/Victorian XV against Australia in March 1886. His 16 runs, for a child, caught all the distinguished and experienced eyes who were there.

An average student, Darling's attentions were absorbed by games. As well as cricket, he represented Norwood in Australian Rules. But his father, notwithstanding his introduction of a bill into the parliament in 1870 to grant a lease on the parklands that would become the Adelaide Oval, was no fan of sports, at least not for his son. Darling Senior decided that Joe ought to join the family wheat business, sent him to Roseworthy Agricultural College, had him work in a bank, then packed him off to one of the Darling farms.

Giffen said Joe had been 'buried in the backblocks', and encouraged the prodigy back into cricket. At 23, having ripened in the bush, Darling returned to Adelaide. He married a grazier's daughter, and they talked John Darling into backing Joe's purchase of a sporting goods store in Rundle Mall. That summer he played his first game for South Australia.

Six games later, he was playing for Australia. He greeted his colonial teammate Ernie Jones in the national team's changing room, to be told that an initiation ritual involved wrestling with the miner-cum-brickie. Darling won the batsmen's applause by slamming the paceman to the floor.

Changing rooms nicknamed him 'Paddy', after the boxer Paddy Slavin. Darling did bear the pugilist an uncanny resemblance, but his strength in hand-to-hand combat gave the nickname a second layer. Compactly built, with intense close-set eyes, he was unorthodox in one regard. No left-hander had scored a Test century to that point. In 17 years Billy Bruce had come closest, but left-handers were rare and, in orthodox circles, despised. They were thought to play across the line among other insurmountable weaknesses. When it came to learning how to bat, left-handed boys were encouraged to use the strong hand to grip the top of the handle, and face the bowler like a right-hander.

Darling stood up to Tom Richardson, on the wrong side of the bat, through the 1894–95 and 1896 series. He was a new type of batsman. Most Australian players were one-dimensional, either blockers or sloggers. Giffen was a blocker, Lyons a slogger. Iredale was a little more cultured, but Bruce, who opened with Harry Trott, was a slogger. Trott could be a blocker one day, a slogger the next. Alberto was a slogger to a fault. But Darling was a bit of both, able to tailor his attitude to each ball. In his fourth Test, Darling had achieved a singular honour in Sydney, charging Johnny Briggs and launching a drive 100 metres over the Paddington End onto the tennis courts. It had taken him just four Tests to do what none of the sloggers – Massie, Bonnor, Lyons, Albert Trott and so on – had achieved. He had scored the first six in Test cricket. Many had scored

Joe Darling on the drive

fives, by putting the ball over the fence, but only Darling had put one out of the ground. But when Harry Trott asked him to open Australia's batting in 1896, Darling became a staunch defender and would end his batting career with a reputation for dourness.

Darling's first tour couldn't have contrasted more with that of his younger schoolmate Hill. Harry Trott ensured that Hill got equal pay, but he played like a learner. He walked out at Lord's in front of 30,414 and contributed 1 run to Australia's nightmarish 53. In the lost series, his scores were 1, 5, 9, 14, 1 and 0. He did better against the counties, accumulating 1,166 runs from 40 other innings.

Although the series was lost, the tour vindicated Trott's leadership and restored Australia's competitive dignity. They played 34 matches, including three hard-fought Tests, winning 19 and losing six. Jones (121 wickets) and Trumble (148), together with Giffen (117) and McKibbin (101), gave the team its firepower, while Trott provided excellent value, scoring 1,297 runs at 26.46 and taking 44 wickets at 21.09. As a touring captain, Trott ticked all the boxes. Hill, who played under Darling and Monty Noble, would name Trott the finest he ever served. Trott took the series defeat graciously, saying in his end-of-tour speech: 'Sport is sport, and one ought to take defeat without bitterness.'

Wisden approved: 'The absolute antithesis to Blackham [as captain] was Trott, who, with the exception of Murdoch, proved himself to be incomparably the best captain the Australians have ever had in this country. We have his own testimony to the fact that he was by no means anxious for the post, but almost from the first match it was perfectly clear that he was in every way fitted for it. Of course the continuous success of his side made his duties far more pleasant and easy than those of some previous captains, but we feel quite sure that in a season of ill-fortune he would have earned just as great a reputation.'

The hallmarks of Trott's captaincy were instinct and percipience. He had a knack for making the change to match a bowler's strength to a batsman's weakness. Like Mark Taylor a century later, Trott earnt a reputation for magic. Hill wrote: 'Time and again he got a champion batsman's wicket by putting on a bowler whom he knew the batsman did not like.' Trott so loved his hunches that England players criticised his captaincy as lacking a plan. Trott followed his not inconsiderable gut feeling. Unlike Giffen, he delegated comfortably – perhaps too comfortably, given that, after he had Grace and Stoddart stumped in his first two overs at Old Trafford, he took himself off. But most of all he was, in today's parlance, a people person. At a time when England's players occupied two dressing rooms, Trott, a postman, led lawyers, bankers and plutocrats. His captaincy symbolised the difference between England and the soon-to-be-federated Australia. With the egalitarian signal came a genuinely warm heart. Perhaps Trumble described it best: 'Harry took a personal interest in each player's temperament, his problems and personality.' Even today, in more democratic times, such interest can't always be guaranteed from a captain.

Harry Trott: postman, bon vivant, all-rounder, supreme captain

Trott was a man of honour, too. Worried that McKibbin chucked the ball, Trott under-used him in the big matches, either to spare the bowler's embarrassment or to save the game from controversy, or both. On the way home, the ACC gave him the option of cancelling a visit to New Zealand. But Trott said his team would fulfil their obligations, and the side-trip was an enjoyable decompression from the strains of England.

Trott's re-election was beyond question for 1897–98, but four tours of England had wrought havoc on this convivial man's liver. His health declined as his girth grew. His 104 in January 1897 against NSW would be his last century; by 1897–98, a few hours' batting in fierce heat was too much for his congested liver, and complications involved the loss of sight in his right eye.

Trott was not the only player in difficulties. His counterpart, Stoddart, missed the first two Tests due to his mother's death and never regained his old form. Giffen could not come to financial terms with the Melbourne Cricket Club and SCG Trust, who were organising the series. Dimboola Jim Phillips, Trott's old teammate who was now a most courageous umpire, wanted to eradicate chuckers, and had Australia's spearhead Ernie Jones in his sights.

All this opened opportunities for the generation of the Golden Age. In the first Test, Ranji – though incapacitated with an attack of quinsy that turned into tonsillitis – brought a touch of the east to the SCG with his 175. Darling (101) and Hill (96) came of age with their first big Test scores.

The loss in Sydney would be Australia's last that summer. Harry Trott, a bigger contributor as captain than as player, was ill throughout the Boxing Day intercolonial game, and batted through sickness to make 79 of Australia's 520 in the Second Test in Melbourne. His innings was overshadowed by another of his captaincy coups: he promoted the all-rounder Charlie McLeod from number nine to open the batting, and McLeod repaid him with the highest innings in the match of 112.

Phillips called Jones for chucking, the first such ruling in a Test. Trott took Jones off. Phillips had the backing of Spofforth, who had written an article saying that Jones (and McKibbin) 'put the ball, that is they throw only from one point, mostly the elbow', and called on umpires to be brave enough to no-ball them.

Deprived of Jones and lacking faith in McKibbin, Trott had to turn to two novices to square the series. Monty Noble and Hugh Trumble were both tall and angular. Both were to be captains and heroes of the Golden Age.

Montague Alfred Noble was called 'Mary Anne' (for his initials) and 'Boots' (for his boots). He was otherwise a straightforwardly competitive man. Melbourne was his first Test and his fifteenth first-class match. In Australia's innings he had shouldered arms to Richardson and been bowled for 17. He was hard on himself, exclaiming in the changing room: 'I suppose after such a silly display they'll never pick me for Australia again.'

He had reason to be nervous. Despite an auspicious entry into the world – his mother Maria declared that her eighth and last child would be famous when a passing military band played music as he was born in Sydney's Haymarket – Noble had taken time to establish himself for NSW. His father, Joseph, managed a pub in Paddington, where Monty would play alongside Victor Trumper.

He rang the bell at St Mark's Church in Darling Point, and sang solos in the choir until the professional singing success of one of his brothers inflicted him with modesty and he retired from singing except at private family functions.

Noticed at Paddington – where he would score 10,127 runs at 46.24 and take 657 wickets at 15.97 – Noble was taken on a NSW tour of New Zealand as a 21-year-old in 1894 but produced little with bat or ball. No child prodigy, he failed on debut at home for NSW in 1894–95 and was dumped for nearly two years. His first century came in his fifth match, an unbeaten 153 against Victoria at the SCG which included a last-wicket stand of 111 with Bill Howell.

His first wicket for NSW wasn't a bad one: Ranjitsinhji, caught behind at the SCG. Noble also dismissed MacLaren, Stoddart and Hayward, a royal flush of Englishmen, enough to get a surprise summons to play the Second Test of the 1897–98 series.

Tall and gawky, Noble batted with an upright stance and high grip. His bowling attracted attention for its unorthodoxy. Photographs show Noble pinching the seam between thumb and forefinger, a grip copied from visiting American baseballers. Controlling the ball with only two fingers required practice, immense strength and long fingers. It yielded a medium-pace outswinger with the threat of cutting back off the seam.

On a wearing MCG wicket Noble responded with his swervers, getting Ranji again and finishing with 6/49. Australia won by an innings. In a single game Noble had stepped up from a risky youth to an essential team member.

That day in Melbourne he went into partnership with Hugh Trumble, who took 4/53 to complete a match analysis of 8/107. Although similarly long-limbed, Trumble was a different kind of break-back bowler. Noble was faster and spun the ball less but swerved it more in the air. Trumble relied more on loop and dip. Both relished shaping the ball's flight into a headwind, and they shared a Zen-like control under pressure.

Six years older than Noble, Trumble had been around top-level cricket considerably longer. Trumble came from a cricketing family.

Monty Noble looking indomitable

An immigrant from Northern Ireland, his father William had settled in the prosperous Melbourne suburb of Abbotsford, worked as a civil servant and sent his four sons to Hawthorn Grammar. William bowled leg-breaks for South Melbourne and laid out a turf wicket for his boys. In 1884 Billy, four years Hugh's senior, had played the first of his seven Tests.

Billy eventually gave up cricket for legal practice. Hugh had a less demanding job as a bank clerk. At the Melbourne Cricket Club, he created an instant impression. His height would always astonish. At 6 foot 4 inches, or 193cm, with a bulbous nose, lantern jaw and jug-handle ears, Trumble made the caricaturists' art too easy. His approach to the wicket, Noble would write, was 'sidelong and insinuating, with his neck craned like a gigantic bird'. Pelham Warner called him 'that great camel', Giffen 'that giant'. Johnny Douglas, starting his career as Trumble's ended, would state: 'Trumble should not be allowed on a cricket field – his natural place would be up trees in the bush'.

Batsmen soon had more immediate reasons to wish Trumble had chosen some other life. His bowling resembled that of Lance Gibbs, the West Indian off-spinner of similar lankiness. He curled the ball away from the right-handers and spun it back in – not a great deal, relying on flight and changes of pace more than spin to take his wickets. Johnny Moyes later wrote about Trumble's bowling intelligence:

> Trumble was one of the great bowlers of history. He had a flight which annoyed and often perplexed the batsman as the ball would drop a little shorter than seemed probable. He would often attack the batsman's strength by feeding the cover drive until the stroke-maker did not quite get to the pitch of the ball, and spooned up a catch to the cover fielders. Able to stand the strain of the longest day, imperturbable, resourceful, this giant ranks with the immortals of the bowling art.

But Trumble, having bowled alongside Spofforth and Boyle in 1887, had toiled for years to find that control. After topping the domestic aggregates in 1889–90 and taking 7/89 and 8/110 in Adelaide, including Giffen in both innings, Trumble was an easy pick for the 1890 tour. As we have seen, the tour dissolved in alcohol and must have been confronting for the shy Trumble, whose 52 wickets in 28 matches were ineffective support for Turner and Ferris. Alcohol, such a binding agent in Murdoch's earlier tours, had turned into an occupational hazard, though Trumble did have one lighter moment back home for Victoria. Wicketless, he was given beer at lunch and took a swag in the next session, not quite understanding why he was floating on his feet.

Trumble's bowling did not develop rapidly in the early 1890s. In 1892–93 he topped the first-class averages as Victoria won the inaugural Sheffield Shield, but his 1893 tour was again moderate. A double of 7/31 and 7/85 against the Players at Lord's, a century against Oxford and Cambridge Past and Present and a creditable 108 wickets did not paper over his paltry six wickets at 39.00 in the three Tests.

Over the 1890–95 period Trumble only took 11 wickets in six Tests, at 32.72. Yet he was picked to tour England again, controversially ahead of Albert Trott, in 1896.

While Alberto went to England and raged, Trumble rebuilt his career. For the first time he deployed his wit and height to outsmart batsmen in England. After two lean Tests, he took five wickets on the first day at The Oval. For the match, Trumble bowled 65 overs and took 12/89. Twice he got Stanley Jackson. 'You devil, Hughie,' said the aristocrat, 'but I'll pick that slower one sooner or later.' It was not enough to win the match – Australia crumbled for 44 in the fourth innings – but Trumble had finally dug his name into English turf. His 148 tour wickets at 15.81 gave immense satisfaction after the years of struggle and the controversial selection. *Wisden* agreed, making him a cricketer of the year, 'one of the most popular of Australian cricketers'. Some of that popularity was evident in a more relaxed Trumble, as he posed for photographers having a mock 'punch-up' with Syd Gregory in New Zealand on the way home. He also revelled on the voyages, pretending to teach unsuspecting passengers ludicrous moves in deck games, and playing pranks on teammates, once having Jim Phillips enact feverish coughing fits to scare players out of their bunks.

Trumble was on his way. Without great pace or vicious turn, his bowling had needed prolonged study and it took a decade of first-class cricket to turn Trumble into the finished article.

Trumble's ethical conduct, alongside the likes of Darling and Noble, would do much to restore the Australians' reputation. He was involved in a rare skirmish when his Victorian captain Harry Trott ordered him to bowl three deliberate no-balls against South Australia in January 1897. The reason was a law, changed soon after, which said a team with a lead of more than 150 had no choice but to enforce the follow-on. Trott did not want to bat last, so he asked Trumble to overstep to ease the South Australians past the 150-run deficit. Trumble never disowned his actions, but wasn't proud of

An immortal of the bowling art, Hugh Trumble using his height.

them either. 'I had to do it,' he said, 'but I wonder what my father will think of it.' William refused to believe it. 'Hughie wasn't brought up that way', he said, and Hughie wasn't. But he was also brought up to obey orders, and in this instance he placed loyalty to Trott above loyalty to a broader code. Impassioned by the debate his actions caused, Trumble went out and crashed 82 runs at number nine.

By 1897–98, Trumble's palette had broadened: top-rank bowler, batsman and first-slip catcher. His giant frame was a tent pole around which the Victorian and Australian teams staged them-selves. Batting eight for Australia, he played two crucial innings in 1897–98: 70 at Sydney and 46 at Melbourne, stopping the rot with a partnership of 165 for the eighth wicket with Hill. For Victoria against Stoddart's England XI, he made his first century on home soil, 107 in 123 minutes against Richardson, Jack Hearne and George Hirst. His eight wickets in the Second Test, alongside the debutant Noble, engineered Australia's turnaround and initialised the dominant bowling partnership of the Golden Age.

Neither an Adelaide dust storm nor Melbourne bushfires could stop Australia in the Third and Fourth Tests of 1897–98. Their key players were Darling, Hill, Trumble and Noble.

In Adelaide, Darling was batting for the first time before his father, who was still urging him to give this up and get a real job on the land. Before the Sydney Test, to amuse himself, John had offered Joe a pound for every run. He was less amused after Joe's first three innings cost him £144. So John changed the scheme. He said: 'One has to be canny with Joe. He bats better when the silver is up.' So now he only offered Joe a pound for every run in excess of a hundred.

In the usual Adelaide heat, Joe fell to Richardson, but not before he had scored 178. His father, fleeced again, beamed, though he still thought cricket was wasting Joe's energy.

The innings was a 285-minute marvel of sustained aggression. Darling only faltered at 98, when he cut Richardson airily to point. Ranji spilt the chance. Minutes later, Darling swung Briggs over the square leg boundary. Not only had he become the first player to score two centuries in a Test series, but he was the first to raise his hundred with a five (today's six).

He overshadowed Hill, who made 81 in a second-wicket stand of 148 in 98 minutes. This was the Golden Age personified: Darling and Hill carting Richardson, Hirst, Hearne and Briggs, with Ranji, Hayward, Stoddart and MacLaren eyeing off the pitch for their reply.

It was a great day for Australian cricket, an even better one for South Australia. Giffen, cricketing godfather, happily put aside his dismay at not finding a financial arrangement enabling him to play.

At the MCG, Trott again showed his hard nose by insisting on playing under a blanket of bushfire smoke, rejecting Stoddart's request for a delay. Trott said the conditions were 'normal for Melbourne'.

Trott did, however, join Stoddart's protest at what the English-man described as the 'evil barracking' of Australian crowds, especially their racist taunting of Ranji. Stoddart, normally a cool customer, said in a speech, 'I have a right, as an English cricketer who has been out here so often, to make reference to the insults which have been poured upon me and my team during our journey through this country.' In his reply, Trott said, 'I quite agree with Mr Stoddart's remarks about the crowds. They are a perfect nuisance. Yet,' he continued, amid pressure-releasing laughter from the audience, 'we can't do without them.' Trott did, though, suggest that some of the worst barrackers should be jailed 'to set an example'.

The Melbourne Test belonged to Hill, finally out of Darling's shadow with one of the greatest Ashes innings. He entered in the second over of the match, after Charlie McLeod was bowled by Hearne. The pitch, unusually, had been covered, and was described as two-paced. Richardson roared in. Darling, Syd Gregory, Iredale, Noble and the captain were quickly out and Australia were 6/58 when Trumble joined Hill. Immediately Hill nearly ran himself out. From there he began pulling balls from a preposterous width outside the off-stump to the square leg fence. The great Richardson would say that Hill 'made me feel I took up fast bowling for his benefit'.

Hill's style was a novelty. Crouched low with his hands pressed down the neck of the bat, legs spread, he did not appeal to purists.

Because his compactness limited his reach, he was more effective cutting and hooking than driving, though he compensated by skipping lightly down the wicket. Bowlers said he was never 'at home', or stuck on his crease, when they flighted the ball. Aesthetically, Hill would suffer by comparison with Trumper, but photographs of his stance convey a highly coordinated assurance. As Johnny Moyes wrote, 'He walked to the wicket like one who is master of his fate.' Even though Hill was not a captain for most of his career, the example of his batting provided priceless leadership. Moyes wrote that 'as long as [Hill] was there we thought everything would turn out all right.' From Murdoch to Ponting, this is the unspoken power of all the great batsmen-captains.

By stumps in Melbourne, Hill was 182 not out, the highest first-day score in an Ashes Test to that point. Horan wrote that 'Hill's innings will be talked of when the smallest boy who saw it will be white with the snows of time.' The 165 Hill and Trumble added was a record for the seventh wicket, impassable until Rod Marsh and Kerry O'Keefe beat it 76 years later.

Hill, superstitious about being photographed, was mobbed by snappers as he came off, and duly added just 6 runs on day two. But Australia's 323 set up an innings win. The MCG's smoky shroud prompted Ranji to remark that only Australians could be so desperate to win the Ashes that they would set their country on fire to do so.

In Adelaide, Archie MacLaren had equalled Darling's feat of two centuries in a series, which left the Australian opener with something to beat in the Fifth Test in Sydney. Chasing 275 to win in the last innings, with the Ashes safe, Darling went on a blitz. Richardson had surged with 8/94 in the Australian first innings. Darling, while losing partners, raced to a hundred in 91 minutes, the fastest by an Australian in the first 43 years of Test cricket. He blasted 30 boundaries, 20 before he reached three figures. Such an innings could never be chanceless. He was dropped on 17 and 58, and on 50 Richardson hit him on the pads. 'I have never seen a clearer case for an lbw appeal,' said the Surrey Express. No doubt he framed the appeal itself in more direct terms, but he could not sway the umpire, Charles Bannerman. Sections of the crowd broke into fights over the decision, but Darling batted on. He was fourth out at 252, for 160, his third century in the series, and Australia won 4–1, regaining the Ashes lost in 1893.

The year was a vintage one for batsmen: Hill scored 452 runs, McLeod 352, MacLaren 488 and Ranjitsinhji 457. But above them towered Darling's 537 at 67.12, the first to pass the magical 500 in a series. England played one last match at the end of their tour, against South Australia. They might have found Australia easier. Darling (88 and 96), Hill (124 not out) and Jones (14 wickets) were rampant, and South Australia won by eight wickets. For the first time in SA cricketing history, Giffen was surplus to requirements.

As Darling had risen, his Test captain had gone into eclipse. Amid the run feast, Harry Trott totalled only 28 in three innings after the Second Test. By the last match he could barely see through his right eye. He played no first-class cricket for the next three years. In 1898–99, with John McLeod, he led a VCA rebellion to secede from the moribund ACC, but Trott now lacked the authority to match his Falstaffian girth, and he was voted down. He was suffering from physical and mental illnesses brought on by alcohol abuse, and after complaining of 'irrational fears' he was admitted to Kew Asylum, where he stayed, on and off, for two years.

9

THE GOLDEN AGE

IF it's true that bowlers win matches and batsmen save them, Australia had been competitive in the first 20 years of Test cricket mainly through the quality of its leather-flingers. Since Gregory's tour of 1878, the English had admired the great bowlers who emerged from Australia. Less so the batsmen.

Australia had produced wave after wave of bowlers: Spofforth, Boyle and Palmer, then Turner and Ferris, the evergreen Giffen spanning generations, and now Ernie Jones and Hugh Trumble. In batting, however, Murdoch remained the only Australian who ranked beside English masters such as Grace, Shrewsbury, Stoddart, MacLaren, Steel, Ulyett, Hayward and Ranji. Little wonder that the balance of results still tilted England's way, and little wonder that Australia had not won a series on testing England wickets since 1882.

Among Australian captains too, Murdoch was still pre-eminent, notwithstanding his sorry mid-career exile. Of the eight other captains up to 1899, three (Horan, Massie, Giffen) had been stand-ins, while Scott and McDonnell were failures. Gregory and Trott were better leaders than players. Blackham, the longest-serving, was so unwilling that he resisted the job for 14 years. It was under Trott (and Giffen's mentorship in Adelaide) that the next great captain-batsman stepped forward. And yet, although he took Australian teams on three tours of England and was the complete role model, Joe Darling's life also bore out the *Register*'s assessment that 'cricket in Australia is far from the stage where a first-class man can afford to devote his lifetime to it'.

Darling would never exceed his marvellous 1897–98 batting under Trott. The next summer began tragically. Playing for Adelaide against Port Austral, he scored 235 not out before being excused because one of his sons was very sick. Darling and his wife Minna would have 10 sons and five daughters, but in November 1898 their infant son died. When the Shield season started, South Australians wore black armbands.

By then, Darling was respected not only as a player but as a leader. Notwithstanding their clashes, he had inherited his father's work ethic and authority. The Darlings took no nonsense. It was a saddened, and hardened, Joe who returned to the South Australian team as captain in December 1898. With Giffen playing under him, he scored 27 and 70 and South Australia beat a NSW side featuring a very fluent young right-hander from Paddington who stroked 68 before suffering a nosebleed and getting out. Few who saw him, however, were in any doubt: Victor Trumper was coming.

After a sombre Christmas, Darling went on another run binge. Playing in the first match at Brisbane's Woolloongabba Oval, he made 210. Government offices closed as 10,000 fans streamed to the Gabba. South Australia's win, by an innings and 284 runs, would be their biggest over the northerners for another 90 years.

With Harry Trott interned at Kew, Darling was the unanimous choice as Australian captain for the 1899 tour. Darling and his co-selectors Syd Gregory and Hugh Trumble proposed a modified selection process. Normally the touring squad would play fundraisers against a Rest XI before leaving. This time, Darling, Trumble and Gregory picked 11 players and designed the three matches against the Rest as a selection trial for the last two places.

Darling celebrated his captaincy by scoring 104 in the first trial match. Victorian Frank Laver and South Australian Affie Johns were picked from The Rest. The young Trumper scored 6, 46, 46, 26, 75 and 0 for the Rest, getting 'picked' as first reserve.

Sydney newspapers campaigned for Trumper's inclusion in the squad proper, and the flexible Darling, after witnessing Trumper's sweet 75 in the last game, convinced Gregory and Trumble to take a 14-man squad, with Trumper a junior member on half-pay. It would prove a history-changing selection.

So Darling sailed on the SS *Ormuz* with five new tourists to England: spinner Bill Howell, Trumper, Charlie McLeod, Laver and Noble. Compared with earlier tours, the group promised much. At home they had beaten England 4–1. The stage was set for the first Australian team to regain the Ashes in England since the trophy's genesis. For the first time, a five-Test series would take place on English soil, although, in deference to the all-powerful county schedules, each Test would be limited to three days.

The real Golden Age – these ideas needing English audiences for full verification – began with a whimper. Darling's team lost to Essex and Trumper made a duck. Soon Iredale was in bed with measles, Hill needed surgery to remove a growth from his nose, and Jack Worrall was down with an injured knee. Nonetheless, Darling held his course. Trumper scored a promising 82 in the win over Lancashire, Howell took 10/28 against Surrey, the first time an Australian bowler had performed a clean sweep in England, and Noble took 7/15 at Leicester.

The First Test, begun amid fervid anticipation at Trent Bridge, ended in a draw but was a transformative event. Noble, who, like his fellow banker Hugh Massie, had hit a century in his first innings in England – an unbeaten 116 against South of England at Crystal Palace – opened the batting and made 41 and 45, the first of numerous pivotal innings in the series.

Grace, at 50, opening England's batting, was even more unsettled by 'Lightning' Jones than three years earlier. In the field, the doctor was more hindrance than help. Clem Hill clipped 52 and 80, and the old man couldn't stop his cuts past point. Grace declared to Stanley Jackson, 'It's no use, Jacker, I shan't play again.'

England were lucky to get away with a draw, luckier still to have former Test man Dick Barlow umpiring. At one point, Barlow went up with the fielders in appeal before remembering who he was. He soon forgot again, when, on 30, Ranjitsinhji was clearly run out by Laver. Ranji walked, but Barlow called him back. 'You're not out!' he cried, to the Australians' shock.

The 1899 Australian team. Back row, l to r: J Worrall, CE McLeod, H Trumble, FA Iredale, F Laver, VT Trumper; middle: Major B Wardill (manager), E Jones, J Darling (c), WP Howell, C Hill; front: JJ Kelly, MA Noble; absent: SE Gregory, AE Johns.

Darling, no jolly green glad-hander, protested to Lord Harris during the next break. Harris agreed, saying Barlow had 'misplaced loyalties to his old team', and made sure the former player had umpired his last Test. It was too late for the game, though: the recalled Ranji went on to make a match-saving 93 not out.

The Second Test at Lord's completed the transformation. Grace's last appearance had coincided with Victor Trumper's first, and no handover could have been more powerfully symbolic. After a first-Test duck, Trumper painted Lord's with a sumptuous 135. Hill made the same score.

A comparison of their 135s probably encapsulated their careers. Hill came in at 2/28 and dug in with Noble for the hard stuff. They set the game up for Trumper's wizardry. The English were beguiled by Victor, but Hill, batting in a tougher situation, had a more decisive impact. Charles Fry wrote: 'Even his free and enterprising strokes must be called "careful".'

Noble contributed a vital half-century. Australia, playing its three young aces from the front, charged to 421 in response to England's 206.

In England's first innings, only Jackson and the audacious Gilbert Jessop could withstand Jones, who took 7/88. In their second, the combined greatness of Fry, Ranji, Johnny Tyldesley and Jessop mustered 12 runs. If not for MacLaren's 88, one of the greatest innings by one of England's greatest batsmen, the match would not have gone to a fourth innings. As it was, Australia only needed 26, which Darling, appropriately, polished off. *Wisden* concluded that the match 'furnished one of the most complete triumphs gained by Australian cricketers in England since Gregory's team came over and astonished us in 1878'.

The win's importance was confirmed by a wet summer and inconclusive three-day Tests. That Darling's team held its lead was due to Noble's strategic efforts. In a blink, Giffen's successor had emerged. Like Giffen, Noble was a fanatical athlete, filling his spare moments with push-ups and his boat trip with hours on the skipping rope. In the Third Test, Noble made a pair. So upset was he by getting out first ball to Jack Hearne, the middle wicket of that bowler's hat-trick, that Noble walked off in the wrong direction. Australia, helped by the weather, saved the match, but it seemed nothing could save them at Old Trafford until Noble came in at three for 14 in the first innings. For 190 minutes he defied the attack. Having struggled with his usual front-foot play, Noble played mostly back, watching the ball off the slow wicket and deflecting it from his pads. Darling sent Noble out to open the second innings. Noble told his teammates, 'You won't see me back here for some time.' He kept his promise, taking 320 minutes for his 89. The crowd sang the 'Dead March in Saul' and booed him off. He was lampooned for scoring '1000 runs in 1000 years'. But he saved the match, and the precious 1–0 lead. In the Fifth Test, he played another match-saving innings, 69 not out, and topped the aggregates with 367 at 52.43, complemented by 13 handy wickets. Ranji marvelled at his late 'curl', and Fry wrote: 'He has made a complete study of the art of deceptive variation of pace and of the art of deceptive flight.' Neville Cardus would measure Noble's style subtly, writing that he was 'in the classic school through and through' but also showing that 'it is possible to be classic without being pedantic'.

The only Englishman to master Noble in 1899 was an Australian, and in the least classic style. Albert Trott, playing in exile for Middlesex, deposited Noble over the Lord's pavilion. At one end was the all-rounder on his way to becoming the Mr Perfect of Australian cricket. At the other was the all-rounder on his way to becoming a sideshow hitter and tragic lost talent. That day, but that day alone, was Alberto the victor.

Darling had won back the Ashes in England, against as strong an English team as ever played. His place in history was assured by that fact, but it was his and his team's demeanour that won admirers. The *Review of Reviews* wrote: 'The passion for cricket burns like a flame in the Australian blood and … the passion is intensified by an unfilial yearning on the part of young Australia to triumphantly thrash the mother country.' This was the eve of Australia's federation.

In his assessment, Dimboola Jim Phillips focused on cricket. Darling's team, he wrote, 'play more in unison, they exchange views in the dressing room, and their captain is thereby materially assisted in many of his plans'. Nothing more telling was said about Darling's style. He was an autocrat with ears, a dictator whose followers were devoted and loyal because he did not appear dictatorial. It was a happy team. For all his abstemiousness, Darling took his boys to music halls and let the puckish Hill sing songs in the field. Diverse in class, they didn't distinguish between amateurs and professionals, unlike their opponent, which was still maintaining the anachronism of dual changing rooms.

On his fourth England tour, Trumble's double of 1,183 runs and 142 wickets prompted Grace to call him 'the best bowler Australia has sent us'. From one who had faced Spofforth, Turner and Jones, it was a stunning claim, but it was justified that season. In the Test series, Trumble's 232 runs and 15 wickets were highlighted by a 5/60 at Headingley and 44 at Old Trafford, both turning the momentum Australia's way. There were more prolific players than Trumble, but none who better timed their contributions.

Most romantic about the 1899 team, most captivating, was the arrival of Trumper. For a youngster taken to England almost as an afterthought, he was the brightest star. The English fell in love with Trumper in a way they reserved, thereafter, for Bradman and Warne. Harry Altham called him 'the cluster of the Southern Cross'. Pelham Warner wrote, 'He was the artist batsman who reduced the flower of English bowling to the level of the village green … when he walked out to bat every blade of grass bowed to him.'

Against Sussex, Trumper made an effortless 300 not out in 380 minutes, surpassing Murdoch's 286 as the highest score by an Australian in England. *Wisden* gushed, calling it 'from first to last being of the most perfect character'. What enthralled England most was the speed of his feet. It was said that there was no such thing as a 'good-length ball' when Trumper was batting; he rendered everything 'Trumper-length'.

Trumper's Achilles heel was, as Darling observed, his constitution. 'Unfortunately,' Darling wrote after the tour, 'owing to the fact that he did not enjoy the best of health Trumper had many bad days, but when fit and well there was only one cricketer in it as champion of the world, and that was Trumper.'

Although Trumper appealed to the poetic, Hill made more runs. *Wisden* wrote:

> Without doubt he was the best bat in the Australian team … The way in which, on a hard wicket, he could turn balls to leg has to be seen to be believed. No left-hander has ever depended so much on skill and so little on punishing power in front of the wicket.

Darling's own role cannot be ignored. After Trumper's triple century, Darling decided that the youngster should get a full share of tour profits. As it cost all the others to bring Trumper in, it is testament to Darling's fairness and authority that nobody begrudged Trumper a penny of his £800.

Darling fined five players for missing the start of the Notts game to visit a tobacco factory. Even though they thought the match was delayed by rain, they accepted their fines. When the firebrand Jones declared that he was going to take three days off during a county game (this was allowed if he was not playing, but not if, as was the case, he was 12th man), the team wanted Darling to send Jonah home. A meeting was called, at which a vote would be taken. Darling sat the fast bowler down and said that the team would vote to expel him. The only way Jones could avoid this, said the eminently reasonable captain, was to stand up before they voted and apologise. Jones bristled and complained and uttered threats, but he had been outwrestled by Darling once before. There was no certainty the players would really have expelled their main bowler, but Darling got the man to apologise, and the vote never took place.

Darling was equally hard on the English. When Wilfred Rhodes, a great all-rounder but not the best fielder, was England's 12th man at Trent Bridge, Stanley Jackson called on the nimble Johnny Tyldesley to substitute. (It was a ploy England would try again, to devastating effect, on Ricky Ponting in 2005.) Darling refused outright. He said Rhodes was in the XII and must field. Darling got his way.

For all the glitter of Trumper, Hill and Noble, the top scorer with the best average on the 1899 tour was Darling. His 1,941 runs at 41.29 had never been bettered, not even by Murdoch. It was Darling, not Trumper or Hill, who became the first Australian cricketer to be waxed up in Madame Tussaud's. His team won 16, drew 16 and lost three, the best-yet Australian tour, and they had beaten the best-yet opponent.

Joe Darling's remaining cricket career was dedicated to tours of England. At the end of 1899, brought down by influenza, he decided to spend more time with Minna, who was on the way to producing a team-and-a-half of 15. Still pressured by his father, Darling concentrated on his sports store. But the store was withering and John Darling bought a 10,000-acre property called 'Stonehenge' in Tasmania's eastern midlands, pleading Joe to take his family there and live what he considered a wholesome, useful life.

Joe complied. He announced his move by sending a telegram to the South Australian *Register*: 'Have purchased property; intend residing in Tas.'

With one bound, Joe was free. For two years he played no first-class cricket, until the first Test of 1901–02, when he batted at number eight and scored 39 as his team was thrashed. He was dismissed by Sydney Barnes, the Lancashire League outsider embarking on a career that would crown him the greatest English bowler of all.

On a sticky in Melbourne for the Second Test, 25 wickets fell on the first day. Barnes (6/42) skittled Australia for 112, but Noble (7/17) was even better as England replied with 61. Darling, surveying the carnage, had a brain wave, guessing that the pitch would improve greatly the next day. All he had to do was stick in some tail-enders to survive the last half-hour, and opportunities might open up the following morning. So he virtually reversed the batting order, leaving only himself, bravely, at the top. Barnes again rattled the Australians, but they went to stumps with the cream of their batting – Trumper, Hill, Noble, Reg Duff and young Warwick Armstrong – still in reserve.

The second morning, on a dry pitch, proved Darling's genius. Hill made 99, Duff 104 and Armstrong 45 not out. Duff added 105 with Hill for the ninth wicket and 120 with Armstrong for the tenth. Stranger low-order combinations cannot be imagined. Noble, again supported by Trumble, took six more wickets for a career-best analysis of 13/77. Trumble's hat-trick of Arthur Jones, John Gunn and Sydney Barnes, to finish the match, was the sixth in Tests.

Having drawn level, Australia gained a lead they would not surrender in the Third Test at Adelaide, when they chased down 315 in the fourth innings. Hill, following his 99 in Melbourne, made a remarkable 98 and 97 while Darling's 69 in the run chase showed his talent was undimmed by semi-retirement.

Hill's unique run of 90s took him past Darling and Trumper as the leading Australian batsman. Since the 1899 tour, he had dominated three domestic seasons. In 1900–01 he scored 620 runs at 103.33 including his career-best 365 not out against NSW in Adelaide. Singularly, he had brought up his triple-century with an eight. On 292 he drove straight, completed an all-run four, and Iredale's wild return ran off for four overthrows. The New South Welshmen gave Hill three cheers; the SACA struck him a gold medal. For the state, his score wouldn't be passed until an import called Bradman did so 35 years on.

Hill scored another thousand runs in 1901–02. His run of 90s was also bizarre for some of his dismissals. In Adelaide, his first-innings 98 ended when he was caught by Johnny Tyldesley on the oval's concrete running track. Tyldesley called Hill back, thinking the inner edge of the concrete track was the boundary. But Hill reminded him of the local rule: for ground balls, the inner edge of the concrete was indeed the boundary, but balls in the air needed to clear the fence. On 97 in the second innings, he disrupted a bail with his foot or bat when he tried to bunt the ball away. Hill took this, too, with good grace.

Trumble, coming off his Melbourne hat-trick, saved better for Adelaide, staunching England with nine wickets. His second innings performance, off 44 overs in the absence of the injured Noble, showed his strength in adversity. The game, and potentially the Ashes, had been slipping away but Trumble kept England's stellar line-up down to 247. Still, their lead was 314. Australia invested all its hopes in Hill until he was out for 97, and were ready to give up when Trumble joined Darling at 4/194. Trumble, towering over his toylike bat, was the man for the occasion. His unbeaten 62 sealed one of the great run chases.

Darling decided he had had enough cricket; he would go back to Tasmania. But he would be up for two more England tours. In a way, Darling became a conditional captain. But it wasn't caprice; it was necessity. He could not live otherwise. His father had threatened to cut him, and his 15 children, out of his will.

With Darling returning to Tasmania and the Ashes still up for grabs, the Australian team voted the beanpole Trumble as captain for the Fourth Test in Sydney. In one sense it was risky: Trumble's captaincy experience comprised a handful of games for Victoria. In another, it was a no-brainer. Trumble was unflappable, good-humoured and in superb all-round form.

If only for democratic reasons, it was only fair that one of the guild of great bowlers had the captaincy. The belief that bowlers were too preoccupied with their work, too close to the action, too physically committed (and too slow in their thinking) to be captains had taken root by 1902. Giffen's four Tests as captain seemed to prove that bowlers were better at taking orders than giving them. Along with this grew a cricketing class culture: within changing rooms, bowlers played the role of enforcer, joker, eccentric, bonehead, brawn and proletarian hero, while batsmen were the ruling class.

Hugh Trumble,
the two-hat-trick man

Trumble was atypical. Educated, restrained, measured, polite and tirelessly good-natured, he was not a bowler's bowler. Given the chance, he might have made a great Australian captain. That he did not owed more to circumstances than personality.

As captain, Trumble was the senior man in a team of gifted but still immature stars: Trumper, Hill, Noble, Duff, Armstrong and the Victorian left-arm swinger Jack Saunders, making his Test debut.

After losing the toss in Sydney, Trumble used Saunders liberally. The left-armer took 4/119 as England made 317, Australia reached near-parity, then Trumble let Saunders loose on a wearing pitch. The debutant took 5/43 as England collapsed for 99. Even without Darling, Australia's fielding and team spirit were superior. Trumble had looked after the shop responsibly, extending the 2–1 lead to an unbeatable 3–1.

Even though Saunders had injured himself, Australia did not miss a beat in the Fifth Test in Melbourne. Trumble and Noble bowled 114 of Australia's 132 overs. Trumble's success disproved theories about bowler-captains not knowing how to deploy themselves. Australia fell for 144 on a sodden wicket, but Trumble (5/62) kept England to 189. Hill's 87 underpinned Australia's 255, but England had ample time to chase 211 on an improving pitch.

England were two for 87, with MacLaren and Tyldesley in charge, when Noble got going. He was a little chastened, having been carted for four fours in an over by Gilbert Jessop in the first innings. But now Jessop was out, and fresh batsmen found Noble unplayable. He gave the English a second Melbourne nightmare in a month. His 6/98 raised his series tally to 32 wickets, second in history to Giffen's 34 in 1894–95. Trumble took 28. The next best was Saunders's nine.

Trumble never had a chance to extend his two-from-two record. Days after the Melbourne Test, both teams sailed for England on the SS *Omrah*. A tour to England was still the main affair for Australia's cricketers, so Darling was back at the helm.

As in 1899, Darling's 1902 team started slowly. Against Middlesex, they were bamboozled by Bernard Bosanquet's apparent leg-spinner that turned the other way. The wrong'un was born, to the dismay of Trumper, Darling, Hill and Noble. Australia collapsed for 36 in the First Test at Edgbaston, rain saving their skin, and 23 against Yorkshire. Hill drove a ball at Trumble in the nets and dislocated the bowler's thumb, putting him out for two months. It wasn't the worst result for Trumble. On the eve of the tour he had married Florence Christian, and his trip through England was doubling as a honeymoon.

When the 1902 Australians arrived at Lord's, *Wisden* called them 'a somewhat forlorn and dispirited set of cricketers'. If they could have gone home, a majority would have liked to. Darling and Noble had flu. Saunders had an inflamed eye and tonsillitis. Trumper was customarily ill. 'Doc' Rowley Pope again substituted as a player. Rain was ruining gate receipts.

But Darling, even sick, was calm and optimistic. Bad luck never affected his spirit. As the weather lifted at Lord's, so did his team's health and outlook. Trumper, Hill, Duff, Armstrong and Noble found form and they escaped with another draw. At Sheffield, where Bramall Lane hosted its one and only Test, Australia collapsed on another sticky and Darling became the first Test captain to record a pair. When he called for volunteers to bat second time around, the first hand to shoot up was Trumper's. Darling said, 'I don't want you, Vic. I don't want to lose good wickets on this gluepot.'

Darling looking like a leader

But Trumper insisted, and made 62 in 50 minutes, an innings that, along with Hill's 119, changed the course of the series.

Australia won, due in no small part to Darling's cool head on the last day. Before England commenced their fourth-innings chase, the pitch was illegally rolled. Instead of protesting, Darling told his bowlers to knuckle down and stop complaining. He was helped by Trumble's return from thumb injury, flu and honeymoon. The giant took 4/49 to help Noble roll England.

The series, one of the most famous in history, achieved its greatness in the last two Tests. At Old Trafford, *Wisden* wrote, 'At the end of the first day [Australia] looked to have the game in their hands, and at the end of the second it seemed equally certain they would be beaten.' Darling won the toss and batted on a wicket that was soft rather than sticky. The English bowlers might have pitched too short, but every ball was Trumper-length. The great Sydneysider put on 135 with Duff in 78 minutes. At lunch, Duff was out for 54 but Trumper, joined by Hill, was already past 100. Hill and Trumper must have been a dizzying sight together. When Hill was struggling, Trumper would take over the strike. A return of the favour was unnecessary.

Fifteen wickets would fall on the day, but Trumper made 104 – against Rhodes, Bill Lockwood, Len Braund and Jackson. *Wisden* said Trumper did not make 'a mistake of any kind. His pulling was a marvel of ease and certainty'. MacLaren spread the field, but Trumper drove Jackson over the sightscreen. MacLaren growled: 'I couldn't ruddy well set one of my long fields out there, could I?' It was the first century before lunch on the first day of an England–Australia Test, a feat only matched twice since.

Darling also chipped in with a half-century in Australia's 299. Skilful as ever, he could turn the switch to attack when needed. His 51 contained the first two sixes – hits out of the ground – in Tests in England. Then Trumble and Saunders captured five Englishmen before stumps, the difficulty of the wicket underlining the greatness of Trumper's century.

But the next day, Jackson (128) and Braund (65) turned the match around, and Lockwood and Rhodes decimated Australia's batting from Trumper all the way down. Syd Gregory and Darling resisted until stumps, but the Australian captain should have been out before scoring. He top-edged a pull off Braund straight to Fred Tate, a controversial bowling selection ahead of George Hirst. Tate spilt it. Had he taken the catch, Australia might not have reached 40, and the game would have been England's.

Even so, Darling's 37 and Gregory's 24 only added respectability to Australia's woeful 86. Their only hope was that fresh rain on the second evening might have churned up the wicket. More rain threatened: this was Manchester, this was the summer of 1902. But MacLaren was cocky. Chasing 124, England made it to 0/37 by lunch. MacLaren poked his nose into Australia's changing room and said to Darling, 'We've got you this time.' In the spirit of 1878 and 1882, Darling shot back: 'We have only got to shift a few of you and the rest will shiver with fright.'

So they did. Saunders got Lionel Palairet and Tyldesley, and then MacLaren, of all people, after a patient 35, swung intemperately at Trumble and was caught in the deep. Ranji, muddled by Darling's legal-but-less-than-sporting tactic of changing position behind the batsman's back while the bowler was approaching, didn't last long. Jackson and Braund, first-innings heroes, fell cheaply and the avalanche was on. England went from 2/72 to 8/116. With eight to win, keeper Dick Lilley hoisted Trumble to leg and Hill took a memorable running catch.

Poor Fred Tate, whom nobody but the English selectors had wanted in the first place, was the last man in. Tate had vitally dropped Darling and taken 0/44 in the first innings. His match was partially redeemed with the wickets of Gregory and Trumble in the Australian collapse, but he epitomised the cricketer who wanted the ball to go anywhere but to him. Yet here he was, last man in, eight to win … and the rain pelting down, bringing a 45-minute delay.

When the weather cleared, Tate came out with Rhodes. It was Trumble's job to tie Rhodes down and expose Tate to Saunders. Trumble would say: 'With the ball greasy and my boots unable to get a proper foothold on slippery turf, it was the most trying over I ever bowled.' But he did it, and Rhodes couldn't get the single.

So Tate was left facing the dangerous Saunders. Would he be a hero? He swung the first ball to the leg side – four! England only needed another boundary to win. On the fourth ball, Tate saw stars and tried to repeat the shot. The ball kept low, and bowled him. Australia had won by three runs, 'one of the most memorable matches,' *Wisden* stated, 'in the whole history of cricket'. Darling and his heroes were jubilant: they had retained the Ashes. Tate was inconsolable, weeping in the changing room. He promised revenge. 'I have a little lad at home who will make up for it,' he reportedly said. He did not play another Test, but his son, Maurice, would play many. Not least of Maurice's many achievements was being the first Test bowler to dismiss Don Bradman.

After Old Trafford, The Oval promised an anti-climax. But England won there by one wicket. Trumble was heroic, scoring 64 not out and 7 not out, and taking 8/65 and 4/108. Not even Grace or Giffen had scored a half-century and taken 10 wickets in a Test. Jessop's matchwinning 104 in 75 minutes and the narrowness of England's win wrote that match into legend, but Trumble's all-round brilliance was among the greatest performances by any cricketer in any Test.

Charles Fry summed him up:

> I would prefer not to see Hughie Trumble against me in flannels for the simple reason that he is the most long-headed, observant and acute judge of the game, a perfect master of the whole art of placing fieldsmen and changing bowlers. It is his head – that long solemn head – I should fear in England this summer … not his bowling arm, spinning finger, deft as they are. It is the head, best in the side, that makes the difference for the Australians.

Trumble's last game in England was against the South. He celebrated with a tidy 9/39 and 6/29. His last ball was his 23,987th in England, more than any other Australian. His 207 catches on English soil were also a record. His 587 wickets on five tours were surpassed only by Spofforth and Turner. But they didn't score anywhere near his 3,262 runs.

Victor Trumper made 2,570 runs for the tour, beating Darling's 1899 record by 629, with a scarcely believable 11 centuries. It got to the point where Darling stopped asking if all team members were on the bus. He would only ask: 'Is Vic aboard?'

Hill was overshadowed by Trumper, but on the way home in South Africa he was the saviour. Many of the Australians struggled on the matting wickets, but Hill cracked a century before lunch on the third day in Johannesburg and 91 not out at Cape Town. Trumper, Trumble and Noble were exhausted, but Hill kept grinding out the runs.

The other Australian batsman to add stiffening while the Golden Age heroes were in decline was the imposing Victorian all-rounder Warwick Windridge Armstrong.

Armstrong had had a fair England tour. He played the Test series mainly as a batsman, but his 72 tour wickets, along with 1,075 runs, made him one of *Wisden*'s cricketers of the year. Fry wrote that Armstrong was 'built for driving', and he certainly preferred hitting fours to running. But he was also capable of filibuster if the match dictated. His leg-spinners did not turn a great deal, but off a longish run he could maintain accuracy and think a batsman out. He showed his petulant side when England selected the South African-born all-rounder Charles Llewellyn for the Edgbaston Test. 'I thought we were playing England, not South Africa,' said Armstrong. His upstart comments were not taken lightly, and Llewellyn would recall them as the worst insult he received from a fellow cricketer.

After a draw against a surprisingly resistant South Africa in the First Test there, Armstrong opened with Syd Gregory at the Old Wanderers and carried his bat in the second innings. His 159 not out would be the first of six Test centuries, five more than either Noble or Giffen.

Two years younger than Clem Hill, Armstrong was a later developer. The privately educated son of a solicitor, he had moved from regional Kyneton to Melbourne at 19 to play for the South Melbourne cricket and football clubs. For the Blood-Stained Angels, Armstrong played 13 games including the one-point loss to Fitzroy in the 1899 VFL Grand Final. That summer, he took out his frustrations on the Melbourne Cricket Club, hammering 270. Melbourne, still battling the VCA for control of Victorian and national cricket under secretary Ben Wardill, recruited Armstrong to manage staff and organise practices. He gave up football and became, to all intents and purposes, a professional cricketer.

Within two years he was playing for his country. Not chosen in Darling's Australian team for the first Test of 1901–02, Armstrong won his place with a superb all-round performance against NSW in the Boxing Day match. He dismissed Trumper and Charlie Gregory, then ground out 137. Only Armstrong and his senior partner – Peter McAlister, with 89 – could resist Noble. Batting in the tail for Australia that summer, Armstrong cemented his place in Darling's famous 'reversed order' in Melbourne, adding 120 runs for the last wicket with Reg Duff.

At 23, Armstrong was still establishing himself in 1902. On that marvellous tour he learnt loyalty and resistance. He would build himself in the mould of Darling and Noble and forever look back fondly on 1902. After he led the all-conquering Australian sides of 1920 and 1921, Armstrong said: 'The 1902 side could play 22 of my [1920–21] chaps and give them a beating.'

The 1902 team represented Darling's ideals of leadership in action. *Wisden* commented:

> They would not, with all their ability, have been able to show such consistently fine form week after week throughout a long tour, if the men had not taken scrupulous care of themselves when off the field … Everyone who is at all behind the scenes in cricket knows perfectly well that in the case both of English elevens in Australia and Australian elevens in England, the brightest hopes have sometimes been wrecked through want of self-control on the part of players on whom the utmost dependence was placed. In this connection it is, of course, impossible to mention names, but the famous cricketers who have captained elevens in this country and the Colonies will know perfectly well the cases I have in mind …

The young, svelte champion: Armstrong in 1902

In his own sphere of action, Darling is a born leader. When he comes to England, he comes simply and solely to play cricket, and he has the rare power of being able to keep a whole team up to something approaching his own standard. He has immense concentration of purpose and under his guidance the players were just as keen at the end of three months' cricket as they had been at the beginning of their tour ... All seemed to be fully imbued with the idea that their one duty was to enhance, if possible, the reputation of Australian cricket.

There lay Joe Darling's epitaph, as captain of a team that played 39 matches and lost two. His team was so popular that their tour earnings were £800 a man, plus £250 for the three Tests in South Africa. As a winner of the Ashes on two consecutive tours, Darling has been equalled only by Bill Woodfull, who had Bradman in 1930 and 1934, and Allan Border, who mastered a plummeting England in 1989 and 1993.

10

THE DYING OF
THE LIGHT

DARLING retreated to family and farm in Tasmania, and would not play again until the next tour of England in 1905.

Two old captains were still running around. Restricted by sciatica and the continuing demands of the post office, Giffen had not appeared for Australia since 1896. But even past 40, South Australia's Grace retained his cricketing faculties. He scored a century against NSW in January 1897 and took 10/194 in the match against them in December 1898. He scored the second century on the new Woolloongabba Oval in Brisbane (after Darling's 210) and three half-centuries when leading The Rest against Darling's Test team. Giffen's command performances were becoming sparser, but he routed the English in November 1901 in Adelaide, taking 7/46 and 6/47 for South Australia despite a strained side muscle.

At 43, the strongman had one last chance to torment the Victorians. Up to 1903, Giffen had taken 15 wickets or more in a match five times. No-one before or since has done it more than thrice. In his third-last game, Giffen took the train from Adelaide to Melbourne and captured seven Victorian batsmen for 75 runs. Then he scored 81. Then he took 8/110 in the second innings.

And then, because he was not done, he scored 97 before running out of partners.

There has never been an Australian cricketer like George Giffen, and with today's focus on specialisation, it's hard to imagine another. He batted, he bowled, he caught, he led. He fought for his rights and put opponents offside. He wrote more eloquently than any Test player. Although he did not reproduce his South Australian feats in Tests, he was the first Australian to score 1,000 runs and take 100 wickets against England. Only Monty Noble and Shane Warne have done it since. There is a place for pure statistics to tell their story, with their weight of persuasion that words lack. Giffen is still the only Australian to take 1,000 first-class wickets and score 10,000 runs, in a 251-match career. His nearest rival is Richie Benaud, who, in eight more matches, scored 39 more runs but took 76 fewer wickets.

Giffen was never seen at his best in England, and for that reason probably has not been given due recognition. He played through the dim years of Test cricket, when England would not tour Australia and Giffen would not tour England. But he shepherded Australia back into the lambency of the Golden Age. As captain, in 1894–95, he achieved his highest honours as a Test cricketer and laid the foundations for Darling, Trumper, Hill and Noble.

But it's the records that still stun. Eleven thousand runs and 1,000 wickets. A double-century and more than 12 wickets in the same game, twice. Fourteen wickets or more in a first-class match *eight* times. *Nine* times scoring 100 runs and taking more than 10 wickets in a match. First Australian to take 10 wickets in an innings. Only Australian to score a century and take a hat-trick in one match. Four hundred and seventy-five runs and 34 wickets in an Ashes series. The first double-century in the Sheffield Shield. Only Australian to top the batting and bowling averages on a tour of England. One hundred and seventy-eight runs and 15 wickets in a match at the age of 43 … You could fill pages with Giffen's numbers. He stands alongside Bradman in the records he set for eternity.

Typically, Giffen never retired. His last game for South Australia was in 1907, against Fiji. Aged 48, Giffen took 6/58 in the first innings – overbowling himself, of course – and scored an unbeaten 32. In the second innings he took two wickets but received such a battering from Sokidi Valutu and Meleti Raimuria that he took his cap from the umpire, walked off the field and up the hill to the GPO, changed into his work clothes and never played again.

Giffen spent the First World War in Adelaide, coaching cricketers in the Parklands where his group was known as 'Giffen's Early Risers'. Aside from the brief ban on horse racing during the war, he was a regular at the Morphetville track. In 1922, Clem Hill and Joe Darling were upset by the lack of recognition for Giffen's achievements, and pushed the SACA to organise a benefit match. Hill remembered that he had only been picked for his first Ashes tour, as a teenager, after Giffen's intervention.

In 1922, on the eve of Giffen's benefit, the *Sporting Globe* wrote: 'Excepting our soldiers, nobody has done more to bring this country before the world than the members of our Australian XIs.' Darling, writing to the secretary of the SACA, said Hill, Lyons, Ernie Jones and Darling himself, the cream of Australian cricket, owed their careers to Giffen. Tellingly, Darling also mitigated Giffen's actions in refusing to tour England in 1888 and 1890: '[F]ew people realise how much George jeopardised his prospects in life by playing so much big cricket, and I thought that now he was reaching the age of retirement from the Post and Telegraph Department, then something should be done in the matter.'

A crowd of 26,161 attended Giffen's benefit – a South Australian record – and £2,020 was raised. The SACA, fearing he would take it all to Morphetville, converted the sum into a lifetime annual pension of £150.

Giffen would not live long enough to receive all of it. In mid-1927, aged 68, he went to a postal workers' picnic and bowled at a single stump from 22 yards. Other workers laid bets on whether or not he could hit it once. In 24 attempts, he hit it 21 times. This would be his last astonishment. That November, Giffen died at home and was buried with his parents and sister in West Terrace Cemetery. A bachelor, he left no surviving heirs. He had been married to the game.

On his discharge from Kew Asylum, Harry Trott had moved to Bendigo to recuperate and work as a postman.

Trott appeared much older than 35. When he wandered to the Bendigo Cricket Club to watch practice, and asked if he could have a net, he was thought insane. He wasn't. He was just missing cricket. He played for Bendigo, taking them to Tasmania, and was again representing Victoria by January 1901. His leg-spinners and occasional surprise off-breaks were still crafty enough to take wickets, including, against NSW at the MCG, Jim Kelly, Victor Trumper, and Syd and Charlie Gregory. Trott opened the batting for Victoria occasionally in the 1900s. His 47 and 59 against South Australia in 1903–04 prompted *The Age* to say that he 'batted in quite his old form'. That summer he was also involved in the lowest-ever first-class score in Australia. Trott, who had been in some horrendous Australian collapses – including an all-out 18 at Lord's in 1896 – was in a Victorian team that totalled 15 against England. Six made ducks. Not Trott, who, still at his best in a crisis, top-scored with 9.

In February 1908, when the Victorian team's match against NSW went into a seventh day and clashed with the scheduled fixture against an England team containing Jack Hobbs, Sydney Barnes and George Gunn, the 42-year-old Trott scored 4 and 30 and took five wickets. He was still exerting influence over national selections, but within limits: in 1909, after a tour to Tasmania with Bendigo, Trott pushed hard for the stylish Tasmanian Norman Dodds as Australian wicketkeeper. Dodds was rejected, according to the Launceston *Daily Telegraph*, because of his 'choice of a boon companion' from among the 1907–08 English touring team: a rare case of a player possibly missing Test selection because of suspected homosexuality. The Englishman was never outed.

In 1910 Trott retired from the Bendigo Post Office and moved back to South Melbourne, living at Albert Park and playing for the club, which he led to New Zealand in 1912. He had every reason to be satisfied with his recovery, indeed with his career. Never a champion like Giffen, never as gifted as his brother Albert, he had been Australia's first successful captain after Murdoch. His captaincy had turned the game's history, bringing in Hill, Darling and Noble.

He had done it from the humblest beginnings. 'How many posties born in Collingwood,' he asked, 'ever went so far?'

Yet his poor physical condition never promised a long life. Albert, who had represented England and returned to Australia to coach, was back in London as the First World War broke out. In 1914 he was diagnosed with cancer. He returned to his flat and surveyed his situation: 41 years old, impoverished by a lifetime of cricket, alone, alcoholic, now terminally ill. Not even Bradman would match Alberto's 102.50 Test batting average for Australia, but that memory brought bitterness. He put a gun to his head.

Harry never got over the heartbreak. He died from organ failure three years later. His health problems were real. Albert's were not: Harry had found out, soon after his brother's suicide, that the cancer diagnosis had been incorrect.

If Monty Noble's career ever hit a pothole, it was in 1902. He scored 1,000 runs in England, as he did on all four of his tours, but it was falsely inflated by one innings of 284 against Sussex. His bowling was overshadowed by Trumble and Saunders. In the Tests he struggled with the bat and took 11 of his 14 series wickets in one match at Bramall Lane.

On his return he was hit by friendly fire. Jack Worrall, the Victorian captain and sometime Test batsman omitted from the tour, wrote in an English newspaper that he believed Noble and Saunders bowled with illegal actions. Never before accused of chucking, never called on the field, Noble was stunned. To make matters more awkward, in December 1902, shortly after the publication of Worrall's article, Noble was elevated to the NSW captaincy, and his first game would be against Worrall's Victoria.

The fight was taken up by that other rising tower of power in Australian cricket, Victoria's Warwick Armstrong, who, with Saunders, refused to play against Noble under Worrall. After some strong talk, Worrall withdrew. His career was over. Noble's, as captain, was just beginning. He made a nervy duck in the first innings but 60 in the second. The redoubtable Armstrong, poetically, took a hat-trick.

Captaincy would bring out the best not only in Noble's game but in his character. Wanting more employment flexibility, he had dropped out of banking and trained in dentistry under a prominent Sydney dentist, Henry Peach. Self-employed, Noble could decide his own hours. Unlike some of his complicated predecessors and successors, Noble is an easy character to understand. His description of the captaincy, in his book *The Game's The Thing*, can stand as a mission statement:

> The great leader is the embodiment of all the hopes, virtue, courage and ability possessed by the ten men under his command. If he is not, he is but the shadow and lacks the substance of captaincy. He will not last.

After the disappointments of 1902, Noble became the most complete Australian cricketer since Giffen. He was indubitably a better captain. Noble reached 1,000 Test runs and 100 wickets faster than Garry Sobers, Richard Hadlee and Imran Khan. Ray Robinson wrote that Noble 'must have been the most accomplished cricketer Australia produced as bowler, batsman, captain and fieldsman, at least in the pre-1954 era of all-weather wickets'. That era, needless to say, included not only Giffen, Trumper and Hill but Bradman.

In late 1903, a week after scoring 230 against South Australia at the SCG, Noble was elected captain in Darling's absence. On the first morning of the series in Sydney, Duff, Trumper and Hill were out within half an hour. Noble scored a chanceless 133 in just on five hours. He chose his first match as captain to record what would be his only Test century; but England's 577, thanks to R.E. ('Tip') Foster's 287 on debut, put them ahead.

In Australia's second innings, 292 adrift, Noble rearranged the order to great effect. Trumper, coming in at 3/191, went into harness with Hill, who, burdened by the South Australian captaincy, had been stuggling for form. His shortish frame was attracting weight, and *The Bulletin* remarked that he looked more like a roller than a batsman. But he found his touch alongside Trumper. Hill was on 51 when Trumper drove straight, and the batsmen ran four. To beat the return, Hill ran six yards past the wicket,

Australia's champion cricketer and dentist, Monty Noble

only to hear that the ball had shot past the wicket and Trumper was coming for an overthrow. Hill took off. As the return flew in behind his back, Hill assumed it couldn't have beaten him home. But Bob Crockett, the premier Australian umpire, gave Hill out. When Hill stood his ground, Crockett said, 'You ought to run for the Senate.' The enraged Sydney crowd showered the ground with bottles and chanted 'Crock! Crock! Crock!' Cartoonists would show the Englishmen hiding in cages and manholes. Crockett needed a police escort. Pelham Warner was set to take his team off until Hill finally relented.

Trumper went on to lash 185 not out, but England, initiating a new tour tradition by playing as the MCC, won by five wickets. More Trumper runs in Melbourne, and the return of Hugh Trumble with nine wickets, could not stop another English win, with Johnny Tyldesley and Rhodes starring. Noble tried to conceal his anxiety. All of Darling's work seemed to be slipping away. Called upon by the press to sail up from Tasmania and resume his post, Darling generously said he believed Noble would lead Australia to a 3–2 win.

Runs from Trumper, Noble, Hill, Duff and Syd Gregory ensured a fightback in Adelaide, but Noble was on his own in the Fourth Test in Sydney. Armstrong, unable to handle Bosanquet's wrong'uns and Rhodes's finger spin, or make any impression with the ball, was dropped. Peter McAlister took his place. (Armstrong vented on the poor bowlers of the University club, smashing 438 for Melbourne.)

Surrounded by an out-of-form XI, Noble took 7/100 in England's first innings and scored 59 runs in both digs without losing his wicket, but the mysterious Bosanquet's 6/51 returned England the Ashes they had lost in 1897–98.

In the final match in Melbourne, Australia were playing for more than pride: Trumble made it known that this would be his last appearance. Overlooked for promotions at the National Bank due to his time off for cricket, Trumble was yet another great who had to stop playing to look after his family.

Trumble wasn't needed in the MCC's first innings in Melbourne, when paceman Tibby Cotter announced his arrival with 6/40 and Noble took 4/19. England needed 320 to win, but were rated a fair chance. Trumble was the destroyer for a last time as England limped to 6/101.

Control was his hallmark, and at no time is control at a higher premium than when a batsman is facing his first ball. Batsmen are, as a rule, never more vulnerable than when starting their innings. They are never more likely to get out. Yet for all this, first-ballers are rare, hat-tricks even more so, because bowlers are so seldom able to deliver the precise ball to exploit the weakness. Trumble had already proven himself, in 1901–02, to be a bowler of sufficient control to take a Test hat-trick. Now, in England's second innings, he had 4/28 when Bosanquet, inventor of the googly, slashed at him. The catch was skied to Algy Gehrs. After crossing, Pelham Warner faced Trumble. The signature top-spinner came, looping, tempting Warner to drive, then dipping. Warner popped Trumble a return catch. The last man, Dick Lilley, averaged more than 20 in Tests but was no match for Trumble. Caught on the crease, tricked by a skidder, Lilley was out first ball. Trumble had become the first man to take two hat-tricks in Test cricket. He did it with his last three balls in the game.

Moyes immortalised Trumble's last moments: 'Then he donned his sweater, walked off the field and out of international cricket. No man ever made such a dramatic exit as this, but then Trumble was an unusual man, one of the men who really mattered.'

Encumbered by his own modesty, Trumble would never have so described himself. He plugged on, underappreciated, at the bank until 1911. Ben Wardill's 31-year tenure as secretary of the Melbourne Cricket Club ended, and after the brief tenure of an Englishman, Sidney Tindall, the MCC had an inspired idea. Trumble would occupy the job for the next 27 years until his death in 1938. When he died, not even Bradman was considered worthy to replace him.

Conspicuous with his stetson and long-stemmed pipe, standing out, literally, above the crowd, Trumble was popular and efficient in the job, notably overseeing the expansion of the MCG into the world's largest cricket stadium. He managed a MCC team to New Zealand in 1927 and wrote wisely on the game. He was no towering leader like Darling. But he was the most intelligent of bowlers, the Glenn McGrath of his time. In a superb and revealing passage he wrote for the *Sun News-Pictorial* in 1927, Trumble argued that the era of uncovered pitches was a game of smoke and mirrors:

> It is quite a common occurrence after inspection of a [wet] pitch to find half the side wanting to put the opposition in if they win the toss and the other half wanting to bat … The sticky pitch gives the bowler his day out, but it is not every bowler who can take advantage of it. Bowlers, as a rule, do not keep the ball up enough on these wickets, and what may be a fair length ball on a fast pitch is much too short on a slow-paced one and may be pulled to leg. A bowler cannot afford to bowl any bad length balls on a sticky pitch when forcing batsmen are about and looking for runs … A batsman of intelligence and resource should very soon adapt himself to the altered conditions of English pitches, quite able to hold his own even if the season is wet. The trouble with most batsmen is that they seem to lose heart when the pitch is affected by rain.

There is no better piece of writing about the psychology of cricket. And no other explanation is needed for the fact that Darling's 1905 Australians, Trumble-less, were unable to win in England for the first time in a decade. From the moment Trumble walked off with his hat-trick, the Golden Age was dying.

11

THE END OF
PLAYER POWER

AFTER another dominant domestic season in 1904–05, Noble returned the captaincy to Darling for the 1905 tour. This time the Golden Agers, and perhaps Darling himself, were taking one tour too many. Noble scored another double-century against Sussex and 2,000 runs for the tour, but was ineffective in the Tests. Hill's series return of 188 runs at 20.88 was only marginally better than Trumper's 125 at 17.85.

Darling, who had only played five first-class games in Australia since 1899, batted well, appearing in 51 games and scoring 1,696 runs at nearly 40. He featured in two massive partnerships, 273 with Armstrong against the Gentlemen and 275 with Noble against Sussex. But the Test series was lost 0–2.

Armstrong, who had bounced back from his slump in 1903–04, was now Australia's leading light. His 248 at Lord's against the Gentlemen prefaced an outstanding Test series, with 252 runs and 16 wickets. In a fading Australian side, he was the second-best batsman behind Duff and second in bowling behind Laver. In the drawn Third Test at Headingley, Armstrong took Noble's place as the side's lynchpin, scoring 66 and 32 and taking 2/44 and 5/122.

Armstrong's 1,902 runs at 50.05, including a career-best 303 not out against Somerset, bested Noble, Darling, Hill, Trumper and Duff. *Wisden* said: 'In point of style he has improved out of knowledge since he was here in 1902. All the clumsiness that marred his fine natural powers has disappeared.' His 122 wickets at 18.20 outshone Cotter, Laver, Howell, Charlie McLeod and Noble. But as was often the case with Armstrong, the success came with a smear. In several matches, most notoriously in the Trent Bridge Test, Darling called on him to bowl to the most negative tactics imaginable. From around the wicket, Armstrong pitched ball after ball outside the right-handers' leg stump. In 1905 there were no restrictions on how many fieldsmen could stand behind the batsman. Darling stacked the leg-side field to drain the blood from the match. Armstrong bowled 52 overs, with 24 maidens, and took one for 67. It was said that he aimed at square leg. *Wisden* commented dourly: 'The cricket was very flat and tedious. As a display of stamina and steady skill it was astonishing, but nothing more could be said for it.'

Armstrong was not the first to bowl leg theory, but he and Darling were the first to use it to kill off a Test match. Later it would be adapted, not to restrict but to intimidate. The incident tarnished Darling's reputation; never before had a team of his been hooted in England. He was hooted as well when Cotter started hitting batsmen with bouncers. Fortunately for Darling's good name, he did not stack the leg-side field.

While grizzled, Darling retained his sense of humour. He came across England captain Stanley Jackson at the tour-ending friendly at Scarborough. Darling had called incorrectly at each of the five Test tosses. Jackson, wanting to toss for the friendly, found Darling in the Australian changing room wrapped in nothing but a towel. Did he want to toss the coin? Darling replied: 'I'm not going to risk the toss this time. Let's wrestle instead.' Jackson declined his offer and won the toss again.

The 1905 team took home £900 apiece, but this would mark the end of the rivers of gold. Back in Australia, a new ruling board was about to be established, a more potent successor to the Australasian Cricket Council, which had been wound up in 1899.

The Australian Board of Control of International Cricket was run by two administrators, the NSWCA's Billy McElhone and the VCA's Ernie Bean. Darling had little time for either. McElhone, he said, was typical of the 'freeloaders who appear at NSW matches', who made sure they were fed while the players were kept waiting. Politically, Darling was a remarkable combination of patrician and bolshie, a member of the establishment who stood firmly for players' rights. In 1905, he and Hill told Lord's that the incoming Board of Control in Australia did not represent the players. Their lobbying would have far-reaching ramifications.

The captain retired from international cricket at tour's end, saying he owed his future to his wife, children and adopted state. After so many years of post-Murdoch instability, Darling had re-established the captaincy's template. While Murdoch's departure had left the captaincy with years of turmoil, Darling's successor was a man of similar merits. Yet Noble would also quit in disillusionment. In the Darling–Noble era, while the personal qualities of the ideal Australian captain were being set in stone, the powers of the office were being permanently eroded.

Since Dave Gregory's day, international tours had been owned by the players, backed by private sponsors, and organised, after 1888–89, by the Melbourne Cricket Club. The Australasian Cricket Council's weak attempt to wrest financial control from the players in the 1890s had failed.

The administrators' revolution was waged from 1905–06. Bean and McElhone formed the Board expressly to take the management and finances of tours away from the players and the Melbourne Cricket Club. The need for a unifying body was incontestable. With Australian Test matches collecting receipts of several thousands of pounds, the states were too often squabbling over how to divide the spoils. But Bean and McElhone were distrusted by the players, who saw the threat they posed to their prize asset – the tours to England.

Darling convinced the SACA to stay out of the new Board, and then, during the 1905 tour, he and Hill persuaded Lord's to rebuff the Board's coming invitation to tour Australia in 1906–07. It is a measure of Darling's influence that the MCC did his bidding.

Noble was no innocent bystander. In 1905–06, as the Board was coming into being, the Melbourne Cricket Club was organising a 'rebel' team of Test players to tour country centres. Trumper led a team including Noble, Cotter, Duff, wicketkeeper Hanson Carter and other leading players including 'Sunny Jim' Mackay, the new batting prodigy who scored 902 runs in the 1905–06 Shield season.

In retaliation, the NSWCA banned the rebels, including Noble. 'The Assocation and not the players run the sport,' said McElhone. He asked the rebels to repudiate any links they had with the Melbourne Cricket Club, and they refused.

With the England tour cancelled, the 1906–07 Australian season was in disarray when Darling (back for a few games for South Australia), Hill and other stars said they would not play against NSW until the rebels were reinstated. The ban was lifted but a disillusioned Mackay, regarded as the successor to Trumper, moved to South Africa and was lost to Australian cricket.

By 1907–08, when the English were coming and Noble would be Australian captain, fringe skirmishes were taking place. McElhone fought with the SCG Trust over its fee to stage the Test, and when he balked at the Trust's demand for 18 per cent of the gate takings he said he would move the Test to the Sydney University ground. This time McElhone had overreached. The university replied that the noise would upset the professors and students. McElhone backed down. The Test remained at the SCG, and the Trust received its fee.

Against this backdrop, Noble was attempting to win the public's faith as Test captain. After the Golden Age heroics, Australia had lost the past two Ashes series.

England won its first five matches on tour, but captain Arthur Jones fell ill and Frederick Fane took over for the First Test at Sydney. Noble leading the way with bat and ball, Australia were set 275 in the fourth innings. Noble made 27 as they fell to six for 124, seven for 185 and eight for 219 before an improbable ninth-wicket partnership between Cotter and Gerry Hazlitt gave Australia one of the narrowest wins in history.

Astonishingly, the Second Test in Melbourne repeated the pattern but in reverse, the England bowlers Barnes and Arthur Fielder putting on 39 to give England a one-wicket win, chasing 282. The match, watched by a bubbling crowd of 91,000, should have been tied but, as the English pair became confused going for a suicidal last run, Hazlitt, who had only to lob the ball to either end, threw wildly.

The series broke Australia's way in Adelaide. When Clem Hill did well, Australia did well. His first-innings 87 had underpinned Australia's two-wicket win in Sydney. When he failed twice in Melbourne, Australia lost.

The January temperatures in his home town were seasonably high, hitting 43 degrees on the fourth day and 45 on the fifth. Hill was already under the weather with influenza on the first day, when he made 5 out of Australia's 285. England's team was strengthened by Jack Crawford, a dynamic all-rounder who advertised himself to the Adelaide crowds with 62 to lift his team to a 78-run lead. Then Crawford and Barnes wrecked the Australian top order, dismissing Trumper, NSW youngster Charlie Macartney and Peter McAlister. Hill, too unwell to field during England's innings, was now suffering from heatstroke as well as flu, and did not come in until six for 179. A seventh fell at 180, and Hill was left with Roger Hartigan, a Queensland woolbroker playing his first Test.

Hartigan's boss at Mactaggart Brothers wanted him back at work, and threatened to recall him if the match went for more than two days. Hartigan had done his bit to prolong it already, with a sound 48 in the first innings, and the match was now into day four. Hill repeatedly staggered to the side of the wicket to vomit. Yet the might of Barnes, Crawford, Braund and Rhodes could get neither batsman out. Barnes, after dropping Hill on 22, grew morose.

Hill and Hartigan reached stumps with centuries, and on the fifth morning advanced their partnership to 243. Hartigan's repentant boss telegrammed: 'Stay as long as you are making runs.' Australia added 326 for their last three wickets, Hill contributing 160 in a batting feat of physical endurance probably only matched by Dean Jones's pain-wracked 210 in Madras eight decades later. The *Adelaide Advertiser* dubbed him 'Clement 'Ill'. Hartigan went back to woolbroking and missed the next Test. He only played one more, but later became a long-serving Queensland cricket administrator.

Australia won by 245 runs and Noble, full of pep, came home to Sydney to score 176 and 123 and take five wickets against Victoria. He carried that form into the Fourth Test and Australia regained the Ashes, winning by 308 over a now demoralised England.

The visitors' stand-out was George Gunn. The MCC, in a break with tradition that cheered as many as it alarmed, now allowed professionals and amateurs to share changing rooms and hotels. Gunn, who had come on the tour as manager, to recover from a bout of consumption and check on the marketing of his Gunn & Moore bats, entered the fray as an emergency and scored 462 series runs, with centuries in both Sydney Tests.

Armstrong, who had surprised the English in 1905, was even harder to counter on home pitches. He was Noble's right-hand man, topping the Australian batting averages with 410 runs capped by a patient unbeaten 133 in Melbourne. He also took the last wicket of the Ashes-sealing match and his tally of 14 was second to Saunders's 31.

For Noble, a 4–1 series win brought more than redemption. It gave him the chance to inscribe his style on the Australian team. Noble by name, he did his best to instil a nobility of nature. From point, he discouraged appeals unless the batsman was definitely out. As a signal to umpires that he didn't agree with an appeal, Noble would sometimes roll the ball back along the ground. Sportsmanship was his pride. Once, while batting for NSW, Noble's partner hit the ball into the air and cried out, 'Come on, he'll drop it.' After the fieldsman grassed the chance, Noble did not congratulate his partner but conspicuously rebuked him.

As a strategist he synthesised Trott, Trumble and Darling. He manipulated his bowlers with Trott's skill, shortening their spells to keep them fresh. He analysed batsmen's weaknesses with an elephantine memory, and set fields innovatively, leaving the cover position open to encourage batsmen to drive the outswinging ball. Like Trumble and Trott he was prepared to buy wickets.

Like Darling, Noble was stern. When opposing teams called for a substitute fielder, Noble was wont to ask what was wrong with the injured player. In a Shield match in 1904–05, he objected to a Victorian runner coming out with bare legs, and stopped the game until pads were strapped on. He was a stickler. As Trumble said, 'Woe betide the inattentive or carelessly dressed fieldsman.' Noble also liked junior players to know who was in charge. Once, batting with Stork Hendry, Noble called his partner for two runs but Hendry demurred. Later, Noble said, 'When I say two, I mean two.'

But Noble did not chastise players in front of the team. His style was to let them worry about how angry he might be, leave them to face their own conscience, then have a quiet word later. It has been an effective method for more than just cricket captains.

From Darling he adopted a rigorous off-field code of discipline, yet was also open to compromise. He drank and smoked, but clamped down during Test matches. When Trumper went AWOL in England to look at the White Star liner *Adriatic* and missed a few overs in the field, Noble responded by taking the rest of the players to see the liner the next day. 'You won't find me snooping around while you are off the field,' he told them. 'Do what you like with your spare time but take your cricket as seriously as I do. You are all potential Australian captains so make sure you turn out as such for the Tests.'

You are all potential Australian captains. Noble was not only motivating and inspiring his team, but letting us know that 30 years into the history of Test cricket the office had a prestige that did not need further elaboration.

Through these auspices, by 1908 Noble had the unwavering loyalty of his men. Ray Robinson wrote, 'With his strength of character, he seldom had to put his foot down because his magnetic personality assured him of popularity. He could change bowlers and demote batsmen without hurting their feelings.'

Noble would need every iota of that loyalty. As the 1908–09 season progressed towards the 1909 tour of England, things were boiling. On the surface, Noble was in his prime. Now 35, he was batting better than ever, making two 213s, against Victoria in Sydney and against South Australia in Adelaide. Against Victoria he also bowled 10 successive maidens, including 64 straight dot balls, and hit 69 not out in the second innings. Against South Australia, he followed his 213 with five wickets for the match. NSW, 713, defeated South Australia, 97 and 89, by an innings and 527 runs. The new Giffen indeed.

But the real game was being played behind closed doors.

From Tasmania, Darling continued to fight McElhone, exposing the NSW chief for falsifying the ABC's minutes over the Fijian tour of 1907. McElhone had opposed the tour out of support for the White Australia policy, but later, when this was publicised, attempted to fake the minutes to say he had endorsed the Fijian visit.

McElhone hit back where it hurt: the Board decreed that Darling's 1905 tour would be the last in which the Australian captain was elected by his teammates. The Board arrogated to itself the power to choose the captain.

Darling had influenced the SACA to stay out of the Board until, in 1907, it was guaranteed an annual Test match. But McElhone and Bean double-crossed them, distributing profits from the 1907–08 summer only to NSW and Victoria. In September 1908, a livid Darling spoke at a SACA dinner, praising his home state as the only one that treated players well. *The Bulletin*, McElhone's mouthpiece, retorted that NSW was short of money 'because it has treated the crowd Darling represents [the players] with lavish generosity'. The players, it continued, 'who have mostly been in revolt against [the NSWCA] in late years, ought to get down on their marrowbones and worship it'.

For the 1909 tour of England, the Board was determined to take control. First, it appointed the captain – Noble – and his deputy, Victoria's stylish but ageing top-order batsman McAlister. It also appointed McAlister as treasurer. It imposed some unusual tour conditions: the team would play six days a week, more than previously; rooming arrangements would be fluid to stop cliques from forming; and players would not receive cash advances to buy their kit. These arcane changes meant little to an outsider but raised hell among the team.

Then came the grab for cash. The Board said it would collect all the gate takings, retain 5 per cent of the first £6,000 and 12.5 per cent of the rest, then distribute the remainder equally.

The three senior players, Noble, Hill and Victoria's Frank Laver, objected. But this time McElhone and Bean outmanoeuvred them, asking them publicly to make their case that the plan was less fair than on previous tours. Noble, Hill and Laver were unable to do so. Sections of the press criticised the players for wanting the status of amateurs but the fees of professionals. It was widely pointed out that the Board had recently staged a benefit match for Noble, which, although poorly attended, raised a handsome £2,000 for the captain. If the Board was so grasping, why such generosity?

The Bulletin argued that cricketers should not be paid at all. Other media struck at the magazine's hypocrisy, given that it was campaigning elsewhere against the running down of wages.

Noble was not a tour selector. The Board gave that role to McAlister, Frank Iredale and Hill. Hill's response was to declare himself unavailable: he would not tour England under the eye of McAlister, now perceived as a Board spy. Iredale, the former Test player, was a NSW administrator whose career hopes depended on NSWCA secretary McElhone. McAlister, a capable Victorian batsman, had never quite made the step to Test level. In the 1907–08 series he had scored 155 at just under 20. At 39, his time appeared to have slipped by. Nor was he liked by Noble, Trumper and Armstrong. For the last batting place, Hill voted not for McAlister but for South Australia's accomplished Algy Gehrs, a 28-year-old who had also been picked ahead of McAlister for the previous tour. Gehrs seemed to have a stronger case for selection. In the Australian season preceding the 1909 tour, he had scored 720 runs at 45.00 compared with McAlister's 312 at 31.20.

This time, though, McAlister voted for himself. Hill disagreed. Iredale, paycheck in mind, sided with the Victorian.

Amid the mayhem, Noble did well to get his men all on the one boat. On their departure – finally out of the clutches of McElhone and Bean – Noble pulled a swiftie. Even though the Board had appointed him captain, he told the players that they, the team, always elected their tour leader. Repudiating the Board's appointment, he called for a vote. Of course, he was elected. Then he opened the vice-captaincy to a vote, and the players rejected the Board's appointee, McAlister. They also voted Laver manager, to take control of the accounts from McAlister.

Laver and McAlister, club and state teammates, were now barely on speaking terms. Laver ended the tour by refusing to draw up a balance sheet, let alone hand over wads of cash.

Amazingly, Noble managed to knit the team as a playing unit. The attack of Laver, Armstrong, Cotter, Bill Whitty and Macartney seemed immeasurably weaker than those of past tours, and the team lost the First Test by 10 wickets. But they won the Second and Third, drew the last two, and retained the Ashes 2–1. Noble, whose bowling was now occasional, contributed handily with the bat but relied on Armstrong, Warren Bardsley, Vernon Ransford and Trumper.

The last player chosen had been Bardsley. By the time the 1909 team went home he would be among the first. The son of a school-teacher, Bardsley had been born at Warren on the western plains of NSW but had moved to Forest Lodge, in central Sydney, as a child. Playing for Glebe, Bardsley was a fanatical cricketer on the Giffen model. He practised jujitsu, boxing, skipping and running to increase his cricketing stamina. He carried balls to squeeze. He never smoked, drank, ate meat or bowled. In a career that would make him the oldest Australian captain and the oldest player to tour England, Bardsley minimised his risk of injury by bowling just 54 balls in a 23-year career.

He batted from the textbook: upright, high grip, straight bat. He studied bowlers and conditions as if his life depended on it. He seldom dominated attacks, because that would court risk. His footwork was crisp, his batting fluent but never reckless. He prac-tised from 6 am at Jubilee Oval by Sydney Harbour; his work on

Warren Bardsley: little charisma, loads of runs

dewy early-morning wickets prepared him for English conditions. He was professional before the modern sense of it. He did have to hold down a job, even if his marriage to the game prevented any attachment to a woman. For 14 years he worked as a clerk at the Crown Solicitor's office in Macquarie Street. He walked to the office every day – to help his fitness for cricket.

All that dedication had to lead somewhere, but for five years Bardsley was a second-stringer for NSW, picked only when the Test men were unavailable. He was 26 when he finally played a Sheffield Shield match. Making the bowlers pay for his long wait, he compiled 748 runs at 83.11 in his first full season. He had brought himself into the reckoning for Noble's 1909 tour with 192 against Victoria. It didn't hurt that he put on 304 with Noble.

Bardsley, one of those constantly underrated players, was omitted from the initial squad. He lacked charisma: not only did he abstain from alcohol and tobacco, but he avoided socialising or games. If he was not going to win favour with his personality, he had to do it with his bat. When his chance came, he took it: in six hours of a trial match, against Saunders and Whitty, Bardsley made 264. He was tacked onto the team list.

Following the decline of 1905, Noble's 1909 team was expected to slide further. Hill wasn't around, Trumper was getting on, and Noble was near retirement. That they surprised everyone owed a great deal to Bardsley. Averaging 48.26, he scored 2,172 runs. So methodical was he against Essex, having put on 355 in 195 minutes with Vernon Ransford, that Trumper felt bound to run him out. Bardsley, on 219, had been eyeing Armstrong's record of 303. Trumper told him he had to give someone else a turn.

Australia winkled a series win with the meagrest resources. It helped that Noble won all five tosses. At Leeds, with the series in the balance, he had a hunch that the unproven Macartney – very much a batting all-rounder – could win the match with the ball. 'You go on and get them out and I'll bowl at the other end and keep the runs down,' Noble said. Macartney took 11/85 and Noble tightened the screws with maiden after maiden. (Speaking of maidens, he disciplined Macartney for chatting with females at the fence, moving him to slip.)

In the Tests, Bardsley played consistently but without a half-century until the fifth match at The Oval. Australia led 2–1. Against the mighty Barnes, Bardsley passed 50 for the first time, then 100. He batted for three hours and 45 minutes, making 136. In the second innings, to drive the match to stalemate, he batted for precisely the same time and scored six fewer runs. Unglamorous, Bardsley was effective in the extreme. His 180 stand with Syd Gregory would stand as an Australian openers' record against England until Bob Simpson and Bill Lawry broke it 55 years later.

Wisden anointed Bardsley a cricketer of the year, writing that 'no left-handed batsman has possessed greater skill in scoring all round the wicket'. His two centuries in a Test match had never been achieved: not by Grace, not by Murdoch, not by Shrewsbury or MacLaren or Jackson, not by Hill or Trumper. Just plain Warren, known to his teammates as 'Curly'.

Syd Gregory, aka Little Tich

The tour ended rancorously. Noble came home with one group of players via Colombo, where they played a draw. A second group, travelling with McAlister, lost their match in Colombo and were criticised for carousing. Officially, Laver told the Board the tour grossed £13,228. The Board received £1,003 and the players £473 each, half the previous tour's dividend and well below what Dave Gregory had distributed 31 years previously. But there was doubt about the figures, with the Board openly questioning Laver's and Noble's honesty.

Noble, a captain of unquestionable integrity, had had enough. On 13 January 1910, he wrote a public letter to the Board saying he was retiring to pursue his dentistry practice. Like Murdoch and Darling, Noble felt he was being white-anted by administrators. He had discovered that McElhone was conducting secret negotiations with South Africa over future tours. For this to occur without the Australian captain's knowledge or consent was unprecedented.

Joe Darling's last first-class game, in 1907–08, had been a tough one. Sydney Barnes dismissed him twice cheaply and the English scored 660. That, for Darling, was enough.

In Tasmania he was a member of the Legislative Council from 1921 to 1946, helped form the Tasmanian Country Party in 1922, and was made a CBE. He pioneered techniques in farming merino sheep, did much to eradicate rabbits, and introduced a nutritious breed of clover. He was active in gaining tax exemptions for small farmers and in prosecuting corruption. Always a legislator, Darling maintained his connection with cricket and was influential in changing rules that had been controversial during his time. Thanks to Darling, batsmen needed only to hit over the boundary, not out of the ground, to get six. Thanks to Darling, bowlers could safely fill their footmarks with sawdust during rain interruptions so that games could restart sooner. Thanks to Darling, captains had to exchange team lists of 12 players that excluded specialist substitute fielders.

Through middle-age, Darling played club cricket. In 1921 he hit a century in an hour for Claremont, and the next year, batting for Break-o'-Day, set 203 to win in 90 minutes, Darling led the successful charge with 133 not out. In his sixties, in 1938, he was still pushing for players' rights, lobbying for a fund for retired players. His suggestion was not taken up for another 40 years.

He died from complications after gall bladder surgery, aged 75, two years before Don Bradman's Invincibles toured England. Debate over the greatest teams will go for as long as we watch the game. Darling's 1899 and 1902 teams are too often overlooked.

The number three batsman of those teams, Darling's fellow Prince Alfred Collegian Clem Hill, was left with the leadership of Australian cricket in the wake of Noble's retirement. Though a 14-year Test veteran, Hill was still only 32, and as he had not been on the 1909 tour he was seen by the Board as a mediator – yet another misjudgement.

As we have seen, the appointment of McAlister to the selection panel was seen, by the team, as an act of espionage. Hill watched from home as the team retained the Ashes but ganged up on McAlister. In the next domestic season, the stakes were ramped up when McElhone refused to appoint Trumper, who had waited 11 seasons, to succeed Noble as NSW captain. Instead McElhone appointed the uncredentialled Austin Diamond.

Hill, meanwhile, found his range as a captain in Adelaide. England's dashing Jack Crawford was brought to coach and play, giving Hill some overdue all-round support, as did Hill's brother Solly. Clem scored 609 Shield runs at 152.25 as South Australia won its first Shield in 15 years. Hill's mother owned a cockatoo which chased Clem and pecked at his legs, but whenever it laid an egg he made a century. On 16 November 1909 it laid an egg, and the next day Clem made 176 against McAlister's Victorians, putting on a nose-thumbing 253 with Algy Gehrs (118). Rain interrupted play, and a frog was removed from the pitch.

Hill added another 171 with Gehrs against NSW, scoring 205 in a rattling four hours. Then, McAlister absenting himself from Victoria, Hill went to the MCG and amassed 185 and 43.

In 1910–11 South Africa sent its first tour to Australia. In a batsman's summer of baking heat and flat pitches, Hill and Trumper pressed their point. They, not McElhone and Bean or their puppet McAlister, were the nation's heroes. Hill led Australia for the first time at Sydney in December 1910. He was the only choice, and he had the batsmen he wanted – Trumper and Bardsley, himself, Gehrs, Armstrong, Ransford and Macartney. South Africa's attack, raised on matting wickets, consisted almost exclusively of googly bowlers, in fashion after the success of Bosanquet and Australia's Herbert 'Ranji' Hordern.

Hill told his men that the only response to the googly was to get down the wicket and hit the bowlers off their length. Bardsley made 132 in even time as a reminder that his reputation as a batting tortoise might have been exaggerated, but Hill stole the show, hitting a century on his captaincy debut as he had seen Trott and

Noble do. Hill's 191 included an exhilarating hour of batting with Gehrs, in which the South Australians blitzed 144 runs. Hill's first century took 98 minutes, his entire innings 200 minutes.

Hill's captaincy was never as commanding as Noble's or Darling's. A bit like Jack Blackham, he was focused on his own game, and could seldom calm others' disquiet. When South Africa's Aubrey Faulkner was smashing the Australian bowling – he made more than 700 for the series – Hordern asked Hill if he could leave a gap at cover and feed Faulkner's favourite cover drive. It was a Noble–Trumble kind of move. Hordern bowled three half-volleys which Faulkner drove to the fence. Hill was beside himself. Next ball, Hordern flighted it higher, the ball dipped, and Faulkner drove a low catch to Gehrs. Rather than congratulating Hordern, Hill gasped, 'Well, it came off, but for heaven's sake don't try it again!'

Australia won the series 4–1, Hill (425 runs at 53.13) and Trumper (661 at 94.43) the stars. Trumper's unbeaten 214 in Adelaide, in Australia's only Test loss, was praised in the *Register*: 'Old cricketers rated it the most perfect innings they had seen on the Adelaide Oval.' Hill made another century in Melbourne, and became the first Test batsman to pass 3,000 runs. It would take Jack Hobbs to surpass him.

Speaking of Hobbs, the next season England proved a higher hurdle. Led by Johnny Douglas, who would lose his life in the North Sea trying to save his father, the MCC brought Hobbs, George Gunn, Rhodes and Barnes as well as left-handed bat Frank Woolley and left-arm bowler Frank Foster, brother of the imperious R.E. Foster. Hill and Trumper scored heavily in Australia's win in Sydney, but thereafter the series was all Hobbs and Barnes. England's greatest-ever batsman and bowler, at the peak of their form, made it a rout by the end of January. In Melbourne, Cotter urged Hill to bowl first. But Hill was not an instinctive captain. He looked at past MCG Tests: six times captains had sent opponents in, six times they had lost. Hill batted. Barnes bowled Bardsley with the first ball and served Hill the best over of the great batsman's life. As Barnes would recall: 'I gave him one that was an off-break to him, and then an inswinger. Then I sent him one going away and he let it go. The last ball of the over pitched on his leg stump and hit the off.' Barnes took four wickets for 1 run in his opening seven-over spell.

In Adelaide, Hill made another 98, but Trumper and Bardsley lost form to Foster's leg theory and Barnes's magic. Douglas accused Charlie Kelleway and Hordern of using resin to doctor the ball, and confronted Hill, but he refused to believe Australian bowlers would do such a thing. The crowd hammered the English, but the English hammered the Australians.

The storm between players and administrators, brewing for three decades, needed the trauma of home defeat to bring it to breaking point. A record 342,275 people would watch the five Tests, which only exacerbated tensions between the players – who were attracting so much new interest and income – and the Board, which claimed the revenue. The previous summer the Board had increased the Australian players' match fees to £25 per Test, plus railway and hotel expenses. It seemed generous, but it was a bait. The big prize, as always, was control of tours of England, and McElhone had never taken his eyes off it.

In January 1912, midway through the Ashes series, the Board announced that it would appoint the manager for the upcoming tour. This was revenge for McAlister's humiliation. Ever since 1909, the Board had been trying to requisition Frank Laver's tour diaries for the true state of the accounts. Laver, saying his diaries were 'mementoes' containing private information, hid them. McElhone decided he would never again allow the players to outfox him.

In reply, six senior Australian players, led by Hill, wrote to the Board saying its decision to appoint the 1912 manager was unconstitutional. The six wanted to elect their own manager, or they would not go.

Crushing losses in the Second and Third Tests did not help their cause. The selection panel of Hill, McAlister and Iredale was contemplating changes. Hill wanted Macartney back in for Sydney University medical student Roy Minnett, who had made 90 in the First Test but precious few since. Hill telegrammed McAlister, who replied that Macartney could come back into the team, as a replacement not for Minnett but for Hill!

The telegram was leaked to the press. Hill arrived in Sydney on 2 February for the most frank discussion in the history of Australian team selections.

Hill arrived at Bull's Chambers, in Sydney's Martin Place. McAlister was there, with Iredale and Board administrator Sydney Smith. They argued over the Fourth Test team and the 1912 tour squad. Hill finally lost his temper, saying to McAlister: 'You've been looking for a bloody punch in the jaw all night.' Hill later recounted:

> I told [McAlister] that if he kept on insulting me I would pull his nose. He said that I was the worst captain he had ever seen, and as he had aggravated me beyond endurance, I gave him a gentle slap on the face.
>
> He said I had hit him when his hands were down. I said my hands were down now, as I put my hands behind my back. He rushed at me like a bull, and then I admit I fought him. Messrs Iredale and Smith held him back, and as I went out he called out that I was a coward, but as the others prevented him from leaving the room, the matter ended.

That was a concise record, but the fight appears to have been more like 12 rounds than one. Iredale said Hill and McAlister were boxing and wrestling for 20 minutes. Smith thought McAlister was going to be thrown to his death through the window. They forced a table so hard against Iredale that it pinned him to the wall. Finally, Smith said, 'I grabbed Clem's coat-tails and pulled him away from Peter. Frank leaned across and grasped Peter and what might have been a nasty scene was avoided.'

Iredale recalled, simply: 'They went at it hammer and tongs.'

McAlister made no public comment.

The Fourth Test in Melbourne started one week later, by which time the brawl was front-page news. McAlister got the selection he wanted, Minnett playing ahead of Macartney. The MCG crowd showed its allegiance by giving Clem Hill three cheers when he walked out to bat. The result, however, went much as it had through the series: Hill failed, Hobbs and Rhodes put on 323, Barnes and

Foster destroyed Australia, and the only home player to do himself any credit was Minnett, who scored Australia's sole half-century.

Another loss followed in Sydney. Hill, who had quit as a selector, boycotted the 1912 tour. He wrote in *The Sydney Morning Herald*: 'There are some things a man can't stand. If they go too far I will retire from the game altogether. I do not want to do it because as I have said before, I want to go to England with the team, but they leave no other course of action.'

He was joined by the rest of the Big Six – Trumper, Armstrong, Ransford, Cotter and Carter. Thus Trumper, who had been Hill's deputy, gave up the chance of becoming Australian captain for a tour of England on a point of principle.

Armstrong, the future Australian captain in the Big Six, had a history of enmity towards the VCA. He had supported Darling's lobby at Lord's to lock out the new Australian Board in 1905. In 1905–06, he had withdrawn from a Shield match as the VCA was not offering him the same pay as McAlister. He had refused to play for Victoria under McAlister's captaincy.

Noble unleashed three years' worth of pent-up anger at McElhone and the Board in the *Herald*. The Board was 'a democratic body being ruled and governed by a despot' – McElhone. Noble supported the concept of a Board but was 'strongly against the present personnel'. The Board had 'absolutely failed' to 'bring everybody into line', had 'not been credited with one single act of conciliation or forebearance', and had 'held the pistol of coercion at the heads of the players the whole time, and gradually taken from them all their privileges'. As a result, he wrote, 'we now have the spectacle of a non-representative team going to England'.

Hill also attacked McElhone, writing: 'If it is considered desirable that the control of Australian cricket should be placed in the hands of one man, by all means do it openly, but do not pretend to invest the Board with control when you know one individual controls the Board.'

Pelham Warner, England's cricket supremo, tried to solve the impasse by involving the Australian Prime Minister, Andrew Fisher, the Governor-General, Lord Denman, and several state governors, but the Big Six were solid, while McElhone saw this as the final battle. Through sacrificing the 1912 team and ending the Test careers of Hill and Trumper, McElhone got his way.

Clem Hill's legacy in Australian cricket is easy to summarise. For his cricket, he was the greatest record-setting batsman before Bradman and the greatest left-hander before Neil Harvey and Allan Border. For his captaincy, he was the man whose career ended when he punched out a fellow selector and boycotted an England tour.

Nobody would claim that Hill was a great Australian captain. He played his best cricket under mentor-teammates such as Trott, Giffen, Darling and Noble. Like Trumper, Hill was content to pile up runs while leaving leadership to others. Like Trumper, he was ready to take the captaincy if it ever came to him, but by the time it did it was too late to protect the players' power.

Syd, the smallest and most likeable Gregory

Sydney Edward Gregory, the shortest and most likeable of the famous family, played under the radar for Australia for 22 years. He was simultaneously the luckiest and unluckiest cricketer of his era. Lucky, because he got to play 58 Test matches, touring England an unsurpassed nine times, without ever being consistently a Test-quality batsman. Lucky, because he got to hold the highest cricketing office. Unlucky because, holding that office by default, as a strike-breaker, he was known as a scab captain. Unlucky because, through no fault of his own, he led an undisciplined team on a chaotic tour and would be the least effectual of captains.

In 1870, Syd was born in the cottage his father Ned occupied at Moore Park. He played for the Sydney club, then Waverley, but it was on name rather than achievement that he was chosen on Murdoch's 1890 tour. Syd played 33 matches and averaged 11.92, impressing all as a good fellow, a fine fielder but a work in progress as a batsman. His finest near-hour was to bat scorelessly for 50 minutes against Nottinghamshire, saving a draw. He grew a moustache, helping him look like an adult, and became the first second-generation Test cricketer. The problem was, many thought that was the reason he was picked.

When the English toured in 1891–92 Syd's unbeaten 93, at number eight, against Lohmann, Grace and Briggs, for NSW, earnt him a Test in Adelaide. He failed twice and was dropped.

His continued selection for England tours remains something of a mystery. He scored 114 in seven innings for NSW in 1892–93 but was picked for Blackham's tour. The Gregory name remained powerful, with Uncle Dave a continuing influence. Syd averaged 23.22 in England, making his maiden first-class century, but averaged 15 in the Tests. His 57 at Lord's, to help the 'Little Dasher' Harry Graham restore Australia's fortunes with a stand of 142, was Gregory's career in microcosm: a rearguard action in a lost cause, one good innings to save his place.

In 1894–95, his one good innings was his career-best. In the first Test in front of family and friends, 'Little Tich', as he was nicknamed after Harry Relph's diminutive vaudeville character, rattled off 201 in 270 minutes. A public collection raised £103, and NSWCA president George Reid said: 'If we had left the list open for a week, I believe we'd have got enough to set him up for life.'

Syd must have wished they had. He had worked as a post office clerk, but, his hopes raised by his double-century, he quit to start the first of a number of retail ventures. His shop in central Sydney would be the first of his business failures.

His 1896 England tour, under Trott, was his best. He topped the averages with 1,464 runs at 31.82, ahead of Darling and Hill. He made 182 runs in the Test series but, typically for him, it included one score – 103 at Lord's – and many failures. Gregory was a pioneer of the 'one-percenters', stealing runs through perceptive calling and surprising foot-speed. In the field he was one of the best cover-points who ever played, quick across the ground, sure in his pick-ups, and able to fire a flick-throw from below shoulder height, neither overarm nor underarm, effecting the kind of run-outs that left batsmen scratching their heads. At 40, in Charles Turner's benefit match, Syd would run out two batsmen in consecutive balls with direct hits from cover.

Gregory's notable innings continued to be interspersed with failure. In five Tests in 1899, he recorded one century – 117 to help save the draw at The Oval after hearing the news that his father had died – but little else.

When Australian pitches improved around the turn of the century, Gregory made 176 in Adelaide and 168 in Sydney. As befitted the middle-order role, he went out to attack. The pressure of accelerating the game and entertaining the crowds – Ranjitsinhji said no Australian batsman 'showed such resource and variety of strokes' – also contributed to his failure rate.

For ten series, Gregory was on the brink of omission but kept saving himself. In 1903–04, after famously dropping Reg Foster on 51 on his way to 287, Syd saved himself with a slashing 112 in 122 minutes to set up Australia's win in Adelaide. But by 1906 his career seemed over. His benefit match, in February 1907, raised £788.

The benefit was more necessary than most. Among all the trials of working life suffered by the early cricketers, Syd's were the worst. He owned sporting and men's goods shops in Bondi Junction, King Street and Pitt Street in Sydney. While he travelled, the shops failed. In 1903 he was declared bankrupt after his partners absconded with goods and money. Discharged in 1905, he found work as a clerk with the Water Board.

Financial need drove him back to the game, and in 1907–08 he began his Indian summer, scoring 201 and 63 against Victoria and being recalled to Noble's Test team, making unlikely runs against the rampant Barnes on sticky Sydney wickets. His 1908–09 domestic season was the best of his life, with 547 runs at 68.37. He hit two centuries after Christmas and got another tour to England, another chance to make some coin.

George Reid, the man who had passed the hat around (if not quite for long enough) in 1894–95, again came to Gregory's aid. After Gregory played his record 50th Test match in 1909, Reid, now Australia's High Commissioner in London, staged a collection and presented him with a silver cup containing 200 sovereigns. Universally liked, Syd was seldom feared by bowlers, and after another poor tour his playing career was pronounced finished.

Not quite. After Noble's walk-out and Hill's punch-up, Syd was fingered as a 'Board man' in early 1912. With an eye to giving him the leadership of the tour, McAlister and Iredale selected him in the Fifth Test of the 1911–12 series. Opening the batting (Gregory is one of three Test cricketers, along with Vinoo Mankad and Wilfred Rhodes, to bat everywhere from one to eleven), the 41-year-old made a creditable 32 and 40.

And so, again on the brink of bankruptcy, Syd Gregory became Test captain, one of only five in a 15-man squad who had been to England before. Technically he was crossing the picket, although, like Tom Horan and Hugh Massie in 1884–85, he was not seen that way by the strikers. The Big Six never held a personal grudge against Gregory. They saw him as a victim of circumstance.

On the field, Gregory's team was not quite as bad as portrayed. A wet English summer hosted a triangular series between the three Test nations. Australia beat South Africa 2–0 and lost to England 0–1. Three Tests were ruined by rain. Gregory made 72 runs at 12.00, while Charlie Kelleway, Charlie Macartney – seasoned Test cricketers by now – and Bill Whitty held the team together. Leg-spinner Jimmy Matthews took a sensational two hat-tricks in one day against South Africa at Old Trafford, but was one of numerous players who let their captain down with drunken exhibitions on three continents. Gregory tried to impose discipline, but he was not that type of man and the team lacked the ballast of Hill, Armstrong, Ransford and Trumper. One anonymous teammate wrote:

> Syd Gregory, who is one of the finest fellows that ever played the game, has done his best, both by example and by personal persuasion, to keep the men in check, but they got beyond all control, and have completely defied his authority. Syd however is too good a fellow to 'squeal'. He says nothing, but he feels a lot, and I believe he is deeply hurt about the matter.

Trumper, working in England as a journalist, knew which way things were going and declined invitations to rescue the team. Outside the Tests, they played 31 first-class matches and won seven.

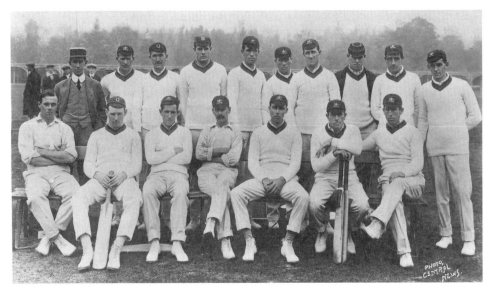

The 1912 Australian team led by Syd Gregory. Back row, l to r: CJ Crough (manager), RB Minnett, E Hume (visitor), C Kelleway, ER Mayne, SMH Emery, DBM Smith, WJ Whitty, H Webster, GR Hazlitt; front: W Bardsley, JW McLaren, TJ Matthews, SE Gregory (c), CB Jennings, CG Macartney, W Carkeek

The only batsman who took any glory from the tour was Warren Bardsley. Honest and simple, Bardsley cleaved to authority. On the 1909 tour, he had unquestioningly sacrificed his wicket when Noble told him to, and never begrudged Trumper for running him out. But that did not necessarily endear him to the inner circle. When Hill, Armstrong, Trumper, Ransford, Cotter and Carter formed the Big Six, by rights it should have been the Big Seven. Bardsley was the only star left out of the rebel group. But they weren't sure they could trust him. He was such a quiet, obedient individual, he could as pliantly follow Billy McElhone as Clem Hill.

So Bardsley went on Gregory's 1912 tour, one of the Board's men. Bardsley remained Bardsley. He led the batting with 2,365 runs at 51.41, scoring two centuries against South Africa. He was not part of the group who disgraced themselves in the USA. He came home separately, on the teetotal express. His abstinence was as effective on the pitch; as Johnny Moyes wrote, Bardsley was expert at 'the most difficult of all things – which ball to leave alone, especially on a biting wicket'.

Bardsley was so potent in England that a serious proposal was canvassed to ban left-handed batting. With the leg-before-wicket law under review, it was felt that left-handers complicated matters. Right-arm bowlers also found them very hard to get out if they could not pitch the ball outside leg-stump. *The Times* said the proposal was 'not unworthy of consideration'. A proposed banning date of 1925 was set, to give current left-handers time to change or retire.

Some in England felt that Bardsley was going to dominate the game like no other, and had to be stopped. Not even Hill had sparked such a response.

At home, Billy McElhone was playing the victim. Given a banquet by the NSW government at Sydney Town Hall, McElhone said he had 'heartburnings' over the tour and the boycott by the Big Six, but it was 'inevitable in any movement for reform'. He hoped 'that no private bodies of any nature would ever try again to regain control of cricket'. For 65 years, his hopes would be fulfilled.

But the tour was an embarrassment. The Board-appointed manager, George Crouch, was even less useful than the captain. McElhone telegrammed Crouch to bring the players home early. Crouch, a Board puppet but without the strings attached, did nothing.

As they came home, the Australians got worse. In Ireland, they brawled so badly on their boat that the stewards refused to serve them liquor. Cricketers fell drunk on deck and could not be revived. The *Sun* wrote, 'it is alleged that the cricketers referred to became continually intoxicated … and on several occasions made public exhibitions of themselves … The night before the steamer left Auckland, a gang of roisterers kept the whole ship awake … Other incidents during the trip from Vancouver served to make every true Australian on board feel ashamed.' The team lost a game to Philadelphia, the last time that was allowed to happen.

Three players – Matthews, Barlow Carkeek and Dave Smith – were carpeted and did not play for Australia again. The most durable legacy of Syd Gregory's time as captain was the Board permitting itself to exclude players from future tours for non-cricketing, that is disciplinary, reasons.

Syd Gregory lived another 17 years, dying where he had been born, in the shadows of the SCG. His Test average was 24 and he made four centuries in 100 innings over 22 years for Australia. Though no fault of his own, his captaincy would go down in infamy. He could boast a longevity that nobody could deny. His record of 58 Test matches would not be broken by Bradman or anyone from Bradman's era. It would take until 1956 and Ray Lindwall for another Australian to play more Tests than Little Tich.

The 1912 tour might have been a debacle, but the Board did wrest financial control from the players. It did push the Melbourne Cricket Club to the margins. The Big Six might have made their stand, but on the main issue they lost.

Here Armstrong emerges, far from his image as irresistible colossus, as an accommodator. Personal loyalties were far from clear-cut. Syd Gregory, for instance, was a close friend of Armstrong's. Back in 1906, Armstrong had been instrumental in helping Gregory discharge his bankruptcy. Armstrong, though loathed by Ernie Bean, was able to win favour from other Board members. So in the years following the 1912 tour, while Armstrong was stripped of the Victorian captaincy – Bean and McAlister demoted him below Vernon Ransford, bizarrely another of the Big Six – Armstrong was emerging as the next captain of Australia.

Bean's role is murky in the extreme. In November 1912, when Gregory's Test men were returning, Bean asked Victorian fast bowler Jim Kyle to find a replacement for Armstrong as Victorian captain. Kyle refused, saying, 'If this goes on in big cricket, I don't care if I ever play for Victoria again.'

But by the end of February 1913, Bean had ousted Armstrong. Neither this nor the recurrent malaria he had picked up in Malaya in 1909 affected Armstrong's cricket. In 1913–14, he scored 202 not out against Queensland and 132 against South Australia. Ransford fell ill before the game against NSW in January, and the Victorian captaincy fell again to Armstrong, who sought a guarantee for the rest of the season. Bean and McAlister refused. So from lunch on the first day, Armstrong refused to play as captain. In a bizarre compromise to keep him playing, Bean and McAlister gave him back the captaincy – for just one match. Unsurprisingly, Victoria came last in the Sheffield Shield for the third season in a row.

In 1914, cricket in Australia was in the doldrums again. Crowds and gate takings had fallen back to 19th-century levels. These periods of contraction, first around 1890 and now in 1913–14, coincided with economic downturns. The public was showing its feelings towards the quarrelling at the top.

A spirit of emergency brought about reconciliation in 1914. Hill was restored as an Australian selector. For the planned 1914–15 tour of South Africa, the national selection panel of Hill, Bean and Les Poidevin nominated Armstrong as captain.

The war between Board and players having been settled in the Board's favour, the real war was just beginning. Armstrong's ascent to the captaincy would have to wait another six years.

The war years saw the end of cricket for Hill and Trumper. After 1912, Hill had continued playing for South Australia. In 1912–13 they won their third Sheffield Shield. In early 1913, Hill and Trumper put on two last great shows at the SCG. In the Shield match Hill scored 138 and 77, Trumper 201 not out and 25. A month later, in Trumper's benefit, Hill, leading The Rest, hit 66 and 34. Trumper, leading NSW, made 126 not out and 61. Two years later, Trumper was dead at 37, his kidneys stricken with nephritis, and Hill was one of his pallbearers.

Although he was involved in the most notorious fistfight in Australian cricket, Hill was no antagonist. He was approached to lead 'rebel' private Australian teams to England and Canada, but backed off. When McElhone receded from Board management to become Lord Mayor of Sydney, Hill reconciled with the authorities and was a Test selector until 1926. He was watching with his wife, Florrie, when Jack Hobbs passed his record of 3,412 Test runs. When the crowd cheered, Hill was unaware of what the fuss was about.

After the First World War, Hill played on occasion to raise money for South Australian cricket. With Darling he promoted the overdue benefit for Giffen (in which Bill Woodfull and Bill Ponsford, two coming giants, played their first game together, both making centuries).

Like his mentor Giffen, Hill was a keen horse racing man. He took up a position with the South Australian Jockey Club as steward, then handicapper. In 1937 he moved to Melbourne to be the Victorian Amateur Turf Club's handicapper. Declining health prompted a move to the seaside near Geelong, where he worked as the turf club's handicapper. Catching a tram on Collins Street, in Melbourne, in September 1945 the 68-year-old fell. He died from his injuries on 8 September. By this stage he had seen Bradman break all of his records. He had also seen the Board of Control achieve its final victory. But Hill was a man of peace, and there is even a photo, taken in the 1930s, of himself, Noble, Armstrong and others standing in an amicable group with Peter McAlister.

Monty Noble was another pallbearer at Trumper's funeral. In 1914 he toured New Zealand with an unofficial Australian team. Like Hill, after the First World War, to help regenerate the game, he came out of retirement to lead his state. In 1919–20, he played against Queensland but injured his leg and his runner, Ted Adams, who would be Town Clerk of Sydney, was run out. Adams never forgave himself for so ending the first-class career of one of Australia's greatest captains.

Noble gave up dentistry and became both a manufacturer's representative and member of the SCG Trust. He was one of those who oversaw the grandstand that, in 1938, was given his name – the first time this honour was bestowed on a cricketer. Noble wrote books and journalism, and as a broadcaster took part in the 'phantom' radio coverage of Australia's overseas Tests in the 1920s and 1930s. He was so trusted by the NSWCA, post-McElhone, that he was the state's sole selector. In the dental chair, he had once treated Bill Ferguson, who not only became Australia's tour baggage handler for almost half a century but also sent his sister to the surgery. She became Noble's wife and the mother of their four children.

When the Second World War broke out, Noble, 67, served as a volunteer dentist for the Australian Army in Liverpool, on Sydney's outskirts. He had been in that post for a few weeks when, during a social cricket game, he suffered a heart attack. He died later at home in Paddington. As a citizen of cricket, he knew no peer. But the 30-year war between administrators and the Australian captain had been lost on his watch. His player-power coup on the 1909 tour would be the last. It is no little irony that Noble, the strongest of characters to hold the captaincy, would also be the last of that kind. After him, the Board would be, literally, a Board of control.

12

OUT OF THE ASHES

ARMSTRONG, Australia's captain-designate, sat out the First World War. He was well into his thirties and, while cricket-fit, suffered from malaria and eye infections. Although he was that beloved Australian creature, the drinker who could hold his drink, Armstrong's steady diet of whisky and poor food inflated him far above what anyone could call a fighting weight.

The cricket captain to emerge from war was a soldier. Herbert Leslie Collins enlisted in 1915 and wore the uniform in Palestine and France. An accountant's son, Collins was born among the workers in Darlinghurst. A full decade younger than Trumper and Noble, he was able to watch them close-up when they played for Paddington. They were established Test stars by the time Collins rolled over his careful left-arm finger-spinners for the club. Quiet and wiry, he was one of cricket's students, taking in every last detail. Arthur Mailey would call him 'Squirrel', as his eyes were thought to shine brighter in the dark.

Useful club form for Waverley saw Collins selected for NSW in December 1909, but it took him three seasons to become a regular, blossoming on a trip to Hobart when he survived four chances on his way to 282 in 290 minutes.

During the year before the war, he found consistency as NSW's opener, and was third in the national averages. He was then chosen for an unofficial tour of New Zealand, where he got to know the likes of Armstrong. But he was overlooked for the ultimately cancelled Test tour to South Africa.

In January 1915, Prime Minister Billy Hughes made an address to Australia's sportsmen: 'As you have played the game in the past, so we ask you to play the greater game now. You are wanted in the trenches now far more than you were ever needed in the football and cricket fields.' Unlike Armstrong and some other cricket stars, Collins heard the call. While Armstrong's age and size mitigated against enlistment, sections of the New South Wales and Victorian public were engaging in a new type of competition, with the northerners claiming more willing soldiers among their sporting stars, of whom Collins was one of the higher profile. After scoring 15 and 1 against Victoria at the SCG, he left for Palestine with the Australian Light Horse.

Collins drove supply trucks to artillery positions. Even if he never held a gun, the face he came out of the war with expressed hardship. Two months after the armistice, order number 1539 of the AIF set up a Sports Control Board to occupy the thousands of personnel waiting in England. The response was unexpectedly robust, and more than 12 Lord's net sessions were needed to select a squad. Collins, a lance-corporal, was picked under the leadership of Captain Charles Kelleway. His teammates included all-rounder Jack Gregory and batsmen 'Nip' Pellew and Johnny Taylor. Collins found the young NSW wicketkeeper Bert Oldfield living in dingy London lodgings and unwilling to play, but Collins lent him gear and talked him into a trial. The first-choice wicketkeeper, Ted Long, was so impressed by Oldfield that he demoted himself.

The Marylebone Cricket Club, after supporting the AIF's proposed tour of the English counties, withdrew its promise of Test match status for matches involving a combined England XI. Then, due to poor behaviour and unrest among the players, General Birdwood sacked Kelleway and replaced him with Collins. Seven men of higher rank would play under him, but Collins's quiet intensity sparked trust in all.

Largely a goodwill exercise, the tour achieved much more. It uncovered a superstar in the rangy blond Gregory, who bagged 942 runs and 131 wickets in 25 matches. Gregory managed to bat with Long, a bunny, for 90 minutes without scoring to save a draw against Sussex, and to put on 54 for the last wicket, with the same partner, to beat Yorkshire.

The tour also unveiled an astute leader and sound opening batsman. Collins's innate patience was enhanced by war. He topped the batting with five centuries and 1,615 runs at 38.45. He bowled more than 700 overs and took 106 wickets, including 8/31 against Somerset. His team won 12, drew 12 and lost four. Visiting South Africa on the way home, Collins scored 235 and took 5/52 in the first of two unofficial Tests in Johannesburg. His team won both. The *Cape Argus* admired his captaincy, saying 'in the art of placing a field [Collins] had little to learn from the average international eleven'. His team, the *Argus* said, was 'hard to beat due to their skill, their keenness, their combination and their batting'.

On return, the AIF team conducted a short summer tour around Australia, Collins advertising his form with 135 against Queensland and 129 against NSW. It was expected that the AIF team would feed its stars into the first-class scene. But the trauma of war and family needs sent most back to their pre-war commitments. The tour, played before big crowds, generated healthy profits all taken by the Sports Board; the players subsisted on their army pay of six shillings a day.

Collins slipped from AIF cricket back to NSW, scoring 109 of his 117 before lunch in his return game, against Queensland. Not commonly a fast scorer – he was described as 'apparently strokeless' – leaving the army broke Collins's shackles, if briefly.

His next season, 1920–21, would be his best. His AIF record made him a natural choice as NSW captain. England had declined an invitation to send a team in 1919–20, deeming it 'unseemly' so soon after the war. A team came under Johnny Douglas in 1920–21.

A case of typhoid on their voyage meant a week's quarantine in Fremantle on arrival, and they never played to their potential. Collins made a century as NSW welcomed them with a sound beating, and was made Armstrong's Test vice-captain, although, oddly, he was a selector while Armstrong was not. One explanation is that Ernie Bean was another of the selectors. The war had done nothing to dilute the Victorian feud.

During the war, Armstrong continued to work and play for the Melbourne Cricket Club. In the first two post-war seasons, he averaged 57 with the bat and 22 with the ball, despite a weight of 22 stone (140kg) and continuing attacks of malaria and fibrositis.

Not a well man, Armstrong was fit enough for Test cricket. Early in the 1920–21 season, he scored 53 and took 4/60 against South Australia. Fibrositis caused him to hand over the Victorian captaincy to Vernon Ransford, and Bean and McAlister tried to convince their third selector, Matt Ellis, that Armstrong was past his prime. When Ellis disagreed, Bean's and McAlister's derogatory notes about Armstrong were leaked to the press. Armstrong responded by pulling off his greatest run-scoring feat, a double of 157 not out and 245 against South Australia, becoming the first Australian to total 400 runs in a match. He also took three wickets, a fair way to quash rebellion.

So six years after being awarded the captaincy, Armstrong became Australia's 41-year-old Test captain. In the First Test in Sydney, Australia opened with a modest 267. When England batted, Armstrong gave the new ball not to Gregory but to the slower Kelleway. Crowd and players looked at him quizzically. But, as Ray Robinson wrote: 'The sight of ['Jack'] Russell's bails flying first ball satisfied most people that a tactical genius was in command.'

England made 190, and vice-captain Collins scored a faultless 104. Armstrong then massacred the English bowling with 158, lacing 17 fours through a field that was spread to the pickets. Giving himself the ball, he then took the key wicket of Jack Hobbs to start the dominoes falling.

The series, unearthing an exciting new guard of Gregory, Arthur Mailey and Ted McDonald, and restoring the interrupted careers of Charlie Macartney, Collins, Warren Bardsley and Jack Ryder, was a triumphal march for the last remaining Golden Age veteran. In the Second Test at his beloved MCG, Armstrong made 39 and took 2/50 and 4/26. Collins, dropped off the fourth ball of the match, made 64 and Gregory belted a century down the order. By Adelaide, the Ashes were regained on the back of Collins's 162, Armstrong's 121, and contrasting centuries from Kelleway, in seven hours, and 'Nip' Pellew, in two.

The merits of Armstrong's captaincy have long been debated. Gregory remembered his time under Armstrong as his happiest. Mailey chafed under his defensiveness, saying Armstrong 'bluffed' rather than 'cajoled' batsmen out. Other teammates rated his tactical sense below that of Collins, Trott and Noble. It's true that Armstrong had such personnel that the proverbial drover's dog could have led them to the Ashes. But Armstrong had a certain aura. Better to be lucky than good.

His feud with Bean continued. During the Third Test Armstrong's left thigh was battered and bruised by England paceman Harry Howell, and after travelling to Sydney with the Victorians for their commemorative hundredth match against NSW, Armstrong was unable to walk. He had his teammate, Dr Roy Park, confirm his unfitness. But Bean, having heard rumours that Armstrong was seen at Randwick Racecourse, didn't believe him. Armstrong declared himself fit for Victoria's next match, against the English, but McAlister and Bean dropped him.

If player power was dying, people power was alive. Armstrong was three Tests into leading Australia to its most successful, and most-watched, Ashes series. He was in career-best form. Bean might have picked a better moment. A public protest at the Melbourne Town Hall featured politicians, including Victorian Senator James Guthrie, who said: 'I once caught McAlister out and now I'm going to boot him out.' Martin Hannah, MLA, perhaps over-egging it, told the crowd: 'Kaiserism is not dead.'

A protest was planned outside the MCG. Bean retaliated by banning pass-outs. Still, 8,000 chose to leave their seats and protest for Armstrong rather than watch Patsy Hendren cart the Victorian bowlers. The crowd inside the MCG chanted Armstrong's name and called out, 'Give Ernie Bean a bowl!'

Victoria lost. Armstrong, meanwhile, in a nicely timed gesture, was fulfilling a promise to play against the 'Boys of Mentone', school children aged six to 15. He represented a team of three against an opposition of 18. He took 16 wickets but was bowled for 13 as his three went down. The boys gave him a pipe, and he presented them with a ball used in the Nottingham Test of 1909.

Back for the Fourth Test at the MCG, affected by malaria and the whisky he had taken to subdue its symptoms, he dropped himself down the order. England had made 284, and Australia were 5/153 when Armstrong breached the gate. Legend had it that the teetotaller Bean gloated at Armstrong from the pavilion, as if to say, 'I've got you now.' After Armstrong had finished with 123 not out, it was said that Bean took to drink.

Bean attempted a Board coup, but failed by one vote to have Armstrong replaced by Collins as captain for the 1921 tour of England. Once appointed, Armstrong argued hard for the Victorian paceman Ted McDonald. In his one lasting tactical innovation, Armstrong believed that not one but two express fast bowlers could share the new ball. In Gregory and McDonald, he believed he could rout the English before the ball was marked.

Like George Giffen, Armstrong tried to improve his condition by stoking the fires on the *Osterley*. McDonald, who joined him, got his weight down and his fitness up. Armstrong remained at 22 stone. Robinson wrote: 'No ball that Armstrong drove, and no deckchair he sat on, was ever the same again.'

As far as the captain's power went, it was not 1909 anymore, still less 1902. Armstrong went as a contracted Board employee, with the Board's Sydney Smith – witness of the Hill–McAlister brawl – looking over his shoulder. Folklore has him as a strong Australian leader, but even 'Tup' Scott and Percy McDonnell had more power.

Armstrong might have won the battle for popularity over Ernie Bean, but the administrators had won the war. Men like Bean and McElhone, who embodied the amateur sports administrator of the 20th century, saw themselves as the permanent custodians of the game and players as fly-by-night opportunists. Even such a massive entity as Armstrong was, in their view, a paid labourer with little regard for the greater good. The conflict between stiff-necked, middle-class voluntary administrators and charismatic sports stars would be repeated by new faces playing the same old roles through more than a century of Australian cricket.

Armstrong, who needed a fight like he needed whisky, turned his aggression on the English tour organisers. Calling them 'a mob of novices', he ordered Smith to rearrange the fixtures to allow travel days on the eve of Tests. He also persuaded Lord's to allow players to drink in their changing rooms, not just the bar.

The scale of the players' victories was shrinking. Armstrong was not. At the International Cricket Conference, he argued for eight-ball overs (the norm in Australia since 1918), extra rolling of rain-affected pitches, and the appointment of umpires on the morning of matches, rather than earlier, to remove the temptation of betting. Lord Harris questioned whether there was any betting, and Armstrong replied that if his lordship had a spare £500, Armstrong would put it on the next Test for him.

On the field, Australia continued their domination. Macartney made a first statement by scoring 345 in four hours against Nottinghamshire. Gloucestershire looked weak, and Armstrong said he was 'going to get among these cheap wickets'. Instead, to his team's amusement, he was hit to all corners. Grudgingly he gave the ball to Mailey, who took 10/66.

In the five-Test series, Australia would use 13 players to England's 30. In Gregory's third over of the First Test, an English newspaper remarked, 'he destroyed the morale of English cricket for the best part of a season'. His wickets in that over were Knight, Tyldesley and Hendren, who said he 'would have gladly endorsed [the ball] with my initials and the date if in the heat and horror of the moment I could have recalled either to my memory'.

Armstrong and English captain Johnny Douglas at the toss in the 1921 Ashes series, shortly before Douglas was axed.

Armstrong's team secured the Ashes in seven and a half days of play. Gregory, McDonald, Bardsley and Macartney were supreme, Armstrong chipping in where necessary with 152 runs at 30.40 and eight wickets at 26.50. His highlight was the Ashes-capping Third Test at Headingley, where he scored 77 and 28 not out and took 2/44 and 2/6. On the tour, he achieved the 1,000 runs–100 wickets double for the third time.

The English didn't, by and large, like him any more. His team was too dominant and he was too unapologetic. Despite their success, he projected an irascible, often contemptuous authority. The growing animosity came to a head during the Fourth Test. The first day had been washed out, leaving two days. England's captain, Lionel Tennyson, the poet's grandson, replacing the sacked Douglas, decided to declare at 4/341 half an hour before stumps. Armstrong had bowled the last over. But Australia's wicketkeeper, Hanson Carter, told Armstrong that in two-day matches, as this Test now was, declarations must be made at least 100 minutes before stumps. While argument raged, Armstrong sat and smoked his pipe. The crowd booed him. Robinson described it as 'the most hostile demonstration an English crowd ever gave Australians'. But

Armstrong and Carter were correct. Play resumed, with England having to bat. Armstrong bowled the first over. In the tumult it was not noticed that he became the first and only Test bowler to send down consecutive overs, inadvertently breaking one law while observing another.

As the Fifth Test at The Oval meandered towards another draw, Armstrong's arrogance overflowed. He told his bowlers that England's Phil Mead was such a slow scorer that 'I won't ask you not to get a man out, but as long as Mead remains at the wicket we cannot be beaten'. Mead was allowed to make 182 not out in five hours, mostly against Australia's batsmen. Armstrong wandered the outfield reading the paper. Asked why, he replied: 'To see who we're playing.'

He received a comeuppance, of sorts, when his team was beaten in two late-season festival matches at Scarborough and Eastbourne, meaning that the 1921 team did not beat the 1902 record. Armstrong was happy not to surpass cricket's – and his own – Golden Age. For the rest of his life he was an enthusiastic extoller of the past, claiming that Don Bradman and Bill O'Reilly could not have achieved much against Darling's 1902 team.

In 1921, there was one last fight for Armstrong. The tour had grossed £35,644. But the Board took its cut, then sent the home-bound team on a short tour of South Africa. Armstrong did not play, handing the captaincy to Collins. Each player brought home £700, comprising a tour fee of £400 and a bonus of £300 – still less than Dave Gregory's men had brought home in 1878.

One Board vote from the captaincy, Collins served Armstrong steadily. He broke his thumb stopping a hot one at silly point in the First Test, missed the Second and Third, but batted for nearly five hours at Old Trafford as he inched his way to 40 to save a draw.

With Armstrong in a Durban sanatorium, injured and disgruntled about still being overseas, Collins became Test captain in Johannesburg. He put into practice his methods from the AIF tour: he sat alone at the end of each day thinking through events,

Herbie Collins, unruffled,
cutting in England

studying opponents' weaknesses. A man who would gamble on two
flies going up a wall, he refused to play cards with his teammates. A
chain smoker, he seldom drank except to celebrate a win. Fielding,
he would not shout or remonstrate. He just asked his men to watch
him between every ball for a subtle nod or jerk of the thumb.

After a quiet Test series in England, as captain in South Africa he
scored 548 runs at 60.88, including 203 in the Second Test. Joining
him late, Jack Gregory creamed 100 runs off 67 balls in 70 minutes
in a partnership of 209 in 85 minutes. Collins's men had the better
of two draws, then an easy win in the decider at Cape Town, where

he showed a sense of humour as captain, sending out Carter and Mailey to 'chase' the one-run target.

Australia's other star in South Africa was a pent-up Jack Ryder.

Outside those who paid the ultimate price, Ryder's career was more disadvantaged by the war than any other Australian. Ryder, it's safe to say, hit his physical peak around 1913–14 and never fully regained it.

When, cut off by war, many Australians' interests contracted to the local, Ryder became a hero of his suburb. Collingwood people are proud of their own, and the phrase 'favourite son' might have been coined for Ryder. The second son of a Methodist carpenter, he grew up on the hard streets of the inner-Melbourne suburb and trained as a bootmaker. A fast-growing 183-centimetre all-rounder with a pointed nose, receding chin and smiling eyes, he was spotted by the new Collingwood club at 17 and was taken in a hansom cab to their first district game in 1906. Not for 43 years did Ryder stop playing. For 25 years no vote was needed to elect the club captain.

A boom youngster for Victoria before the war, he had driven the ball so hard he broke stumps at the bowler's end. He bowled outswingers at a stiff pace, surprising batsmen with his bounce, and took his best figures in 1912–13. Had a Test team been picked, Ryder would have been the first on the boat. His one first-class season had yielded 521 runs at 43.41 and 35 wickets at 15.64.

An all-rounder had arrived in the class of Giffen, Noble and Armstrong. Ryder was proceeding towards a Test debut on the proposed 1914–15 tour of South Africa, when his all-round brilliance defeated local rivals Fitzroy in a VCA district final watched by 20,000.

When war cut down his cricket hopes, Ryder switched from bootmaking to travelling as a boot salesman. He married the daughter of a confectioner and they had two children. He played cricket locally but did not join up. According to a 1995 biography written by Marc Fiddian, Ryder never spoke, even to his family, about not enlisting. That war left as much silence among those who did not go as among those who did.

Ryder emerged from the war years a quiet, even taciturn man. Though his enthusiasm for cricket was undimmed, he remembered those lost six years with a regret that was, in the circumstances, better left unspoken. He returned to first-class cricket at 29 and made his Test debut at 31, his best bowling years behind him. In his First Test, in Sydney in 1920–21, batting at nine and eight, he was run out cheaply in both innings; Ryder, who lunged down the wicket to drive and kept on coming, often confused his partners.

Although he made three centuries that season for Victoria, Ryder was no favourite of Armstrong's. On the 1921 tour, Ryder did not play a Test. Armstrong could point to Ryder's less-than-overwhelming five Tests in Australia, but there were rumours that the 1921 team was divided between the indulgers and the abstainers. Ryder was among those – which included Mailey, Bardsley, Johnny Taylor, Tommy Andrews and manager Sydney Smith – whom Armstrong called 'the lemonade crowd'.

What might also have contributed to a schism was Ryder agreeing with English critics about Armstrong's high-handedness. When Armstrong cut short the match against Yorkshire so the team could travel to the next Test, Ryder, for whom the Yorkshire game was a rare chance to play, disagreed. The Press Association wrote that Ryder and Edgar Mayne, who also missed out on a Test, 'were so disgusted with their treatment by the selection committee that they wouldn't play for Victoria' when they returned home.

While Armstrong was grumpily laid up in Durban, Ryder finally got his chance and went berserk, scoring 78 not out and 58 in the First Test, 56 in the Second, and 142 in the Third. His Test average on the South African tour was 111.33, and in the Third Test he also took the first two wickets.

Too much a Victorian to carry out his threat to move, Ryder averaged 101.83 the next season. Victoria won the Shield. Ryder was not even the top batsman: Frank O'Keeffe, having a dream run, made 708 runs at 118. But Ryder achieved the highest individual score with his 242 in 304 minutes opening the batting against South Australia, who hadn't won a Shield match since the war. He also took seven wickets at the SCG, showing that his bowling days were not completely finished. If ever a player went out and scored runs in anger, it was Ryder in the days following the 1921 tour. Not that he ever spoke out. His scoring said enough.

Armstrong, who played a handful of games in 1921–22, received a cheque of £2,500, raised during the previous summer's protest, from Billy Hughes, who said: 'When Warwick goes into the field, the Englishmen are half beaten; when he takes the ball, they are wholly beaten.'

And that was it. As Australian agent for Peter Dawson's Scotch whisky distillery, Armstrong set off on the accumulation of what would be, by his death in 1947, a sizeable fortune. His last cricket was for Melbourne, for whom he played until 1927, leading the club to New Zealand. He and his wife Aileen moved to Darling Point in Sydney in 1934, where he worked for the James Buchanan distillery and declaimed the inferiority of current players.

Armstrong's legacy needed no defender. He did enough of that himself, and statistically his position was impregnable. He had played in the two most successful Ashes tours, in 1902 and 1921. He had introduced the two-pronged pace attack. As Robinson wrote, 'In confidence, dominance, willpower and ability to get his way, Armstrong is the nearest Down Under approach to W.G. Grace.'

Yet, as great a cricketer as Armstrong was, he presided over the steady decline of the players' entitlement to the full rewards of their labour. He had been outmanoeuvred by the Board and outdone by circumstances. He left the captain's role weaker than he found it. The clamp of Board control – the victory of McElhone and Bean over Darling, Noble, Hill and Armstrong – would remain tight for 56 years after Armstrong played his last Test.

13

THE FALL

UNDER Collins's increasingly influential captaincy, NSW won the next Sheffield Shield. Mailey would write: 'I learnt more of the psychology of cricket from Collins than all the hundreds of cricketers I met. Without being perceptibly diplomatic, he could carry the burden of responsibility yet transfer the credit to those he thought deserved it most.'

With Armstrong having retired, there was no demur about Collins succeeding him. When Arthur Gilligan brought an MCC team in 1924–25, Collins was the senior batsman in a young team, a level of pressure he had not previously faced. At home for his first Test, he won the toss and batted. Maurice Tate, son of the ill-fated Fred, was making a dynamic first tour of Australia. After Bardsley was out for 21, Collins proposed to shelter his debutant partner, the young Victorian Bill Ponsford, from Tate. It was slow going, and never truly convincing, but both batsmen survived to put on 190 and Collins, with 114, hit his 1,000th Test run in his 12th match, a world record, making up for lost time. Clem Hill said: 'That's the toughest bowling I've ever seen on the first day. If Tate had had any luck, your whole team could have been out twice before lunch.'

The Test reached a seventh day, three of the four innings passing 400, before Australia won by 193. Collins missed the third day due to the death of his sister, and Bardsley deputised. Wickets had improved due to covering at night. It made sense, but Archie MacLaren howled against a rule which, he said, 'put gates first and cricket nowhere'.

Australia's rediscovery of the series was Ryder, who so thrived on rejection. In the three years after his 142 in Cape Town, Ryder had not played a Test. Brought back for Adelaide in 1924–25, he watched Collins, Gregory, Taylor and Victor Richardson fail. Ponsford and Arthur Richardson offered some resistance, but Australia were five for 118 when Ryder went in, and soon six for 119. With Maurice Tate and Roy Kilner bowling menacingly, Ryder played it safe. After stabilising the innings with Andrews, Ryder lashed out with the tail, thrilling the Adelaide crowd with his booming drives. In 395 minutes he gave one chance, on 145, a drive that struck mid-on Tich Freeman's wrist so hard he went off. When he saw his swollen wrist, Freeman fainted.

Ryder's unbeaten 201 made his point. In England's reply, he took the prize wicket of Herbert Sutcliffe. With Australia struggling again but wanting to set a target in the second innings, Ryder cracked 88 in two hours, becoming the first to score a double-hundred and a half-century in a Test. Australia needed all of his 289 runs, winning by just 11.

Collins, talking with Macartney, leads the 1926 Australians onto the field.

Australia won the series 4–1, yet with Hobbs, Sutcliffe, Woolley, 'Patsy' Hendren and Percy Chapman in their batting, and Tate leading the bowling with a record 38 wickets, England were on the road back. With cricket being broadcast on radio and played before record crowds, more than a million spectators watched the tour, enriching the Board if not the players with gate takings of £95,171.

Collins's batting luck ran out through the series, but his shepherding of Ponsford helped produce a star. Others to flower under Collins were Victor Richardson from South Australia, Gregory, Oldfield and Mailey. It helped that Collins won the toss in four Tests. Gilligan, who called Collins 'Horseshoe', showily got down on his knees to check Collins wasn't throwing a two-headed coin.

Collins, deep into his thirties, had led the transition, and perhaps now was the time to step aside. But his batting came good again in the lead-up to the 1926 tour, with two centuries as he led NSW to its 17th Sheffield Shield in 30 seasons. At 37, Collins was up for it, and up to it. He didn't guess that he had played his last game in Australia.

One incident during the 1924–25 series had raised eyebrows. On the last morning of the Adelaide Test, England needed 27 with two wickets in hand. The series was still alive and the match was on a knife-edge, with Gilligan and Freeman comfortable at the wicket. At the team's hotel, Mailey recalled, 'a fabulous-looking racecourse man, smoking a cigar, called to see Collins'. Collins spoke to the man, then led him to Mailey.

'This fellow says it's worth 100 quid if we lose the match,' Collins said. Then, without changing his expression: 'Let's throw him downstairs.'

Mailey noted the size of the man. Collins reconsidered: 'I'd better ring the hall porter, then.'

Mailey told the story to attest to Collins's honesty. But it would later acquire a sinister undertone. Collins was a professional punter, so was he a target for match-fixers? When the team took the field that morning, Gregory would obviously bowl from one end, and at the other Collins was expected to choose the safe Kelleway over the riskier Mailey. He chose Mailey. It seemed a curious choice until, needing 18 to win, Gregory dismissed Gilligan and Mailey drew a nick off Freeman. Australia had won by 11 runs, but Collins's tactics would be held against him.

Collins helped to select the 1926 touring team. After the controversial omission of Alan Kippax, who had scored 585 runs at 83.57 that season, an omission Monty Noble called 'a crime against the cricketing youth of Australia', Australia lost its trial series against The Rest, but Collins showed faith. Six of the squad were to be first-timers in England.

The English summer was wet, and the team was affected by colds and flu, rained-out matches and the General Strike. Collins had a lean tour, hampered by neuritis and arthritis. His tactics were risk-averse, and Australia drew nine of their first 11 games, many of them rain-affected.

Collins was working with shrinking resources. Gregory, deprived of his partner McDonald, who had moved to Lancashire, struggled with a bad knee and would not take a wicket in the first four Tests. It was left to the spinners, Mailey and a New Zealand-born Victorian leggie named Clarrie Grimmett, to carry the attack, while Macartney and Bill Woodfull did the heavy lifting for the batsmen.

Marred by rain, the First and Fourth Tests were drawn. The Second and Third, played on docile wickets, would have needed more than the allocated three days to reach a result. Collins, suffering from neuritis, had to hand over the captaincy to Bardsley for two Tests.

Bardsley had been chugging along, Bardsley-like, since the war. In 1921, he scored 2,005 runs at 54.18 – pretty much the same produce as in 1909 and 1912. The world had ended and begun again, but Bardsley was Bardsley. His mild eyes sheltered behind the pulled-down peak of his cap, and he seldom moved a muscle if it didn't lead to the accumulation of runs. Even Collins, that stony-faced statue, was moved to the point where he said, 'Cheer up, Bards, it can't be that bad!' But Bardsley believed that by expecting the worst he could always be prepared. Even in his forties he arrived at grounds early to inspect slope, weather, angles of the sun, every last detail, in Robinson's words, 'casing the joint for stealing runs'.

Like many whose careers were interrupted by the war, Bardsley had kept his game young. For the 1926 tour he was picked as vice-captain, narrowly, over Ryder. In a fading team, Bardsley was seen as a proven quantity.

Bardsley didn't score another 2,000 runs – he made 'only' 1,424 – but he averaged nearly 50 again. In a wretched, rainy English summer he provided a ray of sunshine at Lord's, his unbeaten 193 his highest Test score. Harold Larwood had battered his hands and he gave four chances. But he carried his bat and saved the Test. The next best Australian score was 39.

Two captains, two openers: Collins (L) and Bardsley.

Captain at Headingley, Bardsley's experience was scant: he had led NSW in six matches, 15 years earlier. Nobody had accounted for the possibility of his being captain.

The burden affected him. Rain had fallen for four days in Leeds. He tossed with Arthur Carr, lost, and was sent in against Tate on a gluepot. Tate pitched it up, Bardsley prodded, and Sutcliffe held a brilliant catch in slips.

The match was drawn, with Macartney, Woodfull and Arthur Richardson making centuries.

Fittingly for a man whose touchstone would be his modesty, Bill Woodfull had been a slow starter in cricket. The third of a Methodist minister's four sons, he was named William Maldon, for the town of his birth in rural Victoria. As a child he and the family moved to Jack Ryder's Collingwood, where a backyard turf wicket became Billy's sporting nursery. But he suffered from rheumatic fever as a child, leaving him with permanent joint pains.

Woodfull attended Melbourne High School, where he would later teach maths and serve as principal. Cricket remained secondary. He was no machine, no Giffen or Bradman. Deceptively scholarly in appearance, doughy and placid, he first played for Victoria at 24 as a mature-age student. In his second match, against Western Australia in Perth, he batted for four hours before being run out for 153. With the other Bill, Ponsford, breaking the world record first-class score with 429 in 477 minutes against Tasmania, Woodfull established an opening partnership. The first time they batted together, the Bills put on 133.

With pitches better prepared and bowling stocks thin, these were batsmen's years. The real dasher was Macartney. Collins, Bardsley and Ponsford were accumulators, and Woodfull was something of a stodge. Crouching low, with his hands spread apart on the grip, barely lifting the bat for a backswing, he was built for survival. He concentrated on impregnability and breaking bowlers' spirits.

While Ponsford continued to break records and entered Test cricket in 1924–25, Woodfull waited – and made bowlers wait, making a five-hour 117 against NSW and a half-century against the MCC. On

Victoria's 12-match tour of New Zealand, he added three centuries including 212 against Canterbury. In none did he get out.

Approaching 30, Woodfull knew the 1925–26 season would be his make-or-break time. In nearly 10 hours of batting at the MCG, spread over four days, he subjected the South Australians to his tour application, scoring 97 and 236. Another century against NSW got him onto Collins's 1926 boat.

It was predicted that Woodfull would be overrun by the new breed. Few saw him as a future regular. Instead, with Collins's team fading, Woodfull was a revelation. Like Hugh Massie he made 201 in his first match on English soil. At The Oval he nudged his way to 118 against Surrey; his first boundary was his last scoring shot. Though Arthur Gilligan said he had 'no flash and not much sparkle', he scored 1,672 runs at 57.85, top of the aggregates and averages.

Bill Woodfull, the late bloomer

Woodfull was not judged good enough for the main XI until the Second Test, at Lord's, and then only in the middle order. But when Collins succumbed to neuritis and Bardsley stood in as captain, Woodfull got his chance at the top. After Bardsley was out first ball, Woodfull made 141. He would never be out of an Australian team until his retirement.

At Old Trafford, with Collins still out and Bardsley still captain, Woodfull and Macartney made centuries again. A fourth maudlin draw resulted – or failed to result. Bardsley's brief interlude as Australian captain, at 43, presaged a quiet end for a quiet man. After the tour he played no further first-class cricket, but would become a state and national selector.

Bardsley, who did not marry until he was 62, was a cricketer's cricketer, and a cricketer of substance. He was the first Australian to score 50 first-class centuries, and the last before Bradman. His English record, of nearly 8,000 runs and 27 centuries, would stand until Bradman. In a time of tempestuous souls, only once did he receive a rebuke from authority. On the 1926 tour, Bardsley was fined by team management for wanting to play in too many matches. He was the type of player, said Bert Oldfield in a classic of understatement, 'who believed that he needed all the practice he could get'.

England's combative captain, Arthur Carr, was having an even worse 1926 series than Collins. At Headingley, he had dropped Macartney fourth ball, and the Australian champion made a century before lunch. For the decider at The Oval, England replaced Carr with the dashing Percy Chapman, whom Neville Cardus described as 'every schoolboy's summer night's dream of the ideal cricketer'; he was ultimately to drink himself to death. Carr would enjoy a different fate, as Douglas Jardine's key co-conspirator of the Bodyline strategy.

In mocking honour of Chapman's elevation, Mailey turned out for the Test in a dinner jacket. He evaded disciplinary action by taking six wickets. 'Five wickets,' he said, 'wouldn't have done it.'

England also recalled Wilfred Rhodes at 48. The decider was balanced until, between the second and third innings, rain fell. England were contemplating Gregory on a drying wicket, but Collins let them off by choosing the innocuous off-spin of Arthur Richardson, to whom Hobbs and Sutcliffe feigned respect as the wicket settled. By the time Gregory came on, they were set. They added 172, both making centuries, and England's 436 put the Ashes out of reach. Despite Collins's brave 61 in what would be his last Test, Australia were never in the hunt. For the first time since 1912, England held the Ashes, Rhodes eking out 42 valuable runs and taking 4/44 to nail the Australian second innings.

Some speculated that Collins's bowling Richardson instead of Gregory had a nefarious motive. Hunter Hendry believed Collins threw the match, and Noble held 'suspicions'. For losing the Ashes, Collins was vilified when he returned home. Not only was he stripped of the Australian captaincy, but also those of NSW and Waverley.

Yet to rig a result, Collins would have needed many accomplices. Was Arthur Richardson trying not to get a wicket? Richardson's bowling had helped Collins win the Melbourne Test of 1924–25. And what of the rest? Was the whole Australian team colluding? The batsmen who were out for 125 in their second innings, Woodfull, Ponsford and Macartney? Grimmett and Mailey, who bowled 97.5 overs between them? It beggars belief. The Adelaide incident shows that a bookmaker knew Collins – but also that Collins rejected his advances. And Gregory had not taken a wicket in four Tests. It wasn't strange that Collins chose not to bowl him. The most logical explanation is that Australia were outplayed under pressure, and were over-reliant on too few performers.

The post-1926 clean-out swept away Clem Hill as a selector and Sydney Smith as manager, but for Collins, the loss had lifetime consequences. Cricket was his one source of success; ostracised

Collins, unpadding after a net in 1926

from the game, he fell back on his addictions. Mailey once said that Collins's 'hunting grounds were the racetrack, the dog track, Monte Carlo, baccarat joints in Kings Cross, a two-up school in the Flanders trenches and anywhere a quiet game of poker was being played'. On tours, Collins would bet on what train would arrive next, how many carriages it would have, and how many windows. He bet on ribbon-cutting contests on sea voyages. Under Mailey's light pen, it sounds fun. But it wasn't fun for Herbie Collins over the next 30 years. He became a bookmaker, but failed. He became a stipendiary steward – surely unthinkable if he was thought to be corrupt – but failed there too. He became a commission agent for punters and bookies, low on the gambling foodchain. Once he had gone to Covent Garden to hear opera. In England he had sung tenor at parties, but as he entered his forties the only parties Collins attended were in poker dens.

In 1933–34 a benefit was played for Collins, Kelleway and Andrews. It raised £500 for each, but Collins was soon appealing to the NSW Cricketers' Fund. The NSWCA treasurer Edwin Tyler wrote in 1931: 'I have to report that I interviewed Mr H.L. Collins in regard to his present financial position. He informs me that he has been right up against it for a considerable time, has tried in every possible way to get employment or means of earning his live-lihood, but has failed almost completely. He has an invalid mother who has no hope of recovering. So short has he been of money that on occasions he has not been able to buy the necessary medicine, and more infrequently they have been short of food.'

The fund supplied him until 1938. He married at 51, to a bookie's daughter 27 years his junior. They had a son, and Collins re-enlisted with the army, working at Victoria Barracks. He spent his nights gambling, and by 1950 was divorced. Collins's soldier-cricketer-bookmaker existence has been romanticised. But now we know more about gambling and more about that war, his photographs show a man shadowed by sadness and the memories he could not share. He died of lung cancer in 1959, penniless and forgotten by his one-time peers. The fall was complete, the romance erased.

14

A BATTING PARADISE

THE average age of Australian cricketers, and their captains, has never been higher than in the 1920s. Armstrong captained at 41, Collins from 32 to 36, Bardsley at 43. They led men in their thirties and forties, who were, like their captains, prolonging interrupted careers.

The last captain of the 1920s, Collingwood's Jack Ryder, got the job at 39. Under him the situation bordered on ridiculous: Australia selected two spin bowlers, Don Blackie and Bert Ironmonger, who were nearing 50. In the race to regenerate, England was winning. Certainly Hobbs was still playing Test cricket at 46, but in the bowling stocks, England was producing Maurice Tate, Harold Larwood and Walter Hammond, in the prime of life. By 1928, Australia's firepower lay with a lame Gregory, whose productive years had also been shortened by the war.

In and out of the Test team under Armstrong and Collins, Ryder had become the undisputed champion of Victoria. His leadership showed a certain ruthlessness. In 1923, after bowling the MCC out for 71, Victoria ground to 6/617 before Ryder declared. In protest, the English stonewalled. Their openers, William Hill-Wood and Geoffrey Wilson, went so slowly for 85 overs that Ryder had Arthur Liddicut bowl underarm.

Work kept Ryder out of cricket for the start of the 1926–27 home season, and he handed the Victorian captaincy over to the rising leader and fellow teetotaller, Woodfull. On Christmas Eve in the big match of the summer, Victoria bowled NSW out for 221, Ryder taking 3/32. The match paused for Christmas Day and the Sunday of Boxing Day, then Victoria got going. At stumps on 27 December, they were one for 573. Now that Sheffield Shield rules allowed for the optional covering of pitches, bigger scores were more frequent. It also said something for the decline of Australian pace bowling. Woodfull 'missed out' with 133, but Ponsford was 334 at stumps. On 28 December he added 18 more, and Hendry went from 87 to 100.

Coming in at two for 594, Ryder showed that he was not one of those batsmen who suffered from having to wait. Woodfull said Ryder's innings contained 'the most terrific hitting I think anybody has witnessed in cricket'. Eight decades later, even the likes of Gilchrist and Richards cannot have hit as hard, for such a sustained time, as Ryder that day. In four hours he hit 33 fours and six sixes, at a time when the MCG was bigger and the bats were weaker. He went from 63 to 210 between lunch and tea. His first hundred took 115 minutes, his second hundred 74 minutes and his last 95 runs took just 56 minutes. At one point he said to his batting partner, Bert Hartkopf, 'Don't take any notice of me, I've gone mad.'

The astonishment of his 295 has not receded with the years. Nor has that of Victoria's 1,107. When Ryder was 275, leg-spinner Tommy Andrews said to his captain Alan Kippax, 'I know Ryder's weak spot!' The next four balls went for four, six, four and six. Going for another six to reach 300, Ryder holed out. Mailey commented later, 'Very few chances were given but I think the chap in the tweed coat dropped Ryder in the shilling stand.' Mailey gave several versions of the same story, one of which is that if the old gentleman in the brown derby hat at the back of the grandstand had held his catches Mailey would have had them out days sooner.

Victoria won the Shield that season and the next, Ryder playing under Woodfull, who had also led an unofficial Australian team to Malaya. In 1927–28, perhaps the high (or low?) point in the

The King of Collingwood, Jack Ryder

years of the batting paradise, Woodfull scored 43, 31, 99, 191 not out, 106, 94 and 81 not out. Yet his 645 runs at 129 were dwarfed by Ponsford's 1,217 at 152.12, among them an innings of 437 to sneak past his own world record. North of the border, a couple of youngsters called Jackson and Bradman were breaking through. Even with a 284 on a short tour of New Zealand, and a season's average of 133 for his new club Carlton, Woodfull would never be seen as their equal for sheer mercilessness.

In Victoria and nationally, there was a two-year debate over the captaincy merits of Woodfull and Ryder. In 1928, with a glittering English team on its way, Ryder was appointed Australian captain over his younger state captain. Woodfull generously stepped aside from the Victorian role to let Ryder lead. But such was the confusion in the Board, a debate went on for hours over whether Woodfull or Vernon Ransford, aged 44, should be chosen as Ryder's vice-captain – until someone helpfully pointed out that Ransford was not in the XI.

Ryder's form was better than ever, with centuries against South Australia and NSW, and the Board considered that they needed a father figure for an inexperienced team. Gone were Collins, Macartney, Bardsley, Taylor and Mailey – the nucleus of the mid-1920s teams. Gregory and Kelleway were on their last legs. Australia had some promising new batting talent, but the bowling stocks were threadbare. Too much depended on Grimmett and the elderly Ironmonger, who would bowl a combined 178 overs in the First Test in Brisbane, at the Exhibition Ground.

In the race for post-war regeneration, England had won. Hobbs anchored a star-studded line-up of Sutcliffe, Hammond, Jardine, Hendren and Chapman. Larwood, Jack White, Hammond and the magnificent Tate were a superior bowling attack. Ryder was leading lambs to the slaughter.

Slaughtered they were in Brisbane, by 675 runs. Gregory, twisting his knee trying to take a catch in his 41st over, confessed tearfully to his teammates that he was finished. At 33, he was Australia's youngest bowler. His foil Kelleway went down with food poisoning. After England made 521, it rained, and Australia could do no better than 122. Cruelly, Chapman batted again rather than enforce the follow-on and set Australia 741, which the home team managed to reduce by 66. Woodfull alone stood fast. In this season he began collecting his nicknames: Old Steadfast, The Rock, Unbowlable and The Worm-Killer. There's not much else we need to know about his batting. Within 51 overs Australia were all out. Or not *all* out. Woodfull was still there, on 30, looking for partners.

When Jack White had Bradman caught for 1 in that disastrous second innings, Tate called out: 'What do you mean by poaching my rabbit?'

It was a humiliation the young batsman would never forget. Bradman's success derived in some part from an insatiable desire – and ability – plus a healthy chip on his shoulder and an elephantine memory for snubs. From his earliest years in Bowral, where his father George, a carpenter-cum-farmer, had moved from Cootamundra for the health of his wife Emily, Donald George was looked after by his elders. For the local team, he used a cut-down bat to make his first impression against adults. Soon he was making centuries, and double-centuries, against fully grown bowlers. Sometimes, as against Bill O'Reilly's Wingello, it was against fellow prodigies.

Leaving school at 14 to work under his sponsor, the local real estate agent Percy Westbrook, Bradman's eye was trained on sport. It might have been tennis – equally honed by his drill of hitting a golf ball against the brick stand of his family's water tank – but by his late teens cricket had won. The NSW selectors requested he come to Sydney for a trial. Then, a snub: a 29-man squad was picked, without Bradman. This he would never forget.

'Proving the doubters wrong' is the most fatigued of clichés, but for Bradman it remained fresh and stinging, a lifetime's motto. Mountains of runs taught the state selectors not to hurt him again. He moved to work for Westbrook in Sydney, then took a train to Adelaide when told that Jackson, with a boil on his knee, would miss a Shield match. Bradman scored 118 against Grimmett, and another four centuries in the next eight games, including a monolithic 452 not out against Queensland (which could have been a forgotten 80 if the bails had fallen off when Alec Hurwood hit his stumps). He gave half-chances on 264 and 345. In the end, the Queenslanders were so grateful to have been there that they chaired him off. With wickets covered, the balance tilted unfairly the batsmen's way, but even in that context Bradman stood out. Within a year he was picked for Australia.

English mockery in Brisbane was followed by his omission for the Second Test. There was epic debate about who left Bradman out. Warren Bardsley claimed he was outvoted. Later, Ryder took some responsibility, saying he felt Bradman was young and would not suffer from being 12th man. He also wanted to shield the prodigy from Tate, Larwood and White. Ryder said: 'I only wanted some pace.'

The selectors gave him Don Blackie, an off-spinner who was two days older than Bert Ironmonger. Australia's bowlers were crushed in Sydney by Hammond's 251. Their reply suffered a bad start when Alan Kippax was bizarrely given out bowled. England had appealed when a bail was seen on the ground; George Hele, at the bowler's end, turned down the appeal. The English turned to square leg, where Dave Elder gave Kippax out. In the changing room, Victor Richardson tried to persuade Ryder to intervene, but Ryder dallied and the moment passed.

After the contentious dismissal, Australia stuttered. Ponsford was put out of the match by a Larwood snorter, and 12th man Bradman fielded for a combined 652 English runs. Ryder said: 'He did a good job too, but I had the impression he didn't want the position again.'

Again it was only Woodfull, with 68 and 111, who helped Ryder stave off humiliation. The selectors dropped Ponsford and restored Bradman for Melbourne, but another defeat followed. Four Australians made centuries, including Woodfull and Bradman, but Hammond's 200 and Sutcliffe's 135 guided the tourists to an Ashes-retaining win, their seven for 332 being the highest fourth innings score in an Ashes victory. What made it worse for Australia was that much of it was made on a vicious Melbourne sticky while

Ironmonger, against whom they might have been lucky to get past 100, was hand-mowing his regular strip of park for St Kilda Council.

In the remaining Tests, Australia showed improvement. Hammond made another two centuries in Adelaide, where Jackson announced himself with a sumptuous 169 and Ryder hit 63 and 87, but Australia fell 12 runs short of an unlikely win.

As captain, Ryder was a yielding diplomat. In Melbourne, Grimmett said Douglas Jardine had obstructed him from taking a catch. Ryder defused the situation by not appealing for obstruction, instead sending Grimmett to his mark. When Larwood was jeered for bowling short to Ironmonger in the MCC v Victoria match and the English staged a sit-down in protest, Ryder declared the innings closed rather than let the tension build. Perhaps, in the Australian tradition, another captain might have joined any of these fights. An Armstrong, a Dave Gregory or a Joe Darling probably would have. But it wasn't Ryder's style, and in the context of the series, humility was a defensible approach.

Ryder had become the first Australian captain to lose his first four Tests, but such was England's strength and the flux of the home team, not to mention his own herculean efforts with the bat, he was not widely blamed. Australia had lost to a team of genius. Tate, Hobbs and Sutcliffe were already on the highest rung, but Larwood and particularly Hammond were instant superstars. Hammond made 905 runs, a world record that would stand for precisely 18 months. Australia gained great heart from a final Test in which Woodfull and Bradman made centuries and Tim Wall – Ryder had been 'given some pace' at last – took eight wickets. The Test took eight days, but Australia won and the players chaired Ryder from the MCG.

These were hard times for Australian cricket, but Woodfull, with another century in the Fifth Test, capping a series of 491 runs at 54.56, at the top of the order against one of England's greatest attacks, was leading the quest for respect. Johnny Moyes waxed lyrical, calling Woodfull 'almost unbowlable. His backswing was a mere gesture to convention, like a man opening the door an inch or two, then closing it hurriedly so that nothing could enter.' It wasn't pretty, but desperate times weren't calling for display. Woodfull's three centuries were the first time such a feat was recorded on a losing side. Ponsford, the record-breaker, was no longer even a Test cricketer. When Hammond disturbed Woodfull's stumps in the last Test, it was the first time he had been bowled in a year.

Not even such a series could exhaust him. In Victoria's match against the English, between the Fourth and Fifth Tests, Woodfull was on the field for every minute of the four days, scoring 275 in a draw as dull as it was worthy.

While helpless to stem England's supremacy, Ryder had fulfilled his brief to oversee generational change. His Test average was 51.62 and the 1928–29 tour was an unprecedented financial success, with nearly 1,200,000 spectators paying £95,820 to watch the exciting Englishmen.

Ryder had unfinished business in England, after two disappointing tours. In 1929–30 he averaged 50.18 for Victoria, leading Woodfull. A national selector himself, Ryder was looking forward to the 1930 tour. But he misjudged his role in the transition. His fellow selectors, Dr Charles Dolling and SCG Trust chairman Dick Jones, considered that he was part of the old guard, not a bridge to the new. Ryder was sitting at the SCG waiting to bat when he was handed the Ashes team list. The name with the (c) beside it was Woodfull. Nowhere was Ryder. He was stunned. Stork Hendry, sitting next to him, said: 'You make a hundred and show those bastards sitting in the stand what a mistake they've made.'

As usual, Ryder functioned best when rejected. He spat out 100 runs in the next 172 minutes, and followed it with 168 against Queensland. There were public protests, the prisoners at Pentridge threatened to riot, but Ryder said nothing, either publicly or to his former friend Jones. Ryder never spoke to him again.

He watched Woodfull and Bradman lead Australia on a summer of wonders in England. Ryder maintained his dignity, never speaking out against his omission and continuing to play alongside Woodfull for Victoria until 1932. He was given a benefit at the MCG, netting £2,463, and won another Sheffield Shield. In his last game, at the Gabba against Queensland, Ryder scored 71. He pulled a ball so hard that it sent the square leg umpire, Jim Orr, to hospital for three stitches, a painful way to end a 30-year umpiring career. Eddie Gilbert, the lightning Aboriginal bowler, who had been no-balled 13 times for throwing three weeks earlier in Melbourne, ended Ryder's Victorian career.

Ryder is one of those cricket personalities whose name features as prominently after his retirement as before it. In 1935–36 the Maharajah of Patiala asked an Australian entrepreneur, Frank Tarrant, to organise an Australian tour to India. The Maharajah would pay expenses and would not try to poach any current Test players. The Board of Control rejected the request, but after five months of public pressure, it relented. The Maharajah of Patiala's team played 23 matches in India, with Ryder as captain and personnel including Macartney, Hendry and Ironmonger. They lost three times and split a series against an All-India XI 2–2, in which Ryder scored Australia's only century, 104 on matting at Bombay. By all accounts it was a pleasant tour, and Ryder ensured Australian–Indian cricketing relations started well by refusing to attend any functions where Indians were not entitled to the same privileges as the white men. He predicted that India would, one day, be a cricketing power.

For 24 years, from 1946 to 1970, Ryder would be an Australian Test selector, respected for his judgement, fairness and persuasive skills. Among those whose careers were kicked along by Ryder were Bill Johnston and Keith Stackpole, Australian stars separated by two decades. To Johnston, Ryder suggested he try bowling his faster ball eight times an over. To Stackpole, Ryder said that having a bat in his hand that was all the cause he needed to teach the bowlers who was boss.

In his eighties, Ryder was still a selector. At 87, he led the parade of former players during the MCG Centenary Test, having travelled to the ground each day by train. Three weeks later, he died of heart failure. His service to his club and state left a grandstand and a medal named in his honour. On the day of his funeral, local shopkeepers shut their doors for the passing of the King of Collingwood.

15

THE WOODFULL ERA

WHEN the Board decided to make Bill Woodfull captain of the 1930 tour ahead of Ryder, he was so upset that it took several delegations before he would agree to have his appointment ratified.

Eight years younger than Ryder, Woodfull was the first Australian captain from the post-war generation. Gone were the remnants of player power and the memories of the 1912 brawl. Woodfull led a team that was under the Board of Control's firm control. In place of the shop steward and managing director, the new prototype of the captain was a mentor, a father figure, a tactician and an onfield inspiration. Compared with the captains of the 19th century, his range of influence was dramatically shrunken. He was a sporting leader, not an alternative government. In return, the captain enjoyed heightened social prestige: Woodfull would be a confidant of the King of England. But the power was gone. The captain no longer had any control over finances.

Woodfull might have had cause for pessimism over the 1930 squad. 'Woodfull's Kindergarten' contained only four from the previous tour: himself, Ponsford, Grimmett and Oldfield. Names such as Bradman, Kippax and Jackson were disdained by the English, notably Percy Fender, who predicted that Bradman's habit of playing across the line would be found out on greener wickets.

One feature of the Australian captaincy had not changed: a tour of England was the litmus test and ultimate challenge. Woodfull, a teetotaller whose only vice was a fondness for bridge, established his style immediately with his young group. Ray Robinson wrote that 'the kernel of Woodfull's captaincy was the way he got the utmost from each man. Their esteem was their response to his personal qualities of commonsense, straightforwardness, tolerance, consideration and unselfish service to his side.'

Armed with that esteem, they went to work. Bradman, still 21, made the first of what would become routine tour-opening centuries against Worcestershire, on his way to 1,000 runs before the end of May. Worried about his bowling ranks, Woodfull requested either Ironmonger or NSW's leg-spinner Hugh Chilvers. The Board turned him down, regarding Grimmett and Queensland's Percy Hornibrook as sufficient.

Woodfull's vice-captain, having been a contender for the captaincy, was South Australia's Victor Richardson. No less than Giffen or Bradman, Richardson's sporting achievements dizzy the mind. He represented Australia in baseball, and South Australia in football, baseball and golf. He won a South Australian tennis title and played A-grade lacrosse and basketball. He won three SAFL premierships with Sturt as a rebounding backman, and in his first year playing in the centre he tied for the Magarey Medal for South Australia's best and fairest footballer. As a young man he attended some form of practice every night, and sometimes more than one.

As a cricketer he was a swashbuckler, a handsome, Brylcreemed, pencil-moustached 1930s star who thrived on a tour of America and counted Joan Crawford among his fans. When it comes to Richardson, cricket is part of the story but far from the full story.

His father, Valentine Yaxley Richardson, was a house decorator, and the Richardsons lived across the road from Joe Darling, who coached Victor and his elder brother, Osma Voy. They went to Kyre College (now Scotch) and received instruction from Karl

Quist, father of the Australian tennis player Adrian. When the First World War broke out Victor was working in the South Australian Government Produce Department while Osma went to France. Killed at Pozieres in 1916, his loss left a permanent mark on his brother, who lived as if wanting to complete two lives in the space of one.

Victor was a born leader, and Woodfull won the Board's vote ahead of him only narrowly. From 1921 Richardson had skippered Sturt and South Australia. The former he would lead for 21 years, the latter 14, until a coup and a Bradman stopped him.

Through the 1920s, Richardson carried South Australian cricket as Giffen had. On his first-class debut in 1918–19 he hit 72 and 48 off Victoria's Armstrong, Ryder and McDonald. The next season, against the same exalted opponents, he hit 134 and made Vernon Ransford's tour of New Zealand. In the unofficial Test match in Auckland, Richardson cut and hooked his way to 112 as his team made 663 at 6 runs an over. On this occasion, as always, he was a popular socialiser. His father had been head of a Temperance Alliance and Victor did not have a drink until he was 27, but thereafter he knew one end of a champagne bottle from the other and made up for lost time.

Richardson led a South Australia of almost comical weakness. In the decade to 1925–26 they managed a solitary first-class victory. Richardson often made centuries in losing sides; in Sydney in 1924–25, he scored hundreds in both innings against Gregory and Mailey but still lost.

He made his Test debut under Collins in Sydney, following 42 and 18 with a century at the MCG in his second Test. In the first cricket match to attract more than 200,000 spectators, Richardson was given a life on 67 and went on to 138 in three and a quarter hours.

Consistency eluded him, however, and by the Fourth and Fifth Tests he was 12th man. He missed selection on the 1926 tour, but consoled himself with induction into the American Sports Hall of Fame for his achievements as a baseballer. Accordingly, he was a superb fieldsman, his throwing and close catching better than any Australian since Syd Gregory. A *Sydney Morning Herald* headline once asked: 'Is Richardson Human?' His batting stance, low and crablike, was the only ungainly thing about him.

The late 1920s set an unhappy pattern for his batting. Able to dominate first-class bowlers, even in beaten sides, Richardson was seldom able to carry that ability up a level. In 1926–27, his South Australians won the Sheffield Shield for the first time in 14 years, a tremendous achievement and a triumph of leadership in having lured Grimmett from Victoria. But, picked as the captain of The Rest against Australia, he failed twice. Two seasons later he cracked 231 in 307 minutes against the English in Adelaide, hoicking Larwood into the stands, but again missed out in the Test trial. Brought into Ryder's team for the Second and Third Tests, he scored 27, 0, 3 and 5 and was dropped again. Between the Tests he made 115 for South Australia against Queensland.

Two centuries in the next season saw him picked for Woodfull's 1930 tour as vice-captain. The South Australian contingent thought he should have been captain, but while he had more charisma and enterprise than Woodfull the sticking point would always be his ability to hold down a Test spot.

Bradman was not an immediately happy tourist. Some senior players didn't make him welcome, and played practical jokes on him. Stork Hendry had him take his shirt off and play the piano (at which Don's sister Lillian had taught him), but instead of appreciating his skills his teammates joked about the muscles popping out along his ribs. We know Bradman didn't forget these things, because he talked about them for the rest of his life. He would write, after his retirement: 'When I was a young boy from the country in a team of world-famous players they wouldn't speak to me. They seemed to resent me.' When it came to being teased, he didn't have much of a sense of humour.

The Australians went undefeated until the First Test, the first four-day Test in England, when they hit a red-hot Tate and an English team still overwhelmingly confident from the previous two series. At Lord's for the Second Test England seemed to be gaining control once again as Ranjitsinhji's nephew, KS Duleepsinhji, emulated his uncle with 173 on debut. Chasing 425, Woodfull and Ponsford built the platform. Having put on 162, during the third day's lunch break they were presented to George V, who said Woodfull was his favourite Australian cricketer. Ponsford was out immediately after the break, but then Bradman came in, and Woodfull helped him add 231 runs in two and a half hours. Just before the close, Woodfull was stumped for 155, his sixth century in nine Ashes Tests. Lest Woodfull harbour any delusions of becoming the foremost batsman, Bradman advanced to 254, what he considered technically his best-ever innings, cut off by a fabled catch by Chapman at gully. Sir James Barrie, author of *Peter Pan,* who was watching with Neville Cardus, said: 'But why is Bradman going away?' Cardus: 'Surely, Sir James, you saw that marvellous catch?' Barrie: 'Yes, but what evidence have we that the ball which Chapman threw up in the air is the same ball that left Bradman's bat?'

With 6/729, Australia had reversed the momentum of two series. Grimmett wheeled away for six English wickets, leaving Australia with 72 to win. Three men fell quickly and the terror of collapse loomed, but Woodfull carried his team through without further loss.

Woodfull (*far left*) leading his 1930 team onto the field at Worcester, among them Victor Richardson (*third from left*) and Don Bradman (*behind Richardson's left shoulder*).

Their sails full, Australia had begun their new era at Lord's. On the first day at Headingley, Woodfull scored a handy 50 but Bradman a handier 309, which he increased to 334 the next day. The Yorkshire crowd was generous: when Bradman passed 'Tip' Foster's 26-year-old record of 287, the noise was so immense that play had to be stopped. The match was drawn with England well behind, and Old Trafford was rained out, but at The Oval Sutcliffe's careful 161 was straws in the wind before the tornado of Australia's 695: Woodfull 54, Ponsford 110, Bradman 232. Percy Hornibrook, with 7/92, completed the decisive 2–1 win.

More than seven decades later, Bradman's 974 at 139.14 remains world-beating. There was a mercilessness about his batting that always defied ordinary understanding. In skipping down or across the wicket, his muscles were stronger than metal springs, his skeleton made of something lighter than bone. His wry lips stretched in a half-smile that disguised an instinctive harshness. In 1930, he was able to regard 100, or 150, or 200, as if they weren't so important. He clearly loved batting – film footage shows him as light and enthusiastic as a jack-rabbit, his strong bottom hand whirring his bat in rotary motion – but he also loved grinding opponents into submission. He humiliated Tate, England's best bowler since Barnes. Fender had openly doubted his ability to play across the line in English conditions, so Bradman went to Fender's Surrey and hit 252 not out. He placed his shots so Fender would have to chase them. This relentlessness set him apart: he never seemed to tire, never threw his wicket away, never had that joyous release of having done the job. He sometimes batted so long and was so tired that teammates had to strip off his pads and clothes. No matter how tired, he kept his focus. There is no difference between him and all the others except that he kept scoring runs. Johnny Moyes wrote, 'His figures are so fantastic and overpowering that they can never be ignored.' His sheer appetite raised him to the pedestal occupied only by Grace. When diarist, theatre critic and cricket-lover James Agate had written of Grace, he could have been foreseeing Bradman: 'There's lots can do it now and then, but the Doctor, he just keeps on doing it.'

Woodfull's 345 at 57.50 was second to Bradman. Grimmett took 29 wickets. Bernard Bosanquet met him during the tour and asked, 'Am I responsible for you?'

More than the runs and wickets and series win, the ages told the story. A complete reversal had taken place since 1928–29. England's average age was now 35. Hobbs (47), Woolley (43) and Hendren (41) were in their twilight. Chapman had been dropped before the Fifth Test, somewhat controversially as he had been averaging 43. Although Australia had three in their mid to late 30s – Grimmett, Victor Richardson and Oldfield – the team's average age was 28 and Bradman was still 22.

Richardson had again failed to quite measure up. His 98 runs in the Tests at 19.60 saw him dropped again when Australia returned home. His 832 tour runs at 26.83 were also underwhelming. It didn't help that Richardson said publicly, 'We could have played any team without Bradman, but we could not have played the blind school without Grimmett.' It was fair that Grimmett receive due recognition, but Richardson might have been over-egging it by discounting a national hero's 974 runs.

Modern celebrity, as Bradman found out in 1930, extracted its pound of flesh. He wrote his life story for the London *Star* and by the end of the tour was fined £50 of his 'good conduct' money. Bradman wouldn't forget, and the fine started an ongoing sniping battle with the Board which did not end until he became a member of it.

In a move orchestrated by his new employer, sportsgoods retailer Mick Simmonds, Bradman came home separately from his 1930 teammates and undertook a one-man promotional tour around Australia. There are two lines of thought on this, not necessarily incompatible. One is that Bradman was an aloof, self-centred individual who placed his own rewards on a separate plane, the Bradman who, in 80 Test innings, was only run out once, and only another three times in 258 more first-class efforts. The other is that the pressures of celebrity were so great that he had to insulate himself in order to preserve his mental clarity for the purpose of making runs and winning matches – for his teams. Both arguments can coexist. It's unkind to criticise Bradman's character. He was a shy teetotaller who did not want to participate in what he called 'beer drinking contests'. That was his right. But the fact that he saw team bonding as 'beer drinking contests' suggests that he never fully understood his colleagues either.

The 1930 Ashes contest was the first of Woodfull's five series as captain. Hosting the West Indies and South Africa in the next two summers, his team steamed on an engine constructed of Bradman's runs. Woodfull moved to the middle order against the West Indians, failed in three Tests, then returned to the top and scored 83. Opening, he averaged 70.17 against the South Africans, second to Bradman, making 161 in Melbourne and three half-centuries. But England were coming back, with new players and new plans.

Bodyline, or 'fast leg theory' as England's new captain Jardine called it, was a method by which Larwood, Bill Voce and Bill Bowes bowled short-pitched balls at the batsmen's bodies with fieldsmen stacked, both close and deep, on the leg side. Joe Darling called it 'Bradman theory', acknowledging its intention. Larwood felt that Bradman had backed away from short balls during his 232 at The Oval in 1930. But Bodyline would inevitably capture the wicket, sooner or later, of any batsman, regardless of his name or his approach.

Leg theory had been around since Armstrong and before, as a means of choking scoring. That too was unsportsmanlike. What England did in 1932–33 was to add physical intimidation to the negativity.

The confrontation started before the Test series. In November, at the MCG, the English played a non-Test Australian XI, led by Woodfull. Bob Wyatt was leading England instead of Jardine, who had gone fishing. More than 109,000 people watched the four-day game, then a record for a non-Test. They saw Wyatt use his bowlers conventionally, then change tactics, stacking the leg field and directing a short-pitched attack at the body. Woodfull scored a direct hit in the chest. The Australian XI won the match, but England had tested its rocket.

Each of the Tests is the stuff of fable. In Sydney, with Bradman absent ill, Woodfull was out hooking but Stan McCabe submitted his claim to greatness with 187 not out. A round-cheeked, attractive strokeplayer from the Mosman club in Sydney, McCabe had to ask his father to stop his mother from jumping the fence and attacking Larwood and Voce. After his innings, still one of the greatest on Australian soil, McCabe said honestly, 'I got away with it this time, but I was lucky and could never do it again.'

At 38, Victor Richardson's Test career was thought to be over. Bodyline resurrected it. His 231 off Larwood four years earlier was remembered, and he was in form, with 134 against the MCC and 203 against Victoria. His aggressive and mature personality was considered, rightly, suited to combat fast leg-theory. So optimistic and belligerent, so vivacious in the field, he would add more to the changing room than runs or catches. Living up to Cardus's moniker of 'The Guardsman', Richardson stood by McCabe for two precious hours in Sydney and gave 49 to their partnership of 129.

But it was all for nought. Aided by centuries from Sutcliffe, Hammond and the Nawab of Pataudi, England won the Test easily. A slower pitch awaited in Melbourne, and Bradman was back. He came in at number four, and his first ball was a slow bouncer from Bowes. Bradman leapt into position to hook, was through his shot too early, and bottom-edged it onto his stumps. Jack Fingleton's 83 helped the hosts to 228, the highest score of the match. Playing his third Test match, the tall, fastish NSW leg-spinner Bill O'Reilly spooked the English, taking 10 wickets to even the series. Bradman's second innings 103 not out was also instrumental.

Defeat pricked Jardine, and a bone-hard Adelaide pitch gave Larwood the requisite assistance. On Friday the thirteenth of January, 1933, Jardine won the toss and batted. By this stage the English captain had been asked not to enter the Australian changing room. He could knock, but not go in. Woodfull's role in this is intriguing. Clearly he resented the English tactics, and there was no warmth between the captains. Woodfull was no instigator of hostility, but nor would he deny his men their righteous anger. England made 341, having been four for 30 and lucky that Australia had only one fast bowler, Wall, who took 5/72. His opening partner was O'Reilly, supported by Grimmett and Ironmonger. Never can Australia have had an attack so ill-fitted to the conditions.

Woodfull opened with Fingleton to conventional fields. Gubby Allen had Fingleton caught behind, then, with the last ball of his second over, Larwood's bumper hit Woodfull above the heart. The Australian captain dropping his bat, clutching his chest and reeling from the wicket is the most enduring image of Bodyline. But Larwood's ball was not bowled to a Bodyline field. Allen, who refused leg-theory fields, delivered the next over, a maiden to Bradman. The great provocation was not so much Larwood's hitting Woodfull but what happened next: Jardine held up play to set up his leg cordon. Having hit Woodfull, he changed the field to signal a constant attack on the body.

Larwood's second ball to the leg-theory field knocked Woodfull's bat from his hands. There were 50,962 in the Adelaide Oval that Saturday, and it was said that if one of them had jumped the fence the rest would have followed. They booed the English every ball. Bradman was Bradman, of course, but Woodfull was beloved, and seeing him hit was even more incendiary than seeing Bradman stopped.

The Battle of Adelaide went England's way. Woodfull made 22 before being bowled by Allen. Bradman and McCabe made 8 each, the recalled Ponsford a fighting 85, Richardson 28 and Oldfield 41 before being famously, if accidentally, hit by Larwood and his skull fractured. Mounted policemen entered the ground to discourage a riot, though one of the police said to a spectator that if he jumped the fence he would not be stopped. Not since 1879 had an English team come so close to physical injury at the hands of a maddened crowd. If the South Australians had rioted it would have made the SCG invasion look like a pillow fight.

At the end of play, England's managers, Pelham Warner and Lionel Palairet, came to the Australian changing room where they found Woodfull receiving treatment on the massage table.

'I don't want to see you, Mr Warner,' Woodfull said. 'There are two teams out there on the oval. One is playing cricket, the other is not. This game is too good to be spoilt. It is time some people got out of it.'

For one who was so reserved and diplomatic, there is an irony in these being Woodfull's most famous words. He did not intend them to be publicly aired. An insider leaked his outburst without Woodfull's knowledge and certainly against his wishes. But its reporting led to the lancing of the boil. Things could not continue as they were, and the broadcasting of Woodfull's true opinion led to the exchange of telegrams between the Board of Control and Lord's in which the English were accused of 'unsportsmanlike' behaviour, to which the MCC sniffily threatened to call off the tour. Unpleasant though it was, only an open argument could bring Bodyline to an end.

Australia's 222 was far from enough, and a strong second innings gave England an insurmountable lead. Chasing 532, Australia folded before more fast stuff – except for Woodfull, who reprised his gallantry from Brisbane in 1928–29 by again carrying his bat, for 73 not out in Australia's 193.

It is incredible that two days after the hammer-blow to his chest, he played probably his greatest Test innings. Ronald Mason wrote of the innings as 'four hours of grinding patience and weariness and unsubmissive courage … avoiding the bumpers when he could and letting them hit him when he couldn't.' Woodfull's ability and courage as a batsman have seldom been given their full due.

Woodfull's captaincy template was complete: as a batsman he led from the front, and as a mentor he nudged from the rear. He didn't micromanage tactics, instead setting a general course and letting the players work out their own methods. He did not read newspaper reports, but at the end of each day read out his bowlers' figures, letting the numbers speak for themselves. The loyalty Woodfull's men paid him was a response to concrete actions, such as when O'Reilly confessed to being afraid to bat. Woodfull said, 'I want you above all not to get hit,' and excused him if he backed off. O'Reilly recalled: 'What a relief! Could any shivering batsman ever have been presented with a more reassuring exit than that?'

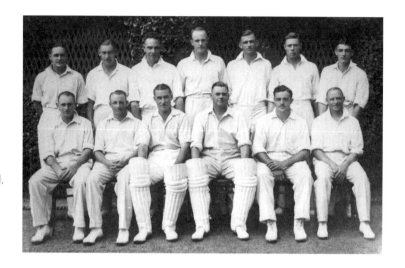

The Australian team that played in the Fifth Test of the 1932–33 Bodyline series against England. The side was captained by Bill Woodfull. Back row, l to r: LS Darling, PK Lee, H Ironmonger, WJ O'Reilly, TW Wall, EH Bromley, LPJ O'Brien; front: SJ McCabe, DG Bradman, WM Woodfull (c), HH Alexander, WAS Oldfield.

In Brisbane Australia lost again, this time by six wickets. With that Test went the Ashes. Jardine, unapologetic and unbending, ordered more Bodyline. Vic Richardson counter-attacked with the innings of his life.

Although he did not score heavily, Richardson was enjoying his finest hour. He played in all five Tests, opening in the last two, and never – literally – took a backward step. For a batsman who had struggled for consistency at Test level, his scores were remarkably even: 49, 0, 34, 32, 28, 21, 83 and 32 before a pair in the Fifth Test pushed his average below 30. Richardson was the one Australian player who opposed the Board's decision to send protesting cables to the MCC. In Richardson's view, Australian batsmen should stop whingeing and get behind the ball. His criticism of Bradman was implicit. In Brisbane he backed up his words with an innings that deserved three figures, but it was not Bodyline that got him out. Typically quixotic, he was stumped, running down the wicket to Hammond.

England had, as well as Bodyline, a star-studded batting order which only failed once. The final Test in Sydney gave England a 4–1 series win. Woodfull made another half-century.

Between those games Woodfull was a pallbearer at the funeral of Archie Jackson, dead from tuberculosis at 23. Amid Bodyline and the Great Depression, the photograph of Woodfull, Richardson, Oldfield and their teammates carrying Jackson's casket is a portrait of tough men's terrible grief.

For the second time, Woodfull, in a 4–1 loss at home, was Australia's supreme batsman. Bradman and McCabe had higher series averages than Woodfull's 305 at 33.89, but Bradman missed the First Test and his backing away from Bodyline to slash short balls over slips had an air of abandonment. He made runs but did not inspire his team. McCabe, as he predicted, did not get lucky again after Sydney. Richardson and Fingleton played to their limits.

Ponsford, as throughout his career, was found out by the highest-quality bowling on spicy wickets. He plundered more big scores than Woodfull, but history has made a glaring error in judging Ponsford a better opening batsman. Compared with Woodfull, Ponsford was a flat-track bully. In the toughest circumstances, Woodfull was repeatedly superior.

Woodfull batted for more minutes (1,145) and faced more balls from the English pacemen than any other Australian, took more punishment, and still scored respectably. More than this, it was his sportsmanship that set Australia on higher moral ground than England. Has this ever happened outside Bodyline? It was Woodfull who refused to retaliate. True, he lacked the bowling arsenal to win the series, but fast leg-theory is such an effective tactic that Woodfull could have used it with Wall and Victoria's Bull Alexander and given Australia hopes of winning. He declined. Alexander sent down a bumper at Jardine in the last Test, hitting the Englishman on the hip to the crowd's great joy, but Woodfull spurned leg-theory fields.

His sportsmanship was never on finer display than in the Fifth Test, when Larwood broke a toe. Jardine, as tough on his own as on the opponent, ordered Larwood to bowl the last five balls of his over. All Larwood could do was stand and roll his arm over. Of all the points Woodfull could have made, he chose dignity: he politely patted each ball back to the bowler. Larwood left the ground to a thundering ovation from a crowd that had identified the true villain. They were also standing for Woodfull. As R.C. Robertson-Glasgow

Not an unlovely batsman to watch, Woodfull could flash when in the mood.

wrote, 'Of all the protagonists in that fiercest controversy, I should say that he alone came out of it with reputation heightened and personal friendships increased.'

Now 35, a senior maths teacher at Melbourne High School, recovering from a series in which the bowling assault deserved the name, Woodfull might have been thinking of retirement. But it was not his way to leave wounds to heal by themselves. He wanted to be active in cricket's rehabilitation. Amid the Depression, Bodyline crowds had set records. Cricket has rarely had such a grip on the national interest. In 1933–34, Woodfull had one of his best domestic seasons with 818 runs at 62.92. The laws had been amended to ban 'intimidatory' bowling, though its policing remained subjective. Battling neuritis, Woodfull hit four centuries. In the biggest match of the year, Victoria against NSW in Melbourne, Woodfull showed that his sportsmanship was undimmed. NSW's Fingleton, on 86, was given run out while gardening. Woodfull recalled Fingleton. The opener went on to 145 but Victoria, dominant throughout Woodfull's years, won another Shield.

Australia's proposed 1934 tour to England, which Woodfull was appointed to lead, was an uncertain venture. English county captains had voted to ban intimidatory bowling, and Jardine retired, but the MCC would not give Australia guarantees that the tactic would not be used. Woodfull's men stopped in Hobart, Perth, Colombo, Port Said, Naples and Nice, some taking a side trip to gamble in Monte Carlo and watch tennis in Paris. They sealed a pact not to comment publicly about Bodyline. Their refusal led to an English journalist, Trevor Wignell, calling them 'the silent, sneering sixteen'.

Early in the tour, Bradman, now vice-captain, began to suffer from a series of illnesses and Woodfull inexplicably lost form. By the First Test the captain volunteered to stand down, but Bradman, and a restorative 172 not out against Lancashire on Test eve, convinced him to play. Two traumatised teams struggled through the early Tests, but after Woodfull, inconvenienced by 'Wimbledon throat', dropped himself down the order in Old Trafford and scored his series-best 73, and Bradman regained full health, the contest broke Australia's way. Bradman and Ponsford dominated the later Tests, O'Reilly took 28 wickets in his first rubber in England and Grimmett 25 in his last, and Australia won 2–1. Woodfull thus became the only Australian captain to twice regain lost Ashes in England, each time clinching them on his birthday.

Bodyline remained a nasty undercurrent. Elements in English cricket, watching Bradman and Ponsford put on a series-winning stand of 451 at The Oval, felt thwarted. Among those were Arthur Carr, the former captain who had been one of the initial planners and conspirators, at Nottinghamshire. His bowlers were Larwood and Voce, the latter of whom played in Australia's county match at Trent Bridge near the end of the tour. Carr unleashed the big left-armer to leg-theory fields. In the first innings Voce took 8/66, all caught fending. Whatever else can be said about Bodyline, nobody claimed it didn't work. An enraged Woodfull told the Notts secretary that if Voce bowled short to leg-theory settings in the second innings, the Australians would leave Nottingham. Carr backed down, and was soon stripped of the captaincy. Voce developed a 'leg strain', and the Australians faced legal bowling, to constant booing.

The one Australian batsman who stood up to Voce, making an unbeaten century, was young Queensland opener Bill Brown. Observing him on the 1934 tour, Robinson labelled Brown 'the most serene batsman I ever saw play for Australia'.

Born in Toowoomba, Brown played four seasons for NSW before returning to his home state. His dairy-farming, hotel-owning father had suffered catastrophic business failure during the First World War, and moved the family to the inner-western Sydney suburb of Marrickville when Bill was two. Coming of age during the Great Depression, Brown left school at 14 but only found temporary work. His attention, in any case, was on cricket, in which he soon established the keynotes for a 14-year Test career: constant practice, textbook neatness, a preference for the on-side, and playing within his limitations. His pleasant oval face bespoke sober reliability, a good partner in board games or business. Never would it be said of Bill Brown that he wasted an ounce of his potential.

From Queensland via Sydney,
Bill 'Nugget' Brown

After running himself out before he faced a ball in his first-class debut, Brown had finished his second season behind only Bradman in the national aggregates. He got to see Bradman close-up during stands of 294 against Queensland and 192 (in 96 minutes) against Victoria, in what would be Bradman's last match for NSW.

Bradman also got to see enough of Brown, who made 154 and 205 in those matches. When consulted on a third opener for the 1934 Ashes tour, given the virtually identical records of his NSW teammates Fingleton and Brown, Bradman plumped for the latter, suspecting Brown's straightness and quiet charm would be assets on and off the field. Brown immediately set about justifying his borderline selection, hitting a century on his second outing and joining his skipper in a partnership of 281 in the last match before the First Test at Trent Bridge, where, batting in the unfamiliar number three slot above Bradman, he made a four-hour 73 to lay the foundation of Australia's win. For the Second Test, Ponsford was injured and Brown moved up to his favourite position against the new ball. He would remain Australia's first choice as opener until 1946. In a Lord's Test in which no other batsman passed 40, Brown recorded 105. True, he made most of his runs before rain ruined the wicket and Hedley Verity ruined the order, but he was so convincing and correct that when Ponsford came back, Woodfull moved himself down the order to leave Brown in place. During his 1,308-run tour, Brown vindicated Bradman's intuitions about his character and skill.

Woodfull's team ended the 34-match tour with one loss, virtually a repeat of 1930. His overall statistics were also much the same, with 1,268 runs at 52.83. But his Test returns had been comparatively lean, and he decided that at 37, with the game healing and the Ashes retained, it was time to hand over to the next generation. Bradman, who had come home separately from the 1930 team for a personal promotional tour, thus sparking resentment that would follow him for decades, was again separated from the team, this time in hospital with a life-threatening gangrenous appendix.

Woodfull went out a winner in every respect. Offered a knighthood for services to cricket, he followed Dave Gregory's example and refused. 'Had I been awarded it for being an educationalist,' he said, 'then I would have accepted it, but under no circumstances would I accept it for playing cricket.' Australia's only cricketing knight, then, would be Bradman, who had no such qualms about the importance of the game.

There is a good case for Woodfull to be thought of as Australia's best cricket captain. He had Bradman, of course, who made any captain look good, but he managed his team through five series with the skinniest pace-bowling reserves. He depended on O'Reilly and Grimmett, but he had to. He is not known as the most innovative tactician, and Mailey did not think much of the fields he set for leg-spinners, but in the evolution of the office, and in the circumstances of the time, it was his personal courage and maturity rather than his results that earnt him his reputation. Jack Pollard said Woodfull's players 'had an affection for him only equalled by Ian Chappell among our great skippers'. Outside the changing room, the admiration for Woodfull was universal.

Woodfull would become the model for Australian cricket captaincy for half a century. Instead of his ability to make his men wealthy, the captain's role was now defined by personal qualities shown in crisis. Woodfull, as captain in 1932–33, underwent the biggest crisis of all, and showed himself sporting, courageous, and above all decent. It is impossible to think of a finer human being who has been captain, and all of those who follow him suffer, to some degree, from the comparison.

His last first-class game was a joint testimonial with Ponsford in 1934–35. Woodfull made 111, the pair amassing the last of their 20 century partnerships. He also took a rare wicket. Their career statistics – Woodfull 13,392 runs at 65.00 with 47 centuries, Ponsford 13,819 at 65.18 with 49 hundreds – are indistinguishable. Ponsford made two quadruple-centuries, a triple and more doubles, but given the conditions and the testing they faced in 1928–29 and 1932–33, there can be little doubt that Woodfull was the more substantial batsman. He would certainly not see a more worthy captain in his life, which ended in 1965 with a heart attack on a golf course near Tweed Heads, a result, his widow Gwen said, of the assaults his body had suffered 32 years before.

16

THE BURIED IDEA

WOODFULL'S heir-designate might have been Bradman, but his immediate successor turned out to be one of Bradman's antagonists.

Victor Richardson, left out of the 1934 tour, might have been finished in Test cricket but for Bradman's burst appendix. With Bradman missing the 1934–35 season, Richardson was the popular choice to lead a tour to South Africa the next summer.

He had led an Australian team overseas before, Arthur Mailey's exhibition tour of the USA in 1932. They went to Hollywood, where Boris Karloff played, Douglas Fairbanks dropped in, and Joan Crawford watched Richardson attentively. Bradman, using the tour as his honeymoon, scored nearly a third of Australia's 10,000 runs and played happily under Richardson's festive leadership. Richardson gave him plenty of bowling, and Bradman's leg-breaks notched more than 100 wickets in 50 matches.

After his fine resistance in Bodyline, Richardson was given an unofficial tour to New Zealand in 1933–34, but it was called off when the players read contracts offering just 15 shillings a day.

Despite his success as captain of South Australia, he was being undermined in Adelaide. Richardson was a factory foreman type of captain. As far back as 1924, he had led players' delegations to the SACA demanding 'loss of time' payments on top of the pound-a-day playing fee. His demands made him enemies on the SACA board, and by 1933 the SACA committeeman Harry Hodgetts, a stockbroker and fraudster, went behind Richardson's back to offer Bradman a six-year employment contract and the state captaincy. This, after 13 years leading a weak state single-handedly, was Richardson's reward. Of course, few South Australians criticised the SACA for bringing them the best. Richardson and Grimmett, neither one a friend of Bradman, played on under a cloud of dissent.

Vic Richardson at Durban with his eye on South African Herby Wade's coin

Bradman's illness was another twist, giving both state and national captaincies to Richardson. The craven Hodgetts, at a farewell function in Adelaide, said what a fitting reward it was for Richardson 'at the end of his career'. Clem Hill, from the back of the room, called out: 'End of his career? Bunkum!'

O'Reilly would say that playing under Richardson was the happiest touring experience of his life, and it was not just a snipe at Bradman. Richardson did lead happy tours. At a civic function in Kalgoorlie, the mayor said to Richardson, 'I want to wish you and your team, Mr Chipperfield, all the best of successes in the Olympic Games.' Richardson loved telling the story. In South Africa, he took his men to visit the grave of Jack Ferris, the great left-armer of the 1880s who had died of typhoid fever in the Boer War. Against Griqualand West at Kimberley, Richardson refused to take no for an answer when local officials refused his bowlers beer on the field. Richardson walked off and got the drinks himself. Not that he was prepared to let Bacchus rule. When a player complained of being hung-over, Richardson told him he felt like that every morning, so the player had better get out there and get on with it. His grandsons, 40 years later, might have said the same thing.

Wherever Victor Richardson led Australian teams, in New Zealand, the USA, Canada, England (as Woodfull's deputy in 1930) and South Africa, the nearest they came to losing a game was a tie in Bristol. Ray Robinson said, 'Richardson's teams always fielded as if they were winning – or thought they had a chance.' This tour was particularly meritorious, as the South Africans were fielding their strongest-yet team which had recently beaten England at home and away. This would be the first five-Test series in South Africa and the first complete one there on turf. The hosts were typically confident, but in the First Test at Durban, McCabe, Arthur Chipperfield and O'Reilly starred in a nine-wicket win. O'Reilly, out of sorts, was itching for a bowl in the second innings but Richardson ignored him, vocally doubting his abilities, until he finally let the Tiger loose. Within a session O'Reilly had taken a matchwinning five wickets.

In Johannesburg for the Second Test, Australia were 2/274, chasing another 125 to win, when the weather closed in. McCabe,

Richardson (*fourth from right*), with his happy tourists. His hand is on Stan McCabe, while to his immediate right are O'Reilly and Brown.

playing the second of his three great Test innings, had crashed 189 not out in 197 minutes. He hit the ball so hard that in an unprecedented action, the South African captain Herby Wade appealed against the light. The umpires let him take his frightened fieldsmen off and the match was drawn. The teams later staged a baseball game, climaxing when Grimmett took a miraculous catch with his non-gloved hand to give Australia a one-run win.

Australia won each of the remaining Tests by an innings. Their bowling at Cape Town, dismissing South Africa for 102 and 182, was remarkable considering Ernie McCormick asked to lay a wreath on the Newlands wicket as 'it's the deadest thing I've ever struck'. Grimmett took 10 wickets, passing S.F. Barnes's world Test record of 189. In the one series of the 1930s that Bradman missed, Australia were more dominant than in any of those he played. Grimmett took

44 wickets and O'Reilly 27, and the batting strength rested on the NSW opening combination of Brown and Fingleton.

Seeing an opportunity to replace the retiring Woodfull and Ponsford, the pair had shared stands of 249, 124, 64, 130, 177 and 205 for NSW the previous season. Brown's on-side play, with several varieties of leg glance, was wondrous. Robinson 'never doubted there were 90 degrees in the quarter of the field between square leg and the wicketkeeper's left boot, until Brown made it look as if there must be more.'

Touring South Africa under Richardson, Brown was consistency personified, making four half-centuries then 121 in the Third Test. In successive Tests he and Fingleton put on 93, 105, 233 (the first time Australia passed 200 in a Test without losing a wicket), 99 and 162.

Richardson's captaincy was part of the dominance. In the First Test at Durban, with South Africa threatening to set a target, Fingleton told Richardson he had little to do in the field. Richardson moved him to short leg, and so the O'Reilly 'leg trap', which would capture dozens of Test wickets for the leg-spinner, was founded.

In the Fifth Test, again at Durban, Richardson took five catches, a world record. But his batting yielded an undistinguished 84 at 16.80. His tour was a success in other ways. Three decades later, when Ian Chappell was selected to tour South Africa, his grandfather pulled him aside and said, 'Be careful of the women over there. Some of them could be your cousins.'

Richardson was a notably tolerant leader. On the eve of the Fourth Test in Johannesburg, he let some players breach their contracts by flying to Kruger National Park as long as they returned the same day. His team was one of the most popular to leave our shores. Against Transvaal, local fans were so incensed by their batting hero Bruce Mitchell's slow scoring that they implored O'Reilly to bowl underarm. Instead, to great cheers, O'Reilly sent down a perfect leg-spinner, pitching outside leg and hitting off. As rain bucketed down while Australia needed four runs to win, visibility down to zero, the local bowler Eiulf Nupen bowled four wides on purpose to let them win.

Richardson (*third from right*), leads his team on at Cape Town.

Harry Hodgetts might not have been the best person to say it, but the tour was indeed a fitting sign-off for Richardson. He came back to Adelaide to find Bradman recuperated and ready to lead. He led his South African tourists against a Bradman XI to start off the 1936–37 season, and lost, due mainly to Bradman's 212. It was widely assumed that Richardson would quit rather than play under Bradman, but he did not. In Bradman's first match in charge of SA, against Victoria, Richardson put on 83 with him.

The following season Adelaide staged a joint benefit for Richardson and Grimmett. Neither had much time for Bradman, nor he for them. Bradman was instrumental in ending Grimmett's Test career on 216 wickets. In a rain-interrupted match, Grimmett bowled the

Don for 17. Richardson said Grimmett had done them both out of a thousand pounds in gate takings.

Richardson lived for another 30 colourful years. When his first wife died in 1941, he enlisted with the RAAF and spent the war in India. He remarried and became an expert cricket commentator on ABC Radio and for 12 years was Radio 5AD's sports editor. His working career, including stints as a sales rep and insurance executive, capitalised on his winning personality. He was also an innovative thinker. In 1952 he said: 'Limited-overs matches [should be] introduced to encourage faster scoring.' He took the idea to an interstate conference, which rejected it.

Richardson died in 1969, five years after seeing the eldest son of his daughter Jeanne play Test cricket. A year later Ian's younger brother would also represent Australia, and a decade later a third. Richardson's legacy, already recognised in the gates named for him at the Adelaide Oval in 1967, would ramify within and beyond the field of play. In his pugnacity, Richardson was both a relic of one age of player power and a forerunner of another. He was also the first embodiment of the contrarian streak in Australian cricket, the anti-Bradmanism that would find its full flowering in his eldest grandson.

17

BRADMAN

TO paraphrase the novelist Mary McCarthy on Venice, there is nothing to say about Don Bradman that has not already been said – including that statement. His life story is so embedded in Australian legend that its repetition is superfluous. Unlike any other captain, his life has had so much light cast upon it and his personality been so publicly dissected that what is required is not to illuminate him but to narrow the spotlight.

Compared with Australia's great captains, one observation about Bradman stands out. He was not a born leader. Whether it's Dave Gregory, Billy Murdoch, Joe Darling, Monty Noble or Bill Woodfull, and even some of the lesser captains and stand-ins such as Hugh Trumble and Victor Richardson, their leadership potential was recognised early. Sometimes they had to share captaincy, as Woodfull and Ryder did, and sometimes it came late, as with Bardsley. But always they led teams at lower levels before they became Test captain – particularly if they were the champion batsman.

Not Bradman. It really does stick out. Neither of the two greatest batsmen of the golden age, Hill and Trumper, were particularly eager captains, but both led their states and Hill led his country. The young Bradman, in clear contrast, made an effort to avoid captaincy.

The reason is obvious, and sensible, but it came to colour his captaincy: he recognised that his capacity to score runs was paramount to any team he played in. This is an important element of his self-knowledge, but it would cost him.

Until 1935, Bradman wanted to be left alone to score runs. He was a boy genius, looked after by the men, and his transition to a position of responsibility came late.

As the Depression deepened, Bradman batted like the hungriest man on earth. Of his many statistical monuments, one stands out. In all but one season from 1928–29 to 1937–38, he topped the Australian first-class aggregates. The exception was the Bodyline year, when his 1,171 runs at 61.63 were eclipsed by England's champion Sutcliffe. Every other year Bradman was first, often averaging 40 or 50 more than the next man.

But he was no captain. At NSW, he played under Alan Kippax. When Kippax was out, Oldfield led. For Australia, Bradman slotted in under Ryder, then Woodfull. The first time Bradman led a team was as a relatively seasoned 25-year-old, when he deputised for Woodfull in 1934 in England. The responsibility coincided with stress, anxiety and illness that nearly killed him.

Had he reached for captaincy, it would have come sooner. When Hodgetts lured him to his Adelaide stockbroking firm on a six-year deal worth £700 a year (£500 if he was overseas), captaincy experience was part of the offer. The Australian leadership, after 1934, was his. But Bradman had to wait out his long recuperation, as well as ongoing arguments with the Board over whether he could continue to supplement his income writing for newspapers, before he could lead a team.

Even then it was fraught, because, as we have seen, Richardson and Grimmett were not members of Bradman's cheer squad. For Bradman it was hard coming into a new state as the puppet of an unsettled administration, displacing a charismatic local hero. Bradman was upsetting a lot of homebred applecarts. Would captaincy, and the maze of local politics beneath it, affect his batting? Was this why he had resisted it?

In his first Shield game as captain he scored a century. In the next match he hit 233, in the next 357. That answered that. When

Richardson retired, Bradman seemed more at ease, knocking up 369 against Tasmania to rub out Hill's state record by four runs. He seemed all right with captaincy.

A regenerating England, missing Sutcliffe and Larwood but with Hammond and the menacing Voce, came to Australia in 1936–37. Having his own team meant Bradman could bring in the leg-spinner Frank Ward in place of Grimmett. Australia's batting would revolve around himself, McCabe and Fingleton. An even series beckoned, and the captains, Bradman and England's Sydney-born Gubby Allen, were expected to restore the friendliness of the pre-Bodyline years.

Bradman would later confess he had 'no special ability as captain' and that, while he never lost a series, he 'lost a great deal of sleep'. His first Test, in Brisbane, portended ill. He lost the toss and England, underwritten by Maurice Leyland's 126, scored 358. McCormick, Bradman's spearhead, broke down after taking three wickets in eight overs. A Fingleton century and Bradman's 38 could not cover the cracks in a weak middle order, and Voce ripped through the home team twice. The obligatory Brisbane downpour soaked the pitch in the fourth innings, and Australia's 58 (Bradman a duck) was embarrassing.

The worst of the weather followed Bradman's men to Sydney. In blazing sunshine Hammond hammered 231 not out before a storm prompted Allen's declaration at 6/426. Voce was again unplayable on the sticky, and Bradman was one of four ducks in Australia's 80. Following on, 324 was an improvement but insufficient to make England bat again. Captain at last, Bradman was facing a white-wash. Voce, whose rearing left-arm pace was downright terrifying on wet wickets even without Bodyline fields, had taken 17 wickets in two Tests at fewer than eight apiece.

As captain, Bradman was showing an unhealthy desire for control. Trying to overrule O'Reilly's field placements, he met understandable resistance. Trying the same for Grimmett in South Australia had, Robinson wrote, been 'like an editor telling a cartoon-ist what to draw'. Bradman erred in placing the ungainly O'Reilly at short leg when McCormick was bowling. Martinet or miscalculator?

The young Don

Whatever his motive, Bradman was big enough to accept O'Reilly's plea to be moved.

After 28 Tests and 98 first-class games as an observer, Bradman was finding captaincy harder than it looked. He finally won a toss in Melbourne, but Voce's dominance continued. Under gloomy skies, more gloom: Bradman fell for 13 and only McCabe's 63 kept Australia afloat until rain swept the ground at six for 181. Bradman saw enough of the wet wicket on the second morning to declare at 9/200 and get the Englishmen in. For once the weather went his way. Morrie Sievers, his only medium-fast bowler, took five wickets. Then a curious game of cat-and-mouse started between Bradman and Allen. While the pitch was still wet, Bradman was in no hurry to bat again, so he instructed his bowlers to adopt a defensive line. Allen, thinking the same way, figured his best chance was to declare. But he waited until nine for 76 to get the Australians back in, 40 minutes before stumps.

Here Bradman showed a desperate rat-cunning in the class of Dave Gregory and Joe Darling. First, he feigned uncertainty over what Allen had done, and sent a messenger to see if a declaration had been made. 'Of course the little blighter knows!' Allen exclaimed. Bradman's delaying reduced 40 minutes to 35.

Borrowing a page from the Darling playbook, Bradman decided to reverse the order. He sent O'Reilly and Fleetwood-Smith, two of the worst batsmen in Test history, to open against Voce and Allen. He encouraged Fleetwood-Smith by saying, 'You can't hit the ball on a good wicket so you won't be able to edge it on this.'

O'Reilly spooned his first ball back to Voce, but Fleetwood-Smith, joined by Ward, survived until stumps with a crucial 0 not out. He never hit the ball. He told Bradman he 'had this game by the throat'.

On the third morning, with the Ashes and Bradman's fledgling captaincy in the balance, he kept sending out non-batsmen. Fleetwood-Smith was out to the first ball he hit, but Keith Rigg, who later nominated this as the innings of his life, held the fort with a vital 47 until Fingleton came in at six and Bradman at seven. They started their partnership at five for 97, just 221 ahead on an improving deck.

Who knows what would have happened to Bradman's career, and captaincy, had the next few hours turned out differently? He dug in, playing for survival. He and Fingleton made it to the close at five for 194. The next morning, under cloud, they went on to a world record sixth-wicket partnership of 346. Bradman, heavy-headed with flu, made a methodical 270, Fingleton 136. Bradman's 458-minute innings was his longest in Test cricket in Australia. The final lead was 688. Too ill to field, Bradman looked on as O'Reilly and Fleetwood-Smith finished the job for a 365-run win.

With Ward unimpressive and Grimmett still prolific for South Australia, there were calls for the master's return. Bradman and the selectors refused, but this was the least of his problems. Apparently without his knowledge, the Board chairman Allen Robertson had summoned O'Reilly, McCabe, Len Darling, Leo O'Brien and Fleetwood-Smith, all Roman Catholics, for a carpeting over fitness, alcohol consumption, and undermining the captain. Bradman denied knowledge of the meeting, and it is possible the Board acted covertly to protect him. In any case, O'Reilly answered the lecture by asking Robertson if the players were being charged with misconduct. When Robertson said no, O'Reilly said, 'This is all tiggy touchwood then,' and left.

McCabe was forced to make a public statement asserting faith in Bradman's captaincy. Bradman, obviously hurt, reacted in his customary way, with 212 in the Adelaide Test, his runs the difference between the sides, then 169 in the decider in Melbourne, where his men were as ruthless as he was. McCabe and Jackie Badcock made hundreds, and O'Reilly did the rest. The selection of fiery Victorian Laurie Nash, who had injured some Englishmen in a tour match, sparked fears of a bumper war, but Bradman used Nash more psychologically than physically. Nash took five wickets but his bouncers were generally more a threat than a promise.

The 1936–37 series was the first a team had won from 0–2. It should have cemented Bradman's authority as captain. His tactics in the Third Test had turned the tide and the recovery of his batting had been all-important. But his cleverness in dropping himself to number seven in Melbourne was criticised as cowardly and selfish

– not something a Woodfull or a Richardson would have done. Bradman responded that he was not Woodfull or Richardson. He was, without any false modesty, too important to risk.

'The captain's job,' he would write, 'embodies the welfare of the team, and if his own personal success is an integral part of victory he should act accordingly … Some were unkind enough to suggest that my purpose was to avoid batting on a wet wicket. Of course it was; but only because such avoidance was necessary in the interests of the team.'

'L'état,' as Louis XIV said, 'c'est moi.' Bradman was saying the same: 'The team is me.' This is not very satisfying as a general theory of captaincy – it is so monstrously self-centred – but it was the most effective view if and only if the captain was Bradman. Any other captain could justifiably be accused of cowardice. But Bradman's 'cowardice' was for the team's benefit. The captain only embodied the welfare of the team because the captain was Bradman. He stands guilty of the accusation, but he was also correct.

The 1938 tourists, here in Launceston, are smiling. Why? They have Bradman (*third from left*).

This did not placate his critics. Again he was vilified for Grimmett's non-selection on the 1938 tour. The ageing Oldfield also missed selection. A batting-heavy team struggled to win matches. Bradman's own form sparkled, with 1,000 runs again in May and a century in the First Test at Trent Bridge. McCabe's 232 there was the best innings Bradman ever saw, but it could not produce a victory and Bradman's six-hour 144 not out in the second innings was needed to salvage a draw. McCormick could not fix his dragging back foot and left an immense workload for O'Reilly. The series meandered until the Fourth Test at Leeds, where Bradman made a first-innings 103 and Australia sealed the Ashes. Both teams loaded up with batsmen for the timeless dead rubber at The Oval, and Bradman injured his ankle bowling during England's 7/903. Even then, Hammond only declared when he received medical advice that Bradman could not bat. Australia's loss, by an innings and 579 runs, was their heaviest of all time, but they had retained the Ashes.

Bill Brown, having moved to Brisbane to sell cars and lead his native Queensland, was lucky to be picked for the tour. Leading a losing state team affected his batting. He only saved his Australian spot by caressing 132 against Bradman's South Australia.

But, as in 1934, he justified the Don's faith. His 1,854 runs at 57.93 on the 1938 tour were second behind you-know-who. *Wisden*, making him one of its five cricketers of the year, approved his 'charming skill, coolness, thoughtfulness and certainty'. Nottingham spectators were less enthusiastic during the First Test, when Brown's tedious 133 earnt him his boos as he followed Bradman's instructions to save the Test. But Lord's was again his happiest hunting ground. There is something apt in this irreproachably nice man performing so ably at cricket's home. With McCormick's confidence shattered by no-balls, Bradman needed his batsmen. Brown's 206 not out at Lord's, in front of more than 20,000 in the ground and 17,000 viewers on new television sets, saved another match and eventually the Ashes. His 512 runs at 73.14 in the five Tests produced the only series, between 1929 and 1948, in which Bradman was outscored by a teammate.

Although Bradman was such a towering figure, he enjoyed a fraction of the power held by Dave Gregory, Murdoch and Darling. International cricket was controlled by the Board, which paid the tourists a set fee of £600 plus a 30-shilling per diem. Without a profit share, they were earning less than Gregory's men of 1878. The loss of financial control meant that if Bradman wanted to capitalise on his talent, he had to accept personal sponsorship and journalism opportunities, which had led, in 1930, to the initial breach between him and his teammates. The Board had divided and conquered. Bradman's personal side-deals only entrenched the Board's final victory.

Not that Bradman was a lapdog. At the end of the 1938 tour, he asked that his wife Jessie be allowed to join the team. Woodfull's wife Gwen had come in 1934 and Bradman was asking for the same. The Board refused. Bradman, who had already made Jessie's travel arrangements, was angry and distraught. His men, seeing the state he was in, cabled the Board. It reconsidered, and the argument was settled – as long as the players fielded their wives' travel expenses out of their own pockets. This was what player power had come to.

Bradman's captaincy on the tour was unremarkable, but he was limited by his bowling stocks. Not since 1924–25 had Australia fielded a top-class fast bowler. Bradman did what he could, though that often meant bowling O'Reilly to exhaustion. But he didn't ask his chief bowler to do anything he wouldn't have done himself. On his first tour as captain Bradman averaged 115, surpassing even his tallies of 1930 and 1934.

O'Reilly, the lifelong rival and critic, had a mature and almost impersonal explanation for their differences, writing later: 'On the field we had the greatest respect for each other. But off the field we had not much in common. You can say we did not like each other but it would be closer to the truth to say we chose to have little to do with each other. I don't think that this arose from the ego-laden encounters of our younger days. It was more the product of the chemistry arising from our different backgrounds. Don was a teetotaller, ambitious, conservative and meticulous.

I was outspoken and gregarious, an equally ambitious young man of Irish descent.'

It is well put, as it encapsulates the differences without laying blame. But it does pinpoint Bradman's shortcomings as captain. He could not help his personality. The greatest captains can transcend these differences and inspire their men nonetheless. Woodfull was also an ambitious, meticulous teetotaller, but his Irish Catholic teammates would have died for him. There was something about Bradman that some players in the 1930s didn't like. They respected him, and knew he was the best thing that they had going for them, but they didn't love him, and in the final analysis of the Australian captaincy, the very best have engendered a kind of love.

This friction between Bradman and his players would only be solved – and perhaps *could* only be solved – by an eight-year break.

18

THE SECOND COMING

THE 1938 tour had left Bradman disinclined to tour England again. Ready to quit the game and leave Adelaide, he applied for the Melbourne Cricket Club secretary's position in 1939 after Hugh Trumble's death, but was beaten by one committeeman's vote in favour of Vernon Ransford. During the Second World War Bradman aimed to enlist with the RAAF but tests on his eyesight, of all things, showed limitations and he was placed with the army as a physical trainer. Worsening fibrositis invalided him out.

War would, however, provide an opportunity for a future Australian Test captain. Just as Herbie Collins had established his leadership during the previous war, so did Lindsay Hassett in this one.

The youngest of a Geelong real estate agent's six sons, Arthur Lindsay Hassett was another sporting all-rounder. At Geelong College he was a champion at Australian football, tennis and golf, but his tininess favoured cricket. Hassett's height is usually recorded as 5'6", or 168cm, but that must have been in platform shoes. Photographs show him looking up to Bradman, barely five-six himself.

Perhaps because of his leprechaun stature and beaky humorist's mien, it took Hassett years to be treated seriously by selectors and opponents. Still at school, he made 147 for Victorian Country against the 1930–31 West Indians, and at 19 he made his first-class debut facing Grimmett. Hassett announced himself splendidly, swinging his first ball to the leg-side boundary. Two balls later Grimmett had him lbw.

His progress was slow in Victorian cricket, and it was almost five years after his debut that he scored his maiden century, against a New Zealand XI at the MCG leading a successful fourth-innings chase of 293.

Bradman liked him well enough to take him to England in 1938, and Hassett started in Bradman-like fashion, with 43, 146, 148 and 220 not out. His Test contributions were more modest, his best a stoic 33 at Headingley when Bradman was out and Australia looked like collapsing in search of 107. Such was the tension, Bradman and McCabe stayed in the back of the changing room rather than watch.

In his twenties, Hassett was a dasher and a prankster. On that tour, he deposited a dirty goat in the hotel room of McCabe and O'Reilly. Hassett was relaxed enough to play the late cut early in his innings, and was such a straight driver that three times in his first three seasons he caused partners to be run out from deflections off the bowler.

In the last three seasons before the war Hassett, like Bill Brown, was peaking. With an average of 70, he scored nine centuries, including a pair of 122s against NSW in the last Shield game. Not even Bradman ever scored twin centuries against O'Reilly, whose dander was raised as the impish Victorian kept lofting him down the ground.

When war broke out, Hassett answered the call, becoming a gunner in the 2/2 Anti-Aircraft Regiment in Egypt and Palestine, a risky position. Hassett was famous, however, among his fellow diggers, and organised three AIF matches in the desert in October 1941, beating an Alexandria XI, the New Zealand Base XI, and the Gezira Sporting Club XI.

In 1942 he returned to Australia, married Tessa Davis and went off again to New Guinea. Although a warrant officer, he was the obvious choice in 1945 to lead an Australian Services XI including spinner Cec Pepper and batsman-cum-journalist Dick Whitington. They played five 'Victory Tests' against an England team containing Len Hutton, Wally Hammond, Bill Edrich and Cyril Washbrook, honourably drawing the five-match series 2–2. The results were secondary to the rejuvenating effect on Britain. In bombed-out Sheffield, 50,000 turned out to watch England win. The Third-Test crowd at Lord's was 84,000 over four days. As the Australians remained on their soldiers' salary, this left plenty of surplus for British charities. The tour also launched the excitement machine Keith Miller's mutual love affair with English crowds. Hassett wrote: 'This is cricket as it should be. These games have shown that international cricket can be played as between real friends – so let's have no more talk of "war" in cricket.'

Hassett in aggressive mood

Had the tour finished after the 48 games in England, it would have been a success to rival Collins's in 1919. But it dragged on for six weeks through India and Ceylon, breaking Hassett's team. Two bowlers went home with fatigue and the rest struggled on amid poor umpiring, low pay and difficult conditions. The team won two from seven first-class games and lost a three-'Test' series 0–1. Graciously, Hassett said, 'We have come to India to play cricket, not win trophies.'

His diplomacy was stretched against East Zone in Calcutta, when nationalists stormed the field. Rather than panic, Hassett cadged a cigarette off the rebel leader and chatted amiably about the anti-England cause.

At home, the team was driven on through a six-game swing of lacklustre cricket, losing to NSW and Victoria and drawing four other matches.

Bill Brown had also seen active service, as an RAAF pilot officer in the Pacific. The war had been cruel to Brown's cricket. After his magnificent 1938 tour, he scored 1,057 runs at 105.70 in the next home season, an average that would be called Bradman-like if Bradman himself hadn't averaged 153.16. With 84, 67, 61, 99, 12, 174 not out, 95, 168, 1, 81 and 215, Brown single-handedly lifted Queensland off the bottom of the Shield table.

He was still on duty in the Philippines during Hassett's Services tour, and was still there in November 1945 when Queensland selected him, as captain, for the first interstate game after VJ Day. Arriving less than 24 hours before play, Brown walked calmly onto the Gabba and scored 84 and 31, going on to make 604 runs at 46.46 in the short season.

In its first meeting after the war, the Board decided to fulfil an obligation to New Zealand to compensate for a cancelled 1940 tour. Bradman was unsure about coming back. Invalided out of the armed services, he was also facing financial devastation. In 1945, Harry Hodgetts's stockbroking firm was exposed as a sham: the SACA powerbroker had been cooking his books. Bradman, whom the bankrupt firm owed £762, started his own firm, Don Bradman and Company, so promptly that questions were asked in Adelaide's financial circles about his backing.

Bradman presented the Board with his report on the 1938 tour, but declined to tour New Zealand. Hassett was the logical replacement, but some members of the Board were uncomfortable with his fun-loving personality and popularity among the players. The last thing they – and Bradman – wanted was another Richardson.

Discussing the 1938 tour, Bradman painted a glowing portrait of Brown, far less threatening or charismatic than Hassett. Jack Pollard wrote that Brown's captaincy 'was like the man himself, sound, considered and lacking in flamboyance and with the talent at his disposal, highly effective'. On the advice of a possibly jealous Bradman, the Board gave Brown the captaincy ahead of Hassett, who received one vote out of 13.

The courtly Brown would have to manage some strong personalities. Bill O'Reilly, the master, was talked into touring despite a long-standing knee injury. The young Victorian batting, bowling, Mosquito-flying all-rounder Miller was already a star from the

Victory Tests. Sid Barnes, a Sydney street urchin whose batting turned him into a dandy of the city and clown of the cricket field, would open with Brown.

Brown was lucky that the gap between Australian and New Zealand cricket was great. He only had to keep the bus on the road. His team beat the provinces, and in the Test at Wellington Walter Hadlee called correctly but chose poorly. It was, as they say, a good toss to lose. Within a session on a bumpy wicket New Zealand were all out for 42, O'Reilly taking 5/14, Ern Toshack 4/12, and a young rugby league-playing Sydney fast bowler called Ray Lindwall picking up his first Test wicket.

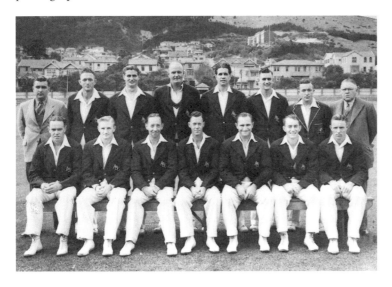

The 1945–46 Australian team that played New Zealand in Wellington. Back row, l to r: W Watts, D Tallon, KR Miller, WJ O'Reilly, ERH Toshack, B Dooland, EC Yeomans (manager); front: IW Johnson, CE McCool, AL Hassett, WA Brown (c), SG Barnes, KD Meuleman, RR Lindwall.

After Brown and Barnes added 109, Australia made a meal of their reply, getting to 8/199 before Brown decided the wicket was bad enough to get the hosts back in. O'Reilly ripped through them again, but aggravated his knee injury. It was left to Brown to decide which of his youngest bowlers, Colin McCool or Ian Johnson, received the opportunity of taking the last wicket. Brown, typically cautious, tossed a coin and McCool took the wicket with his second ball.

While the tour was completed without mishap, Hassett was always the more natural leader. When the team complained about its insulting allowance of £1 a day, Brown was unable to get more out of the Board. He wasn't one to rock the boat.

Stung by bad luck in business and begged by the Board, Bradman agreed to play Test cricket in 1946–47 against Wally Hammond's tourists.

After the eight-year break, Bradman was a different captain. Early in his career Bradman had happily played under older men, such as Woodfull and Kippax. Between 1936 and 1938 he was trying to lead contemporaries who had achieved a great deal and were, to some degree, jealous of him. His leadership in 1936–38 never quite transcended those personal rivalries. After the war, Bradman finally got his ideal: a team of youngsters who would follow him blindly.

O'Reilly and McCabe were done, but Australian cricket emerged from war with Miller, Lindwall, Hassett, Morris and Barnes. Brown having broken his thumb, Hassett became Bradman's vice-captain.

England, understandably, were weakened, but mercy had no part in Bradman's nature. In the first post-war Ashes Test, on a fine Brisbane morning, he appeared caught at second slip off Voce for 28. Bradman didn't walk. Umpire George Borwick said the ball had bounced. Hammond exclaimed: 'That's a bloody fine way to start a series.' Bradman went on to 187, putting on 176 with Hassett. The day set the course of Anglo-Australian cricket in the immediate post-war period.

Australia won by an innings, and the captains spent the summer barely on speaking terms. Test cricket was back on. War had not diminished Bradman's bitter memories of 1928–29 and 1932–33. He had chased Hammond's cuts and drives for unforgettable days. His desire for revenge was unquenchable.

Bradman made 234 in the Second Test, the same as Barnes, as they put on 405 for the fifth wicket. The 1946–47 series was a near-whitewash, but there was plenty of interest in the array of emerging talent. Bradman's men had the makings of invincibility, but among the English were also signs of hope. Denis Compton, Len Hutton, Bill Edrich and Cyril Washbrook were coming through to take over from Hammond, on his last cricketing legs. In Alec Bedser they had a bowler whose swing and cut could even, at times, master Bradman. Their gloveman Godfrey Evans was equal to Australia's Don Tallon.

Hassett, Bradman and Barnes were the only Australians with pre-war Test experience. Hassett enjoyed a superb season with 1,213 runs at 71.35. He led Victoria to the Shield, scoring 200 against Queensland and 190 against NSW. At 33, he was in a delayed prime. Like Macartney, Collins, Bardsley and Armstrong after the previous war, he was making up for lost years.

Three future captains made their Ashes debuts in 1946–47. The finest batsman among them had the least auspicious start.

Arthur Morris, 24, stepped onto the Gabba as Australian opener on 29 November, 1946, and within minutes was caught by Hammond off Bedser for 2. It would be the first of 18 occasions Bedser dismissed him in Tests.

Not needed for the second innings in Brisbane, Morris failed again in his Second Test, at home in Sydney. Around this time he took up smoking. Often it took the captaincy to trigger the habit, but Morris wasn't going to wait. In the Third Test, in Melbourne, Bedser got him for a third straight failure.

The selectors stuck with him, knowing the riches he promised. Born in Bondi, son of a schoolmaster, Morris spent most of his childhood in Doug Walters's future birthplace of Dungog, in the valley of the Williams River, north-west of Newcastle. The chunky, sandy-haired boy's talents were quickly recognised – as a left-arm unorthodox spinner – and he was representing Newcastle Boys' High School at 13.

Moving back to Sydney's south-western suburb of Beverly Hills, he bowled spin, played rugby league and was captain of Canterbury Boys' High School. While a student he represented the St George Club, home of O'Reilly, where the Tiger, who knew a little about these things, noticed that Morris was not the best spinner but deserved to be higher in the batting order than number eleven.

Giving spin a break, Morris became impermeable and adaptable. His left-handed technique was compact, based around back-foot

Arthur Morris, future Team of the Century opener

play but with enough improvisational flair to make fields hard to set. He was a nervous starter and preferred not to take strike, but was also unafraid to hit over the top once set. By 16 he was at the top of the St George order and a century against Sydney University got him into the State Seconds. Two years later he was wearing NSW colours. Watched by teammates O'Reilly, McCabe and Victor Trumper Junior, Morris started his first-class career in a manner that had never been achieved: 148 in the first innings, then a breathless 111 in the second. Four matches later, he came up against a fired-up young Miller, who decided to knock his head off. Miller's over went for 24, most of it in hooked fours – the most expensive in Miller's life.

After Japan attacked Pearl Harbor, Morris was deployed to the Army's Movement Control Unit in New Guinea. Still on duty in 1945, he missed Hassett's Services tour and the 1945–46 domestic season. Morris had every reason to feel robbed. Who knows how many Test runs he could have scored between 18 and 24? But he came back to state cricket without a chip on his shoulder, and began destroying opponents.

Failures in his first three Test innings, however, put his selection in doubt. With the Melbourne Test hanging critically, Morris got it right. Bedser dismissed him yet again, but not before he had scored 155.

So began a rich four-year run of almost uninterrupted success. Morris scored chanceless twin centuries, 122 and 124 not out, in the Adelaide Test, then another half-century in Sydney as the series was won 3–0.

The second future captain blooded in 1946–47 was a Victorian all-rounder who caught Bradman's eye. Ian Johnson scored 47 in Brisbane, then, flighting his off-breaks in Sydney, had Hutton caught behind with the third ball of his first Test over. England recovered before Johnson took the last five wickets. His 6/42 would remain his best Test figures until 1955.

Patchy form in the rest of the series suggested a career of occasional rather than regular greatness. Johnson's background was thoroughly establishment. His father Bill, a prosperous North Melbourne wine and spirit merchant, had played one game for Victoria before becoming a Victorian and Australian selector and a good friend of Bradman's in the 1930s. Ian, 10 years Bradman's junior, attended Middle Park Central School and Wesley College, where he matured rapidly as a footballer and quarter-mile runner, a sound middle-order batsman and an off-spinner who bowled with an elbow permanently bent by a schooltime fracture. Dark of eye and large of tooth, like a well-bred black colt, he was playing first grade for South Melbourne by 16, for Victoria by 17.

In top cricket, Johnson batted handily without overwhelming any attack, took every chance that came his way at slip, was a mature and congenial presence, and bowled with a containing accuracy, now and then breaking through for three or four wickets.

During the war, he married Lal Park, the daughter of one-Test batsman Dr Roy Park, and flew Beaufighters for the RAAF 22 Squadron in the Pacific. Returning to Victoria he played his best cricket, scoring 88 against NSW's O'Reilly, Toshack and Lindwall, taking 6/27 and 4/17 against Hassett's Services XI, before his 6/88 against Queensland sealed a Test debut under Brown in New Zealand. He wasn't needed for much more than fielding, but was the kind of solid, versatile, reliable fellow that Bradman liked to add ballast to the brilliance of Lindwall, Miller and Bill Johnston. Bradman was also a fan of Johnson's bowling, admiring the surprise floating off-spinner Johnson was able to turn off the palm of his hand.

But no Australian post-war debutant would have the impact of Raymond Russell Lindwall.

Fast bowling is so central to the mythology of Australian cricket that it is easily forgotten how long, from the 1920s to the 1940s, it lay dormant. Tim Wall and Ernie McCormick were all Woodfull, Richardson and Bradman could bring to the table. Australian bowling of the 1930s depended on leg-spin.

Meanwhile, the next great fast bowler was growing up in southern Sydney. Lindwall was the son of a Water Board employee who died when Ray was a boy. As an 11-year-old, Ray was taken to the Sydney Test of the Bodyline series where he adopted Harold Larwood as his model. Not Bradman, not O'Reilly, not Woodfull – but Larwood. Lindwall was a tough, physical kid who wanted to inspire fear.

He learnt cricket in the backstreets of Mascot and Botany. At St Mary's Star of the Sea School, Hurstville, he hit his first century, though he said his best innings was an unbeaten 75 on a Bexley street where there were 120 fieldsmen. A genuine all-rounder, at 15 he achieved the improbable feat of scoring 219 and 110 in a single day in separate matches: for Oatley juniors in the morning, then for Carlton Waratahs seniors in the afternoon. He played rugby league, sometimes alongside his gifted brother Jack, and earnt a footballer's face. Timed at 10.6 seconds over 100 yards, Ray was a hard-running fullback who would play first grade for St George and, according to some, sacrifice Kangaroo honours when he chose cricket.

While attending Darlinghurst Marist Brothers College, Lindwall joined the St George cricket club, where like Morris he came under O'Reilly's sway. O'Reilly's advice was to give up football, not work so hard on his batting, lengthen his run, and bowl as fast as he could.

Lindwall wasn't a simple tearaway. From his earliest days he would stand out for the thoroughness of his preparation and thinking. He performed stretching routines and trained hard before it was de rigueur. He developed a flowing run-up and a dragging, whippy, round-arm, delayed delivery that had journalists fancying themselves poets. Of recent bowlers, he resembles England's Darren Gough, who had the same late whip of the wrist and low action, with a touch of Pakistan's Waqar Younis. Like Dennis Lillee and Glenn McGrath, Lindwall was expert at analysing batsmen, developing a plan, and bowling to it. He got through his overs quickly and, in his peak years, gave more pleasure than any other bowler of the era.

Lindwall played the last first-class game before Japan bombed Pearl Harbor, then left a clerical job to fight in the Pacific, the legacy of which was malaria and dengue fever that would trouble him through 15 years in cricket.

Thirty-three wickets at 24.03 and 134 not out at number nine against Queensland ('smashing drives and perfect square cuts', raved *The Sydney Morning Herald*) earnt Lindwall a Test debut in New Zealand. He bowled so fast that the batsmen wanted crash helmets. He took 39 more wickets in the summer of 1946–47, when Bradman wound him up and let him go at the English. Still only 25, hardened by war and obedient to his disciplines, Lindwall loved to see the whites of a batsman's eyes. He did not use the bouncer as much as Larwood, but when he did it flew at the throat, exploiting surprise as much as pace.

In his first home Test, he fell ill with chickenpox. He made his first impression in the Third Test in Melbourne, hammering 100 runs in 113 minutes, adding 154 in 88 minutes with Don Tallon in a joint exhibition of the most ferocious driving seen for decades in a home Test when the match hung in the balance. Lindwall ended England's first innings at Adelaide with three wickets in four balls, took 10 wickets on a green flier for NSW, then went on a tear with the second new ball in the last Test in Sydney, taking 7/63 and 2/46 and leaving the English with something to remember.

Ray Lindwall, not a man to be messed with

Bradman was not only an Australian captain, but an éminence grise. His consent to play on after the war was seen as an act of generosity. As a reward, he was promoted to the Board, replacing Hodgetts as the SACA delegate. Bradman spoke strongly on player welfare issues, such as the provision of single hotel rooms on tour and the type of balls used. He advocated changes to the lbw law in bowlers' favour.

But even with Bradman as a director, the captain's influence was a shadow of its former self. The Board made more than £100,000 from England's 1946–47 tour, but Australian players got £40 a match. Bradman was personally responsible, through his career, for a 91 per cent increase in attendances and gate receipts. Yet the most powerful cricketer who ever played was reduced to arguing for concessions on hotel rooms and lbws. Billy McElhone and Ernie Bean must have been laughing in their graves.

A win followed over India, on its first Australian tour. The Indians were openly proud to be bowling at Bradman when he accomplished his hundredth first-class century. His Test scores were 185, 13, 132, 127 not out, 201 and 57, retired hurt for his only time in Tests. The only kindness he showed was to visit the Indian changing rooms to offer advice.

Bill Brown, now 35, had been eclipsed by Morris and Barnes. But Bradman pushed for his restoration to Test cricket as his deputy in place of Hassett, and as opener in place of Barnes.

Dedicated to every facet of the game, in his early years Brown had trained with professional sprinters to improve his running between wickets. Wedded to the 'one-percenters', Brown had a reputation as a great run-stealer. But as far back as 1935, it had cost him when, batting for NSW against Queensland at the SCG, he had been run out by Ron Oxenham after backing up too far at the non-striker's end.

India's Vinoo Mankad had observed Brown's speed, but did not want to ambush him in a Test. In the warm-up match between India and an Australian XI at the SCG, Mankad paused his bowling action and warned Brown that he was backing up too far. Mankad said that if Brown kept doing it, he would run him out.

Brown didn't listen. Two overs later, Mankad carried out his threat.

India's next game was against Queensland, and again Mankad told Brown he ought to stay in his crease until the bowler had released the ball. Mankad did not run him out that game, so Brown thought the Indian would not carry out his threat in a Test.

In the Second Test at Sydney, Brown was on 18 when Australia was struggling on a rain-affected wicket to chase India's 188. Morris – also warned by Mankad, but he had taken heed – was lbw to India's captain, Lala Amarnath. Just before stumps on a gloomy day Brown moved out of his ground as Mankad bowled to Bradman. Mankad ran him out.

Bill Brown at his preferred end of the wicket

Although there would be debate over Mankad's sportsmanship, the SCG crowd applauded him. It was clear that Brown was trying to gain unfair advantage and had not listened to repeated warnings.

If the batsman had been another type of character, the controversy might have muddied relations. But Brown phoned Mankad to accept blame. The term 'Mankading' stuck to the Indian rather than the Australian, but Brown was the one at fault. Brown even saw the humour in it: later that season, giving himself a bowl for Queensland, Brown pretended to 'Mankad' South Australia's Reg Craig. Brown had the last laugh, claiming Craig a few balls later, one of his six career wickets.

Brown's response to the 'Mankading' was gentlemanly, but his dismissal showed a rare lack of professionalism. His keenness to run got the better of him. In the end, the series ended poetically. Brown, who missed the Third and Fourth Tests with a recurrence of his thumb injury, was back for the Fifth, in Melbourne. The match started after a minute's silence for the assassinated Mahatma Gandhi. Brown, in his farewell home Test, was a run short of what would have been his last Test century when he was caught out of his ground. The fielder who whipped in the quick throw? Vinoo Mankad.

A change to the laws in 1947, enabling the bowler's back foot to drag across the crease as long as it landed legally, took a yard off the distance between Lindwall and the batsman. It wasn't what the Indians needed. Lindwall had a knack for removing openers in the first or second over of an innings. On a belting batting pitch in the Fourth Test in Adelaide he was irresistible, taking 7/38 in a match in which 20 previous wickets had cost the bowlers 1,055 runs. Bradman's 201 was the leader, but Hassett (a career-high 198 not out), Barnes, and India's Vijay Hazare and Dattu Phadkar also made centuries. Yet Lindwall could destroy a batting line-up in the most benign conditions.

One batsman who could not cash in on that Adelaide deck was Australia's 19-year-old debutant, Neil Harvey, who made 13 coming in at four for 503. It must have seemed an eternal wait after spending the previous two Tests as 12th man, making sure Bradman had enough to drink as he piled up more runs.

Harvey knew he could master these Indian bowlers: he had made two half-centuries against them that season. For Victoria, he came in at three for 11 with a jaunty air which, Pollard wrote, 'bowlers all around the world later learned to worry about', and scored 87.

Short, dark and neat, Harvey was built for cricket: a 171cm, 66kg packet of pure coordination. Like Bradman, Harvey had weak eyesight and couldn't read scoreboards clearly from the centre. It didn't matter. Coming to the wicket without a cap or hat, dapper and compact, Harvey saw the ball like nobody else.

Many of the captains, as we have seen, came from cricketing families, but there was no cricketing family quite like the six Harvey boys of Argyle Street, Fitzroy. Their father, Horace, had played club cricket in Newcastle and Broken Hill, once scoring 198. Now he constantly challenged his sons to beat him.

Before Neil came Mick, Harold, Ray and Merv. After him came Brian. Having trained their reflexes on the cobbled lanes of Fitzroy, all played first grade, four played for Victoria, and two, Merv and Neil, played for Australia. Ray and Neil also achieved national selection as baseballers.

Every back-alley game was a Test match. Neil was the only left-hander, but his brothers didn't hold it against him. They taught him one rule, which was that the ball was there to be hit. Wonderfully orthodox, he scored at a slogger's rate, often a run a minute; St Kilda never forgot the hammering he gave them in 1951, 254 in the first innings and 126 in the second, scoring as fast as any of the big hitters yet without playing a shot that couldn't be found in the textbook.

A wicketkeeper-batsman at school, Harvey stepped into Fitzroy's firsts at 14, and as soon as the war was over he was ready for a Victorian debut in Tasmania. In his first game at Launceston he scored 18, a sighter for the following week, when, at Hobart, he stroked 154 runs in 169 minutes.

A month later he was facing NSW's Lindwall, Ernie Toshack and Ginty Lush on the SCG. A first-innings duck didn't deter him. In the second he scored 49 at a run a minute. A few weeks later, meeting the English, he contributed 69 to a rapid-fire century partnership with Hassett.

Merv played Test cricket before him, making 31 and 12 as Sid Barnes's replacement, respectable but not enough to get him another Test. The next year, Neil went past him.

After Neil's 13 on debut, Bradman told him he would be retained for Melbourne. Bradman had faith in him. Feeling an attack of fibrositis coming on, the captain retired on 57 and gave Harvey his chance on a docile track. Harvey played with care, still a child alongside Brown, Hassett and Sam Loxton; after three hours, on 95 he turned the ball through square leg and Lindwall helped him run five lengths of the pitch. Harvey, at 19 years and 19 weeks, was Australia's youngest-ever Test centurion. His 153 was his second first-class century. He was going to England.

19

THE INVINCIBLES

BRADMAN was initially reluctant to lead the 1948 Ashes tour, but was persuaded by responsibility to his team and to Ashes cricket, and by financial incentives. He arrived in England with 17,000 food parcels from the state of Victoria, but the cricket tour was no charity mission. The Australians were there to continue the revival of cricket, but any team of Bradman's was in England to win.

Starved of pace in the 1930s, he relished returning with equipment the calibre of Lindwall, Miller and tall left-armer Bill Johnston. Bradman favoured his fast men, bowling them when they wished, and giving them confidence-building advice. To Lindwall he merely said, 'You will play in the first Test, and in the meantime watch the no-balls.' He had seen McCormick's confidence destroyed by no-balls in 1938, and treated Lindwall as a racehorse he needed to keep relaxed. Miller, who needed no help relaxing, rumbled the English with bat and ball. But Lindwall was the spearhead. Bradman used him in spells no longer than five or six overs. Twenty-seven wickets in the series, a record for an Australian paceman, were the result, capped by a spell after lunch on the first day of the last Test at The Oval of 5/8. His 86 wickets on tour made him one of *Wisden's* Cricketers of the Year.

The contest for the opening batsmen's roles on the 1948 tour was three-cornered between Morris, Barnes and Brown.

Working as a clerk at Sydney Town Hall, Morris had been worried that he wouldn't get time off to tour England. He switched to work as a promotions and sales officer for a motor parts distributor, joining the long stream of Australian cricketers who shaped their working life around their cricket. The key was finding an employer happy to have a famous cricketer on their part-time payroll.

Unexpectedly, the Board had named Morris on the tour selection panel, but the left-hander ironed out any debates with 138 in the tour opener at Worcester and, a week before the first Test, 184 against Sussex.

No further argument was necessary during the Tests. Morris scored 31 and 9 at Trent Bridge, 105 and 62 at Lord's, 51 and 54 not out at Old Trafford, then failed (to Alec Bedser again) in the first innings at Headingley. England took charge of the match on the fourth day, setting Australia an impossible 404 to win on a dust-bowl. The record for a fourth-innings chase was England's seven for 332 in 1928–29. Morris, whom Bradman had held back from launching a charge in Adelaide in 1946–47, was let off the chain. He dominated an opening stand of 57 with Hassett (17), then put on 301 in four hours with his captain. Bradman described Morris's 182 as 'the most wonderful innings', his own unbeaten 173 as 'a supporting century'. Morris's assault on Jim Laker's off-spin was savage and significant: Laker would not play another Test for two years.

Cardus, who had criticised Morris's 'loose technique' in Australia, now said his 'batting is true to himself, charming and good-mannered but reliant and thoughtful'. Morris was ruthlessly powerful all around the wicket, and his 196 at The Oval was described by Bradman as 'an unforgettable innings of skill and power'.

A blistering 290 in a day at Bristol capped off Morris's tour tally of 1,922 runs at 71.18, third behind Bradman and Hassett. It is often overlooked that Morris was the most Invincible of the Test batsmen of 1948, scoring 696 in the series.

Barnes also prospered alongside Morris, so the loser in the openers' shoot-out was former captain Brown. Now 36, he passed 1,000 runs in England for the third time. He averaged 57.92 – even better than 1938 – and scored eight centuries, one in every three games. But appearing in the middle-order at Trent Bridge and Lord's finished him as a Test player and he was dropped for Sam Loxton. Brown would retire to a sportsgoods business in Brisbane, becoming a national selector briefly before shying away from the limelight, but stepping forward again late in life as a proud and beloved ambassador for the Invincibles.

Ian Johnson, another of Bradman's favourites, did enough to complete his assigned job: frustrating opponents while Lindwall and Miller were recharging their batteries. Sometimes he did better, taking 7/42 against Leicestershire, but his overall tally of 85 wickets, third behind Johnston and Lindwall, reflected a heavy workload more than penetration. On soft English wickets, where finger-spinners needed to 'ping' the ball, Johnson was too slow to trouble the best batsmen. After seven wickets at 61 in the first four Tests, a reluctant Bradman dropped him for the Fifth.

Neil Harvey was on the tour as a development project. Harvey, said Bradman, had 'the brilliance and daring of youth, and the likelihood of rapid improvement'. Among the Invincibles, Harvey had to demonstrate his improvement in the county games first. Against Surrey, he helped Loxton chase 122 in 58 minutes so the team could get to Wimbledon to watch John Bromwich in the singles final. Against Yorkshire, at six for 31 chasing 60, Australia came closest to being Vincible. But Harvey was the settler, seeing them home without losing another wicket.

His reward came at Headingley, when Barnes was hurt. Centuries from Washbrook and Edrich gave England 496, and Morris, Brown and Bradman were out by 68. Harvey swished nervously. Miller walked down the pitch for a chat. Harvey didn't stop playing his shots, but with Miller's guidance he selected them more wisely. The pair put on 121 before Miller was out for 58. Still more than 300 behind, Harvey put on another 105 with Loxton, bringing up a century in his first Test match on English soil. In the second innings, after the miracle partnership between Bradman and Morris, Harvey struck the winning runs. As an introduction to Test cricket in England, it could have been worse.

Triumphant and vindicated, Bradman finished his career with what a Japanese artisan might call the flaw that defines perfection. His second-ball duck at The Oval, making Eric Hollies cricket's most famous non-entity, could have been scripted to show that an average of 100 should remain eternally beyond reach.

Asked if he saw Bradman's duck, Morris loved to say: 'Yes, I saw it. I was at the other end scoring 196.'

Bradman, beloved in England, here with Sussex captain Alan Melville and a few friends

Leading a team of gifted youngsters, Bradman had his most enjoyable tour. Little wonder. He counselled his team to be unified and happy, both of which came easily. The Invincibles surpassed the great teams of 1902 and 1921 by going through the tour without losing. It can be argued that the 1902 team faced better opposition. It can also be argued that the 1948 team would have beaten anyone sent out to play them.

In five books Bradman tried, unnecessarily, to fence his legacy beyond argument. It was both unnecessary and counter-productive, for, as Alan Gibson wrote of Bradman's *Farewell to Cricket*, 'he seemed to go through every slur cast on him during his cricket career, and reject them all. This insistence on personal innocence marred an otherwise splendid book.'

No objective assessment of Bradman's captaincy is possible. His personal story is too warped by myth, and his record as a captain carries too many asterisks. Were the Australians that good, or were the English too war-ravaged to compete? Could Bradman have steered a team, tactically, without the ballast of his own runs, or is that question unfair? There is also a sense in which Bradman stands outside history. As far as the institution of the Australian captaincy is concerned, its social status had never risen higher than when Bradman was its steward. In 1948 he met George VI and the lord mayor of London. He was a full-fledged dignitary, as exalted as a monarch. He set the captaincy on its path to being likened to a head of state, and in 1949 he would become a knight, the first of a cascade of honours over the next 52 years. After retirement, he was selector, Board director, and twice Board chairman. He was the most dedicated volunteer, but by the 1970s, as we shall see, he had migrated fully from the poachers to the gamekeepers. He clearly enjoyed being in control.

From Bradman's point of view, control had been a long time coming. In his December 1948 benefit match, he lifted a catch to Colin McCool on 97. 'Accidentally', McCool fumbled it and kicked it all the way to the boundary. Bradman went on to make 123 before making a mistake that stopped him converting his start into a double, or a triple, century.

20

A ROOM WITH THE LIGHT SWITCHED OFF

A^N underrated aspect of the Invincibles' tour was Hassett's vice-captaincy. With one century in the series and an average of 44.29, and a tour output of 1,563 at 74.42, Hassett was one of many useful cogs. Beyond his batting, his playfulness was a perfect leavening for Bradman's authority. It was Hassett, not Bradman, who led a late-night group of Miller, Johnson and Johnston to drop in on a random mansion in their tuxedos, testing the English nobility's talent for hospitality and finding it far from wanting.

When Denis Compton had his bat knocked out of his hand by Lindwall while attempting a run, Hassett refused to run him out. Such unasked-for sportsmanship did not endear Hassett to Bradman. But Hassett couldn't help being who he was: merciful and light-hearted. In the Third Test at Old Trafford, Hassett, at fine leg, dropped Washbrook twice off Lindwall. Borrowing a bobby's helmet and holding it as a bucket, Hassett called out to Lindwall to keep on trying.

In 1949–50, Australia was due to tour South Africa. Whoever got the job would lead Australia into a world Robinson compared to 'a room with the light switched off'.

While Hassett might have expected a clear run at the captaincy, he found the Don meddling, talking Bill Brown into standing even though the 1948 tour had effectively finished Brown as a Test batsman.

The new captain would be voted by telegrams sent to the Board. It is not known how Bradman voted, but the Board was deadlocked 6–6 until the final telegram came in. Only by that margin did Hassett win the captaincy. It is astonishing, looking back, that there was any debate at all.

Hassett's pre-tour troubles were not over. Selectors Bradman, Ryder and Chappie Dwyer shocked Australia by omitting Miller, Barnes and Toshack. Barnes and Miller were thought victims of Bradman's animosity. Showy, spontaneous, headstrong and brilliant, they were types Bradman only abided as long as they were producing runs and wickets. The minute they were injured or their form dipped, they were out. In Barnes's case, his omission would cut short a career with a 63 average. For Miller, the interruption would be temporary. Bill Johnston was injured in a car crash in South Africa, and Miller was able to join the team.

Predictably, once out of Australia the players would describe the tour as their happiest – shades of Richardson in 1935–36. Finally given a chance, Hassett showed himself the equal of any Australian captain for getting the best out of his men. He never had a bad series. The stories of his congeniality and intelligence are such that, if this writer could take a pick of any Australian cricket captain to have over for dinner, Lindsay Hassett would be it.

His Test captaincy started on Christmas Eve 1949 in Johannesburg. Suffering from tonsillitis, he watched two wickets fall for no runs. His rescue effort of 112 – possibly his finest Test innings, produced when his captaincy must have seemed at stake – led Australia to ultimate victory.

The series belonged to Harvey, but Hassett could take some credit for unleashing the young genius. Harvey's 178 won the Second Test in Cape Town, backed up by wickets for Lindwall

Hassett, double-breasted and in charge, arriving in England with his 1953 team.

and McCool. Then, at Durban, Harvey inspired one of the most improbable wins in cricket history.

Replying to South Africa's 311, Australia capitulated for 75, unable to cope with Hugh Tayfield's off-spin after a downpour between innings. Somehow, = resistance from Australia's tail convinced Hassett's counterpart Dudley Nourse that the wicket was improving. Rather than enforce the follow-on, Nourse batted again on the mud. Johnston and Johnson ripped through them, but not too quickly. Fearing that Australia would have to bat while the wicket was still drying, Hassett ordered Miller to slow down, keeping the South Africans in for an extra hour rather than taking the last wickets. Hassett also showed how his sportsmanship and his cunning could coincide. When Jack Nel was run out, Hassett recalled him, saying quite ingenuously that Johnston had obstructed his attempt to make his ground. This – and Nourse's slow-wittedness in not declaring – bought Australia just enough time. On an improving wicket Harvey's 151 led the chase for 336, achieved with five wickets to spare, despite Australia's having been four for 95.

The Fourth Test was a draw, Hassett facing criticism for allowing Jack Moroney to score two snail-paced centuries, but in the final match, at Port Elizabeth, Hassett, Harvey and Morris batted Australia to a crushing 4–0 win.

On the first post-Bradman tour, the Don was not missed. Harvey scored a record 1,526 runs on the tour, 660 of them at 132.00 in the Tests. 'Rarely in Test history,' Miller would write, 'had brilliance, grace and consistency been so effectively welded in one batsman'. Hassett's men desperately wanted to prove themselves without Bradman, and Harvey gave them their core. He equalled Bradman's record of four centuries in a series. His 151 at Durban is one of the greatest innings by any Australian. The South African crowds, who had never seen Bradman, adopted Harvey. The love affair was mutual: he met a South African girl, Iris Greenish, whom he would marry four years later.

Harvey wasn't the only future Australian captain to play his best cricket under Hassett. Ian Johnson's 66 runs and six match wickets in the First Test at Johannesburg provided critical support. In Australia's amazing win in Durban, Johnson captured 5/34 as South Africa collapsed. All up Johnson took 77 wickets, the only time he topped Australian bowling aggregates on his six overseas tours.

His legitimacy beyond question, Hassett would hold the captaincy for four years. His batting was supreme by 1950–51. His early season 179 against Lindwall, Miller and NSW was described by *The Age* as 'a brilliant parade of rapid-scoring shots in the "classic" style.'

Hosting Freddie Brown's Englishmen in the First Test in Brisbane in 1950–51, Hassett pulled off a chess grandmaster's coup and one of the most astonishing victories of all.

After winning the toss on the Friday, Hassett's team scored 228, unable to capitalise on a good wicket. Tropical storms stopped play until halfway through the Monday (Sunday being the designated rest day), when, Hassett wrote, 'it was inevitable that we were in for thrills'. Thrills there were. England got to one for 49, then lost six for 19. Brown, having spent a few minutes at the wicket before being caught off Miller, saw his chance and declared 160 runs behind. Australia duly collapsed as the ball spat off the wicket. Out of a juggled order of Johnson, Moroney, Morris, Harvey, Miller, Loxton and Hassett, only Harvey made double figures.

After 13 completed overs, Hassett considered the unthinkable. An hour and a half remained in the day. It seemed absurd to be declaring at seven for 32, but Brown had set the precedent at seven for 68. Was a lead of 192 enough? While the wicket remained poor, it should be. But if Hassett let the tail bat on, Brown might do to him what Hassett had done to Dudley Nourse at Durban, letting the innings drag on until the wicket improved.

So Hassett the gambler declared – just 71 minutes after Brown had closed the England innings.

'Your move, old chap,' Hassett smiled.

The Englishmen also led with their tail-enders, and lost six for 30 by stumps. But the match was far from over. Brown had held back his best: Hutton, Compton, Brown himself and Godfrey Evans. By the next morning the pitch had indeed improved, but only Hutton batted as if it had. Compton, entering a horror series, fell first ball while the others, jumping at shadows, perished to give Australia a 70-run win. Modestly, Hassett said, 'I have little doubt that winning the toss meant winning this game.' In the last Test in Australia on a genuine sticky, Hassett showed the nous of a Joe Darling.

Hassett topped the Australian aggregates that series. Due to his rapport with Brown – who was the size of two Hassetts – it was an exceedingly friendly summer. England, on the rise, were the equal of an Australian team entering its long decline, but due to a measure

Neil Harvey: champion

of bluff and winning the 'big moments', Hassett winkled a deceptive 4–1 win. England's eight-wicket consolation in the last Test in Melbourne, their first Ashes Test win since 1938, did something to break the Australian spell.

Hassett's genius also consisted in patching over key players' loss of form. Morris scored 25, 0, 2, 18 and 0 in the first three Tests. Four times he fell to Bedser, having particular trouble with the outswinger that cut back into his pads. Morris was so aggressive, wanting to punch the bowling through the on-side, that he was sometimes ill-equipped for late movement. Bedser and his twin Eric were staying as Morris's guests in Sydney. Alec presented him with *Better Cricket* by Jack Fingleton and Lindsay Hassett with the passages on batting marked. In the next Test, in Adelaide, Morris showed himself a good student, hitting 206 in Australia's win. He returned the book to Bedser with passages underlined on how to bowl.

By 1950–51, it was clear that the 32-year-old Ian Johnson wasn't going to turn into more than he already was. He took seven wickets at 44.43 and averaged less than 17 with the bat. He provided one highlight, hitting 77 in a partnership of 150 with the rampant Miller in Sydney, but remained a selectors' favourite and seemed entrenched. In the NSW–Victoria match in January 1951 Miller, who had moved to Sydney, sent down a stream of bouncers at Johnson and Hassett, ostensibly in frustration at their defensive batting. But Miller was also beginning to chafe at the Victorian grip on the Test captaincy.

Nearing 40, Hassett doubted whether he would tour England in 1953. But no captain had yet been born who would retire rather than lead his men onto the boat.

In the meantime he had to contend with the West Indies and South Africa. These were the years when Anglo-Australian cricket began to lose its centrality: India and Pakistan became Test-playing countries and the West Indies and South Africa produced some of their greatest teams. In 1951–52, John Goddard brought a

West Indian team that had just beaten England 3–1. Their batting lynchpins were Barbados's Three Ws – Everton Weekes, Clyde Walcott and Frank Worrell – and their bowling was based around the loop and guile of Alf Valentine and Sonny Ramadhin. They were the complete Test team, albeit, somewhat surprisingly, without a pace spearhead.

Hassett repeated his talent for getting a lot out of a little. Lindwall, consistent but struggling with long-term injuries, bowled Allan Rae with the third ball of the series and Walcott with *his* first ball. The first two Tests could have gone either way, but they went Australia's, with wins by three and seven wickets. Hassett's 132 in the latter game was pivotal. On the eve of the Third Test in Adelaide, Hassett pulled out with a thigh injury. Morris, about to become Australia's 24th Test captain, was out of form, then the victim of bad luck and Board mismanagement.

Morris had a good reputation as a captain, having led NSW since 1947. When Lindwall disagreed with his tactics in a Shield match, the calm Morris did not confront him, instead taking him aside for a quiet word. If he was criticised, it was for a lack of ruthlessness. He sacrificed himself in run-outs, and was accused of taking sportsmanship too far when he forbade his pacemen from bouncing Victoria's tail-ender Doug Ring. When Morris's bowlers asked if they could change their tactics, Ring was 88.

On his first appearance as Australian captain, Morris was over-taken by events. Barnes had been chosen, but the Board had secretly quashed his selection on unspecified non-cricketing grounds. Then, when Hassett pulled out, the Board refused a replacement batsman. Australia's team list had five batsmen, Lindwall at six, and the hobbling Hassett as 12th man. Morris went out to toss without having inspected the wicket. He won the toss and decided to bat, but rain delayed the start by half an hour, and the covers were found to have leaked at one end.

Within 26 overs Australia were out for 82, Morris bowled by Worrell for 1. Bill Johnston struck back with 6/62 in the West Indies' 105, and Morris reversed the Australian order as the wicket dried. On the second day the pitch calmed down, but Morris's 45 was one of the better scores in Australia's 255. Ring made 67 but the batsmen let Morris down. On Christmas Day, the West Indies achieved their first Test win on Australian soil, and a shaken Morris handed the reins back to Hassett.

In Melbourne, a tight Test hung in the balance when Australia were set 260 to win. Hassett stood alone, making 102, but when he was trapped by Valentine Australia were 38 runs short with a wicket in hand.

Ring, the spinner, was a bowler who could bat usefully and hit hard. Bill Johnston was a bowler who could only bowl. Hassett, after taking a short dose of Johnston's ineptitude, took a shower. When he came out, the Australian tail-enders were surprisingly still batting. Amid unbearable tension, they sneaked towards the target as the visitors fell apart. Ramadhin went off injured, and a mishit got Australia across the line. Hassett leapt for joy and his towel fell to the floor.

In the final Test, in Sydney, Hassett showed his ruthless side, allowing Lindwall to bowl 25 bouncers in 40 balls. It was intimidation, clearly, but without the stacked leg-side field was not technically Bodyline. Lindwall, a complex man, had a mean streak but when he hurt a batsman he got 'so upset I could hardly sleep'. Nevertheless, his assault dealt a lesson that the West Indians, lacking pacemen to retaliate, would remember.

Australia's decline from the peak of 1946–50 was evident the following season, with a 2–2 draw against Jack Cheetham's South Africans. Lindwall, Miller and Johnston had led the attack for six years now, and were showing the effects. Ian Johnson was finally dropped and said he was ready to retire. Hassett, at 39, managed 163 in Adelaide and a series average of 43.25, but the batting was otherwise totally dependent on Harvey, whose 834 runs at 92.67, including 109 in Brisbane, 190 in Sydney, 84 and 116 in Adelaide, and 205 in Melbourne, eclipsed Bradman's record of 810 in 1936–37 for a home series.

Morris, struggling for a big score, looked to be headed for a restorative century in the last Test in Melbourne. When Morris was 99, Harvey stroked the ball into the covers and called for a suicidal run. Morris hesitated, but Harvey was committed and Morris sacrificed himself. Harvey thanked him with a double-century.

So desperate were Australian audiences to see new blood, Harvey's double-century was overshadowed by his 17-year-old partner. Joining Harvey at a comfortable three for 269, NSW's Ian Craig was applauded from the gate to the wicket. Carefully he studied the bowling and picked his way to a half-century. The scarcely hoped-for century loomed until he popped a catch.

Not to worry. If anyone had said that 53 would be the highest score of Craig's career, they would have been escorted to the nearest mental health unit. In the second innings, as his team slid towards defeat, Craig held his nerve for 47: a neat hundred for the match.

The excitement can be seen in the press reports. The hard-shelled Hec de Lacy, writing in the *Sporting Globe*, lost his head: 'Craig made only 53 but he made them like a champion. He showed no signs of a swelled head, no flashness. Craig sold himself to his public for what he is – a level headed fellow with dynamite in his willow and purpose in his life.'

Craig, a banker's son, had attended North Sydney Boys' High School and excelled at rugby and baseball. By 13, he was playing for NSW in under-16 baseball and Mosman in cricket. He was a slender, wispy individual with a scholar's high forehead, polite manners and a deep voice. He weighed fewer than 10 stone (63kg) when chosen for NSW in February 1952, aged 16 years and 249 days. Playing South Australia, he only got the ball as far as the SCG boundary three times but stayed in for a four-hour 91. Dozens of centuries were clearly on their way. The *Daily Mirror* wrote of his 'very sound defence, ideal temperament, and touch of elegant grace'.

The following season, still a schoolboy, Craig shone alongside Morris, Miller and Lindwall. Against the Springboks he fed the cavernous national hunger for a new Bradman. In 377 minutes, giving hard chances at 4 and 133, he stroked and glided his way to 213. The *Sunday Herald* marvelled at 'the timing of his varied strokes, and especially through the covers and past point. These strokes were made with effortless ease.' Notwithstanding his physical lightness, Craig outscored Miller, who contributed 58 to their stand of 159.

Miller was one to warn against the pressure being heaped on Craig, while inadvertently adding to it with his encomium to the innings: 'For a boy of his age, it was unbelievable. He hit almost every shot in the meat of the bat, very little that was streaky or off the edge, and had composure through it all that many veterans could not have matched.'

Dick Whitington, old enough to know better, wrote:

> The promise of Craig must have been as beautiful and promising as the sight of the stars over Bethlehem to the wise men. Here at last was a young man who could change the horizon of the cricket world and cause cricket lovers to flock to watch him as they flocked, like so many children from Hamelin town, after Bradman.

Hassett knew his team was reaching a difficult stage. Youngsters such as Craig, Richie Benaud and Colin McDonald were still wearing L-plates. In the background, Barnes had been running a libel case hoping to find out why he had not been picked against the West Indies. Attendances had slid since 1950. For the Fifth Test, Miller and Lindwall were dropped to 'freshen' them for the coming Ashes tour. Australia lost badly.

Hassett's captaincy would be slightly marred by his last 12 months. His efforts to maintain the aura of the Bradman years could only stretch so far. He arrived in England with a tired team, shadowed by a press corps including Bradman and Barnes, both writing for English papers.

The Board gave Hassett some difficulty by appointing Morris ahead of Miller as vice-captain. To liven up state cricket, NSW had replaced Morris as captain with Miller. Morris had been the first man to captain NSW 26 times, but Miller, the drawcard, hungry for leadership, had taken over with immediate success. So in snubbing him as Australia's vice-captain, the Board left Miller feeling, not without reason, that certain people at the top didn't trust him.

One youngster on his first tour of England was walking on air. Having been working as a clerk for John Fairfax and Sons, Richie Benaud had just been made a reporter on the Sydney *Sun*. He married Marcia Lavender before leaving Sydney and on the pre-tour swing through Tasmania produced his best first-class performance. Against a Combined XI he smashed 167 not out in 187 minutes, taking 25 off Craig's first over. Then he captured seven wickets and followed up, in Perth, with an unbeaten century in even time against Western Australia.

Benaud was still an experimental choice. A product of Sydney's western suburbs, he was the son of Lou Benaud, a Penrith leg-spinning schoolteacher who once took 20 wickets in a club game. Richie attended Parramatta High School and represented the Cumberland club. A big-swinging middle-order batsman when picked for NSW, Benaud had his skull fractured when he took a bouncer between the eyes. An operation and a season later, he was catching Hassett's eye, trapping him lbw in a Shield match. Then, following his maiden first-class hundred, he won a call-up to the Test team for the last match of 1951–52.

Benaud's first days of Test cricket were hardly auspicious, with 3 and 19. Finally allowed to bowl late in the West Indies' second innings, he got one through Alf Valentine's less than impregnable defence to end the match.

Benaud would test the national selectors' faith. In the early 1950s Australian cricket was not oversupplied with talented youth, so his performances – 734 runs and 38 wickets in his next domestic season – were beacon-like. But his Test career stuttered. Twelfth man in the first 1952–53 Test against South Africa, in the second he scored 5 and 45 and took two wickets. He was hospitalised during the third, hit on the mouth while trying to field a John Waite square cut. In the fourth Benaud took 4/118, just enough to get him chosen for the 1953 tour.

Since Grimmett and O'Reilly, it was believed that Australian leg-spinners held the key to success in England. Benaud had a rhythmic, high action. He did not spin the ball a great deal, but practised assiduously and worked on batsmen with unerring control and just enough variation to trap the unwary. He went to England as Hassett's secret weapon, but couldn't stay under wraps for long. In the tour opener at Scarborough, Len Hutton taunted him for batting for his average. Benaud took the bait, showering the crowd with 11 sixes during a 110-minute unbeaten 135. His uninhibited strokeplay made him an instant attraction. A tall, tanned, handsome 22-year-old, sleeves rolled up and shirt unbuttoned to the chest, with an irrepressible enthusiasm for the game, he was everything an Australian was meant to be and a forerunner of more liberated times.

The 1953 team drew their first four Tests against an England led by Hutton, his country's first professional captain against Australia since Arthur Shrewsbury in 1887. Graeme Hole failed as an opener in the rain-affected First Test, and thereafter Hassett put himself in the firing line. At Lord's, in his first innings as a Test opener, Hassett scored a brave 104, stricken by cramps, his right arm bandaged after being hit by a bumper. Miller's 109 and Morris's 89 put Australia in control, and four quick wickets late on the fourth day had the Australians celebrating.

Hassett with his 1953 team. The front row alone has five Australian captains: Craig (*extreme left*), Hassett, Morris, Harvey and Lindwall. The middle row has another: Benaud (*second from left*).

Too soon. On the last day Trevor Bailey (71) and Willie Watson (109) defied Miller, Lindwall, Johnston, Ring and Benaud, and the spirit of the 1953 Australians ebbed. After the draw they faced press criticism for off-field 'indiscretions'. The Board asked the manager, George Davies, for a report on such happenings, but Davies refused.

The youngsters fell away. Craig, just 17, was scrutinised even more heavily than Bradman had been in 1930. In Bradman's case the attention had followed the runs, whereas with Craig it both anticipated high achievement and rendered it out of his reach. Despite relentless practice his tour was poor; with 429 runs at 16.50 and no Tests.

For Benaud, the tour was all promise and little output. His scores in three Tests were 3, 0, 0, 5 and 7. He took two wickets at 87 and was dropped.

After Lord's, further draws followed in Manchester and Leeds. Harvey made 122 at Old Trafford but was unable to land the killer blow. At Headingley, Hassett sent England in, the first Australian captain to do so in England since Noble in 1909. It seemed an inspired move as Australia took a 99-run first-innings lead. The Ashes appeared won until England engaged in some cynical time wasting as Australia chased 177 in 115 minutes on the last afternoon. Morris, Harvey and Hole crashed 111 in the first 70 minutes, making a win seem inevitable. Then Bailey took more than 11 minutes to bowl each of his last two overs. The Australians protested, but nothing in the laws compelled prompt play. In those last 45 minutes the game stood still and Australia fell 30 infuriating runs short.

Hassett won his fifth straight toss at The Oval, but his team only made 275, tied down by the suspiciously quick off-spin of Tony Lock. Hassett's men, convinced Lock chucked, were doing all they could to keep their anger in check. England took a 31-run lead and five months of pressure finally told. Lock took 5/45 on a dusty turner and England won by eight wickets, recapturing the Ashes for the first time since Bodyline.

Much of Hassett's trouble stemmed from the ageing of his pacemen. Lindwall had lost speed, but could recast himself from tearaway to professor, picking batsmen apart with mini-campaigns. He had used a season in Lancashire to prepare for the 1953 tour. He took 26 Test wickets at 18.85, but Miller took only 10. While Lindwall toiled, Miller ran hot and cold. Together, they had lost the fear factor.

Hassett, who gave himself and Morris the last two overs at The Oval, made a gracious public speech, saying 'England deserved to

Morris, about to put on an
exhibition in 1953 with
England's champion Len Hutton

win, if not from the first ball at least from the second-last over'. Privately, the story was different. Hassett told Hutton that England had done well considering 'Lock chucked half our side out', and the exasperated Australians destroyed a wall clock in their dressing room. They lost only one game on the tour, the one that counted most.

Notwithstanding a frustrating result for Australia, the 1953 tour produced bigger crowds and greater profits than 1948. Crowds amounted to 1.5 million, and the £90,000 surplus was a record. Until the last days, Hassett maintained his charm, asking the mayor of Nottingham, 'If I pull your chain, will you flush?' and receiving an MBE from the new Queen. His team maintained a running gag of getting Bill Johnston a Bradman-like average: once he got his tour aggregate to 102 runs at Hastings for once out, Hassett quickly declared before Johnston could get out again.

Morris, whose 1,302 tour runs at 38.29 were well short of his best, had two consolations. One was to bowl Bedser at Old Trafford, comprising half his career Test wicket-taking tally. The other was to meet Valerie Hudson, a showgirl he would marry soon afterwards. Australia lost the Ashes, but it wasn't all bad for Morris.

Miller would remark that the tour left Hassett 'with more genuine friends through the game than any other cricketer'. Retirement followed, and a benefit before 46,859 at the MCG. The funds raised were second only to Bradman's. Hassett's Test tally was 3,073 runs, also second to Bradman. He scored a century every five innings, all after the age of 32. As a captain and a man, Hassett was second to nobody. Having owned a sportsgoods shop since 1949, he would be part of ABC Radio's cricket coverage until 1981. Robert Menzies said he should have entered politics, if only for his interjections. Hassett moved to Batehaven, on the NSW south coast, where he loved fishing, and died there in 1993. He was admired for the style and adaptability of his batting, but loved for the qualities of character that Dick Whitington summed up in his biography of Hassett: 'A man who, because he loves cricket, came to be a cricketer; … a cricketer who, because he loves life, came to be a man whose company all men seek.'

21

THE HOUR
BEFORE DAWN

SELECTORS in the early 1950s failed to learn the lesson of the 1920s, when leading players tried to extend war-interrupted careers into their late 30s and early 40s. To keep picking them was merciful, but short-sighted. Eight to 10 years after both wars, Australia's ageing, fading teams were overtaken by English opponents who were quicker to rebuild.

Had the Board and selectors been tougher, they might have given Hassett, Morris and Johnson a nudge towards retirement by 1952. The new generation of Harvey, Craig and Benaud could have taken leading roles while Lindwall and Miller were still fit and firing. Miller or Harvey could have been made captain in 1952–53, and a smooth transition been achieved.

But Hassett and Morris deserved compensation for the lost years, and Australia had kept winning until 1952. It was not foreseen that Morris, the world's best opener from 1946 to 1951, would go into sharp decline. Miller grated on the Board, and on Bradman. There was something about Harvey that did not convince Bradman and the Board that he could couple the roles of champion batsman and captain.

England, meanwhile, were forced by three successive Ashes series losses to jettison the old and usher in the generation of Peter May, Denis Compton, Tom Graveney, Colin Cowdrey, Fred Trueman, Brian Statham and Frank Tyson. In an echo of the late 1920s, a rising English team just edged Australia in England and then routed them in Australia. It fell to Ian Johnson to be the Jack Ryder of his time.

In 1953 Johnson's career had seemed finished. Covering the Ashes tour as a journalist for radio 3AW, he recognised that his Test days were behind him. Not so fast, said Hassett. Knowing he had Bradman's backing, Hassett suggested that if Johnson worked hard enough on his game to get picked in the Australian team for England's next tour, in 1954–55, his claims would be looked on kindly. The Board had no appetite for a Miller or a Harvey captaincy.

Hassett had already handed over the Victorian captaincy, a task Johnson acquitted with his usual efficiency. Out of the Australian team, Johnson trained hard and rediscovered the best of his bowling. In the pseudo-Test match of the 1953–54 summer, between Hassett's XI and Morris's XI at the MCG, Johnson took four wickets in each innings, then 5/97 against Queensland, 6/46 against Western Australia, and 12 wickets in Adelaide. He was the top wicket-taker of the season, and even though Miller was winning Sheffield Shields as captain of NSW, Johnson's 6/66 against the MCC in a pre-Test trial in November 1954 bore out Hassett's prediction. Having justified a Test recall, Johnson was the Board's preference as captain.

Next to Miller's achievements, Johnson's were scant. His appointment betrayed the Board's fear of charisma and its higher regard for its own needs than for the players'.

Would Australia have done better, in 1954–55, under Miller? Would *Miller* have done better under Miller? They could scarcely have done worse. But to idealise Miller is to overlook his behaviour under Johnson, which was not always befitting a vice-captain. Furthermore, Lindwall's long peak was over and Harvey, majestic in the first two Tests, was thereafter barren. Morris was spent. Benaud, Alan Davidson and Ron Archer were still being picked on potential. England had arrived at that happy moment when a very good batting order was joined by some devastating pace bowling. Johnson, as captain at 37, with only 12 games as Victoria's skipper and a few seasons as South Melbourne's, was the patsy.

None of this could have been predicted from the First Test in Brisbane, which Australia won by an innings. Morris scored his last Ashes century and Harvey 162 after Hutton had sent them in. Johnson, with five wickets, was one of an Australian bowling group that shared the spoils.

But Brisbane was an illusion. Johnson injured a leg before the Second Test in Sydney, Miller was also injured, and for the second time Morris was the stand-in captain.

Winning the toss, Morris sent England in. It appeared to be a good decision when the tourists fell for 154. But Australia's 228 (Morris 12) was not quite enough, and Peter May's century left a fourth-innings target of 223. Against Tyson, transformed into a typhoon, and Statham, Morris failed again and only Harvey, with 92 not out, scored more than 16. It was a deeply disappointing performance and reversed the momentum of the series.

With Johnson back in charge, the batsmen seemed to lose heart when the MCG pitch began to crack and shoot. They capitulated for 111, a score they repeated in the next Test in Adelaide. Johnson, batting at ten and bowling as a support man, made little contribution and it was observed that the Australian team was playing with a disturbing meekness against the power and fury of Tyson and Statham, hard to accept for a home audience that had not seen defeat since 1932–33. Johnson seemed a fringe figure who did his best but lacked the great Australian captains' ability to lift their team with bat or ball.

Johnson said Australia was declining into a 'bottomless pit'. The Board reappointed him to tour the West Indies in 1955. Against all predictions, his leadership was about to enjoy its finest hour.

The challenge was as much political as sporting, which suited Johnson's capacities. The previous year, England had toured the West Indies calamitously. Losing the series, their tendency to hobnob with white colonial elites rather than their mostly black opponents left a Caribbean mood verging on rebellion. Johnson's

Australians were expected to be much the same. The White Australia policy was publicised in the West Indies as if to say these players would be, if possible, even more racist than the English.

Such a climate, with so little to lose, brought out the best in Johnson. The Caribbean challenge also suited Miller's democratic temperament. Johnson steered his team away from whites-only functions, preferring to socialise with the black West Indian players, pointedly inviting them to join card games in Australia's changing rooms. Johnson, whose journalistic experience gave him a deft touch in public relations, avoided the touring English journalists in favour of the West Indians, who, he wrote, 'conveyed our friendliness to their readers and told them to forget about the White Australia policy'.

Surrey's David Sheppard, captain of the Duke of Norfolk's MCC XI, tosses with Ian Johnson before the 1956 tour opener at Arundel, Sussex.

The crowds, he said, remained 'extremely volatile. They'd laugh their heads off one minute and next be crying for your blood. The important thing was when they abused you not to show resentment. You had to laugh with them, not at them. By doing so you could change their hot temper to genuine friendship.'

For future West Indies tours, Johnson wrote the manual. Respect the locals. Keep your sense of humour. Accept umpiring decisions. No whingeing. Sound familiar?

There was every incentive to lose heart. Davidson injured ligaments before the First Test in Kingston. The West Indies Board chose the white Denis Atkinson as captain instead of the black Frank Worrell, and a loudspeaker-equipped car circled Sabina Park protesting the decision. Australia played well, however, and won by nine wickets. Miller gained some satisfaction by conducting most of the onfield leadership while Johnson was receiving treatment for a leg injury. But Johnson achieved the symbolic public relations coup when, mobbed by spectators as he came off, he picked up a black child and carried him on his hip. It became the image that defined the tour.

The Second Test in Port-of-Spain was a high-scoring draw in front of record crowds, Johnson again asserting himself by stemming dissent at the umpiring. In the Third Test in Georgetown, Johnson produced his best-ever bowling performance into a strong breeze. He deceived Jeffrey Stollmeyer into patting back a full-toss in his first over, and went on to wreck the hosts' batting with 7/44. Three of his wickets were stumpings, as charging batsmen were deceived by the ball dipping into the wind. So often maligned, Johnson had come up with the spell that won the series.

Miller had been enjoying the Caribbean hospitality and performing ably. He and Johnson seemed to be getting on better. In that wonderful adherent of friendship – misbehaviour – they were both in trouble with the Board after taking control of a commercial flight from Trinidad to Tobago. Both former RAAF pilots, they knew what they were doing, but when a livid Board found out it censured them and inserted a clause into future player contracts specifically prohibiting them from flying aircraft.

But tours are long, and the concord broke in the Fourth Test in Bridgetown. Miller made a century in Australia's 668, as did Lindwall, whose runs and 20 wickets were silencing those, including his one-time mentor O'Reilly, who had been calling for him to be put out to pasture. Australia appeared to be cruising towards victory when the West Indies were 6/146. Atkinson was joined by the wicketkeeper Clairmonte Depeiaza and Miller was having some success bowling slow-medium off-cutters. Lindwall was weary, so Johnson walked up to Miller and said, 'Give me some pace.' Miller flat-out refused. Atkinson and Depeiaza lasted until stumps, when Miller unleashed at Johnson, saying, 'You couldn't captain a team of schoolboys.'

All the resentment was coming out. Johnson could have appeased Miller, but knew, in the heat of the moment, the only way to respond to a bully.

'Come on, step outside then,' Johnson said, rolling up his sleeves. Miller declined the invitation and the team saw a new side of their captain.

Atkinson and Depeiaza put on 347, still a world record for the seventh wicket. Miller worked to rule and Lindwall told Johnson he couldn't bowl. Australia only scraped a draw thanks to Johnson's rearguard top-scoring 57 in their second innings.

The air cleared by a fight, Australia dominated the final Test in Kingston, Miller the star with 109 and eight wickets. Australia won the series 3–0 and were undefeated on the 12-match tour. Harvey continued to fertilise the new world with 650 runs at 108.33. Weekes, Walcott and Worrell combined scarcely matched him.

One of the 'lost tours' of the 1950s due to poor media coverage, this was Johnson's triumph. Sir Hugh Foote, the governor of Jamaica, wrote to Robert Menzies, 'The good which they have done is beyond praise or calculation.'

Rating his personal qualities as highly as his runs, the selectors had sent Morris to the West Indies. His 157 in the tour opener at Kingston and 111 in the drawn Test at Port-of-Spain were telling contributions, but he was playing with the heartbreaking knowledge that his wife, Valerie, had an aggressive cancer. On his return, Morris would retire, aged only 33, with a Test average of 46.48 including eight centuries against England, the most outside Bradman. He had scored a century on his first appearance in four different countries, showing his unique combination of technique and unflappability. He would lead an exemplary life in retirement: he played briefly for a Commonwealth side against India in 1963, was a Sydney Cricket Ground Trustee across two decades, remarried, worked in public relations, received an MBE, and retired to Cessnock, not far from where he learnt his cricket as a child. The war had robbed him of thousands of Test runs, but, as Morris was quick to point out, it robbed others of more.

Johnson's West Indian exploits had secured his reappointment, but going to England in 1956 was a tour too far for himself, Miller and Lindwall. None of the senior men played well and discipline was non-existent. Miller failed to show up for the start of the match against Hampshire, and Barnes, writing for English papers, mocked Johnson as a 'non-playing captain'.

One of the worst Australian tours had started promisingly. Only a loss to Surrey, Laker capturing an ominous 10 wickets, blemished the first weeks. Most of the batsmen scored centuries before the First Test at Trent Bridge. At Lord's Australia won convincingly, thanks to half-centuries from Colin McDonald and Jim Burke, a rattling 97 from Benaud, and 10 wickets from Miller.

The cracks (literally) appeared at Headingley, where the wicket was Test-quality only for a day. The toss decided the game. Peter May was the instrument of Australia's defeat, putting the correct number of rotations on the coin before scoring 101. Laker and Lock ran through the Australians twice as the pitch crumbled.

Bert Flack's wicket at Old Trafford was, if anything, even shorter-winded. He said he thought he had prepared a fast track, but clouds of dust rose as it was swept on the first day. May won another toss, England made 459, Lock removed Burke and then Laker took 19 straight wickets, Australia's tour imploding with scores of 84 and

205. When Flack sent a bat into the Australian changing room with a request for signatures, it was sent back with a note: 'Sorry, head groundsman. No comment.'

It was a worse tour even than it looked. Only rain saved Johnson's men from another defeat at The Oval. No Australian batsman scored a century in the five Tests. Harvey made 197 Test runs at 19.70. Miller was incapable of rising above his disrespect for Johnson, and was at the end of his tether as a cricketer.

Benaud, on his second tour, did little better than on his first. His domestic feats in Australia had assumed a Giffen-like quality, but so did his Tests in England. The selectors kept picking Benaud like an investment that had gone too far to wind back. In the West Indies, there had been flashes of his domestic form: three wickets in four balls to end the Test at Georgetown, a stunning century in 78 minutes at Kingston. Then there was a match-changing 97 in Australia's only Test win of 1956. But Benaud the entertainer was inhibited by the negative tactics of an embattled team. At Headingley, with Australia battling to run down the clock on a disgraceful wicket, Benaud took centre 18 times during an innings of 30 that he tried to stretch out to eternity. Few in England could understand what the Benaud buzz was all about.

Johnson's pep talks were often dismissed by his players for their unrealistic optimism, and his tactics when behind in a match, of replicating England's ploy of slowing down the over rate and batting defensively, inspired nobody. Yet again, he had lacked that most fundamental weapon in an Australian captain's armoury: outstanding, team-lifting talent with bat or ball. Seeing how slow the pitches were, Johnson exhorted Davidson and Archer to bowl spin, a move O'Reilly described as 'pitiable'. No bowler took more than Archer's 61 wickets, and no batsman scored more than Burke's 1,339 runs. Both were the lowest leading aggregates on record. Nine wins from 31 games was the feeblest output since Syd Gregory's hobbled side of 1912. The Board didn't help, by refusing to let any of the Australians playing county cricket replace Johnson's injured bowlers. In typical cravenness, washing its hands of the mess it had created, the Board tried to scapegoat Johnson after his return by digging up his claimed allowances from the 1954–55 summer and sending them to the Victorian tax department.

After five months of misery in England, what better than a four-Test tour of Pakistan and India? The Board might have resigned en masse for the sheer stupidity of the scheduling, but that would not help Johnson and his team.

After their English commitments, the team dispersed for a month of holidays. When they reconvened in Rome for a flight to Karachi, they were a more united bunch, but their first Test, on matting, was farcical. In 53.1 overs on the first day, Australia scored 80 runs and lost 10 wickets. Fazal Mahmood, who had represented India before partition, took 6/34 with his medium-pace cutters. Johnson was Australia's best bowler, taking four wickets in Pakistan's 199. The massive Pakistani crowds must have been delightedly perplexed as Australia then batted for another 109 overs to score 187. Fazal took another seven and the home team won by nine wickets. They required 9 runs on the last day but the stadium was still packed. Worst of all, Ron Archer, who was being talked of as a future Test captain, damaged his knee when his spikes caught in the matting, an injury which effectively ended his career.

In India, the Australians lifted. Wonderful bowling from Benaud (7/72) and Lindwall (7/43) ensured a win in Madras, where Johnson scored 73. He was injured for the drawn Second Test in Bombay, where Lindwall became captain. (Miller missed his last chance, down with injury.)

Though a thoughtful and unexpectedly successful captain of Queensland for two summers, Lindwall did not covet the Test job. Johnson, Miller and Archer were injured, Davidson played with an upset stomach, and Benaud had a fever. On a dead track at the Brabourne Stadium, Lindwall used eight bowlers as India crawled to 251. Centuries from Burke and Harvey gave Australia 137 overs to bowl India out. But with himself and Benaud the last bowlers standing, Lindwall could only get an Indian out every two hours.

In Calcutta, Benaud took 11 wickets to seal a 2–0 series victory. It says something that his awakening as a Test cricketer came on a tour when half the team was sick, transport and accommodation were rustic, and opponents were brimming with self-confidence. Australian Test cricket began its upswing on that tour, and so did Benaud. In those hot and hectic Tests, on the tail of a second disappointing Ashes tour, Benaud found the resources to express himself, finally, on the Test stage.

Again Johnson had led a meritorious comeback overseas. Though overshadowed by his Ashes defeats, these series redeemed his captaincy. In his last Test in Calcutta, he passed the 1,000 runs–100 wickets double. He received an MBE and became secretary of the Melbourne Cricket Club for 26 years, a member of the Victorian Parole Board, an OBE and a CBE.

Were Ashes cricket all that mattered, Johnson's captaincy would be a failure. But the 1950s were the years when cricket became a more international game. Seven nations now played Tests. As Johnson's tours to the West Indies, Pakistan and India showed, Australian captains' success would now be judged not only by performances at home and in England.

Despite two Ashes defeats, Johnson as captain had the last laugh.

22

THE NEW BREED

FOR Ian Craig, fulfilment had remained just over the horizon. After his harrowing 1953 tour, he put on a show in Hassett's benefit match at the MCG, lifting four sixes off one Ian Johnson over. Leaving school, Craig concentrated on his pharmacy studies and was completing mandatory national service when Hutton brought out his 1954–55 team. It might have been beneficial for Craig as he re-emerged in 1955–56 with a tighter technique and broader range of strokes.

Chosen for Johnson's 1956 tour, Craig, now 20, was still the baby. His performances improved: 872 runs at 36.33, a century against Somerset, and a four-and-a-half-hour vigil on Laker's Manchester dustbowl when Colin McDonald was the only other to last an hour and a half. Craig played in just the last two Tests, when the series was sliding into despair, but the tour was final proof that Australia needed a new breed.

Craig's stoicism bade well. He posted handy scores in India, and came home to lead NSW on Miller's retirement. They won a fifth straight Shield, Craig contributing two centuries. But amid this success was concern. He gave the impression of physical vulnerability. Though a top-notch school rugby player, he was no bare-chested Benaud or robust Lindwall. Unlike those bronzed Aussies, the sun never seemed to touch Craig's high, pale forehead. Superficial impressions were waiting for supporting evidence, and when he was hospitalised with tonsillitis in England, some wondered if he was strong enough for a long career.

The Board was determined to ram him into the captaincy. His main rival was Harvey, but having played for Victoria under Hassett and Johnson, Harvey did not taste captaincy until 97 domestic matches into his career. His first match as Victorian captain was against Lindwall's Queenslanders. Harvey won the toss and chose to bat on a sporty wicket at St Kilda (the MCG was recovering from the Olympic Games). He top-scored in both innings, with 108 and 53, but Victoria lost by an innings. Against NSW he fared better. Benaud's batting was guiding NSW to victory, and instead of going negative Harvey brought the field in for Lindsay Kline's spinners. Benaud took the bait but miscued. Victoria escaped with the first tie in Shield history, and Harvey was credited with outwitting Benaud.

Ian Craig, young, gifted, unlucky

As captain, Harvey enjoyed a marvellous season, with 836 runs at 104.50. In a trial for the looming South African tour, Craig came down again with tonsillitis and Harvey's team won easily. It gave him every right to expect the top job, but instead the 22-year-old Craig was chosen.

Harvey was usually master of his emotions and he would serve Craig as an effective, loyal deputy. But immediately after Craig's appointment, Harvey was leading Victoria against Craig's NSW in Sydney. Minutes before the match, McDonald broke his nose in the nets. Craig offered to let Victoria call in a replacement. Bluntly, Harvey refused. He didn't want any favours. Instead he went out and opened himself, and batted for five hours. In his 209, the *Daily Telegraph* wrote, Harvey 'used the brilliance, judgement and concentration of a Bradman'. When the selectors were heaping so much pressure on Craig to be the next Bradman, they had as good as they were going to get right under their noses.

Craig led a non-Test team to New Zealand in the late summer of 1957. The team, a statement for the future, included Harvey, Benaud,

Peter Burge, Les Favell, Norm O'Neill and Bob Simpson. They were expected to take their £2 per diem with gratitude. Having observed the poor fitness of Johnson's 1956 team, the Board ordered a new training regime. A lazy lap before nets had sufficed, but now Board contracts were demanding a tougher run, exercises before breakfast, warm-ups and warm-downs, short walks rather than a trip to the bar after play, and the somewhat bizarre requirement to 'keep away from wrestlers, weightlifters and violent exercise fanatics'.

In New Zealand Craig's team played seven, won five and drew two. He made a century in the unofficial Test at Christchurch and gave bold after-dinner speeches, observing New Zealand cricket's 'inferiority status' and suggesting they improve their pitches.

Having fulfilled the Board's hopes, Craig was appointed to lead a Test tour to South Africa. He finished his pharmacy diploma, went to England to work and gain experience with the Marylebone Cricket Club, and flew direct to Johannesburg to meet his men: Benaud, Harvey, all-rounders Davidson, Simpson and Ken Mackay, opener Jim Burke and left-arm paceman Ian Meckiff the best of them. Since their previous Test, they had lost aeons of experience: Miller, Johnson, Bill Johnston, Morris and Lindwall. But Craig, who had led NSW at 19, didn't seem, at 22, too young to lead Australia.

For a man who never played for Australia again, Craig's one tour as captain was a shining success. They won the five-Test series 3–0 and were undefeated in 20 matches. For the first fortnight Craig was manager as well as captain, the Board's appointment, Jack Jantke, having suffered a heart attack. Harvey missed the first month with a broken finger and bowler John Drennan broke down immediately before the First Test, but no obstacle was insurmountable for Craig's fresh young team.

None was younger than the NSW all-rounder Robert Baddeley Simpson. Born into a family of Scottish migrants in the working-class Sydney suburb of Marrickville, Simpson attended Tempe Boys' Intermediate High and played for St Clement's Church of England as an over-the-wrist spin bowler. His father Jock had played football for Stenhousemuir in Scotland, and was one of a militant group of printers at the *Daily Telegraph*. Bobby's mother Sarah was from

Falkirk. Jock passed on his sporting talent and willingness to stand his ground to Bobby and two elder sons, who all played first-grade cricket.

Bobby was the classic sporting prodigy: at 15 he played in Petersham-Marrickville's firsts, and at 16 for NSW. Twelve months later, as 12th man against Victoria, he found himself on the field early in the Victorian innings and was told by Miller to stand in the slips cordon. Simpson was a fast outfielder with a good throw but no slips background. Miller didn't care. Within half an hour Simpson had caught Neil Harvey; he pocketed two more, and the career of arguably the world's greatest ever slips catcher was underway.

Simpson's chances to play for NSW had been limited to when the Test players were unavailable, but when chosen he soon excelled. His first century came in his third season, on a grassy SCG wicket against Victoria when no other batsman passed 50. Simpson presented himself in the Benaud mould, a penetrative leg-spinner who played shots in the middle-order. Against Hutton's MCC in their first state match, he showed he was up to international standard, taking six slips catches, and in the return game was cruising at 98 when, amid the lightest of drizzle, Hutton led his team off. The dumbstruck umpires and batsmen remained. If it was gamesmanship to unsettle the teenager, it worked: when the Englishmen came back, Simpson charged Johnny Wardle and got himself stumped. It would be 10 years before he would make England pay.

Simpson was ignored for Johnson's tours to the West Indies, England and the subcontinent. In the nets he had his nose broken, leaving him with a face that perfectly represented his pugilistic nature. He had been studying accountancy and working for the NSW Water Board, but a cadetship with a Perth newspaper, and the promise of being a big fish in a small cricketing pond, lured him west in 1956. In his first season he batted three, averaging nearly 50 and flourishing under Ken Meuleman.

Rewarded with trips to New Zealand and South Africa under Craig, Simpson was part of the Australian rebuilding program. But after scoring 60 and 23 not out in the First Test, his batting tailed off and he did not bowl. For three years he would be unable to break back in.

The new generation was Benaud, Davidson, Meckiff, Burke, Kline and Mackay, who all contributed in South Africa. Wally Grout took a world record six catches in the second innings of the First Test, establishing himself ahead of Barry Jarman as the next decade's gloveman. Jarman, the son of a Hindmarsh market gardener, had belied his heavy build to show great talent in football as well as cricket. Like Harvey, Jarman was an apprentice fitter and turner until cricket diverted him to a more flexible occupation, running a sports store in central Adelaide.

When Craig and Benaud were pondering which gloveman to play in the First Test, they agreed there was nothing between the pair. Grout, nine years older, had more experience. Both were good-natured and humorous behind the wicket. Finally Craig asked which keeper Benaud felt more confident bowling to. Benaud said Grout, marginally. And there it was: for a decade, including five tours and six home Test series, Jarman would be Grout's understudy.

The 1957–58 series belonged to Benaud, continuing his turn-around on the subcontinent. In his first 24 Tests, Benaud had averaged 21.44 with the bat and 34.44 with the ball. In the second half of his career, those averages would be adjusted. Richie, who had separated from his wife Marcia, was fully dedicated to cricket

Craig (*left*) in South Africa with Slasher Mackay and the champion of the tour, Richie Benaud

now. Bruce Dooland had taught him the flipper in England – the in-dipping, shooting sucker-punch – and Benaud practised it for a year before trying it. He loved to vary the height and pace and positioning of his delivery, but O'Reilly counselled him to bowl the leg-spinner as his stock ball, only using his flipper, wrong'un and top-spinner as shock weapons.

His tour began with a bang, 117 not out against Rhodesia at Salisbury and 53 wickets in his first seven games. He scored 122 in the First Test and took nine wickets in the Second. He took five wickets in the Third and in the Fourth scored 100 and collected another nine wickets. In the final innings of the series in Port Elizabeth, he rolled the South Africans again, taking 5/82. His series totals were 329 runs at 54.83 and 30 wickets at 21.93. Nobody since Giffen, not Miller or Davidson, not even Noble or Armstrong, had enjoyed quite such a dominant all-round series. In Port Elizabeth he made Clive Van Ryneveld his 100th Test wicket with a big-turning leg-break that pitched on leg and hit off. Just prior to that, he had trapped Trevor Goddard playing back to the flipper. Then, with a top-spinner, he whizzed through the wall-like defence of Jackie McGlew. There was nothing Benaud couldn't do.

Except captaincy. Benaud was thought to be too fond of the off-field life, too much Miller and not enough Bradman. Under Craig, Benaud seemed to be proving that his potential would be best realised without the burden of captaincy.

A 3–0 win was a great result for everyone – except, notably, Craig and Harvey. Craig walked onto the New Wanderers for his first innings as Test captain, the score two for 40, with, he said, 'the whole of Australia on my shoulders'. He made 14. Stressed, he took up smoking. Only in the Third Test at Durban, where the ground had been too wet for practice, did he make a real contribution as a batsman, a fighting 212-minute 52. Miller, in the press, asked if Craig the captain might have to drop Craig the batsman.

He did not, instead lowering himself beneath the in-form Benaud and sacrificing his wicket to elevate the run rate. He showed a gift for improvisation as well as sincerity and tact. He was a complete captain – except he couldn't make enough runs.

Harvey, meanwhile, had his first poor series against South Africa, scoring 131 at 21.83. Formerly a teetotaller, he took up drinking. Deputising for Craig against Natal, he chastised his teammates for not scoring fast enough. A year later, when his claim on the captaincy appeared undeniable, these bumps would be remembered.

The team came home in 1958 with many questions answered. But what to do about Craig? As captain, he had recrafted a successful team out of the debris of 1956. As a Test batsman, he had averaged 14.71. The question was difficult, but ultimately academic, for Craig contracted hepatitis and spent the next winter recuperating. He tried to pick himself up for the 1958–59 Ashes season at home, but two ducks showed that a return was premature.

The obvious replacement was Harvey, who had just moved to NSW. He had been selling sportsgoods in Melbourne until a better sales job, with a glass and diningware company, turned up in Sydney. Recovered from his less-than-happy South African tour, he scored 160 against Queensland on his NSW debut, then 149 against the touring MCC.

As Craig's replacement, Harvey seemed a no-brainer. The Johnson and Craig periods had demonstrated that the old Australian way – make your champion your captain – was *the* Australian way.

Harvey led an Australian XI against May's Englishmen at the SCG. England came as unofficial world champions, and there was talk of rounding up a World XI to give them a contest. Their batting bristled with the textbook talent of May, Colin Cowdrey and Tom Graveney. Their bowling, led by two express pacemen in Brian Statham and Fred Trueman, had Peter Loader as back-up and the 1956 series winners, Laker and Lock, for long hot days. Their wicketkeeper, Evans, was the acknowledged world number one.

May hit 140 in the tourists' 319, Harvey a duck in the Australians' 128. May set the Australian XI 449 to win on a track with craters gouged by the pacemen's footmarks. Lock hurled in his dubious finger-spinners, and Harvey's 38 was a lonely top score in his team's 103.

With Australia already underdogs, such a defeat prompted a Board rethink. Bradman, always more convinced of Harvey as a batsman than as a leader, pushed for Benaud. Benaud's captaincy experience added up to three games for NSW and a few seasons for Cumberland. But Bradman swayed the Board. It was cruel to the genius Harvey, vice-captain now under three different men, and Benaud's first task was to make the dreaded phone call. 'I'll be playing for you, Richie,' said the gutted Harvey.

The 1958–59 Ashes series, which Australia won 4–0, has been touted as a revival of entertaining cricket. But by any reckoning it was a tedious series, blighted by slow batting. Benaud's attacking instincts would not be seen in his team's style of play for another two seasons. But Australia beat England, which they hadn't done since 1950–51, and that was all that mattered. And Benaud, with 31 wickets at 18.84 and 132 runs at 26.40, was the star turn.

It was the first series to be televised in Australia – the last session of each day's play was shown on the ABC – and the tube loved Benaud. With his uninhibited reactions, his full emotional range from laughter to grief, he was the Arnold Palmer of his sport.

Benaud, the new national hero

Before the series, Bradman told May: 'I only hope we can give you a good match.' Benaud, recognising that his team lacked man-for-man talent, bridged the deficit by knitting his team together. He started a tradition of team-only dinners on Test eves and made a priority of team morale, setting a template that would become standard practice.

Playing with an urgency England lacked, Benaud's team stated their intentions on the first day in Brisbane, rolling the visitors for 134. The damage was done, as it would be throughout the series, by Benaud and his two left-armers, Davidson and Meckiff. A team effort with the ball again humbled England's finest and set up an eight-wicket win.

So often had initial wins been reversed during Ashes series, it was expected that May's men would rebound. England's captain scored a fine 113 on a grassy Melbourne strip, but Harvey's 167 – a tribute to the man's character – more than countered it, Meckiff took nine in the match and Australia won by eight wickets again.

A draw in Sydney, highlighted by Benaud's nine wickets, was followed by thrashings in Adelaide and Melbourne, McDonald starring with centuries in the last two Tests.

Benaud also had a fairytale in store. In the two years since Lindwall had been dropped, Benaud had been observing the 36-year-old champion trying to recover his outswinger in state cricket. With limited personnel, Lindwall had led Queensland to six wins in eight matches, missing out by one bonus point on taking their first Shield.

The Arnold Palmer of cricket:
Benaud in South Africa

He exercised with a pulley to restore his outswinger, and took 53 wickets at 24.73 over two seasons. Benaud personally encouraged Lindwall to keep plugging away in hopes of a Test recall.

The fairytale came after Lindwall had destroyed England's top order for Queensland, then done well against Western Australia, NSW and South Australia, receiving a standing ovation in an Adelaide heatwave. When Meckiff was ruled out of the Fourth Test in Adelaide with a badly bruised heel, Lindwall was reinstated. Second ball in, he fizzed a straight one at England opener Peter Richardson, and had his first Test wicket since 1956. He dismissed Cowdrey and Trevor Bailey in the second innings, then, in the Fifth Test, got the obdurate Bailey in his first over on both innings. In so doing, Lindwall passed Grimmett's Australian record of 216 wickets.

Fairytales and Benaud's charisma aside, cricket was showing its ugly face. In Brisbane, each day averaged 130 runs. 'Barnacle' Bailey's seven-hour 68 was matched, if that is the word, by Burke's four-hour 28. Slow over rates compounded negative batting, and the series saw some of the most monotonous cricket imaginable, only four days producing more than 200 runs.

The English press took exception to losing, and subjected the actions of Meckiff, Gordon Rorke and Keith Slater to a purity crusade. Meckiff and Slater were accused of chucking, Rorke's dragging back foot of breaking the no-ball law. Television was here, but slow-motion replays were not. The new medium whipped up a hysteria of complaint that Benaud, calmly, interpreted as a diversion from English disappointment.

Thanks to television and the home team's wins, the series was popular beyond its cricketing merits. Crowds of 780,000 watched the five Tests, and, helped by a £5,000 TV rights fee from the ABC, the Board made a profit of £44,984, of which it distributed £85 per Test to each Australian player.

With happy memories of the subcontinent, Benaud cheerfully led his team back in 1959–60. This tour would be longer: three Tests in Pakistan and five in India. After a two-day stopover in Singapore, the team landed at Dacca, East Pakistan (now Bangladesh), four days before their First Test. Benaud sent Kline to supervise the stretching of the mats. Kline was heard exhorting the groundsmen: 'Pull, you bastards, pull!'

Australia put a squeeze on the Pakistanis, Benaud ordering Mackay to bowl at the stumps to a ring field. Slasher applied the tourniquet so expertly that his 64 overs in the match produced 7/58, while Benaud's 77.3 yielded 8/111. It was grinding cricket. Benaud kept asking Davidson for 'one more over', until the penny dropped for Davidson that the 'one more' had gone on for another hour. Benaud's enthusiasm and humour kept his team floating above the heat, and they followed an eight-wicket win in Dacca with another, by seven wickets, in Lahore. There was sniffing at Benaud's habit of wrapping a successful bowler in celebratory hugs, but he was a substantial cricketer, not just a cheerleader. Again, he carried the attack, never asking Davidson and Mackay to shoulder more work than himself, and ended up with 47 wickets in the eight Tests from 546.2 overs. Davidson was also heroic with 41 wickets from 393.2 overs, and Harvey and O'Neill contributed welters of runs. Sublimating his disappointment over the captaincy, Harvey made 96 in Dacca, 114 in the defeat of India in Delhi, and 102 in the draw in Bombay. He batted not for self but for team. When he and O'Neill were chasing a win in Lahore, Pakistan were slowing the game down by tardily changing position as the strike changed. Seeing that the right-left combination was giving Pakistan that opportunity, Harvey sacrificed himself. The game sped up, and Australia had time to win.

Harvey's fielding remained unquestionably the team's, probably the world's, best. Patrolling the covers, he was worth 30 or 40 an innings. Back in 1951–52 he had pulled off four run-outs in a Test, including two off successive balls. Once Harvey picked up the ball, said Simpson, who rated Harvey the best fielder he saw, the batsmen 'might as well take it easy. There was no point in hustling, for it was simply a question of whether he hit the stumps or missed.' More than anyone of his time, he hit. He could catch, too. In the Kanpur Test, Nari Contractor swung Davidson towards Harvey on the leg-side. Ducking and turning, Harvey somehow managed to catch the ball in the fold of his knee.

Wins in Delhi and Madras outweighed the loss in Kanpur. Benaud was criticised for negative tactics by not chasing a win in Calcutta, but his team was fighting exhaustion and dysentery, Gavin Stevens to the point where he nearly died, and the captain was not prepared to risk leaving the subcontinent with anything less than two series wins.

Lindwall played three more Tests, pushing his aggregate to 228 wickets. He passed one of the oldest records, Syd Gregory's 58 Test match appearances: astonishing that a fast bowler, who missed eight years of Test cricket during the war, should become Australia's most-capped player. But Lindwall was an extraordinary individual, an acme of blond, understated, fit, skilled, immensely determined Australian manhood.

Lindwall, who gave more pleasure to spectators than any other fast bowler of his time

Lindwall finished his first-class career with a slow off-break for Queensland against Western Australia at the Gabba in February 1960. He played several more seasons with Northern Suburbs, while helping his wife Peg run their florist business. With private teams, Lindwall would enjoy tours of New Zealand, the West Indies, Rhodesia and Pakistan in the 1960s, before becoming a Queensland and Australian selector. He died at Greenslopes, Brisbane's Repatriation Hospital, in 1996, the great bowling captain who, at his one turn in charge of Australia, was, in his words, 'a captain without bowlers'.

23

THE RISE OF THE HARD MEN

WHILE Benaud led a resurgent team, Ian Craig had recovered his health. Benaud had graciously acknowledged that he was only carrying on the renovation work started by Craig in South Africa – but had Craig's time passed?

Craig possessed a toughness not often recognised. Rather than passively wave farewell to the captaincy, he spent the next three years trying to fight his way back. He was still only 24. When Benaud was on Test duty, Craig led NSW to more Shield success. Craig scored 82 against Queensland and masterminded an innings win by sending the northerners in first; he scored half-centuries in both fixtures against South Australia. He then took a 1959–60 reserve Australian team to New Zealand, taking his record as captain of Australian teams to 17 wins and 10 draws.

But Benaud was now the king. He returned from India for the last Shield game of 1959–60, taking the NSW captaincy back from Craig, and produced his best-ever figures: 54 runs and 12/148 in a nine-wicket win. *The Sydney Morning Herald* said he 'spun the ball like a top'.

The game was facing growing criticism about slow batting, slow over rates and chucking. Its popularity had received a transfusion from television, but this also attracted even more attention to the excesses of defensive play.

Now secure as captain, Benaud resolved to do something about the game itself. With Frank Worrell, captain of the West Indians touring in 1960–61, he made an informal agreement to play entertaining cricket and to hell with the results. The series, and Benaud's part in promoting it, has been documented to exhaustion. It helped that the West Indians bristled with personality: Worrell, Wes Hall, Rohan Kanhai, Garry Sobers, Conrad Hunte, Joe Solomon, Cammie Smith, Lance Gibbs. It also helped that the First Test in Brisbane had the most exciting finish in cricket history.

Benaud's contribution to the tie was telling. Directing traffic, he moved catchers in at the first sniff of weakness, and left them close when the West Indian batsmen tried to spread them. At tea break on the last day, when most watchers thought Australia, six wickets down, would settle for a draw, Benaud told Bradman that he was going to chase a win. 'I'm very pleased to hear it,' Bradman said.

Benaud personally led the Australian chase, adding 134 with Davidson and only getting out, hooking, in the last over. Three balls later Solomon threw down the stumps for the second time from side-on and the match was tied.

The 1960–61 series is unique in that Benaud and Worrell genuinely committed their teams to playing cricket how they would love to play it. They were rewarded with the tie in Brisbane, the most exciting draw in history in Adelaide, when Kline and Mackay held out for 110 minutes, and a series that was squared 1–1 until the last moments of the last match, in Melbourne, when Mackay and Johnny Martin got Australia home by two wickets. Not since 1902 had a more exciting series been contested. Johnny Moyes wrote that the West Indians' effect 'was amazing: they turned the world upside down; they arrived almost unhonoured and unsung; they took away with them the esteem, affection and admiration of all sections of the community. They proved what so many of us had declared – that people will go to see cricket played as a game and an entertainment.' Some 90,800 spectators turned up for the Saturday of the last Test, while half a million people flooded the streets of Melbourne to give both teams an emotional farewell.

Benaud's top-order star of the Calypso Summer was the reinvented Simpson, brought back after Jim Burke's retirement. Given his second chance, Simpson would become the dominant Australian batsman for seven years. For sheer willpower, he knew no equal. He entrenched himself as an opening batsman, beginning the series by starring in the Tied Test with a first-innings 92, and finishing it with the same score, this time smashing 18 runs from Hall's opening over. His 10 innings produced 445 runs at 49.44; Benaud also sometimes used him as a surprise bowling weapon and he removed Sobers twice in the decider.

Since his Test debut under Craig, Simpson had been riding a rocky road, mostly ignored by the Test selectors. He played with Accrington in the Lancashire League, outscoring Sobers, then, carrying the responsibility of a new marriage, changed his technique. On Harvey's advice he stood more side-on to counter the moving ball. Harvey also suggested he go to the top of the order. Simpson excised several attacking shots, including the hook, from his game, which he now based around the straight drive, the square cut and a rainbow spectrum of back-foot deflections. He changed to shorter-handled, heavier bats. Now 24, he had been a first-class player for seven and a half years. No longer the child star, he feared he was already a has-been. He reduced his bowling and sharpened his slips catching. He caught balls against his chest, or with the base of his fingers rather than his palms, and had tremendous concentration and anticipation. But catching would be secondary to a new, life-or-death dedication to batting.

In 1959–60, omitted from the Test tour, Simpson's intensity was Bradman-like. He was on the field for an entire Shield match against NSW in Perth, scoring 236 not out in 590 minutes and taking 5/45 in NSW's second innings. The next week he made 230 not out, in 494 minutes, against Queensland. *The West Australian* wrote: 'Figures indicate but do not show fully the amazing improvement in Simpson's powers of concentration.' In a shortened season, his remaining scores were 98, 79, 98 again and 161 not out. His total was 902 runs, his average 300.66. Not even Bradman had equalled that.

Outside the Tests of 1960–61, he scored 87 and 221 not out for WA against the West Indians, and three other centuries. His 1,541 at 64.20 topped the aggregates. He was also given his first taste of captaincy, leading WA when Meuleman was injured. With a weak team, Simpson got an immediate result: a five-wicket win over South Australia in which he scored 111 runs and took four wickets. Having been held up for so long, Simpson was back on the fast track.

Benaud's Calypso Summer crowned his career, notwithstanding being booed in Melbourne for appealing when Solomon's cap fell on his stumps. Benaud took eight wickets in Sydney, and in Adelaide complemented seven wickets with 77 and 17. He was the complete cricketer: captain, batsman, bowler, fieldsman, an international figure whose smiling intelligence transcended his sport.

Yet he was wearing out. His right shoulder had been so over-worked on the subcontinent and at home that by 1961 he could only brush his teeth and shave with his left hand. When he became captain, he took up smoking. He seldom seemed affected by the pressure, but he would have been inhuman not to feel it.

His 1953 and 1956 Ashes tours remained the gap in his record. On the 1961 tour Benaud would take 61 wickets, second to Davidson, and score 627 runs at 25.08. But his peak years had come between two Ashes tours; England never saw his best. To compensate for his decline, teamwork was again his credo: for the first time, eight bowlers captured more than 50 wickets on a tour.

One of the most interesting newcomers in 1961 was the Victorian opening batsman William Morris Lawry. In a 16-year career, two truths about Lawry were immutable. He was an opening batsman, and he was a Victorian.

The son of a tobacco stripper, Lawry did not come from a cricket family. He was named after William Morris Hughes, the Prime Minister who ran on both sides of politics. Lawry the batsman only went one way. Unlike Simpson, he had one string to his bow, which he played with rigid consistency.

Born in the Melbourne suburb of Thornbury, Lawry attended Wales Street and Penders Grove schools and played for his Presbyterian church for three years before making fourth grade for Northcote at the age of 12. By 16 he was in the firsts, and the day before his 19th birthday he made his debut in the midnight-blue cap of Victoria. He spent most of the next two seasons in club cricket while completing his apprenticeship as a plumber. He was a boy of obsessive interests: cricket, racing pigeons (a family hobby) and also *Phantom* comics, which, when wicketkeeper Len Maddocks discovered a copy in Lawry's kitbag, gave him a nickname that also suited a wiliness masked by small eyes, a peaked cap and a comic-book nose.

William Morris Lawry, The Phantom

Masses of club runs floated him back up to state cricket in 1958–59, and this time he stayed, with half-centuries against Queensland, SA and NSW. The fact that he took five hours to record his highest score of 92 was in keeping with those dug-in times. With an economical backlift, Lawry played the percentages, tucking his runs on the on-side and seldom leaving his crease to the spinners. Sometimes he would venture out, but winning was too precious. His aim was to be the opener with the highest-priced wicket.

His maiden first-class century came the next season, four years and 22 games after his debut, against a second-string WA. He hit the headlines against NSW, scoring 266 in a racy eight hours. The *Sun-Herald* wrote that 'Lawry is no stylist, but he has a magnificent eye, and drives and pulls with tremendous vigour.' It sounds like damning with faint praise, but the statistic – the biggest innings in Australia since the war – was beyond opinion.

Another century against Queensland got him one of the last places on Benaud's 1961 tour. Simpson and McDonald were a settled combination after the Calypso Summer, but each was capable of slipping down the order. Lawry's one-dimensionality worked to his advantage on arrival, when he helped avenge the 1956 team's loss to Surrey with 165, then, at Lord's, scoring 104 and 84 not out against the MCC. Unable to ignore him, Benaud picked him to open in the First Test, a position Lawry would occupy for a decade.

The First Test, at Birmingham, was drawn, Harvey making a dogged 114. Now a 14-year veteran of Test cricket, he had wobbled in the 1960–61 series, but three centuries for NSW had made him one of the first chosen and he was bent on revenge for 1953 and 1956. When Benaud aggravated his injured shoulder in the First Test, Harvey finally led a Test team – onto Lord's, in front of the Queen. Not in some far-flung field, Neil Harvey was captain of Australia at cricket's home.

The match, famously, was played on a strip distorted by a ridge above a buried drain line. Davidson, promising something special for Harvey, took 5/42. England's 206 looked enough when Australia lost McDonald, Simpson, Harvey and O'Neill for 88. Then Lawry played the innings of his life, 130 out of 340. Two things got Lawry through: the soundness of his technique against pace bowling, and a simplicity of mind that was able to shut out doubt and play the ball, not the conditions. The ridge scared everyone except him. He scored precisely 101 runs against Trueman and Statham. Australia's lead was match- and ultimately Ashes-winning.

Harvey made some useful runs, but of more import was the confidence and direction he gave his bowlers. Graham McKenzie, the fluid young West Australian swing bowler on his first tour, rose from the Nursery End with 5/37. Harvey also deployed Simpson's leg-spin to great effect. McDonald offered Harvey tactical assistance but, said McDonald later, 'there was never a need for me to mention anything'.

On such a roguish wicket the Australian chase for 71 was looking shaky when Harvey, out for 4, crossed with Peter Burge and told him to keep playing his shots. Burge took charge, and Australia's win would secure the Ashes.

The recent mythology of the captaincy, built upon Mark Taylor, Steve Waugh and Ricky Ponting, is that Australia always attacks. This has not always been the case, and even under Benaud, a relatively attacking captain, Australia played some numbingly defensive cricket. Even though Harvey only did the job for one Test, he infused his team with the attitude he showed in his batting: when in doubt, go for your shots. Nobody can gainsay the benefits Australia

achieved from Benaud's captaincy, but it is intriguing to ponder on the direction the team might have taken under Harvey.

Under Benaud at Headingley, Harvey produced some of his best batting, top-scoring in both innings with 73 and 53, to stand alone in the ultimately vain battle to stave off defeat.

The teams went to Manchester tied 1–1. A tight match swung England's way in the fourth innings when, chasing 256, they reached 1/150, Dexter flaying Davidson and Mackay. Benaud took a punt and brought himself on to bowl around the wicket. Shane Warne would later make a specialty of bowling into the rough created by the fast bowlers' footmarks, but in 1961 it was a novelty.

Looping leg-spinners were asking to be smacked behind square, but Benaud had nothing to lose. Better a lucky captain, he would later say, than a good one. Or, as Derbyshire fast bowler Harold Rhodes said, 'If you put your head in a bucket of slops, Benordy, you'd come up with a mouthful of diamonds.' Benaud, like Taylor after him, believed in the mystique of his own luck and thereby caused others to believe as well. At Edgbaston, two balls after moving Lawry into an unorthodox short gully for Mike Smith, Lawry had the catch and the legend of Benaud's magic grew another chapter.

Benaud got one to pop on Dexter, bowled May around his legs second ball, and spread such panic in the England changing room that the match was over in a session. England's last nine wickets dissolved for 51 and Benaud finished with 32–11–70–6. It was his greatest afternoon as a Test match bowler.

His other achievement at Old Trafford was to pair Lawry with Simpson. Even after his breakthrough 1960–61 Test season, Simpson gave himself reason to believe he was no favoured son. An automatic pick for the 1961 tour, he had been shifted down the order. His renewal as a cricketer had come as an opener, but he was falling victim to his own versatility. His returns at six were moderate until, in the second innings at Old Trafford, he opened with Lawry facing a deficit of 177. They put on 113, launching Australia's matchwinning lead. Like had found like. Over the next six years, Simpson and Lawry would establish an opening bond that was recognised as the best Australia had known.

Lawry's first tour was his finest. His aggregate of 2,019 was third behind Bradman and Harvey post-war, and has never since been equalled. He scored another Test century at The Oval, after which Bill Bowes wrote: 'Lawry is one of the best players of fast bowling I have ever seen.' With experience going back to Bodyline, Bowes knew his onions.

Lawry's popularity as a reliable and, yes, exciting new Australian opener with a penchant for crunching hook shots would never exceed its 1961 levels. He was known as a practical joker, nailing Benaud's boots to the floor and also swiping one of the Queen Mother's teaspoons, depositing it in the pocket of the put-upon

Lawry in 1961 smashing the English

tour manager, Syd Webb. Such stories would astonish those who later knew Lawry as a colourless, dogmatic warhorse.

Benaud led the tour under a cloud of petty Board politics. Benaud was too friendly with journalists, inviting them into the changing room, for Webb's liking. The Board applied a gag to Benaud, who protested directly to Bradman. Their combined influence was enough to soften the Board. But Benaud would not forget the Board's draconian attitude. As if to drive home their sympathies, *Wisden* named him a cricketer of the year and the Queen gave him an OBE.

Back home, he remained the country's best spin bowler. In 1961–62 he took 47 wickets at 17.97, top of the national aggregates. He also cracked 140 at nearly a run a ball to set up a win over Victoria in the main match of the season.

But the 1961 Ashes tour had shown that the Calypso Summer had not reshaped Test cricket. Australia had marginally faster run and over rates, but back at home the 1962–63 series would exemplify the dour characteristics of Ashes cricket, not the cavalier adventure of the West Indian tour.

Benaud remained supreme, taking a career-best 7/18 in routing the English for NSW. He broke O'Reilly's state record (203 wickets) and Lindwall's Test record (228 wickets) during the summer.

His batting aces were Lawry and Simpson, who set about dulling England's strong bowling attack. In Brisbane Lawry made 98 in 260 minutes, ensuring a draw, and in Melbourne his 57 in five hours was the slowest Australian half-century on record. Dexter, noticing that Lawry rarely played the cut shot, instructed his bowlers to feed it. Lawry kept letting the ball pass. During his vigil Australia lost the initiative, and subsequently the match. In the Fifth Test at Sydney, England set Australia 241 at a run a minute. Lawry batted the entire four hours for 45 not out, so tediously that whenever the ball hit his pads the 'home' crowd appealed to the umpire. Under the pressure of an Ashes series, the enterprise of the Benaud–Worrell accord was a distant memory, and for many spectators Lawry took the blame. The fact that he was playing to his captain's orders was harder for Sydneysiders to believe.

When Davidson tore a thigh muscle in Adelaide and Australia could have chased a win in Sydney, Benaud preferred to settle for draws, a 1–1 series, and the Ashes retained. Without a Worrell to tango with, Benaud chose not to dance. Against the English, for all his expressiveness and desire to attack, Benaud was content to retreat into defence. After Lawry and Burge blocked out the Sydney Test on Benaud's orders, they were booed off. It was a sad atmosphere in which Harvey and Davidson retired from Test cricket.

It would be an exaggeration to say Harvey retired in decline. In his penultimate Test, he took the English bowlers for 154. In his last Shield match, against Sobers's SA, Harvey gave an unforgettable final bow, a 287-minute unbeaten 231. How many players have saved the highest score of their life for their last match? *The Sydney Morning Herald* said his 'batting, with entrancing footwork, a wealth of strokes all round the wicket, and plenty of vigour behind them, was a throwback to his greatest days'.

At 34, his final first-class season yielded 1,107 runs at 55.35. But his sales business was expanding, and he had been touring at the top level for 15 poorly remunerated years. In retirement, Harvey received an MBE, divorced and remarried, and became a national selector for 12 years until 1979. For someone who was so calm, quiet and loyal during his playing days, he emerged as something of a grump, adopting the Warwick Armstrong view that current players were never as good as the old ones and never had been. Consequently, his legacy to the game was somewhat blurred. But perhaps, having been overlooked and underrated, he felt his record needed defending. To those who saw him, no such defence was necessary. After Bradman, he occupied the same rank as Clem Hill, Victor Trumper and Billy Murdoch – the best batsmen Australia had ever produced.

'It takes a star of the first magnitude to gleam in regions bedazzled by the record-breaking of Bradman,' wrote Ray Robinson. Harvey, who would retire with more Tests than any Australian and more runs than anyone save Bradman, made cricket still worth watching in that room with the light switched off.

The other former captain to retire was Craig, who had been continuing to play for NSW. During Benaud's Calypso Summer, Craig's NSW won another Shield. He averaged 84.25 for the season as an opener, and only a back injury, doubt over whether his work commitments allowed him to travel, and the good form of McDonald and Simpson kept him out of a Test return. He made 146 against Queensland in a four-hour blitz with Harvey, 106 against Victoria, 83 against the West Indies and 197 against Western Australia.

Craig was too successful, perhaps, in life outside cricket. His job as production manager at the big pharmaceutical company, Boots, blocked his availability for a third England tour in 1961. He scored another 629 runs for NSW under Benaud, as another Shield was claimed. At 26 he retired, unable to combine cricket with his job, his commitment to the Congregational church as a lay preacher, and a family with three children. The youngest NSW player, the youngest Australian player, the youngest to go on an Ashes tour, and the youngest captain, he was at 23 the youngest ex-captain and, at 26, a first-class retiree before many careers had even started.

In retirement he would head the Bradman Museum in Bowral and be an SCG Trustee for nine years – the youngest ever to hold the latter position.

In the braided cords of the Australian captaincy, Craig belongs more to the 19th century than the 20th. Like Hugh Massie, he was too successful in his working life. Like Henry Scott, he went off to finer things, and whenever he was asked if he regretted his short career, he would assure the questioner that a man who has captained his country and made runs in Test cricket can never have any reason for disappointment.

After the dull 1962–63 Ashes series, Benaud only led Australia once more. The First Test against South Africa in 1963–64 was a bitter affair, with umpire Col Egar taking it upon himself to no-ball Meckiff, who was being recalled to Test cricket after two seasons. Meckiff had been called twice by different umpires but Egar had not found fault with him in five matches. As Egar himself explained late in life, he was acting on what he believed was an implied hint from Bradman to take on suspected throwers in general, and Meckiff in particular, so that Australia would occupy the high moral ground during the 1964 Ashes series if another chucking controversy erupted.

Benaud, a staunch defender of Meckiff in 1958–59, now chose a very brave course. He took Meckiff off. He did not bowl him at the other end, where umpire Lou Rowan might not have called him. But Benaud placed the umpire's authority on a higher plane than his own opinion, or loyalty, or any advantage in the match. Benaud faced a torrent of criticism, even abuse, from crowds and critics, who thought he let Meckiff down. Hassett said Benaud 'took the easy way out'. But when Benaud's action is contrasted with that of another captain – Sri Lanka's Arjuna Ranatunga, who, in the late 1990s, preferred to bring down the game rather than accept an umpire's authority – Benaud's courage achieves an almost heroic dimension. And Meckiff, one of the most decent men to have represented Australia, carried himself with grace and dignity, despite the personal toll he paid.

Benaud had decided not to go on the 1964 Ashes tour, and told Bradman he was considering stepping down for the remaining South African Tests to blood a new captain and defuse the Meckiff issue. Out of the Second Test with a finger injury, Benaud handed the captaincy to the Board's appointment, Simpson.

While Benaud had revitalised the team, the job in 1963–64 was no sinecure. South Africa had the makings of a champion team: Graeme and Peter Pollock, Eddie Barlow, Denis Lindsay, Colin Bland and Trevor Goddard. Australia, on the other hand, had lost its best batsman, Harvey, and its main paceman, Davidson, to retirement. Meckiff, Davidson's successor as the left-arm new-ball specialist, had been rubbed out. Now Simpson was also without Benaud and the injured Brian Booth and Norm O'Neill. He only had half a team.

But if anyone was to enjoy being written off, to actively enjoy it, that man was Simpson. He won the toss and with extreme boldness sent South Africa in on a grassy MCG strip. Simpson worried about leading his team from first slip – the conventional captain's position was mid-off or -on, to talk to the bowler – but he was too valuable not to be first slip. His choice would set an example for many captains.

Barlow made his second straight hundred, but Australia's low-profile attack of McKenzie, Neil Hawke, Alan Connolly, Johnny Martin and Tom Veivers had South Africa out for 274. Unlike Benaud, Simpson used the swing bowler Hawke with the new ball before the pacier Connolly, to great effect. 'Why do we always have to make a mess of things?' asked Goddard after play, a complaint echoed by South African captains down the years.

Simpson batted at three so Lawry could look after his fellow Victorian, the debutant Ian Redpath. The pair put on 219 and Simpson's men ground out an eight-wicket win, the new captain icing the cake with 55 not out in the second innings. Benaud, like Simpson a professional journalist, wrote generously: 'The wonderful performance of Simpson and *his team* [italics added] in this present Test has made it clear to me that we have the nucleus of a very fine team.'

Benaud returned to play under Simpson in the rest of the series, drawn thanks to South Africa's win in Adelaide and rain which saved Australia in Sydney. Simpson marshalled his resources adeptly, if without Benaud's brio. He was also a harder-edged boss, asserting bowling and fielding changes without Benaud's consensual approach.

The 1963–64 Australian Cricketer of the Year was the reserved Sydney schoolteacher Brian Booth, who scored 531 runs at 88.50 in four Tests and 1,180 at 90.76 for the season.

Booth, who had been working his way towards a central position in the Australian batting order for three seasons, had been a first-class cricketer for nine years. There is no initiation story comparable to his. In February 1955, the 21-year-old was teaching at Hurlstone Boys' Agricultural High School. Son of a market gardener from the village of Perthville and born in Bathurst, he was a local star in cricket and hockey. Booth had been spotted as a 14-year-old by city scouts and invited for special coaching, before representing a Combined Country XI and moving to Sydney to play for the mighty St George club.

Brian Booth, dual international, showing his style

Booth was in class when the school's phone rang. It was the NSW Cricket Association. The state team was playing England, and two players had dropped out. Booth was in. He couldn't celebrate, because the game had already started. NSW were batting, and had lost three wickets for 12. By the time he arrived at the SCG, NSW were five for 26. Against Tyson, Bedser and Loader, with absolute calm Booth batted for 235 minutes. His upright style had few embellishments, but his feet moved with such speed and his hand-eye coordination was so sweet that England never had a chance. Only his partners' failure kept Booth from a famous century. He was unbeaten on 74 when the last wicket fell.

Since then, he had taken time out of cricket in 1956 to represent Australia at hockey in the Olympic Games, then commenced a five-year blitz that would make him, for a short time, Australia's champion batsman. As an opener for NSW, he scored three centuries in 1960–61 and held Australia together in the Old Trafford and Oval Tests of 1961. As a touring mate, Booth ruffled no feathers. Out for 99 against Lancashire, all he could do was laugh: the bowler's name was Brian Booth. Popular, amiable and even-tempered, Booth impressed his teammates with his short backlift, exquisite timing and effortless style, scoring mainly through the off-side but adaptable to any conditions or bowling.

At home in 1962–63, he scored a silky 112 in Brisbane against Trueman, Statham, Fred Titmus and Barry Knight, *The Age* approving 'a grand display of solid defence and splendid strokeplay'. In Melbourne, Dexter and his bowlers, seeing Booth's strength on the off-side, bowled at his legs and stacked the field behind his back. In at 4/69 in the second innings, Booth played an entirely different innings. This time he occupied the crease for a day, never losing patience on a low wicket. His 103 didn't save the game but was easily Australia's best, as was his 77 in the draw in Adelaide. His father had nicknamed him 'Sam', and after such innings the sportswriter Robert Gray dubbed him 'Sam Booth, Australia's one-man Salvation Army'.

Booth's next season was his career zenith. He started with 121 against Queensland at the Gabba, then a chanceless, blissful 169 not out in 175 minutes at home to WA. Innings like this led Pollard to say that Booth gave spectators as much aesthetic pleasure as Harvey and O'Neill.

Looking for a weakness in the First Test, Peter Pollock bounced him but was hooked away. After Booth's 169, Trevor Goddard said, 'We didn't mind the leather-chasing, when he played so charmingly.'

Booth's innings was cast into the shade by the Meckiff controversy, and it was little noticed that he broke his hand while fielding. He missed the Second Test but consolidated himself with three more half-centuries and his fourth Test century in Melbourne, where *The Age* said: 'Booth never became jittery against either pace or spin, and he was Australia's anchor man.'

Playing handily under Simpson for the balance of the series, Benaud went out, as he liked to put it, 'while they were still wanting more'. In his last Shield match, against a South Australian team including Sobers, Ian Chappell and Les Favell, Benaud scored 76 and 120 not out. Only 33, he retired after 259 first-class games, with 11,801 runs at 36 and 945 wickets at 24, supplemented by 250 catches, mostly in the gully. He was the first player to score 2,000 runs and take 200 wickets in Tests. Only Giffen, Noble, Armstrong and Miller have comparable statistics, and none left the Australian captaincy as improved as Benaud. Tactically, in every facet from pressuring batsmen with attacking fields – and holding his nerve by keeping them – to popularising the move of declaring shortly before stumps in the hope of a cheap wicket, Benaud was much copied. His management of team spirit, unforgettably putting Davidson's sweater on for him and throwing an arm around his tired shoulders to coax that one last over, has had no equal among Australian captains, except perhaps for Ian Chappell. The first to lead Australia 28 times, against five opponents in an expanding world, Benaud was, for Robinson, 'first among captains I have known', and it's hard to imagine an Australian captain who had such influence for good. Hard also to imagine someone on whom the captaincy had such a good influence.

24

THE FIRST AGE
OF SIMPSON

SET to lead a team to England in 1964, Simpson had something sticking in his craw. He had contributed 361 runs at 40.11 to his first series as captain, but his résumé had a big hole.

Lawry, a year his junior, arrived in Test cricket four years after Simpson but within five Tests had two centuries to his name. By 1964, Lawry, Brian Booth, Peter Burge and Norm O'Neill each had a handful of Test centuries. Simpson, a Test player before any of them and a first-class player for nearly a decade, had none, although he had reached fifty 14 times.

Since work had brought him back to NSW in 1961, Simpson had been on a run glut. He had scored a triple-century, three doubles, and six single centuries – but not one in a Test. In four straight matches in the summer of 1962–63 he scored hundreds, but none in a Test. In the Sydney Test of that summer he ran through the English with 5/57 and had chipped his way to 91 – surely this was his day! – but was bowled by Fred Titmus. Then he got to 71 in Adelaide before Dexter bluffed him out.

All he could do was take out his frustrations on those unfortunate enough to be bowling at him. In the first match of the 1963–64 summer, at the Gabba, he watched Burge knock up 283. Simpson batted for 629 minutes to score a post-war record 359. He gave one chance, at 305. NSW took first-innings points.

He followed it with 246 for a Combined XI against South Africa and 247 not out at nearly a run a minute against his former WA teammates. In three innings, Simpson had piled up 852 runs at 426.00. But there were no Test centuries for him that season.

Lacking Harvey, Benaud, Meckiff and Davidson, Simpson's 1964 team arrived to the news that it was the worst Australian squad since 1912. Simpson said that, this being the case, he would be happy with a 1–0 win. Australia had held the urn since 1959, but on paper – and on covered wickets for the first time in England – with Geoff Boycott, Dexter, Cowdrey and Ken Barrington, England's batting had a look of invincibility.

In a rainy spring, Australia drew six of their first 10 matches. England's attack, revolving around Trueman, and Australia's, around McKenzie, surprised everyone in the first two Tests, but rain had the final say until the Third at Headingley, when McKenzie and Hawke ripped through England and Dexter blundered. Australia were seven down and 80 runs behind, bogged by the spinners, when the second new ball fell due. Dexter took it, and Simpson told Burge, on 38, to counter-attack. Burge's bludgeoning 160 was a great Ashes innings, winning the match and, ultimately, the series.

Simpson still had no Test century. Neil Harvey was once asked why he got out for dashing 50s or 100s when he could have made 300. Harvey replied: 'Who on earth ever wants to make 300?'

Bob Simpson, that's who. Among the great batsmen, there are those who are satisfied with entertaining themselves, their peers and the spectators: Trumper, Macartney, Harvey, Ian Chappell, Doug Walters and Mark Waugh. Others want to bat forever. Bill Ponsford and Don Bradman were reactions against the blitheness of Trumper. And the carefree attitude of Harvey found its answer in the relentlessness of Simpson.

At Old Trafford, Simpson finally got to three figures, late on the first day. He had scored 37 first-class centuries and played 29 Test matches. 'Nobody can describe the feeling of relief that flowed through me when the magical three-digit number went up on the scoreboard,' he said. 'I don't know of any player who was on the international scene as long as I without scoring a century. I was feeling a bit silly about it by this stage.'

Simpson being Simpson, he would still be there at stumps on the second day. It was paralytic cricket. Tedious is too weak a word. Simpson maintained that he was trying to set up a score when the wicket was at its best, to bowl England out twice. But the wicket did not deteriorate, and he stood accused of killing the match.

Worst of all, for the English press, was that he did not declare when he was 265 not out after day two, already the longest innings ever played against England. On the third day he batted on as if suddenly woken, cracking 46 at a run a minute. When he seemed set

Talented, determined, influential, tough: Bob Simpson in his prime

to top Bradman's 334, he was caught behind. 'I did not think I was a good enough player to have broken Bradman's record,' he said. But his 311 was the highest score by a Test captain.

That Test, and the last at The Oval, were drawn and Australia had gouged out the 1–0 win of Simpson's hopes. As for any captain, winning in England was his highlight. He had kept an unusually stable team, the only change coming when an injured O'Neill was replaced by Bob Cowper. Simpson was unbending: at Trent Bridge, when Grout had refused to run out Titmus, who had fallen over after colliding with the bowler, Simpson told Grout: 'Once is enough'. Simpson had a mind, said Robinson, 'no easier to change than a £100 note.'

For all the draws and the slow cricket, the series was watched by a record 354,436 spectators and raised a £30,000 profit for the Australian Board.

Simpson's prestige would never be greater. The decay started with low-level irritants. The Board censured him for making media comments during the 1964 tour, which, as a journalist, rankled with him as it had with Benaud. Simpson would soon be embroiled in a libel suit brought by Meckiff, who objected to Simpson's comments about his action. Then there had been a shock loss to Holland in a one-day match on the way from England to the subcontinent.

Having to go to Pakistan and India on the heels of an Ashes tour would seem brutal, but Johnson's team of 1956–57 had thrived on it, rebuilding themselves in the dust and the heat, and Benaud had led his 1959–60 team with distinction and success.

Under Simpson, some poor habits began to appear. He did not lead subtly or sensitively. He encouraged hard practice and a lifestyle as cricket-obsessed as his own. He found it hard to tolerate idiosyncrasies. This worked well with fanatics such as Lawry, a monomaniac cut from the Simpson cloth. But differences are exaggerated over a long tour, particularly on the subcontinent.

Australia drew 1–1 with India. O'Neill, Veivers and Lawry were laid low with dysentery, Grout fractured his chin, and the

Australians could not rise above some dreadful umpiring. Even the gentlemanly McKenzie said: 'It almost amounted to 11 men playing against 13. The umpires were very bad.' One Australian, asked what he thought of the Nawab of Pataudi's 128 not out in Madras, said: 'Which [innings]? I thought his third was his best.'

Doubtless the umpiring was bad, but poor umpiring was as endemic as hot weather and low wickets. It would become characteristic of Simpson's teams that they responded to bad luck angrily, letting it affect their morale and performance. The tour manager, Ray Steele, was drawn in, and his official report to the Board was described as 'touchy'.

Simpson at least held his technique together – or his technique held him together. In Karachi, for the drawn one-off Test, he scored 153 and 115, the fifth Australian to make two centuries in a Test and the first to do so in Pakistan. Now that he had broken the hundred-barrier, Simpson was turning into a Test batsman of substance. That year, his 1,381 runs broke Denis Compton's world record of 1,159. He scored most of them with a hidden injury, a broken thumb sustained in England.

Coming home, Simpson led NSW to his first Shield as captain, averaging 101.16 with three centuries. But the bad atmosphere among the touring team was hovering. After the Australian summer – featuring a single dull draw with Pakistan – Simpson would lead a squad to the West Indies. Australia's first tour there since 1955 was long overdue, and the hope was that Simpson could build on the goodwill of 1960–61. Instead, his tour fell into an abyss.

Before their departure, the Australian Cricket Society presented Simpson's team with crash helmets. The helmets were thrown away, but the sense of danger remained. In the tour opener against Jamaica, Simpson, O'Neill and Cowper made centuries. So far, so good. But the issue overshadowing the tour revealed much about Simpson's strengths and weaknesses as a captain.

As ever, since the no-balling of Meckiff, the issue of chucking blended an unholy cocktail of opinion and politics. The West Indies' Charlie Griffith, a blatant chucker of his lethal faster ball and a much worse offender than Meckiff, was set to terrorise Simpson's Australians with impunity. Simpson could never quite unshackle himself from grievance, and Griffith's throwing, often hitting the Australian batsmen, deepened his feelings of persecution.

Yet it wasn't Griffith who brought Australia undone. In the two Test losses, it was Hall in Kingston and Gibbs's off-spin in Georgetown who bowled the series-deciding spells. The Australians kept griping about Griffith. Benaud, touring as a journalist, had photos taken of Griffith and wrote: 'He throws. I am quite convinced of this.' In Georgetown, the unacceptability (to Simpson) of the appointed umpires led to a West Indies selector and former captain, Gerry Gomez, standing. Altered rules allowed Hall to bowl to Bodyline fields, stacking five men behind square leg to Lawry. In Bridgetown, Griffith was warned for intimidation after aiming five bouncers in an over at Simpson's head.

Yet while they couldn't let go of their complaints, Simpson and his team also displayed great resilience. Their fielding was brilliant, and if any facet of the game is a barometer of a team's unity it is their fielding. Simpson scored 399 runs at 49.88, including 201 in an Australian record opening stand of 382 with Lawry at Bridgetown. Lawry, emerging from the hell of Kingston to make 368 Test runs at 52, scored 210. Batting is never harder than when the bowlers are not taking wickets, and Lawry and Simpson were forever batting in a crisis.

Simpson's team went down fighting, then won the consolation Fifth Test in Port-of-Spain. At the presentation of the Frank Worrell Trophy into West Indian hands for the first time, Simpson showed his two sides. He complained to Worrell that Griffith had chucked the Australians out. Yet in a good-humoured gesture of friendship he also presented his battered boots to Seymour Nurse, who had mocked their condition. With Simpson, little was ever straightforward or simplistic, and the most self-destructive, grudging attitude often coexisted with – and fed into – a doggedness that spurred him to superhuman feats. He seemed to need the siege mentality, and if the siege wasn't there, Simpson would invent it.

In the opening game of the 1965–66 season, Simpson's wrist was broken by Queensland speedster Peter Allan. His recovery took six weeks, by which time he missed the First Test against Mike Smith's Englishmen.

His replacement was his mild vice-captain, Brian Booth. Booth personifies the theory that the nice guys of Australian cricket were more likely to be stand-in captains than permanent. It should be clear that the ideal of the Australian captain as a paragon of fair play, charity and loving kindness is a complete fiction. Dave Gregory was a rogue on the cricket field, and many of his successors walked the fine line between wanting victory and scorching the earth to attain it.

Like Trumble, Morris and Brown, Booth was too nice to be a long-term Australian captain. But if, in the statuary of captains, he remains in the shadow of the giants surrounding him – Simpson, Lawry, Benaud, the Chappells – as a human being he has no peer.

Since his marvellous 1963–64 season, Booth had been up and down. As Simpson's vice-captain in England, Booth had an unhappy early tour, prompting arguments over whether Jack Potter should be picked ahead of him, until he redeemed himself with 98 at Old Trafford and a series-saving 74 at The Oval. On stormy tours, Booth provided a lighter contrast to his captain, and hit his first ball in the Indian Test series, at Madras, over the fence. A Church of England parish councillor, Booth was a square peg in a round hole during the fractious West Indies tour. He showed his best form in Port-of-Spain. Always an agile outfielder, he ran out Basil Butcher and Garry Sobers and then, against the searing Hall and the kinky Griffith, he stood up with Cowper and put on 252, one of the most courageous partnerships Australia has known. Griffith had sent O'Neill to hospital, and Simpson's unhappiness was turning the series into a bar-room brawl. Booth's 117 was, he said, his most satisfying Test innings.

When Allan broke Simpson's wrist in 1965, Booth was suddenly not a middle-order batsman fighting for his place but the 31st Australian Test captain. He had led NSW twice, for two losses. But Booth had respect. Most of his teammates had seen his Trinidad century. Among the others was a 19-year-old from the antbed wickets of Dungog called Doug Walters.

Booth won the toss in Brisbane and batted. He only scored 17 but the dashing teenager Walters's 155 brightened a rain-marred draw. Lawry also scored 166, but controversially. The English were sure he nicked David Brown to Jim Parks, but Lawry didn't walk, which English pressmen called a 'declaration of war'. Lawry simply did not believe in walking, saying it only tempted the batsman into hypocrisy. He wrote later: 'I despise a player who claims he is a walker and then, when the pressure is on, refuses to walk when he knows he is out.' For Lawry, it was easier to believe that luck evens out in the long run.

As captain, Booth tried to set different standards. Starting a new tradition, he stood outside the changing rooms and shook the hand of every Englishman as they came off. One of the only walkers, Booth also showed his principles when Geoff Boycott clearly handled the ball while batting. Booth refused to appeal, judging it a crummy way to get a man out. The contrast with Simpson couldn't have been more stark.

Simpson scored 59 and 67 in his return in Melbourne, another high-scoring draw, then contracted chickenpox before the Sydney Test. Booth, struggling with his form, was captain again. His thin bowling ranks were spanked by Bob Barber and punished in greyer style by Boycott and John Edrich. Fred Titmus and Brown broke through the Australian batting for an innings win. The English press goaded Lawry, dubbing him the '12th man' in England's winning effort because of his decision not to sacrifice himself when he and Burge got into a tangle.

Booth, with five failures in five appearances, was part of an old guard cleaned out for the next Test. Bradman, for the only time in his career as a selector, wrote to Booth stating his regret. 'I want you to know how much my colleagues and I disliked having to make this move,' Bradman wrote.

Booth played another two years for NSW, another eight for St George. Always more than a cricketer, he refused to play on Sundays and would join Trevor Goddard, David Sheppard and

Booth, too nice to be a long-term captain

Conrad Hunte to speak on cricket and the Christian life. He ran (and lost) in the 1974 federal election, standing as a Liberal for the seat of St George. His chairmanship of the NSW government's Youth Advisory Committee started a number of balls rolling to alleviate the effects of unemployment.

The earthy Wally Grout called him Gabriel, his ribbing containing equal parts affection and respect. Can a man be too principled to survive as the Australian captain? Because he was so upright, was Booth too soft to be a Test leader? If there is any truth in that, it reflects worse on the politics of the game than it does on Brian Booth.

In 1965–66, coming back from 0–1 with two to play was a Bob Simpson kind of situation. After a barren Third Test Graham McKenzie was dropped for Peter Allan in Adelaide, but when Allan pulled up shin-sore at training McKenzie was reprieved. Under Simpson's goading he took 6/48 to reduce England to 241 on a belter. Simpson and Lawry, with the Ashes on the line, set about batting England into submission.

'At a team discussion before the match,' Simpson wrote, 'we had decided we would not allow the English bowlers to dictate as they had done in the previous Test. Bill Lawry and I had privately decided we would try and break up the English attack by stealing and running short singles. From the first ball we played tip and run and within five or six overs the bowlers were becoming cross with the fieldsmen, the fieldsmen cross with the bowlers and so obsessed did they become they virtually stopped trying to get us out and concentrated upon trying to stop the singles. This was just what we wanted and as the fieldsmen moved in closer, we were able to stroke the ball through the gaps.' It was a classic Simpson guerilla tactic, the kind of cricket that relied on nous more than class, the approach he later instilled in teams he coached.

Lawry contributed 119, his second of three Test centuries that summer, to an Ashes record opening stand of 244. It contained 93 in singles. Simpson went on, and on. His first Test century in Australia, seven years after his first home Test, was predictably a big one. In nine hours, hampered by a gastric upset, he made 225, and by the time he was out England were broken.

Cowper's 307 and rain in Melbourne sealed the final draw, and the Ashes were retained. England's running battle with Lawry, on and off the field, was resolved in the Victorian's favour. Against the Englishmen that summer he batted for 41 hours, scoring 592 Test runs at 84.57, doing more than any other Australian to save the Ashes. If they wanted a personal battle, they had picked the wrong man. He made them pay outside the Tests too, scoring 153 and 61 for Victoria and 126 not out for a Combined XI. His total output against Smith's men was 979 at 97.90. Revenge indeed. Then, in the Melbourne district final against Essendon, Lawry batted as if in a Sixth Test. Essendon had made nine for 514. Over three consecutive Saturdays, Lawry batted and batted and batted until his 282 had ensured the trophy went to Northcote. As any good plumber would say: no job too small.

Although Australia had retained the Ashes, the cricket was dour. Neither side enjoyed great bowling depth, and Australia's lack of flair and flexibility would soon be exposed by a superior opponent.

Simpson's 1966–67 tour of South Africa exacerbated trends that had developed in the subcontinent and the West Indies. The umpiring was again dismal, and again Simpson could not leave bad decisions behind. He was snarling so bitterly about one poor decision that the next ball, nicked straight to him, he dropped, a mistake so rare that it lodged in his teammates' minds. Simpson's persecution complex spread. The team lost to Transvaal, Australia's first defeat in South Africa since tours started in 1902. With several of the Australian squad tiring of Simpson's unbending work ethic, their unity fractured. One player turned up at a social function wearing nothing but a jock strap, and a 'wild champagne party' was reported to have taken place on the eve of the First Test in Johannesburg.

The next morning, Australia had South Africa 5/41 but a grand fightback by wicketkeeper Denis Lindsay saw the hosts win by 233. At Cape Town Australia countered, Simpson's 153 propelling a six-wicket win with 24 minutes to spare on the last day. In Durban

Lindsay caned them again and, forced to follow on, Australia lost heavily. Another defeat at Port Elizabeth gave Australia a 3–1 series loss, its first against South Africa.

In retrospect, it is clear South Africa's team was developing into the world's finest. But Simpson's captaincy, so effective in picking young teams off the floor and making the most of limited resources, began to grate during long tours with mature teammates. His own batting was typically solid, with 1,344 runs including 243 against Northern Eastern Transvaal at Pretoria. But his constant criticism of umpires dragged down team morale. Given out in Durban, he stood his ground and glared at umpire Hayward Kidson, to whose appointment Simpson had objected, for so long that Dick Whitington wrote that Simpson's sportsmanship was questionable, his team out of control.

By mid-tour, everything was running against them. In Durban Lawry twice complained about Peter Pollock running on the wicket. Pollock retaliated with a bumper attack. Lawry, always a good hooker, went for his shots but eventually missed. A trip to hospital left him with 10 stitches, but back to Kingsmead he came, batting with a bandaged head for another 146 minutes. Asked later to pick his World XI, Pollock chose Lawry as opener. But Australia were thumped.

The crowds' barracking was often disgusting, and Simpson gave them further ammunition by criticising them as 'unsporting'. He physically confronted a photographer in Johannesburg who was approaching McKenzie. Even Benaud, the mildest of commentators, would sum up the Australians as the 'worst ever' to tour South Africa.

An interesting footnote was the South African board's proposal for a 50-overs match under floodlights. The Australian Board, myopic as ever, declined. But at tour's end a limited-overs international was played. Australia made a respectable eight for 327 in 50 eight-ball overs, but Graeme Pollock flogged them for the last of many occasions that summer with 132 off 98 balls, and South Africa won by three wickets.

Still only 32, Simpson had been a first-class cricketer for 15 years when he decided, in 1967–68, not to go on the next year's Ashes tour. Like Benaud he needed to secure a career and an income. Like Benaud, too, he abdicated the captaincy during a home series, this time against India. Australia had won the first two Tests easily, Simpson making a century in each. His batting was not flagging in the least: including a 277 against Queensland, his season's aggregate of 1,082 at 56.94 was unmatched.

The Board, unkindly, left him out of the Third Test at Brisbane, where Lawry became captain. As tough-minded as Australia had become under Simpson, they were fast haemorrhaging popularity. Lawry, so admired when he first appeared, was losing the nation's love. When Australia hosted India in Brisbane, Lawry's first Test as captain, the five-day crowd of 18,895 was the lowest ever in that city and the smallest five-day crowd in Australia since 1888. India was hardly an all-star outfit, but the unpopularity of cricket reflected Australia's feelings about its team. Lawry, as much as Simpson, embodied an ugliness that contrasted with the romanticised glamour of Benaud.

As Victorian captain since 1961–62, Lawry had shown his relentlessness. In his second full year as captain, Victoria won its first Shield in 12 seasons, Lawry's 133 against NSW the centrepiece of the campaign. As a leader he sapped opponents' hope. In its penultimate match Victoria needed to bowl Queensland out, but the tail-enders were resisting. Wes Hall, batting for Queensland, appealed against the light but was refused. Lawry took the second new ball and gave it to Meckiff. With 14 minutes to go, Meckiff trapped Hall and the Shield was won.

When Simpson gave him the Test captaincy, one of Lawry's first acts was to refuse Chandu Borde's request for a runner. The umpires overruled him. The press and crowds vilified him for taking his will to win too far.

He didn't receive an easy hand, being deprived of Simpson and unable to use his best bowler, McKenzie, who was being rested for the Ashes tour. Lawry lost the toss in his first two Tests but, sent in both times, his team won. In Brisbane it was a tight contest, only 39 runs separating the teams, but in Melbourne Australia won by a comfortable 144.

Lawry's first four innings as captain were 64, 45, 66 and 52. Crowds jeered him for overbowling the Victorians Connolly and Cowper – 'Give Gleeson a bowl, his grandmother's from Geelong!' they shouted – but Lawry didn't hear. He had two wins from two Tests, somewhat against the odds, and his own form was as strong as ever.

The Board allowed Simpson to return for a farewell Test in Sydney. He failed with the bat but, recalling his days as an all-rounder, wheeled in with his skilful leg-breaks and took 3/38 and 5/59, career-best figures that reminded everyone what a gifted natural talent lay beneath the pricklish captain and pragmatic batsman.

25

STORM AND STRESS

WINNING was everything to Lawry, but he was leading Australia into an era where his short-back-and-sides asceticism was past its day.

The team he took to England in 1968 was Australia's youngest ever, eight of the 17 making their Ashes debuts. While it looked like a team for the future, Lawry was entrenched in the mentality of the Simpson years. Much of the tour was blighted by rain. More than 100 hours would be lost, 49 of them in the first four matches and the team's aggregate was half that of the previous tour's. That was not Lawry's fault. Where he could be held to account was in his team's attitude, which was to scramble a win somewhere then hang on for dear life.

They obtained that advantage in the First Test at Old Trafford, where Lawry's 81 was a counter-attacking gem. Walters had his best Test on English soil, and a team bowling effort surprised England twice.

Ahead 1–0, saved by rain from certain loss at Lord's, Lawry took a page out of Simpson's 1964 book. At Edgbaston, defence and rain prevented Australia from losing. John Snow broke Lawry's finger in his first over, so, for the Fourth Test in Leeds, he handed the captaincy to his deputy, wicketkeeper Barry Jarman.

There had been an irony in the preference of Grout over Jarman because of spin, as Jarman built his South Australian career on taking spinners such as David Sincock, Rex Sellers, Ashley Mallett and Terry Jenner. But Jarman was too cheerful to stew over his bad luck. Ray Robinson wrote that 'nature had bestowed on him a double dose of enthusiasm'. Nine years younger than Grout, Jarman had every reason to believe his wait would be short. When this turned out to be incorrect, the dosage of Jarman's enthusiasm was tested.

Barry Jarman and Richie Benaud keep their hopes up as Ken Barrington dispatches the bowling

His Test appearances had been limited to Grout's unavailability: Kanpur in 1959–60, and two home Tests in 1962–63 when Grout had broken his jaw. Jarman took a catch in Melbourne, leaping one-handed down the leg-side to take Geoff Pullar off Graham McKenzie, that would live in folklore. In Sydney, Jarman's catch of Colin Cowdrey back-cutting a Simpson leg-break changed the course of the series.

On the way home in 1964, Jarman played Tests in Bombay and Calcutta when Grout again had taken a ball in the jaw, scoring a crucial 78 in the former game. He also made a handy 33 against Pakistan at Melbourne. The next season, playing for SA against NSW in Adelaide, he whacked a career-best 196 in 265 fun-filled minutes.

Jarman had made a success of his sports store, Rowe & Jarman. When the Pakistanis toured in 1964–65, they had taken thousands of pounds' worth of clothing and equipment on what they said was a credit note from the Pakistan Cricket Board. Jarman sent invoices to the PCB, but when ignored he took them to Bradman and the Australian Board. Other Australian traders were making similar complaints. The Board made noises about chasing the invoices, but did not do so successfully and did not compensate the defrauded retailers. The incident would, however, play a part in the cancellation of Australia's tour to Pakistan in 1969–70, and Pakistani players would not be invited back to Australia until 1972.

When Grout finally retired – at 38 – Jarman became Australia's first-choice wicketkeeper. Rosy-cheeked with sunburn, thickened in all of his parts as if permanently shown on wide-screen TV, he played all four Tests of the 1967–68 series, and as deputy was a jolly foil to the intense Lawry. But just as he was solidly in the Australian team, the curse struck. Taking a ball from McKenzie at Lord's, Jarman broke a finger in three places. Then, when he batted, a rearing delivery from David Brown crushed the same finger against his bat handle.

NSW's Brian Taber replaced him at Edgbaston, but then, when Lawry also broke his hand, Jarman's recuperation accelerated and he took the field as Australia's 33rd captain at Headingley.

Barry Jarman: captain for
one Test

He tossed with Tom Graveney, who, coincidentally, was replacing the injured Cowdrey. The series was poised with Australia 1–0 up, two Tests to play. A draw would retain the Ashes. Jarman had been uncharacteristically quiet in the lead-up. Captaincy at any level was a new challenge for him. Lawry, while assuring him that the team was his, flooded him with advice. Lawry's unremitting obsession with avoiding losing transmitted itself to Jarman, who, having taken up cigarettes to control his weight, was now chainsmoking.

Jarman's only Test as captain was attritional. Both teams batted stodgily, Jarman briefly enlivening things with a lightning leg-side catch of Keith Fletcher off Alan Connolly. Australia made 315, England 302, Australia 312, and so the last innings was set up, a day to play, with England needing 326 to win and Australia 10 wickets. Australia's main hope would have lain with the leg-spinner Johnny Gleeson, but Jarman, at Lawry's suggestion, gave the ball to the containers, McKenzie and Connolly. Gleeson only bowled 11 of 84 overs on a wearing wicket.

Australia did draw the match, so Jarman had carried out his captain's commission. But few were happy about the way they had played. Ian Chappell came into the changing room, hurled down his cap in disgust, and said to Lawry: 'If that's Test cricket you can stick it up your jumper.' Lawry replied: 'We have done what we came over here to do, and that was to win the Ashes.'

At The Oval, after Lawry's 135 in seven and a half hours, English journalist Ian Wooldridge dubbed him 'the corpse with pads'. John Inverarity took four hours for a half-century in the second innings but he was battling hard to save the game. But after yet more rain Derek Underwood bowled England to a series-levelling win.

Lawry's long nose had been hard from the outset. Where Test teams were customarily nominated a day before the match, Lawry followed the letter of the law and named his team an hour before play. Yet Lawry's defensiveness did know limits. At The Oval, he gained much credit for not allowing his batsmen to engage in time-wasting that might have saved the match. True, the Ashes were no longer at stake, but other captains might have been tempted to slow the bowling rate by unsporting means.

Lawry schooled his team, Simpson-style, in the one-percenters. Paul Sheahan won a prize of £100 as best fielder in the series, and Jack Fingleton wrote: 'The flannels of the two teams tell the story. The English leave the field spotless at the knees whereas the Australians have green stains because they fling themselves at the ball.'

Then there was Lawry's indomitable batting, which netted 270 Test runs in a low-scoring series. English journalist John Woodcock wrote: 'Lawry is a great battler and a wonderfully sound judge of length. All too often he has been the rock on which England have foundered.'

Notwithstanding the negatives, Lawry had achieved what he went to England to do.

Late in the tour, Lawry led his men in a mini-rebellion. Tour manager Bob Parish told the Board that the players were not coming home on the scheduled flight three days after The Oval Test. Some wanted to play for extra money in the Scarborough Festival, while others wanted to play county cricket. The Test series had been played in competition with a private 'International Cavaliers' series, in which cricketers were being paid more than in the Tests. Lawry and his teammates wanted to cash in. The Board's response was not to loosen but to tighten the stays, increasing contractual restrictions and inciting a grievance that, in Lawry's case, would turn him from captain into card-carrying rebel within 10 years.

The dispute left a taint of ill-will. Hosting the West Indies the next summer, Lawry's team began poorly, losing the First Test in Brisbane by 125 runs. He was criticised, again, for relying on his medium-pacers rather than the off-spinner Mallett. Another talking point was how umpire Col Egar, so quick to drum Meckiff out of the game, could have been blind to the blatant bend in Charlie Griffith's arm.

Griffith and Hall were shadows of their former selves, however, and both broke down. Once they were gone, so was the aura of West Indian menace. Lawry, who scored 105 in Brisbane, almost doubled it in Melbourne. McKenzie, with 8/71, showed his durability. Lawry made two more half-centuries in Adelaide and 151 in Sydney, Ian

Chappell and Walters also had prolific summers, and the captain, a winner by three Tests to one, declared: 'Revenge is sweet', as it is when sought obsessively. Even with the West Indies in manifest decline, Lawry clung to the bitter memories of 1965, to the point where, if a West Indian batsman wanted an unscheduled drink of water, he objected. He would rather break than bend, and he soon would.

Lawry did get the best out of his men – particularly the many Victorians. Before the Third Test he told Keith Stackpole he wanted him as his opening partner. Stackpole had been failing in the middle order and so had Redpath at the top. Lawry, appreciating the light and shade in a partnership he might form with Stackpole, switched them. Stackpole was so nervous he couldn't buckle his pads, but he scored 58, 21 not out, 62 and 50 and his career was rejuvenated.

The Adelaide Test was an exciting draw, Sheahan and Connolly holding on for 27 balls. When Griffith Mankaded Redpath without warning, so vocal was the Australian response that the West Indian captain, Sobers, came to Lawry and apologised for forgetting himself.

The series saw the full flowering, after six frustrating years, of Ian Chappell. Four half-centuries in the 1968 Ashes series had cemented Chappell into the middle order, but it wasn't until Lawry promoted him to three against the West Indies that Chappell found his niche. Lawry was accused of favouring his Victorians – Cowper, then Redpath – in the pivotal role, and there were questions about Chappell's ungainly technique. Fingleton wrote, 'Chappell is a rare fighter even if he sometimes twists his feet into some agitated knots.'

In his first innings at three, Chappell scored 117, then 165 (the thousandth century in Test cricket), 76 and 96, and five centuries in all cricket against Sobers's tourists. It was a surprise, however, when Chappell was made vice-captain after Jarman was dropped for the Fifth Test. Like Jarman, he had no captaincy experience, having played under Les Favell in Adelaide. But Lawry liked his fight. When Griffth Mankaded Redpath in Adelaide, Chappell took visible exception. His pugnacity marked him out as a street fighter.

The selectors elevated him without knowing what they'd gotten themselves into.

Chappell had attended Prince Alfred College, alma mater of Clem Hill and Joe Darling, but left at 17 to work as a sharebroking clerk and dedicate himself to cricket and his winter sport, baseball, in which, emulating his grandfather Victor Richardson, he represented Australia.

There are many cricketing dynasties: the Gregorys, the Hills, the Giffens, the Trotts, the Trumbles, the Harveys, the Benauds, and, more recently, the Waughs. But no family's influence compares with the Richardson-Chappells. Four Test cricketers, three captains. All four could take their place in an all-time Australian fielding XI.

Richardson had surprisingly little input into Ian's cricketing formation. The adamantine hardness of Ian's father Martin played a greater part. From his sons' accounts, Martin Chappell must have been a mongrel to play against. He toughened Ian against fast bowling by throwing bumpers, with a real cricket ball, off the hard backyard pitch he had laid. When the child faced adult bowlers, Martin scolded him for backing away. The only requisite of batting against Martin was courage. Technique could follow.

Ian Chappell, pre-moustache and full of fight

Ian's coach from an early age was a family friend, Lynn Fuller, who reinforced the Richardson-Chappell attitude with finer points on shot selection, footwork and outcricket. By 19, Ian had scored enough runs and taken enough wickets with his clever leg-spin for Glenelg to get a run for SA. In his second match, a rout by Lawry's Victorians, Chappell's second-innings 59 was the highest home score.

His batting would take a decade to mature. Of average height and weight, his thick lower lip a dead ringer for his grandfather's, he attracted attention for his gestures and fidgets. When he walked onto a field to bat, his collar turned up, he would raise his eyes to the sky and blink repeatedly. He never listened to outgoing batsmen's remarks, preferring to take things as he found them. At the wicket his tics involved adjustments to his equipment, most often his protector, and repeated scratchings of his guard. He took strike with a busy front-on stance and his first movement was back and across, as if preparing to hook every ball. He started and finished his career as a compulsive and mostly productive hooker, with a pause in his middle years when even his grandmother advised him to give the shot a miss.

In 1962, after three games with SA, he went to the Lancashire League's Ramsbottom, but without great success. Batting for SA below a strong line-up including Sobers, Favell, future federal frontbencher Ian McLachlan and Ken Cunningham, Chappell scored 149 in a win over NSW, as well as contributing handily with his wrist-spinners.

In 1963–64 Favell moved him up and down the order until, at the Gabba, at three, Chappell hooked and cut his way to 205 not out. He had found his position: Bradman's, Hill's, Harvey's.

In his first Shield match of the next season Chappell's 127 against Victoria earnt him a Test debut against Pakistan. Simpson put him at third slip for McKenzie's first over. On the third delivery, Abdul Kadir slashed and Chappell, touching a Test cricket ball in play for the first time, took the catch.

He only scored 11, but his season was productive, with 678 at 52.15. It was a shock, then, that he was left out of the 1965 tour of the West Indies. Simpson, not knowing if Chappell could control his hooking against Griffith and Hall, had advised him to delete the shot. From his own experience, Simpson believed greatness came from narrowing the repertoire. Chappell played in some confusion until Bradman asked him why he'd renounced hooking. He told Chappell not to give it up, just to play it better.

Missing an unsuccessful tour might have been a blessing in disguise, but Chappell was out of the Test team until midway through the 1965–66 Ashes series, when after a rich run of domestic form he was brought in with fresh faces Stackpole and Veivers. But then and in South Africa, he seemed more than a Shield batsman, but not quite Test grade. He believed that the Second Test against India in 1967–68, at the MCG, might be his last. After three years and nine Tests, he had still not scored a half-century.

Coming in at three for 246, he was dropped three times. But for clumsy Indian hands, Australian cricket might have taken a different direction. But the good batsman always makes clumsy fielders pay, and Chappell made 151. Having taken three years to establish himself, he would now be a first-choice batsman until retirement.

For all Australia's dominance and Lawry's personal success, in 1968–69 the game was still losing popularity. The series attracted 427,940 fans, compared with 734,892 in 1960–61. In umpires' reports, Australian players were being named for poor behaviour. Lawry would be held responsible for an increasing loutishness. Pollard wrote that Lawry 'typified the loss of decorum among Australia's top players'. The Melbourne Cricket Club historian Alf Batchelder said Lawry personified 'the qualities which made Victorian cricketers hated in other states'.

Lawry was to take a team to Pakistan and India in 1969–70, but when the Pakistan Cricket Board could not guarantee the tour's costs, that leg was called off. South Africa stepped in, and the Australian Board accepted an invitation to go straight from India to South Africa which meant that there would be nine Tests in 15 playing weeks separated by a month for travel and acclimatisation.

The Indian tour was unprecedentedly difficult. Lawry's problems were not, initially, of his making. On the team's first night in India, more than 3,000 demonstrators picketed their hotel in protest at Walters's national service in Vietnam. In the tour match in Bangalore, spectators unhappy at Australia's time-soaking batting showered the field with stones. Lawry had aroused their ire by stopping play when a woman in a sari walked in front of the sightscreen. He would be accused of insulting Indian womanhood. Then, when a stone hit him on the pad, the umpires agreed to bring forward the scheduled close. For Lawry, a draw was too often as good as a win.

Before the First Test in Bombay, there was outcry at the omission of off-spinner Srinivas Venkataraghavan. As appeasement, medium pacer Subrata Guha stepped aside. In the second innings, with Australia needing three wickets to win the match, Venkat was given out caught behind off Connolly when his bat kicked up a spray of dust. Radio commentators opined that Venkat was not out, and

Lawry, they said, should have called Venkat back. Lawry, of course, had no such intention. He had already put himself offside with the crowd, when he hurled down his cap in dismay at the umpires not giving Australia a last over before lunch.

Upon Venkat's dismissal, the crowd hurled bottles, fruit and rocks, and the incoming batsman, Erapalli Prasanna, needed a police escort. A bottle struck Gleeson on the head. A wicker chair hit Lawry. Another day remained, and some of Lawry's teammates thought it best to go off and return on a quieter fifth morning. Fans outside the ground were setting fire to cars and sporting equipment, causing smoke to shroud the Brabourne. Chappell urged his captain to take the team off, but Lawry was supernaturally oblivious, replying: 'Hell, we need a wicket badly.'

Australia got one more wicket and returned to a near-empty Brabourne the next day, the police having barred entry. In an un-Indian silence, Australia took the last wickets and knocked up two for 67 to win. But at what cost? Ajit Wadekar would write of Lawry's lack of 'graciousness' in playing through the tumultuous fourth day. Lawry's view was that he could not risk missing a victory for which his team had worked so hard.

Sheahan made a game century in a Kanpur draw, and at Delhi Australia lost but Lawry produced characteristic heroism, carrying his bat for 49 not out in the second innings of 107.

At 1–1, the series was set up for a pulsating Fourth Test in Calcutta. One night during the match, 30,000 lined up for 8,000 tickets. Jostling turned into a stampede, hundreds were injured and six died. Australia's manager Fred Bennett led an initiative to donate money to the victims' families. But during the match, Lawry stamped himself finally as India's public enemy number one. Stories circulated that Lawry had, on a train out of Delhi, thrown a plate of curry at the wall. In Calcutta, Australia, on top thanks to Chappell's 99 and McKenzie's 6/67, were chasing 42 to win. The crowd rioted, possibly intending to stop the game. If anyone stood between him and a Test win, Lawry was ferocious. Lawry gestured at a photographer with his bat. Reports vary on what happened, but Lawry maintained that he never struck the photographer. The man fell on his camera and broke it, and thereafter the Indian photographic corps wore black armbands in protest.

Australia won, and capped the series with a 77-run victory in Madras. A 3–1 success was a great achievement for Lawry, in the circumstances. He had countered the general criticism that he neglected spinners by letting Mallett have his head. The off-spinner rewarded his captain with 28 wickets in the five Tests. McKenzie took 21. Stackpole, Chappell and Redpath led the batting.

Lawry would later report to the Board questioning security arrangements in India and attacking immoderate elements of the country's administration and media. As usually happened, the Board would scapegoat Lawry and, when his views became public, apologise to India and distance itself from his opinions.

But he left India a winner. Like many a victorious campaign, however, it exhausted the victor. Flying to South Africa, Lawry's men had fewer than three weeks to adapt to a vastly different challenge: Tests on hard, grassy, bouncy wickets against the best fast bowling in the world. Lawry declared that Chappell, who had made scores of 99 and 138 in the Indian series, was the world's best batsman. Lawry saw no need to defend his genuine opinion but Chappell, with a target on his back, was not the only Australian who could not adjust, technically and mentally, so soon.

After some promising early results, Australia capitulated in the Tests. Eddie Barlow made a hundred and Peter Pollock dismissed Lawry and Chappell in his first four balls of the series. From there it was a slippery slope. Australia lost by 170 at Cape Town, and no other Test was that close. They went down by an innings at Durban, 307 in Johannesburg and 323 in Port Elizabeth. Graeme Pollock, Barlow, Lee Irvine and Barry Richards destroyed them with the bat, and Peter Pollock and Mike Proctor with the ball. Chappell recorded 92 runs at 11.50 – thanks Bill! – Lawry 193 at 24.13. McKenzie, spent after India, took one wicket for 333.

It was hardly surprising that Australia lost, but the size and manner of their defeats betrayed a team drained of all unity. They dropped more than 20 catches, 13 off Gleeson. Lawry disputed decisions and bickered with the crowds. Never a great socialiser, he retreated rather than bond with his or Ali Bacher's men. He was thought aloof and petulant. Consequently, some of the Australian players spent more time in factions or with their opponents than as a team. They could barely wait for the thing to end.

There was a hellish moment when an extra Test seemed possible. South Africa wanted one. Why wouldn't they? They asked the Australian Board to pay its players an extra $200 a head. Australia refused. The tour had made more than $250,000 profit. This time, the Board's parsimony was appreciated by Lawry's exhausted rabble.

26

THE ASSASSINATION OF LAWRY

HE win in India a distant memory, Australia was consumed
by the thrashing in South Africa, for which Lawry received his
share of blame. With a tough-looking England team coming under
Ray Illingworth, Lawry set himself to reply in the only language
he knew.

His early season was steady, with 145 for once out against WA.
But the first two Tests, high-scoring draws, renewed criticism of
Lawry's captaincy. Illingworth was scarcely more adventurous, but
not even the emergence of Ian Chappell's younger brother Greg,
with a richly promising debut century in Perth, and a thick-set but
agile wicketkeeper named Rodney Marsh could lighten the feeling
that Australia, and the game itself, was being weighed down by the
tactics of a man who hated losing too much to risk winning.

Greg Chappell's century was truly a breath of fresh air. Selected
as an all-rounder, batting seven and bowling first change, he had
already taken his debut Test wicket, snaring a return chance from
Cowdrey. Faced with England's 397, Australia were 5/107 when
Greg joined Redpath. Snow and Peter Lever were rampant on the
WACA trampoline. Digging in, Greg took 67 minutes to eke out his

first 10 runs and more than three hours to get to 50. Then he took just 58 minutes to cruise to 100, fooling ABC-TV, which had put on the evening news instead of the cricket. When Greg was out for 108, the match was on its way to being saved.

He was a serious insect, sharing Ian's lack of subtlety but without the people skills. Interviewed after his century, he said: 'Maybe I'll be Greg Chappell from now on, not Ian's young brother or Victor Richardson's grandson.'

It is the miserable fate of younger brothers to be compared with their elders – Greg had played under Ian's nameplate on the Adelaide Oval scoreboard – but Martin and Jeanne Chappell's second son was determined to grow up in nobody's shadow. However fine a batsman Ian would turn out, Greg was always going to be better. Coached by Lynn Fuller and Prince Alfred's Chester Bennett, he distinguished himself from Ian by his attention to stylistic details. When Greg got out in backyard games, he would change into new gear and re-emerge as a new 'Test' batsman. While Ian had a rough-and-ready look, Greg was buttoned down. Ian's hair was finger-combed into a tenuous centre-part, while Greg's was an immovable Brillo pad. None of Ian's fidgety, ready-to-hook shuffling for Greg, who stood and walked with a long back that would have been a yoga instructor's joy. When he made his first-class debut in 1966–67 – the summer Ian went to South Africa under Simpson – Greg stroked 53 and 62 not out off unsuspecting Victorian bowlers. He followed up with 61 and 68 not out in the two matches against NSW, 104 in Brisbane, and, the next summer, 154 in batting his team out of a crisis against WA. The runs were one thing, the style quite another. His blood ran cooler than Ian's, his drives, pulls and cuts closer to the ground. He started as a back-foot player in Ian's vein, but his love of the vee between mid-off and mid-on, where he tried to play all his shots early in his innings, made a forward movement imperative. He gave the impression that not even an earthquake could have knocked him off balance.

Greg also started as a leg-spinner like Ian, but two seasons in Somerset persuaded him that he could do more damage with his gangling cut and swing. (He did literal damage for SA one day, killing a seagull midflight and bowling John Inverarity. The umpire, Egar, pronounced the ball dead. The bird was too.)

Under expat Australian Bill Alley at Somerset from 1968, Greg also waterproofed his batting, scoring nearly 3,000 runs in all forms of the game and, with an unbeaten 128 in 100 minutes, the first century in the 40-over Sunday League.

As with Bradman and Trumper, Greg's health fluctuated. Like them, sickness often made him bat better. A few years later, in 1974–75, Greg would battle with tonsillitis and bronchial problems throughout a series in which he scored two centuries, five half-centuries, averaged 55 and took a world catching record. In 1969–70, struggling with flu against NSW, he made a century in 92 minutes. A month earlier, a dislocated thumb didn't prevent twin centuries against Queensland. At the end of the season, he toured New Zealand with a B team under Queensland's Sam Trimble and, alongside the long-haired speedster Dennis Lillee, was the standout young player. One great player was rising. Two, three or four could make something special.

In the Fourth Test at Sydney in 1970–71, after the Third had been rained out, the stalemate broke England's way. Lawry, whose confidence in Stackpole had produced the opener's career-best 207 in Brisbane, now bizarrely backtracked, dropping the Victorian down the order and elevating Ian Chappell, who failed in both innings. Boycott made a century and Snow, menacing in the early Tests, ripped through the Australians with 7/40. Only one man remained undefeated: Lawry, 60 not out in a score of 116, carrying his bat for a record fifth time.

Top-order decency was restored in Adelaide and a new fast bowler was brought in: Lillee, the leonine tearaway from Perth. He was successful immediately, but two more Tests were drawn. Lawry, who could do nothing right in many Australian eyes, was pilloried in Melbourne for declaring when Marsh was eight runs short of becoming the first Australian wicketkeeper to score a Test century.

Lawry tossing with Ray Illingworth, 1970–71

The series remained alive, however, and Australia could still win in Sydney and retain the Ashes for a 13th year. Lawry was looking forward to a final showdown.

The Board had other ideas. They had still not responded to Lawry's stinging report on the Indian tour, lodged 10 months earlier. Bradman, leading the South Australian contingent, wanted to ignore it. He was beaten by one vote on that, and the Board responded in an insipid, uncommitted letter two days before the Seventh Test at Sydney. Bradman, piqued by losing the vote and endlessly irritated by Lawry, now pulled another coup, convincing a Board majority to sack the captain.

The Board did not have the decency to tell him. Lawry found out he had been dumped, after 67 Tests, 5,234 runs at 47.15, 13 centuries and 25 appearances as captain, over the radio.

There were good reasons, but the timing and manner of his sacking carried all the hallmarks of Board arrogance and vindictiveness. Lawry had spoken trenchantly on his players' behalf about the Board's exploitation of them in South Africa. Lawry was not the best Australian captain, although to achieve victory in India and secure the Ashes in England with limited bowling were feathers in his cap. He was an unyielding captain for often desperate times, even if he made them seem more desperate than they were. McKenzie aside, he never had a great bowler, and sometimes McKenzie was all he had. His complexity as a character – unguessable from the single hysterical note of his television commentary – made him one of the more interesting captains in an era when Australian cricket was neither as enterprising nor as tolerant as it could have been.

In no sense did the Board consider the consequences of their actions. Lawry's replacement would be a far greater captain and a bigger headache than any director could have imagined.

Lawry's replacement as opener was 35-year-old Ken Eastwood, whose first Test, against Snow in Sydney, would also be his last. Lawry played on for Victoria for another season. He remained Australia's premier opening batsman, notching a century and four fifties. His final game, in March 1972, was against SA on his beloved MCG. Ian Chappell made 106 as South Australia set Victoria 299 to win. Lawry's last stand went for 190 minutes. His 61 laid a platform as if this were the most important game he had ever played. In future years, he and Chappell would become friends and colleagues, both in the World Series rebellion and as Channel Nine co-commentators. The manner of his sacking showed the two captains that they had far more in common with each other than either had with the Board. Swayed by his friendship with Chappell, Lawry would split from Simpson. New loyalties were always being formed, old ones broken.

But on that last afternoon in Melbourne, Lawry and Chappell were implacable foes. Lawry set Victoria up, and with seven wickets down and 50 minutes to spare, they won the match. To Lawry, all the negative tactics and intensity and inflexibility were in the service of a greater aim: finishing ahead on the scoreboard. Few players so deserved to go out of the game a winner.

27

LEADING IN THE SEVENTIES

I N any story, few devices are more powerful than the buried idea:
the clue that is laid, then left concealed, to grow in the darkness
until its time arrives.

In the narrative of the Australian captaincy, that buried idea was
Victor Richardson. In the 1930s, Richardson represented a stream in
Australian cricket that might be called anti-Bradmanism. As captain
on the 1935–36 tour of South Africa, the free-wheeling Richardson
gave his men the freedom and confidence they would be denied
under the more controlling Bradman. Under Richardson they were
equals, treated as grown men rather than potential trouble. Under
Richardson, they did not have to suffer the two-tiered status that
came with Bradman.

Richardson had Clarrie Grimmett, Bill O'Reilly, Jack Fingleton
and others who were sometimes discontented with Bradman. But
Richardson was not a real alternative. Nearly a decade older than
Bradman, he was 41 when he became captain, and was seldom quite
good enough to command a regular Test place.

Richardson was swept away by Bradman's arrival in Adelaide.
Indeed, Bradman was recruited from NSW in part to force out the
militant Richardson.

On his retirement, Bradman became one of the bosses: Board
director, selector and chairman. The last vestiges of player power

were lost under his authority. From the 1920s to the 1970s, power lay unquestionably with the Board, and even though it managed tours badly and paid the players poorly and irritated a succession of captains, the Board's fundamental control was beyond dispute. If players wanted a better deal, they would – like Bradman – have to seek those deals as individuals. Collective player power had died in 1912.

But the historic grievances never went away. By the end of the 1960s, respect for the silver-haired men of the boardroom was not automatic. Cricket's income had soared without much return to the players. Simpson and Lawry had complained, but the Board regarded player welfare as a second-order issue. If the captain made a fuss, he was dispensable.

It would take an advanced-generation Richardson type to translate discontent into revolution. When we look at the captains, there is only a handful who changed the game. Dave Gregory, certainly, because of the 1878 tour. Murdoch, by carrying on Gregory's legacy. Darling and Woodfull were great captains, but they didn't change the game. Bradman did, but as an individual more than as a captain. Benaud brought a new brightness, but 1960–61 was a false dawn. Simpson would be a towering figure, but more by attrition over four decades than in his first stint as captain.

It can only be said that three captains changed cricket fundamentally: Dave Gregory, Don Bradman and Ian Chappell.

By 1971, Favell's retirement had given Ian Chappell some captaincy experience in SA. He followed Favell's precepts of keeping the matchplay simple and the team enjoying each other's company.

When Lawry was sacked, Australia were only 0–1 down after six Tests, though England were thoroughly on top. Boycott, Brian Luckhurst and Edrich were ruling the new-ball exchanges on one side, Snow and, to a lesser extent, Bob Willis on the other. Rearguard batting from Lawry, Stackpole, Redpath, Walters and both Chappells had stopped a rout, but the Australian bowling had lacked penetration until the debut of Lillee. Carrying the home attack for the first five Tests were McKenzie, 'Froggy' Thomson,

Connolly, one-Test Ross Duncan and Johnny Gleeson. By the time Ian Chappell became captain, all but Gleeson were finished in Test cricket.

Chappell's century in the Fifth Test in Melbourne had been something of a lowlight. Field invasions, a new trend, were now customary when a player raised three figures. Chappell was stampeded, his baggy green cap stolen. He told *The Age*: 'I was petrified I'd fall and be trampled under all those feet. If it hadn't been for a couple of strong spectators who tried to protect me, I'm sure I would have fallen.' Even for the larrikin, there were limits.

For the decider in Sydney, he won the toss and for the first time in his 10 matches as a captain sent the opponent in: a statement of aggression on an underprepared wicket. Lillee, playing his second Test, and Queensland's Tony Dell, playing his first, took early wickets, then leg-spinners Terry Jenner and Kerry O'Keeffe ran through the tail, and England's vaunted line-up was out for 184. But before stumps, Stackpole and Eastwood were out. Two minutes before the close, Chappell himself was in the middle to partner nightwatchman Marsh.

On day two, a Saturday, the Australians were fighting for a lead. Chappell, Redpath and Walters could not build starts into centuries. Greg Chappell was batting with Jenner late in the afternoon, a brave stand taking Australia's advantage past 50, when Illingworth moved into short leg. Snow bounced Jenner and hit him in the head. Jenner had to go off, and umpire Lou Rowan warned Snow for intimidation. Snow and Illingworth objected: he had only bowled one bouncer, they said, and the fact that it had hit Jenner was neither here nor there.

'Crowds will be crowds,' as Dick Whitington wrote, 'and they rarely get their facts straight.' The Sydney crowd turned on Snow, and Illingworth sent his fast bowler, provocatively, to the fence. It rained cans and one spectator grabbed Snow's shirt. Illingworth took his team off, leaving the umpires and batsmen in the centre. With the series at such a critical juncture, Illingworth's motives may be questioned. But the crowd did give him an excuse. After the umpires ordered Illingworth to restart the game or face a forfeit,

Australia lost momentum and were soon all out. England set them 223 to win, which was enough, even without Snow, who broke his hand on the fourth day, to take home the Ashes for the first time since 1958–59.

Chappell's initiation was a prophetically violent affair. Test cricket in the 1970s would resemble war without the shooting, and the wild events of Sydney's Seventh Test would set the tone.

The sowing had been done, but the reaping would take a few years yet. After the pandemonium of the Springbok rugby tour of Australia in the winter of 1971, the Board reluctantly came to see that it would be impossible to provide security for a South African cricket tour the following summer. So Australia hosted a World XI in 1971–72. Ian Chappell had one of his best summers, scoring five centuries and five half-centuries. Before he became captain, his Test average had been 36. In five years at the helm, he averaged 47. He began the series with a century in each innings, and ended it with 111 not out in the Adelaide 'Test', out of 201, one of the best innings of the era. Australia lost 1–2, but the form of both Chappells, Marsh and, particularly, Lillee set Australia up nicely for the 1972 Ashes tour.

Greg had just emerged from a personal batting crisis. Up to 1971–72, he had been scoring so heavily on the on-side that Favell had to remind him 'there are two sides of the wicket'. Bradman suggested changing his grip. Struggling with the adaptation, and a youthful newlywed at 23, Greg was 12th man for the first two Tests against the World XI. Recalled, he made 72 runs in four innings but then made sure he had been omitted for the last time, with 115 not out in Sydney and 197 not out in Melbourne, finishing the series second only to his brother with 425 runs at 106.25.

Already a comradely air was developing among the young team. They were criticised for their casual attire and behaviour, but were more attuned to their times than were their critics. Pollard wrote of Ian Chappell: 'No player has had more influence on Australian cricket over the past 20 years but it is doubtful if he has used his unique position in the best interests of himself or the game.' Time would come down more on Chappell's side than Pollard's.

Ian Chappell leads out the 1972 Australians. Greg follows.

Chappell – who, having missed his flight to join the 1968 Ashes tourists, would have seen the hypocrisy in turning martinet – encouraged team bonding through drinking sessions, and trusted his players. Unlike the controlling Simpson or the tightly wound Lawry, Chappell had a laissez-faire attitude that might have gone amiss in other generations but was perfect for this one. Barry Richards, who watched Chappell from the World XI and later in Sheffield Shield and WSC, said: 'He gave every player a chance to use his own judgment, without making too many demands.'

The 1972 Australians were notorious for the purple jumpsuit Chappell wore on the Lord's balcony and the shared atrocity of mauve safari suits. Sussex beat them for the first time since 1888 when Chappell declared early, setting the county 261 to win in 180 minutes. Transplanted South African Tony Greig led the historic chase, and Australia's tour appeared consigned to the fate of all rebuilding phases.

But England, so powerful 18 months earlier, were already slipping. Lillee's startlingly fast outswing matched Snow in the First Test, which England won narrowly. At Lord's, West Australian debutant Bob Massie became the classic exemplar of a journeyman raised to immortality by Ian Chappell's belief. A humble individual,

Massie swung the ball as if he had it on a string. His 16 wickets, backed up by Greg Chappell's century, gave Australia its first Ashes Test victory in four years.

As with Ian in 1968, an Ashes tour turned Greg's promise into substance. At Lord's, joining Ian at two for seven, already 0–1 down in the series, Greg controlled the pace of the game, subduing Snow for six hours in an innings of 131 that was one of the best of his career.

The Third Test was drawn, and Underwood's left-arm darts destroyed Australia on a fungus-impaired turner at Headingley. The Ashes gone, Greg went for all-out attack at The Oval. Lillee took five wickets in each innings and the Chappells, combining as no siblings had ever done in Tests, scored centuries in a stand of 201 in four hours. *Wisden* crowned Greg one of its cricketers of the year and England swooned at his technical correctness and fastidious bearing, a sign that the Chappell blood wasn't all rough.

Australia still needed 242 in the fourth innings, but Stackpole's 79 and a radiant partnership between Sheahan and Marsh guided them to a win that was celebrated as the turning point of Australian cricket.

The series generated a record gate of £261,283, of which Ian Chappell's players received little more than £1,000 each.

If there was a criticism of Chappell's captaincy, it was that he overbowled his pacemen. Unlike Benaud, who loved Davidson up for that one last over, Chappell mocked his fast bowlers, insulting their manhood when they grew tired. Like his father and grandfather, he liked to goad the best out of others. After working Lillee hard in England, he gave him even heavier duties against Intikhab Alam's Pakistanis at home. Chappell blamed the scheduling – three Tests in three weeks – for the wear and tear on his bowlers, but the Board had some justification in asking why Lillee had requested permission to play a season of county cricket with Derbyshire, a request the Board refused.

Something was building. On the field, Chappell's leadership against a strong Pakistan team was masterly. His first innings declaration worked on the Melbourne Test, said Robinson, 'like yeast'. In Sydney Johnny Watkins, a laughing stock after finding difficulty landing the ball on the pitch, emerged with his bat and helped Massie stage the most unlikely comeback. From eight for 101, 75 runs ahead, Watkins and Massie helped Australia get a lead of 158. Lillee and wrong-footed Victorian newcomer Max Walker did the rest.

Australia's vibrant 3–0 win emboldened Ian Chappell. He was batting superbly, making 196 in the First Test. His popularity with the public recalled Benaud. He requested an invitation to address the Board on issues of player welfare.

In a meeting on 5 January 1973 in Sydney, Chappell deferentially laid out his concerns. Tours of England, he said, were too long and demanding. A player-board liaison officer could be appointed to facilitate communication. Payment incentives and a benevolent fund could be set up to give players a stake in the income they were generating. Captains should be able to report candidly on umpiring standards.

It's easy to picture the scene. Chappell, in wide lapels and flared trousers, earnestly making the best of a rare opportunity to address the old men. And the delegates sitting before him in a grey wall of silence. Chappell wrote later: 'They just did not understand what I was saying.'

Chappell's team to tour the West Indies had been chosen the day before. Sheahan and Mallett could not afford to go. Sheahan described himself as 'a schoolteacher first and a cricketer second'. Mallett, a journalist, did not earn enough from cricket to risk losing his job.

The Board responded to Chappell's presentation over three weeks. It issued the players with orders limiting what they could write, how they could speak to the media, when they could take their wives on tour (only after the last match), when they were required to wear dinner suits, how they had to pay for their own alcohol, and finally – a throwback to Johnson and Miller in 1955 – that they were not to command any aircraft. Such overkill was a thinly coded rebuff. Chappell was being told not just to keep his mouth shut, but that if he didn't keep it shut he would lose his job like Lawry.

But Chappell, like Murdoch nine decades earlier, was building a power base. The West Indies tour ended in triumph. The first two Tests were drawn, and Lillee finally succumbed to the fractures that had been creeping up his back for two seasons. Chappell was now reliant on Walker, South Australia's Jeff Hammond, O'Keeffe and Walters. Massie, injured and out of form, showed his team spirit by teaching Walker his outswinger. Before the Third Test, Chappell sprained his ankle playing tennis, but he did not think the team could do without him at Port-of-Spain. A brilliant Walters century gained Australia a lead, then Chappell, batting in intense pain, squeezed out 97.

Thanks to his fighting innings Australia's lead was 333, but the West Indians were making light work of it at four for 268 at lunch on the last day. Chappell gave his team an earful, telling them to concentrate on what they had done well: tight bowling, enthusiastic fielding, keeping the pressure on. He seemed the only one still thinking of a win. The West Indies needed 66. But five wickets fell for 21 and a fired-up Australia won by 44.

Another Ian Chappell century, and wickets to Walker and Jeff Hammond, sealed a 2–0 series victory in Guyana. Chappell came home unquestionably secure as the captain. Having worked as a sales representative for chocolate and tobacco companies in Adelaide, he now ran his own business, Ian Chappell Enterprises, following Benaud and Simpson into sports media, management and promotional work.

Like all Test cricketers, he needed supplementary income. During the next summer, in which Australia played six Tests, home and away, against a very good New Zealand team, Chappell earned about $4,000 from cricket. His men made even less. They gave the newly renamed Australian Cricket Board good value. Both Chappells plundered runs on the New Zealand leg, becoming, in Wellington, the first brothers to make centuries in both innings of one match. In Adelaide, Ian had equalled his grandfather's record of six catches in a Test.

But in Christchurch he was involved in a clash that would dim his popularity.

The incident started when New Zealand's captain, Bevan Congdon, hit Mallett for a one-bounce four. Umpire Bob Monteith signalled six, and Chappell protested. Monteith reversed his decision, and Glenn Turner, the non-striking batsman, objected to Chappell's intervention. Chappell then unleashed abuse on Turner, including a racial slur directed at Turner's Indian wife.

Chappell's sledging, and his apparent condoning of verbal abuse in his teams, has been well documented. As his career progressed, he grew increasingly short-tempered. By today's standards, with strict codes of conduct and minute television scrutiny, Chappell's lapses, particularly directed at umpires, appear extreme. But in mitigation, Chappell's sledging was generally unpremeditated. Gideon Haigh has written that banning sledging would be as futile as banning road rage. Applied to Ian Chappell's era, that is a fair analogy. Chappell's onfield misdemeanours were the expressions of a man under stress losing his temper. When, later, Australian teams used sledging to supplement and sometimes substitute for their cricketing abilities, Haigh's simile carries less weight. Chappell seldom if ever set out systematically to win games by abusing opponents. There were times, such as in Christchurch, when he lost his cool. His behaviour was shocking, and alienated him from parts of the cricket community that looked back fondly to the standards of a Woodfull or a Hassett. But Chappell was fighting battles that Woodfull and Hassett never dared enter.

In early 1974, he addressed the Board again. This time he ranged over the full scope of Australian cricket, from the Sheffield Shield to junior development to umpiring to one-day cricket to the use of light meters. But when he talked of higher payments for Test and first-class cricketers, he again hit the grey wall. Chappell said his suggestion was 'not well received'. The ACB chairman Tim Caldwell informed Chappell that he should feel privileged merely to be allowed to address the Board who, like the Bourbons, forgot nothing and learnt nothing.

The following year would be Chappell's last as Test captain. England toured under Scotsman Mike Denness, and Australia mauled them 4–1. With Lillee back – a yard slower but a mile smarter – and Bankstown slinger Jeff Thomson finally harnessing his lightning speed, Chappell's dream team, four years in the making, was complete. His counter-attacking 90 on the first day in Brisbane set the tone for the series. Thomson's six wickets on the last day, including his iconic 'sandshoe-crusher' to bowl Tony Greig, did the rest.

Australia's only weakness, until Rick McCosker entered the team to partner Redpath, was at the top of the order. In 30 Tests as captain, only twice did Chappell come to the wicket after a century opening stand. In 27 innings he came in when the total was less than 20. It was not a good era for opening batsmen, therefore a tough time for number threes. 'Australia needed [Ian Chappell's] batting,' wrote Robinson, 'as much as a dowager needs a girdle.'

The 1974–75 series was packed with highlights. Walters's century in the last session in Perth, capped with a pulled six off the last ball, was boy's-own stuff. When Walters came off the field, Chappell acted as if cranky at the risky shot. Seeing Walters turn sheepish, Chappell laughed and wrapped him in his arms. Lillee, Thomson, Walker and Mallett were irresistible, and Cowdrey's return for England as a doughy 44-year-old was extraordinarily brave; that is, unwise. The shellshocked English, on paper a reasonable side, managed only a draw in the Third Test and a consolation win in the Sixth, when Lillee and Thomson were out of commission.

The hallmarks of Chappell's captaincy were now familiar: he imparted no theory, but simply trusted his batsmen to carry out a general strategy of scoring as quickly as possible in order to give the bowlers time to take 20 wickets. Typically, when asked if Lillee and Thomson had intimidated the England batsmen – who were dappled with bouncer-bruises – Chappell put the onus onto the visitors, saying they could have unsettled the bowlers by hitting them down the ground, but chose to retreat into defensive shells. Their bruises were, he implied, their own fault.

The series was unprecedentedly popular, raising $873,441 for the ACB, which paid the Australian players $40,104. This included $200-per-Test bonuses that Chappell had negotiated. He was now earning about $5,000 a season. Lillee, who could only afford to play cricket because his wife worked, said he believed Test cricketers should be contracted on annual salaries of $25–30,000, marginally higher than the national average wage. Alan Barnes, the ACB secretary, spoke for the Board when he replied: 'The players are not professional. They are all invited to play and if they don't like the conditions there are 500,000 other cricketers in Australia who would love to take their place.'

This attitude, which could have come straight from Billy McElhone in 1912, cemented Chappell's resolve. Meeting with ACTU president Bob Hawke, he discussed a players' association. But the idea seemed too radical, even for Chappell, to present to cricketers who feared reprisals from administrators.

Chappell led his men on another profitable Ashes tour in 1975. The English summer started with the inaugural World Cup of one-day cricket, and its final at Lord's was a showcase for the new format, Australia falling 17 runs short of a Clive Lloyd-inspired West Indies. The Ashes series was impaired by rain and the abandonment of the Test at Headingley, when the supporters of George Davis dug up the pitch on the last morning to protest against his conviction for armed robbery (he was released nine months later because of the unsound case against him). Chappell still averaged 71.50 for the series, which Australia won 1–0, and *Wisden* made him one of its cricketers of the year, a long-overdue accolade.

The top personalities in Ian Chappell's team knew their roles. Greg left the mind games to Ian, the raw intimidation to Lillee, the ebullience to Marsh, and methodically went about piling up so many runs that Australia could seldom be beaten. That was his job: run machine. Over the past three seasons Greg had performed his duty to an escalating excess, rattling up 242 at 60.50 at home to Pakistan, 342 at 48.86 in the West Indies, 559 at 69.89 against the New Zealanders, and 608 at 55.27 at home to England. There were landmarks – a career-best 5/61 against Pakistan in Sydney, the first Australian to score 1,000 runs on a West Indies tour, the astonishment of his 380 runs in the Wellington Test, a world record seven caught Englishmen in Perth – but of equal importance, in Greg's

Greg Chappell, second
batsman picked in most
all-time Australian XIs

development, was an offer by a syndicate of Queensland business-men in 1973 to give him the state captaincy and a $15,000 salary. His first season there produced 1,013 runs at 92.09, making him the third player to achieve the thousand for Queensland.

Because of Ian's other priorities – and his trust – Greg led Australia sooner than he expected. On the 1975 tour, Ian played minor matches as a batsman while Greg handled tactics. Ian's ego had no need for total control, and a week before the First Test he tossed against Glamorgan at Swansea before telling his team he was going to field on the boundary while Greg rang the bowling changes.

The ACB made $78,000 on the 105-day tour, after paying the players $2,734 a man. Ian Chappell said it was 'fish and chips money' and announced his retirement.

But only from the captaincy. He would continue as a player. Benaud had done so under Simpson, and Simpson had under Lawry, but Ian Chappell had other plans. He would keep on playing under Greg, but without the captaincy he would free himself to concentrate on the issues that concerned him.

28

TOWARDS THE BRINK

THERE was no need for discussion of the new captain. In a smoothly functioning team, one changed word in the captain's name would achieve the transition.

Greg acknowledged as much, saying: 'The side was running itself. I don't think it would have mattered if Billy the Goose had taken over really. You'd really have to try to bugger it up to ruin Ian's good work quickly.'

As captain against what arrived in Australia as an all-conquering West Indian team, Greg only had to keep doing his regular job: score runs at number four. His brother, liberated from care at three, Redpath, Walters, Marsh, Lillee, Thomson and Gary Gilmour would do the rest.

Greg tossed with Clive Lloyd to decide who would be sent in on a typically underprepared Gabba wicket. Under the curatorship of Alderman Clem Jones, Brisbane was, uniquely, a place to bowl first and see what happened next. Greg put the West Indies in. Lillee and Thomson wrought immediate damage, but the game would have hung in the balance if not for Greg's brace of centuries, 123 and 109 not out. In the second innings, a target of 219 could have been challenging but Greg and Ian made it routine. Greg became the first man in Test cricket's 99 years to score two centuries in his first game as captain.

In Perth, blazing hundreds from Roy Fredericks and Lloyd at six per over, and Andy Roberts's eight wickets more than countered Ian's 156. The West Indies, winning a Test played at breakneck pace, felt vindicated in their death-or-glory policy. After the Second Test they had the momentum and were favoured to take back the Worrell Trophy. But Greg's 52 in Melbourne and, more so, his grand 182 not out in Sydney turned back the tide.

Greg's captaincy was more than just a name change. He attacked new batsmen with close fields, knowing the West Indians' aggressive mood could be tipped over the edge by the temptation of open spaces and the provocation of a silly mid-off. More than Ian, Greg experimented with unorthodox fly-slips and leg-gullies. He broke with five years of Ian's practice by giving Thomson the new ball downwind. Lillee swung the ball into the wind, or took a scuffed ball as a change bowler, and his strike rate increased. Within that series Greg showed a willingness to think outside the square: he sent the visitors in twice and won both matches. Emerging from behind the rigid gait and perfect batting was an innovator.

A 5–1 win over a gifted opponent and a glance at the team statistics demonstrate that the 1975–76 outfit was as dominant as any Australia has put on the field. Greg was at their head in every way, scoring 702 runs at 117.00.

There remained an element of nastiness in the Australian team. For the Fourth Test, the selectors dropped McCosker and brought in Victorian left-hander Graham Yallop. Over the previous 12 months McCosker had been a genial, reliable opener and number three, cruelly denied his first Test century when he was 95 not out the night protesters dug up the Headingley pitch to truncate the 1975 Test there. But in three Tests against the West Indies, McCosker had earnt himself the sobriquet 'Rick the Snick'. With scores of 1, 2, 0, 13, 4 and 22 not out he was the only Australian batsman yet to contribute to what was still a close-fought series.

Ian Chappell, though no longer captain, liked McCosker very much and would later bring him a WSC windfall. Yallop, by contrast, was seen as a fey, upper-class Victorian, not a Chappell kind of man. When Yallop came into the Australian dressing room he could not locate his locker, and nobody offered help. He quickly detected the hostility from Ian Chappell, confirmed when he was told that if he was replacing McCosker he would not be batting six, where he expected, but three. Yallop would write, 'I was not exactly welcomed with open arms into the team.'

Yallop accepted the challenge, feeling, like any Australian under the Chappells, that the choice of sinking or swimming is no choice at all. Yallop scored 16 and 16 not out in Sydney, 47 and 43 in Adelaide, and 57, at six, in Melbourne, where McCosker returned with a century. Yallop, with 179 Test runs at 44.75, could say he had come through his baptism of fire and earnt the respect of his peers.

He would not play another Test for two seasons.

While playing under Greg and scoring 449 runs at 44.90, Ian consolidated his role as the players' shop steward. In South Australia, he echoed his grandfather by leading a players' strike when the SACA wanted to give them a 13th man at a time when it would not pay the laundry bills for 12. The ACB threatened to ban him for wearing striped Adidas boots, in which Chappell was ready to walk away from cricket rather than submit until Adidas decided generously to pay out his contract and excuse him from wearing their footwear. He was warned by umpires after bowling an over of donkey-drops in protest at the new Shield bonus points system. He was warned for 'mooning' the SACA directors' box during a Shield game, when his trousers slipped while he was adjusting his gear (he said it was an accident). At the same time, he was inspiring SA to win the Shield a season after they had come last.

He announced his retirement after the 1975–76 season, but again it was a front for other activities. The West Indian series had been the first to generate a million dollars in gate takings. Ian was paid $4,800. When he 'retired', he toured South Africa with an International Wanderers team, then signed a contract to coach and play for the North Melbourne club. For both he received considerably higher income than as a Test cricketer.

Since Bradman, if a player was unhappy with his pay, he could try to make extra income. Such lone actions undermined the principle that cricket's income was generated by teams, not individuals. In 1975–76, Jeff Thomson accepted a $630,000 10-year deal to go to Brisbane and work for radio station 4IP. If the top players were bought off one by one, there would be no hope of improving the lot of all first-class cricketers.

What was different in 1976–77 was that Chappell, at the end of his career, cared more for the welfare of all players than for himself. What also set this period apart was his discovery of an ally in Kerry Packer, who had been brushed aside when he tried to outbid the Australian Broadcasting Commission for the rights to televise cricket on his Nine Network.

While Ian went off and plotted, Greg's team went into instant decline. Ian's retirement, and Thomson's shoulder injury sustained in the first Test of 1976–77 when he charged into Alan Turner at midwicket trying to catch Mudassar Nazar's popped pull shot, took out two of Australia's main planks. As if spooked, Greg lost his boldness. On the last day of that Adelaide Test, when Australia needed 56 runs in the last hour with four wickets in hand, Greg told Gary Cosier and Rod Marsh to shut up shop. The Adelaide crowd booed them, and him.

Australia won in Melbourne, Greg scoring 121 and 67, but Imran Khan routed them in Sydney with 12 wickets – Pakistan's first win on Australian soil – so the series was drawn 1–1 and the negativity of Adelaide was viewed in its true costly light. After the glories of the previous summer, the Australian team began to look weather-beaten. Greg, as would happen to catastrophic effect four years later, took the team's troubles onto his own shoulders. Wanting to absorb the pressure, he amplified it.

In New Zealand in early 1977, he averaged 34 in a won series, but his action apprehending and paddling a streaker with his bat, while eminently reasonable, undid some of the remediation Greg had achieved between the teams. Greg also showed a growing disciplinarian streak that did not go down well with some senior men. When Greg decreed morning runs, Walters wore a T-shirt saying 'Jogging Can Kill', refused to embrace the exercise, then proved his point by scoring 250 in Wellington.

The March 1977 Centenary Test, a dream-like jubilee for the game, was not all that it seemed. On the field, Australia and England provided one of the great contests. Greg made 40 of Australia's slow 138 after Willis's bouncer destroyed McCosker's jaw. England's advantage was nullified on the second day by Lillee's 6/26. Greg failed in an Australian second innings which was raised into legend by three acts. Blond South Australian left-hander David Hookes, in his first Test, hit Greig for five fours in an over on his way to a 56 that announced, perhaps, the arrival of Australia's next champion. Marsh's unbeaten 110 was the first Test century by an Australian gloveman, aided by McCosker, mummy-like, his misshapen head wrapped in bandages. On the last day, as a tireless Lillee and O'Keeffe wore England down, the Marsh–McCosker stand would turn out to be matchwinning.

The match celebrated the ACB's version of history. Dave Gregory was a sepia-tinted hero. In reality, as we have seen, he had much more in common with Ian Chappell, who, as the Centenary Test was being played, was planning the venture that would realise Gregory's independent ambitions. It had taken the Board until 1912 to quell player power. Now, after 65 years, Gregory's true heir would win that power back.

The gloss of the Centenary Test wore off. Lillee sat out the 1977 Ashes tour with back problems, though it was later revealed that he, with Ian Chappell, was the leading player advocate of Packer's private World Series Cricket. As the still loyal captain, Greg was given an Ashes squad without Lillee, without the omitted Gilmour, and with tyros and experiments including West Australians Kim Hughes, Craig Serjeant and Mick Malone and Victorians Richie Robinson and Ray Bright.

Marsh and Walters set a record for drinking beer on the flight to London, and from there Greg's last England tour would be all downhill. Of 88 scheduled playing hours in the first five games, rain wrecked all but 22. England won the one-day series 2–1, and before the Test series the news broke of WSC.

Thirteen of Greg's 18 tourists were to play for Packer. Two clear factions soon fractured into a rabble. Greg said, during the tour, 'Most of the hotels are so bad they are depressing. They have had a bad effect, especially on the younger team members. Perhaps because the ACB gave the players a pay rise recently, they cut costs in other areas.'

By the end of a calamitous tour, Australia would lose three of five Tests and their matches with Somerset and – a first – the Minor Counties. It was England's biggest home win since Harry Scott's infamous tour of 1886. Greg's batting was one of the few solid bones in a feeble Australian body, but 371 at 41.22 was nowhere near enough. Boycott, Willis and Bob Woolmer (a WSC signatory, along with Greig and Alan Knott) were England's best. By the end of the series, Greig would be sacked as England's captain and Greg Chappell would resign as Australia's.

But Greg was no willing rebel. As much as he agitated for better pay and conditions, he honoured the Test captaincy. 'I understand how people were shocked,' he said, 'because that's how I felt at first. For people to whom cricket was almost a religion, we were heretics.'

In many ways, the reasons Ian had quit the captaincy were precisely what compromised Greg. Both Chappells respected the captaincy's traditions enough to know that you could not be captain while plotting a rebel series. Ian left the captaincy so he could be free to bring about revolution. Greg would be the last big name to sign, and it is conceivable that, had the Board shown an ounce more consideration or flexibility, it could have retained him. Had the ACB done so, it could have wedged the Chappell brothers and given WSC a serious problem. But when Greg wrote to chairman Bob Parish asking to open a dialogue, Parish did not reply. When they came across each other in a London hotel, the chairman snubbed the captain. By refusing to talk, the ACB drove Greg into Packer's arms and ensured WSC's success.

Ian chose his WSC squad of 27, openly snubbing Kim Hughes and Graham Yallop. Hughes, thought to embody the next generation, was a controversial absence. The eldest of five children

LEFT: Greg Chappell with the worst performed (and worst dressed) Australian Ashes tourists for two decades: 1977.

of a schoolteacher, Hughes was born on Australia Day 1954. He showed prodigious childhood talent at Australian football, hockey, tennis and squash. As his family moved around WA, Hughes drew attention for his youth and cockiness. He made up for his size and curly-headed prettiness with a confidence that begged opponents to injure him and teammates to play practical jokes.

In Perth, Hughes came under the sway of Frank Parry, a furniture store owner and brother to the entrepreneur Kevin. Frank became obsessed with Hughes, giving him endless practice and positive reinforcement. Hughes's habit of congratulating himself on spanking shots was a dovetailing of his self-assurance with Parry's Tourettish encouragement.

At club and state level, Hughes tended to blast merry 20s and 30s and get out at inopportune moments, leaving a mess for someone else. His attitude was blithe: he wanted to create memorable moments. The young Hughes inhabited a kind of fantasy. Briefly, he fled the frustration of not making the WA team to try his luck in Adelaide. He lasted half a miserable season before running back to the devil he knew.

His first Shield innings, 119 from 148 balls against a virtually all-international NSW attack in 1975, was described by former Test player Keith Slater as a perfectly constructed innings. But John Inverarity chided Hughes for getting himself out (not 'getting out') just before the tea break.

Hughes added 60 in the second innings, then 102 against the West Indians on the Perth wicket where they would not lose a Test until 2000. He played the off-season in Scotland, took a promotions job for a Fremantle building society, and married Jenny Davidson, his girlfriend from high school. In his second first-class season he blasted 137 not out against Imran, Sarfraz and the best Pakistan attack in a generation. Hookes nudged him out of the middle-order vacancy in the Centenary Test team, but Hughes was picked for the tours of New Zealand and England.

He spent most of those weeks as a spectator. In New Zealand he played no Tests and was out cheaply when he played. An exasperated Marsh tried to educate Hughes to adjust his game to meet the team's needs. Like a patient schoolteacher, Marsh asked, 'So, you've been batting for 240 minutes. How many are you?' Hughes smiled: 'Eight hundred!'

In England, it was his luck to be on the worst Australian tour since 1912. Opinion was divided on whether Hughes rejected an invitation to join WSC or was rejected. His suggesting the former was bravado. For all Hughes's entertainment value, Ian Chappell did not regard him as worthy. Unlike his contemporary Hookes, Kim was not one of the club.

He scored no centuries on the 1977 tour and was only chosen for his Test debut when the series was lost. Greg wouldn't pick him because he was 'too much of a blast-and-hoper', and tour selector Walters, in poor form, would not drop himself. Hughes effectively gave up on the tour, preferring to socialise than watch his team-mates. When he was selected for his debut, he told journalist Norm Tasker, 'Those pricks, now they've made me part of the failure.'

In a game already ruined by rain, he ground out an agonising single in 37 minutes, a wretched debut in a benighted team, before edging Mike Hendrick to Willis. Having wanted to play for Australia ever since he could walk, this misery was all there was to it.

29

THE SPLIT

IT was Ian Chappell's charisma and integrity, and Kerry Packer's money, that lured so many of the top players. The buried idea had arrived. After 65 years of iron-fisted Board control, players were taking their game back.

As captain of the WSC Australians – Greg deferring to him once more – Ian was as courageous and tactically astute as ever. In the 1977–78 season, the WSC Australians lost to Lloyd's West Indians but defeated Greig's World XI, who were buttressed by West Indian players. Ian averaged 43, while Greg, against a World XI bowling attack that combined the best of Pakistan (Imran), England (Underwood) and the West Indies (Andy Roberts and Michael Holding), made a marvellous 174 at Gloucester Park in Perth and 246 not out at VFL Park outside Melbourne.

The public took time to understand WSC, wondering if this was real cricket or an exhibition. WSC also struggled for acceptance in its first year due to the re-emergence of another buried idea.

After handing over the NSW captaincy to Walters in 1967, Bob Simpson had not played first-class cricket. He ran a public relations and sports management firm, organising a well-attended double-wicket competition among the world's best cricketers in 1968–69. For 10 years he continued for Western Suburbs in Sydney, eventually amassing just over 10,000 grade runs and outscoring men 15 years his junior. He topped the Sydney aggregates five times, once more than Victor Trumper.

Each year, Simpson said, state associations courted him for a comeback. At an Angus Steak House in Sydney in 1977, ACB representatives pleaded with him, and he agreed to be their saviour. The cream of Australian cricket, from the Chappell brothers, Walters and Lillee right down to journeymen wicketkeepers such as Dennis Yagmich and Richie Robinson and semi-retirees such as Redpath, were in WSC. The only Test players to remain in establishment cricket, getting ready to host Bishen Bedi's Indians, were Hughes, Gary Cosier, Craig Serjeant, Yallop and Thomson, retained due to the contractual obligations he had incurred in Queensland. A virtual Third or Fourth XI would be playing India. The Board needed a captain. Simpson, with all the cards in his hand, insisted on a rare guarantee: that they appoint him for all five Tests.

In a way that brings back memories of Bradman with the teams of 1946–48, Simpson's captaincy was at its finest. There were no players of his generation to challenge his authority. At 41 he was a fatherly, if not grandfatherly, figure. He was able to tutor and nurture players such as Peter Toohey, Tony Mann, Steve Rixon, David Ogilvie, Wayne Clark, Graham Wood and Rick Darling, who knew they were lucky to be wearing the baggy green cap and would imbibe everything Simpson offered. He was as much coach as captain, and Test cricket was grateful to have him.

The series against India, played in contest with WSC Supertests, was superbly competitive. In Brisbane, Simpson said he was 'more nervous than when I started batting against Wes Hall and Charlie Griffith'. Playing mostly off the back foot, showing street-smarts and pragmatism against the medium pacers and giving master classes against the spinners, he scored 89 in Australia's surprise win by 16 runs. Then, in Perth, two months short of his 42nd birthday, he became the oldest Australian Test centurion at home, scoring 176. Mann's 105 as nightwatchman set up a record chase of 342 in the fourth innings, which Australia got with two wickets in hand. India then retaliated with wins in Melbourne and Sydney.

Simpson celebrating his 42nd birthday with a win over India. Yallop (*to his right*) and Hughes (*behind*) share the joy.

For the decider in Adelaide, the selectors gave Simpson a swag of new players, with Yallop recalled after two years. In yet another wonderful contest, Simpson's 100 and 51 did much to get Australia home by 47.

Simpson, with 539 at 53.90, two centuries, six catches and four wickets, was the player of the series. It was a staggering personal achievement and arguably the high point of his career. Because Simpson was Simpson, and no job could be left half-done, he put his hand up to lead his lambs to the slaughter: to the West Indies, where they would be facing the WSC players who had just massacred the Chappells, Lillee, Marsh and company in Australia. The West Indies Board, putting competition above principle, chose the full terrifying strength of Clive Lloyd, Viv Richards, Andy Roberts, Michael Holding, Joel Garner and Gordon Greenidge.

Simpson, always up for a fight, scored 113 in the tour opener at St Kitts. The 42-year-old captain was awake at 7 am to lead his youngsters on their exercises and drills, but application could only take them so far. The first two Tests, in Port-of-Spain and Bridgetown, were predictably heavy losses. Toohey and Yallop were both hit in the face by bouncers, Yallop becoming the first Test player to wear a full-face crash helmet. Simpson then had to withdraw Bruce Yardley from the attack when umpire Douglas Sang Hue – a WSC employee – called the off-spinner for throwing.

Having done the damage, Lloyd's men could not come to terms with their board to play beyond the Third Test. During a more even contest in Georgetown against Alvin Kallicharan's leftovers, Simpson made 67 and Australia were left with a last-day chase. Simpson said: 'It was so utterly vital I just couldn't watch. We had to win today or the tour wasn't worthwhile anymore.' He said some of his players were facing the prospect of never being picked again for Australia. 'I have never known a situation quite like this. It meant everything to win here.'

They did win, thanks to brave centuries from Craig Serjeant and Graeme Wood, and would very likely have softened the series result to 2–3 in Kingston when Toohey scored his sole Test century, until the crowd, rioting against a run-out decision on Vanburn Holder, coated Sabina Park with bottles and wooden chairs, leaving the Test incomplete.

Simpson's 199 at 22.11 was creditable, but his position, leading into the next summer's home series against England, who had not lost many players to WSC, was complex. Simpson had developed a visceral hatred of WSC, but if the ACB thought he would toe their line they were mistaken. Simpson's dislike for WSC rested more on personal than professional factors. He no longer had many friends among the Chappell–Marsh–Lillee clique and his relations with Lloyd, Richards and the West Indians were openly hostile. But nor was Simpson a Board yes-man. On the morning of the Adelaide Test against India, when he had led such a grand victory, Simpson had fronted the Board to push for improvements in players' contracts and conditions. Among his points was that he, having set aside his business interests to come back and play, should receive special compensation. The Board would not make an ex-gratia payment, so he proposed that his public relations firm be appointed, for a fee, to manage the team's publicity needs. The Board refused. Simpson's insubordination – even at a time when he had saved establishment cricket – was remembered.

In spring 1978, Simpson talked to the Board again. He would lead Australia against England, but only if, as during the previous summer, he was appointed for the full series. This time the Board said no. Neither side blinked, and he retired again, as ever with a sense of betrayal and bitterness.

Graham Yallop's two years out of Australian Test cricket seemed to owe more to the impression he created than his playing record. His father owned a factory, APY Castings, in Melbourne and Graham was sent to Carey Baptist Grammar School, where Frank Tyson had the vision to advise him to give up his preferred fast bowling and concentrate on his batting. After an Australian Schoolboys' tour to Sri Lanka, he worked at Lindsay Hassett's sports store.

Since his Victorian debut in 1972–73, Yallop had scored consistently with a distinctive, wristy style. He shuffled in anticipation and steered the ball with an array of flicks and glides and caresses, but when he middled one of his classic drives he would hold the pose beyond his follow-through.

His bright Test debut in 1975–76 should have guaranteed his place, but his diffident manner pleased neither Greg Chappell nor the selectors. Yallop, who had the moustache but not the attitude to go with it, was the ultimate outsider: left out of the Centenary Test, the 1977 Ashes tour, the WSC signings, and then, adding insult to injury, out of Simpson's team to play India.

Unloved, Yallop's response was to keep making runs for Victoria, which he was now leading. His call-up came for the final, deciding Test of the Indian series, when his 121 secured his first solid run at Test cricket.

Initially, Yallop was selected as Simpson's vice-captain for the West Indies tour. But the disorganised Board, horse-trading between the states, replaced him twice in five days, first with Serjeant and then, to quell a Queensland revolt, Thomson.

Going to the West Indies was Yallop's chance to prove his hardness. In Port-of-Spain and Bridgetown, Yallop took on the might of Roberts, Holding, Garner and Croft at three. His scores, in an annihilated team, were 2, 81, 47 and 14. Then, against Guyana in Georgetown, he repelled Croft with a magnificent 118, unbeaten until Croft speared one from wide on the crease and cracked Yallop's jaw.

Helmets had been presented to Simpson's team in 1966–67, but not taken seriously. Now Tony Greig was trying the rounded headgear in WSC, and David Hookes would do so in response to his broken jaw, courtesy of Andy Roberts, in WSC the next season. Within 12 months helmets would be worn by most international batsmen. Yallop, his jaw partially healed, had more reason than most. He came back against the second-string West Indians and scored 75, 18, 57 and 23 not out. His 317 at 45.29 was second only to Graeme Wood and so impressed the ACB that, when Simpson's demands wore them out in late 1978, they chose Yallop as the 36th captain of Australia.

Graham Yallop, always asked to prove himself

By any reckoning, it was a poor decision. Simpson had saved establishment cricket, but the ACB was so distracted by WSC that it lost sight of what was important. Yallop was a victim of the politics of revenge.

During his two years outside Test cricket, Yallop had received many offers from English counties to defect, but had instead returned to try to break back into his nation's team. At 26, he was the third-youngest Australian captain after Murdoch and Craig. He had his own sportsgoods wholesaling company and had built a house for his young family at Ringwood. He was seen as a patriot, a compliant captain, and the type of establishment son that boards favoured in times of crisis.

Trying to jazz things up, the ACB's marketing department had three skydivers jump onto the Gabba to deliver the coin to Yallop and England's Mike Brearley. The England team was missing only Greig, Woolmer, Knott and Underwood, whereas Australia was

Yallop in full flight

fielding a Third XI further weakened by Simpson's non-selection. Moreover, Yallop's one potential weapon, Thomson, had decided that if he could not break his Queensland contract and play with his mates in WSC, he would not play at all.

Yallop's card as Australian captain was marked within 85 minutes. Like many hesitant men, his first steps were over-bold. Batting first on a green pitch he was one of six batsmen to fall for 26 in those 85 minutes. Australia was looking at a record low until a fast-bowling debutant from Adelaide named Rodney Hogg hit 36 to get them to 118.

When England batted, bad went to worse. Yallop dropped Derek Randall at first slip off Hogg, and moved out of the position. Standing beside the bowler, he fell into long conferences that suggested uncertainty. As England built its lead, Yallop plugged holes. He saw Jim Higgs's leg-spin as too great a risk until the 63rd over, when the horse had bolted.

Facing a big deficit, Australia lost two second-innings wickets for 2 runs. As ever, Yallop's best chance for redemption was with his bat. Against Willis, Ian Botham and Chris Old, he proceeded to play a heroic innings. His partner, Hughes, also tamed his instincts and the pair staved off defeat for a day. It would never be enough, but Yallop's 102 offered hope that his batting could be a talisman for the series.

The Yallop–Hughes stand of 170 in 347 minutes was a false dawn. Australia were routed in Perth, Yallop failing twice. They battled staunchly in Melbourne to register a surprise win, young Sydney left-hander Allan Border making his debut. But England won by 93 in Sydney to sew up the Ashes and a demoralised Australia subsided in the last two Tests.

Hughes's Brisbane century had promised much. Not the type of player Ian Chappell fancied for WSC, he was even less a Bob Simpson type. Against India and the West Indies in the first summer of division, Hughes had been in and out of the team. It wasn't until 1978–79 that Hughes played two consecutive Tests.

His Brisbane 129 declared that a new Kim Hughes had arrived, a player who could protect his teammates and stick around to save a match, or at least try. He batted for eight hours, and the slowness of his scoring was, for once, his highest commendation. His two halves had always been fighting each other: the entertainer and the team man. In fact they weren't equal halves; the entertainer always won. But in Brisbane, after he hooked Willis onto the dog track and Brearley put a man at deep square leg, Hughes resisted hooking. His restraint portended a permanent change, but for the rest of the series he couldn't get past the forties.

Something in his style projected nervousness. He stood tense and upright, his bat tapping the earth like fingers on a typewriter. It seemed to take one extra tap, as if to restrain an explosive force. Defensive shots looked like last-minute compromises, his natural energy drawing him down the pitch, ever forward, to put the bowling back in its box. But such restless energy was not what an embattled team needed. As the third or fourth batsman behind the Chappells and Redpath, playing a role like Walters, Hughes could have been a game-changer. But that time was past. Australia needed a stayer.

So in 1978–79, Yallop's main assets were also his biggest problems. Between the First and Sixth Tests, his own batting could not deliver the kind of inspiration Greg Chappell (or, later, Border) could provide. Yallop scored 41 and 16 in Melbourne, 44 and 1 in Sydney, and 0 and 36 in Adelaide: three starts almost meaning something.

Meanwhile, Hogg was blindingly fast, taking 41 wickets and, with Alan Hurst's 25, keeping Australia competitive. But Yallop could not manage the headstrong Hogg. After his dithering in Brisbane, Yallop tried to plan his tactics thoroughly before each day. But Hogg resented being told what to do and often changed his fields without consulting Yallop. In front of his home crowd in Adelaide, the asthmatic Hogg was having trouble breathing. Yallop, whose plan was to give Hogg 17 eight-ball overs a day, told him to persist. Hogg walked off. When Yallop challenged him, Hogg suggested they settle it behind the members' stand.

A natural introvert, Yallop responded to criticism by over-compensating. Turning authoritarian was no good thing in a losing team, and the team's bellwether, its fielding, disintegrated after a brilliant 1977–78 under Simpson. Yallop's stand-offishness with the media was seen as an arrogance born of fear. He could not win – and he could not win.

Yet amid this misery, in the fifth Test that Australia lost in its worst-ever Ashes series, Yallop scored a breezy 121 off 186 balls, taking the English spinners apart. Australia only made 198 and lost the match by nine wickets, but Brearley gave Yallop the highest praise as a competitive cricketer and unlucky captain. Yallop's 391 runs were more than any other Australian, and more than any Englishman apart from David Gower's 421 – but 223 of them came in two innings.

Yallop's last Test as a captain was at home in Melbourne, against Pakistan, a month after the Ashes disaster. The Pakistan Cricket Board had no qualms about sending its star-studded WSC contingent, including Imran and Majid Khan, Haroon Rashid, Javed Miandad, Zaheer Abbas, Asif Iqbal and Sarfraz Nawaz.

Australia bowled them out for 196 but couldn't capitalise, replying with 168. Majid's century helped Pakistan to nine for 353, but Australia was set for an astonishing and revitalising win on the last day at three for 305 with 77 to get. Then, in 33 balls, Sarfraz extracted some mind-bending swing with the old ball. He took seven wickets for one run, the hideousness of another collapse came over the Australian changing room, and they lost the match by 71.

Yallop, run out for 8, was playing with an injured leg. Replaced by Hughes for the second Pakistan Test, he was out of the job. A season later he was dumped as Victorian captain, a harsh penalty after winning two Shields. But his performance as Australian captain against England left no administrator with any confidence that Yallop was a leader. They were probably right.

30

A BAD MARRIAGE

KIM Hughes would become Australian captain on four separate occasions between 1979 and 1983. The first was as much a surprise to him as anyone else. Queensland's veteran wicketkeeper John Maclean had been Yallop's vice-captain against England, but when Maclean was dropped and Yallop was injured, Hughes was suddenly captain. It didn't bother the ACB that he had never led his state, or that, of his 10 matches as captain of North Perth, he had lost nine.

For the Second Test against Pakistan in Perth, Hughes announced a 'new era', held pep talks, had the team travel together, and mixed up the rooming arrangements to acquaint strangers.

Fresh from 84 in Melbourne, he skipped onto the WACA, won the toss and sent Pakistan in. He promptly dropped Miandad twice as the Pakistani master scored 129 not out. But Hurst's four wickets restricted a defensive Pakistan to 277, and Border's 85 led Australia to a 50-run advantage.

Hughes made 9 in an accident-prone Test. Bowling in the nets, he trod on a ball, twisted his ankle and had to sit out Pakistan's second innings.

In a short and short-tempered series, Australia and Pakistan had already clashed in Melbourne when Hogg had been run out, by Miandad, while gardening. Pakistan's captain Mushtaq Mohammed

Kim Hughes: a new start

355

had tried to recall Hogg, but umpire Mick Harvey overruled him. Then, in the third innings of the Perth match, while vice-captain Andrew Hilditch was deputising for Hughes, Hurst Mankaded the Pakistani tail-ender Sikander Bakht in retaliation. Sikander protested, but Hurst said, 'You've cheated, so you're out!'

Pakistan scraped up 285, Asif Iqbal getting nearly half, leaving Australia 236 to win. The problem with retaliation is that it sets off an arms race. When Hilditch was 29, at the non-striker's end, he picked up a ball rolling past and underarmed it to Sarfraz. Instead of accepting the helpful gesture, Sarfraz appealed. Hilditch became the second Test batsman to be out handled the ball. South African Russell Endean, the only other batsmen out this way, had been trying to defend his wicket.

But Australia won by seven wickets, Hughes was the triumphant new captain, and the Board had a new pin-up boy.

In the second year of WSC, Ian Chappell's team beat the West Indians but lost to a new-look World XI with some deadly new South African components. Ian took his team to the West Indies, where they drew a five-Supertest series 1–1. Against a battery of Roberts, Holding, Garner and Croft, and World XI bowlers of the calibre of Imran Khan, Mike Procter and Garth Le Roux, Ian averaged 40 in his 14 Supertests.

World Series Cricket produced two of Greg's best years. In the Adelaide Supertest he took 5/20 with his cutters, and in the first-ever night match in Sydney he took 5/13. In the Caribbean, in the highest-quality and most competitive five-Test series that will ever be forgotten, his batting was magnificent. His 631 runs, while suffering from Bell's palsy, featured 90 in Bridgetown, 150 in Port-of-Spain, 113 in Georgetown, and 104 and 85 in St John's. No Australian team in the Caribbean would achieve anything comparable to that 1–1 draw for another 16 years. Greg Chappell's statistics alone – 1,416 runs in 14 Supertests – beg for the inclusion of Supertest achievements in Test records.

Once the public understood WSC's competitiveness, the rebel contest gained support. Any Australian team under Ian Chappell was going to compete with technicolour effort. So committed was he that in Guyana, when the crowd rioted, he transgressed not the laws of cricket but those of the land, stomach-punching an official who, Chappell believed, was responsible for the delay that prompted the riot. He pleaded guilty to assault and paid a fine.

Without WSC, Ian Chappell's legacy would have been one decade of staunch batting, half a decade of unforgettable cricket under his captaincy, and a continuance of the injustices that had shortened the careers of Simpson and Lawry. Without WSC, Ian would have been yet another captain who achieved minor improvements in his players' conditions of employment and played under protest.

But because of the Board's intransigence, a complete rupture was the only way for players to win a fair deal. Administrators always wished that men would play cricket for a little bit of money and a lot of love. Only after WSC were players' claims to professional compensation accepted.

It was Packer's money that paid for the revolution, but Packer could not have done a thing without a captain who was both brave and motivated. In its rejection of Chappell's presentations in 1973 and 1974, the Board had ensured its own doom. Led by Bradman, the grey wall had no idea what it was dealing with.

When the compromise came in 1979, the Board lost everything but its baggy green cap. Players in a reunited Australia were treated and paid as professionals. Packer got not only television rights but marketing and merchandising revenue. Night cricket, and full exploitation of the limited-overs game, were among WSC's other legacies.

In 1978–79, after years of escalating profits, the ACB had lost $445,000 as well as the Ashes. The 'compromise' – essentially, the ACB lying down and accepting Packer's terms – coincided with two establishment tours led by Hughes, to the World Cup in England and to India for a six-Test series.

News of the compromise broke two days after Hughes arrived in England. His team, knowing the writing was on the wall, managed only to beat Canada. The prospect of an Indian tour can't have been much fun. Ten of the 15 tourists had never represented Australia overseas. En route to India they needed an emergency stop in Singapore and their first match, against North Zone at Srinagar in Kashmir, was played before more soldiers than spectators. They heard that, at home, Greg Chappell was making Shield centuries, Ian wanted the Test captaincy back, and other WSC stars such as Lillee, Bruce Laird, Marsh and Len Pascoe were among the wickets and runs. Most of Hughes's men knew they were no longer the incumbents, but triallists for the 'real' Australian XI that would take the field against the West Indies at home in November. In addition, Rick Darling, Border, Hurst and Yardley were ruled out of key games with illness or injury, and many others played while sick.

Hughes was no certainty to keep his place. He had scored one century in a dozen Tests, and knew he would lose the captaincy to one of the Chappells. Given the circumstances, that tour of India might have been his finest moment as a cricketer and a captain. He scored 594 Test runs at 59.40, with a century in Madras and half-centuries in Bangalore, Kanpur, Calcutta (twice) and Bombay. Australia lost 0–2 but played with admirable spirit. Yallop also had a fine tour, scoring 167 as an opener in Calcutta, 89 in Kanpur and 60 in Bombay for a series total of 423 at 38.45.

As leader, Hughes achieved what Yallop could not, bringing Hogg into line. Exasperated with the umpiring generally and his 14 no-balls in particular, Hogg kicked down the stumps in Bangalore, then bowled deliberately wide. Hughes sent him from the field, apologised to the umpires and persuaded Hogg to do the same. The only black mark against Hughes's captaincy was his disdain for minor matches, which led to a loss to Australia's weakest opponents, East Zone, at Cuttack.

Captaincy of the reunified Australia was a poisoned chalice compared with what Greg Chappell had inherited in 1975. On the bright side, player payments were vastly improved. Greg had been paid $35,000 a year to play WSC plus a $12,000 sign-on bonus and $5,000 in annual 'consultancy' fees, and he would earn similar money for

Australia now. This compared nicely with the $6,000 a year he had made before WSC. But Packer's PBL Marketing would extract what it paid for. The two years of WSC had imposed an unprecedented schedule of one-day and five-day cricket to feed the television maw. The 1979–80 season would demand an intense program of one-day cricket, plus three Tests against England alternating with three against the West Indies. Greg scored 74 and 124 in the drawn First Test against the West Indies, but few more as Australia lost the other two. Against England, he made a century in Melbourne and 98 not out in Sydney as Australia won 3–0. It was hard to keep track of which series was which, however, and England had refused to put the Ashes on the line for what they saw as an experimental season.

Vice-captain in the reunified team, Hughes kept his place. He, Border and Hogg were the only establishment regulars in the full-strength team. Hughes vindicated his selection with a fine unbeaten 130 against the West Indies in Brisbane, 70 against them in Melbourne and 99 against England in Perth. His 130 in Brisbane, echoing his 129 on the same ground 12 months earlier, came in 378 minutes and was part of a century partnership with Greg Chappell. Symbolic, the partnership was also personal, and the two captains forged a surprisingly durable bond.

It could have been a moment of reconciliation, but Hughes's vice-captaincy riled Marsh, who had been Australia's vice-captain before WSC. Marsh also wanted to be reinstated as captain of WA. Instead, in the spirit of compromise and payback, Hughes received both jobs. Marsh and Lillee each refused to be his state deputy.

Their sentiments were backed by Ian Chappell, playing one last season. Chappell, at 36, was having a rough ride. Having shown an interest in resuming the Australian captaincy, early in the season he was fined in Devonport for swearing at a young David Boon and at umpires. While the ACB had accepted most of PBL's terms, accepting Ian as captain was a demand too far. He only played in the last three Tests, failing in both innings against the West Indies, but making useful runs against England. In his last Test, he scored 75 in the first innings and an unbeaten 26 in the second, helping Greg steer Australia to an eight-wicket win.

By 1979–80, the stress was beginning to get to Greg Chappell. Here he gives Mike Brearley the flick.

His last days as a cricketer were somewhat haywire. In his last match in Sydney, Chappell ground out 158 against NSW. Walters, his old mate, tried to contain him by bowling a metre wide of the off-stump. In protest, Chappell plucked out the stump and hammered it in where Walters had been bowling. It was a humorous gesture, and the crowd applauded Chappell. But such was his disciplinary record, and so sick of him were authorities, that he was sanctioned again.

He made another century in his final first-class appearance, 112 against Victoria in Adelaide, before retiring to a career with Packer. Over time, public opinion has not only forgiven Chappell but elevated him to a kind of cricketing sainthood for his advocacy of the players. Behind his media persona, Chappell became widely appreciated as a generous, thoughtful, compassionate and sincere individual who had lost none of his edge. In 2003, he made considered public criticism of the treatment of asylum seekers and refugees. Among boys who grew up watching cricket in the 1970s, Ian Chappell remains, alongside Dennis Lillee, the folk hero. His support for Terry Jenner in the 1990s, as the former leg-spinner was rehabilitated after a jail term for embezzlement, showed very publicly why Chappell, unlike any other captain except perhaps Murdoch and Darling, engendered a corps of loyal bondsmen.

In 1982, Jack Pollard spoke for the Australian cricket establishment when he wrote: 'All the honours open to Australian cricketers have been given to [Ian Chappell] except the respect of those who revere the game for the standards it sets in good behaviour.'

Time has diluted that view. Chappell's offences against manners, such as banning the wearing of dinner suits on two Ashes tours, seem trivial. What he left the game was far more profound: the realisation of a dream of full professionalism. It shouldn't have taken that long. Without Ian Michael Chappell, it would have taken a lot longer.

31

THE HOT POTATO

No sooner had the relentless home season finished than Greg Chappell's team was sent to Pakistan for three Tests, then to England for a match at Lord's to commemorate the 1880 Test. Paid as professionals, they would be worked as such. Greg had to survive a rare ACB vote to retain the captaincy ahead of Hughes, but this did not inhibit him from making stern recommendations on matters of security, umpiring, weather contingencies and scheduling. Australia lost the First Test, in Karachi, and drew the other two, Greg making 235 at Faisalabad.

Three other captains, past and future, toured under Chappell. Because of his runs in India and his light footwork – and total amnesia of his courage in the Caribbean in 1978 – Graham Yallop was perceived as a specialist against spin. Ignored through the Australian season, he was taken to Pakistan where, alongside Greg Chappell's 235, Yallop made 172 in eight and a half hours at Faisalabad.

While Kim Hughes struggled at times in Pakistan and Lillee took three wickets in three Tests, showing the strain of too much cricket, a genuine star was emerging from the former establishment ranks.

Allan Border's road to top cricket had been far from yellow-bricked. Born at Cremorne on Sydney's lower north shore to a wool-classer father and a shopkeeper mother, four Border sons grew up opposite Mosman Oval. Allan, the second, worshipped

Sobers. Border and his brothers played baseball, but in his teens Allan emerged as the most gifted cricketer, making the NSW Combined High Schools team from North Sydney Boys' Technical High School and playing first-grade for Mosman at 16 as a darting left-arm orthodox spinner who batted handily down the order.

His first and last job outside cricket was clerking in the film library at BP Australia. Born shy, with a face that could get lost in any crowd, struggling to hold down a first-grade place at Mosman, he was drifting from the game until the English all-rounder Barry Knight, who had settled in Australia, persuaded Border to come to his indoor sports centre in Kent Street for some one-on-one tuition through the winter of 1975.

Repetitive drilling gave Border peace of mind: he was a worker. Under Knight, he developed a technique that was, in the old saying, limitless in its limitations. Everything about Border's batting was economical: short backlift, punchy downswing, crisp follow-through. His cross-bat shorts were described as short-arm jabs. All his movements were likewise minimalist: short steps, compact gestures, a tight style in bowling and throwing. He was a late but decisive leaver of the ball. At the crease he crouched with his bat in the air, more like a baseballer's stance, just as his throwing style resembled a 20-yard ping from short stop to first base. The abbreviations of Border's body would contrast with the wristiness of Yallop, the flash of Hughes and the elegance of Greg Chappell. Some observers found him ugly, none of them in Border's changing room.

Playing for NSW since 1977, Border had taken 20 games to make a century. A desperate call-up during the disastrous 1978–79 Ashes series coincided with Australia's only win under Yallop, and Border's unbeaten 60 and 45 at Sydney, amid Australian collapses, should have cemented his place. He grew a moustache, so he would fit in. But losses led to more experimentation, and he was dropped, for the only time, for the Sixth Test.

Having waited so long for a first-class century, he broke his Test maiden in his fourth appearance. His dismissal for 105, bowled by Sarfraz in Melbourne, triggered the infamous collapse.

Criticised for his lack of footwork and tendency to flash late outside off-stump, he answered with runs: 85 and 66 not out against Pakistan in Perth, 162 against India in Madras. His 521 runs in India pushed him into the full-strength Australian team.

Alongside the big boys, Border struggled against the West Indians until Ian Chappell's return spared him some of the heat with a shift from three to six. An unbeaten century against England at three, however, left the selectors confused about Border's best position. For years he would be shuffled around, but Border was unperturbed by unfamiliarity. Going to Pakistan under Greg Chappell shortly after marrying Jane Hiscox, he topped the aggregates, scoring 178 in a provincial match and then, in a career highlight, 150 not out and 153 in a combined 10 hours in the drawn Third Test in Lahore.

Aside from Hughes's batting, the Lord's Centenary Test in 1980 was a damp echo of Melbourne. Hughes batted through five rain-interrupted days to make 117 and 84, innings that made his name in England. Man of the Match, he etched himself into memory by running down the wicket at paceman Chris Old and driving him, off one knee, onto the pavilion. When he charged Mike Hendrick to drive, found the ball too short and instead square cut him, again off one knee. Jack Fingleton said it was the 'shot of the match – could well have been the shot of the century'. The *Daily Mirror* proclaimed him 'The Handsome Young Hero of Australia'. Hughes was compared to Compton, to McCabe, to everyone bar Bradman.

For Hughes his feats were a little too hard to forget. Back in Australia he succumbed to his old habit of premeditating shots, and in 12 first-class innings he failed 11 times to pass 20, the exception being 149 against Queensland. He then made 767 runs in his next 14 innings, celebrating the birth of his twin sons with 213 and 53 not out in Adelaide against India.

Another long triangular season was fraying Greg Chappell's nerves. For the first summer in four years he was spared West Indian bowling, but an even heavier one-day and Test schedule would deepen his sourness. Now concealed behind a salt-and-pepper beard, Greg cut an embattled figure. Crowds fell sharply. The wickets in Sydney and especially Melbourne were disgraceful, making for negative, survivalist cricket. Greg made few runs in the Tests against New Zealand, but Australia won 2–0, saved in Melbourne by a century from the resurgent Walters and some good fortune when umpire Robin Bailhache refused to give Jim Higgs out when he gloved a catch off a Lance Cairns bouncer.

It was a summer of contagious bad tempers. By February, few were surprised when it was Greg Chappell, not just the Melbourne pitch, who cracked up.

After 10 preliminary matches, Australia was set for a best-of-five finals series against Geoff Howarth's feisty New Zealanders. The Kiwis had one of their best sides: left-handers John Wright and Bruce Edgar at the top, a middle order boasting the reliable Howarth, Mark Burgess and Jeff and Martin Crowe, and the redoubtable all-rounders Richard Hadlee and Cairns leading a nagging seam attack. The first two finals were split, meaning at least four would be necessary. Chappell and his men were aching for a rest before the Third Test against India, which would take place in Melbourne after the one-day finals. Thinking beyond that – to an Ashes tour – only wearied Chappell further.

Winning the toss and batting on the porridge-coloured MCG deck, Chappell was at his imperious best until he chipped a ball towards the midwicket fence. Martin Snedden dived full-length to take a catch that for once warranted the epithet 'classic'. But Chappell shunned Snedden's claim, asking the umpires to decide if the ball had carried. In the absence of compelling eyewitness evidence from 50 metres, they could not give Chappell out. He went on to score 90 before Edgar caught him in near-identical manner – off Snedden.

Already peeved, the New Zealanders staged a determined pursuit of Australia's four for 235. Wright and Edgar added 85, but the steady loss of middle-order wickets left them six for 221, 14 short, after 49 overs. Edgar, having passed his century, was at the non-striker's end. Hadlee would face Trevor Chappell, whose medium-pacers Greg seemed to trust.

On a day when neither team could score at 5 runs an over, only a deranged Australian pessimist would have given the tail a chance.

Hadlee smacked the first ball for four, but was lbw to the second. Ian Smith, the blond wicketkeeper, hit a pair of twos before missing a straight one. With one ball to go, New Zealand were eight for 229. Brian McKechnie, the new batsman, was a burly rugby player of no great cricketing talent, but in his delusionary state Greg Chappell saw a muscular Adonis capable of pulling off the kind of act Wayne Daniel had performed at VFL Park during WSC, hitting a six to win the game.

The likelihood was minuscule. It only shows Greg's mental fatigue that he did what he did. Fearing a fifth final, he said to Trevor: 'How are you at bowling your underarms?'

It was a hot Melbourne summer's afternoon at the end of a fractious summer, after six years' constant stress. Marsh was already walking forward, waving his arms, pleading.

'I don't know,' Trevor said.

Would Greg have asked the question of anybody else?

'Well,' he said, 'you're about to find out.'

Greg told the umpire, Don Weser, of his intention. Marsh called out, 'No, mate, don't do it.'

Trevor did it, and more than 50,000 Australians booed their captain. McKechnie threw his bat in disgust. Edgar gave Greg the two-finger salute. Howarth ran on and berated the umpires. Greg, ramrod-stiff behind his beard, strode off. Trevor still seemed not to know what to do, even though he had already done it.

The prime ministers of both countries would condemn the action. More hurtfully for Greg, he was attacked from the commentary box by his brother Ian and by Benaud, who described it as 'the most gutless thing I have ever seen on a cricket field'. At his post-match press conference, Greg stuck to the letter of the law: 'If it is written in the rules of the game it is fair play.'

By the following day he had reconsidered, issuing a written statement: 'I have always played cricket within the rules of the game. I took a decision yesterday which, whilst within the laws of cricket, in the cool light of day I recognise as not being within the spirit of the game: the decision was made whilst I was under pressure and in the heat of the moment. I regret the decision. It is something I would not do again.'

Years later, Greg recognised that in February 1981 he had not been mentally fit to be captain. Blaming the heat of the moment was always going to fall short, as everything a captain does is more or less in the heat of the moment. Greg accepted that he had cracked. As this book has shown, he was hardly the first captain to come apart under the job's unremitting pressure. The disappointment of his team falling away in 1976–77, the enormous personal stress of leading the worst Ashes tour since 1886, his personal doubts about WSC, and the responsibilities heaped on him since reconciliation had bubbled over in one of those spectacular moments that are the very essence of the theatre of sport. If captains didn't come apart mentally – as Greg did that day, as Ian had a year earlier, as Lawry and Simpson had overseas, as a long line had going back to Dave Gregory on the steps of the SCG members' stand in January 1879 – we might not appreciate how close to breaking every skipper has come.

Although Greg would recover his reputation, the underarm incident was the beginning of the last act of his career. Two days after the match, he came out in the fourth final, was booed, and hit 87 to seal the series. He would make himself unavailable for the Ashes tour. A week later, in another dour Test on an atrocious MCG wicket, India's captain Sunil Gavaskar refused to accept an lbw decision and led his partner, Chetan Chauhan, to the brink of forfeit. Only the cool head of their manager, Salim Durani, persuaded Gavaskar to let Chauhan resume batting. Chasing 143 to win in their last innings of the summer, Australia mustered 83. Greg was not the only one at the end of his tether.

Even though the West Indies were Australia's most significant opponent by 1981, Kim Hughes's reputation as a captain was still going to be made by the oldest challenge, a tour of England.

Pollard, no fan of the Chappells, managed to blame both Chappell and Hughes for the chopping and changing, writing: '[Hughes's] inconsistency has made it easier for Greg Chappell to discard and take up again the biggest job in Australian sport … whenever Chappell's business affairs permit.'

Hughes at least had more going for him than Greg had in 1977. Lillee was there, grizzled and balding beneath his headband. Another West Australian, the medium-fast swinger Terry Alderman, was coming through. The batting looked thin without Chappell, and much depended on Hughes, Border and Yallop, recalled again after a strong Shield season.

Having won the one-dayers 2–1, Hughes's Test series couldn't have started much better. He sent England in at Trent Bridge, and Ian Botham, England's captain, seemed crushed by expectation. Alderman and Lillee took 17 wickets and Trevor Chappell hit the winning runs.

In the Second Test at Lord's, another fresh paceman, NSW's Geoff Lawson, ripped through England after Hughes put them in again. Rain made for a draw, but Botham resigned in favour of his predecessor Mike Brearley.

The glory, or nightmare, of 'Botham's Test' at Headingley is well documented. Australia led by 227 and Hughes, who had hit 89, made England follow on. Wickets duly tumbled, and reserves Graham Beard and Steve Rixon put champagne on ice for what would be Australia's fifth win over England in six Tests. Their dominance appeared total when Peter Willey sliced Lillee to a perfectly placed fly-slip to make the score seven for 135. Commentators praised Hughes for his brilliant captaincy, but the captain was rather sheepish as he shook Lillee's hand. The fly-slip had been Lillee's suggestion, and Hughes had rejected it twice before relenting.

Then Botham brained the Australian bowlers in two sessions. He swung at everything and connected. He put on 117 with Graham Dilley, 67 with Chris Old and 37 with Willis. The 130 Australia were set to win was 130 more than they had expected. Hughes was unable to arrest their shock. John Dyson and Trevor Chappell got them to one for 56, but once panic set in it was total. Here was the team's rotten core exposed. Botham's century was lucky, certainly, but aimless and nervous and, in the cruel light of Willis's 8/43, spiritless, Australia lost by 18.

Those 18 runs might have been thousands by the time the tour moved to Birmingham. Hughes was the first captain since Jack Blackham in 1894–95 to lose a Test after enforcing the follow-on. Then things got worse. Botham routed them with the ball, taking 5/1 in 28 deliveries. Then at Old Trafford he blazed 118. Brearley, next to the jitterbugging Hughes, was a Zen master. Perhaps that is all a captain has to do: appear in charge. Marsh and Lillee, if not quite in open revolt against Hughes, gave him little of the support that would have indicated to younger players that they were operating under a unified leadership. Their bets against Australia in Leeds, taking England at 500/1, were, if not a cause, a nasty-looking symptom.

The problem for Hughes, as for every beleaguered captain, was that he was not performing well enough as a player. Marsh and Lillee did try their best – Lillee could always point to his 39 wickets – and assured themselves that by tormenting Hughes they were trying to toughen him up. Lillee bounced and hit Hughes in net sessions. Marsh scolded his impetuosity. The problem was, what might have been an acceptable tough-love routine inside a Shield team destroyed morale when the target was the Australian captain. When finger-spinner Murray Bennett saw what was essentially a form of bullying, he spoke for many when he said, 'There's something missing here.'

In some ways, Hughes was the perfect type to lead Australia; yet his deficiencies were so glaring that his closest mentors might, in retrospect, feel shame for having steered him towards a role for which he was never fit. Paceman Wayne Clark told Hughes's biographer Christian Ryan that if Hughes had been left to bat – if he had been Neil Harvey rather than Greg Chappell – 'he would have gone down in the annals of fucking cricket history'.

Hughes's Ashes tour was a failure. He scored 300 at 25, not enough support for Border's 533 at 59.22. Border's late commitment to his shots suited the swinging conditions. In the last two Tests, with Australian morale and his own finger broken, Border batted for 13 and a half undefeated hours in scoring 123 not out, 106 not out and 84. His average more than doubled those of Hughes, Yallop, Wood and Dyson. Yallop's jitters against Willis and Botham confirmed the notion that he was gun-shy against pace. His only innings of substance was 114 in the Manchester loss. Border was the only success. Lillee, not given to gushing over young players, wrote: 'What a brave player he is! So quiet and efficient about everything he does in cricket, so determined to succeed and so professional.' Border was fast emerging as a cricketing St Jude, a patron saint of lost causes.

And this was a lost one. Australian cricket would hit a lower point four years on, but nothing could match the shock of 1981.

Before the Ashes tour, Hughes had said the ACB 'wouldn't dare' return the captaincy to Chappell. After, there was no alternative. In 1981–82 Greg Chappell became Australia's first part-time captain since Darling. Whereas Darling's commitments kept him out of home series, Greg continued to play in Australia but lent the captaincy to Hughes for tours.

Under Greg at home, Australia beat Pakistan 2–1, Lillee and Javed Miandad nearly coming to blows in Perth, and drew 1–1 with the West Indies, their best result against that opponent for the next decade and a half. Hughes was a grand batsman when someone else was captain. There was an element of truth in what Marsh and Lillee were saying: he should be left alone to bat. Hughes made 106 against Pakistan in Perth, then, on Boxing Day, played an innings that surpassed his Centenary Test double.

The MCG wicket, diabolical already, became nightmarish when the bowlers were Holding, Garner and company. On 26 December, Australia capitulated – except Hughes, who came in at three for 8. His innings was chancier than at Lord's, but, considering the conditions and the opponent and the state of the match, it was his finest. Wickets kept falling at the other end – it really was an unplayable wicket – and Australia were nine for 155 when Alderman joined Hughes. Hughes blazed to his century. When Alderman was out, Hughes had scored 100 of 190 while he was at the wicket. His

In his day, Hughes could master anyone, including the full-strength West Indies

century would assume matchwinning proportions when, in the last half-hour, Lillee tore out the West Indian top four. The image burnt onto the mind is Lillee bowling Viv Richards off the inside edge with the last ball. Hughes's century, however, was something not Richards, Lloyd, Border or Chappell went anywhere near matching.

Chappell's batting was letting him down. Tentative outside off-stump, a fraction slow to the straight ball, he made seven ducks in 15 innings. His 201 in the First Test against Pakistan at Brisbane was forgotten as the nation fixated on his ducks. Finally he recovered with 61 against the West Indies in Adelaide, but after a decade of top cricket he, like Lillee and Marsh, was entering his twilight.

After a short tour of New Zealand, where he scored a series-best 176, Greg could not bring himself to tour Pakistan again and handed Hughes the rough end of the pineapple. Hughes took back the captaincy gratefully, but touring Pakistan without Greg was like … touring England without Greg. Lillee and Pascoe also sat out the tour with injuries. Marsh arrived late, due to his son's illness. Yardley had flu. To make matters worse, Hughes's manager was ACB director and retired umpire Col Egar, the controversy-loving umpire who now embodied the worst gravy-train excesses and political intolerance of the ACB and his home association, the retrograde SACA.

During the First Test in Karachi, Hughes led his team from the field twice when spectators set marquees on fire and threw bottles at the fieldsmen. Hughes said he would take his team home if anyone was hurt, but was undermined by Egar, who gave the Pakistanis contrary assurances.

Australia were terrible. In Karachi Hughes, Border and Dyson made half-centuries, but a second-innings collapse meant a nine-wicket defeat. They dropped six catches. Lawson and Thomson squabbled with the umpires, and when Hughes tried to mollify him Thomson stormed away. The old wars were still raging. Australia were then humiliated in Faisalabad and Lahore. Hughes averaged 25.66 – again unable to make the runs that could have shored up his authority.

It would be no coincidence that Egar was manager of Australia's three catastrophic tours of the 1980s – Pakistan 1982, West Indies 1984 and Pakistan 1988. But Hughes took the rap, handing the captaincy back to Chappell, once again, for the home Ashes series.

This time the handover had less universal approval. There was much disquiet regarding Greg's part-time commitment, and if Hughes's teams had shown the remotest success the Board would happily have given him the captaincy. Instead, Greg regained the job on the casting vote of Board chairman Phil Ridings.

Against England, Greg made his first Adelaide Test century and averaged nearly 50 in a series that was controversial for a crowd invasion in Perth (costing Alderman a badly dislocated shoulder), and celebrated for the wonderful finish in Melbourne, when Border and Thomson added 70 for the last wicket but fell three short. Australia won 2–1, Hughes again blossoming under Greg with 469 at 67, his Sydney 137 the cherry on the cake.

After the Ashes, Greg led Australia in their first-ever Test in Sri Lanka, a big win due to centuries from Kepler Wessels and David Hookes and wickets to spinners Tom Hogan and Bruce Yardley. But Hughes was captain for a disastrous World Cup in England, when his own form was poor and the team won two of six, losing embarrassingly to Zimbabwe. Hughes took an early flight home and Hookes, his vice-captain and a WSC veteran, openly criticised his leadership.

This time it was Greg Chappell who came to Hughes's aid. Greg announced his availability for the five-Test home series against Pakistan during the next summer, but not as captain. For the first time, Hughes would be leading a full-strength team. For once, they harmonised, and Hughes was a star, making 106 in Adelaide, 94 in Melbourne and 76 in Sydney.

However, his batting was overshadowed by the five-times-recycled Yallop, finally allowed to settle in at three. Given the politics of the era, it is bizarre to think of an Australian line-up in which Hughes was the captain, Chappell, Marsh and Lillee were the senior players, and Yallop was the dominant batsman. Yallop's Test scores were 141, 33, 68, 14, 268 and 30. His 268 in front of his Melbourne friends was both consolation prize and crowning glory. He scored 1,000 runs in an Australian summer for the second time in three seasons. For once, Yallop could be said to have proven himself in front of his peers.

Unlike his brother, Marsh and Lillee, Greg Chappell was a compassionate mentor to Hughes. As Australia won the series 2–0, Greg edged closer to Bradman's 6,996 Test runs. He had the staggers until the last Test, in Sydney, when he started cautiously, was dropped by Mohsin Khan, and passed the record with overthrows. A pitch invader knelt before him and kissed his glove: appropriate in a way, for Greg's style had always invited descriptions such as 'regal' and 'majestic'. He went on to 182, bookending his career with centuries. He also passed Cowdrey's world record to take 122 catches. Australia has never had a more skilled and lithe all-round fieldsman.

With Marsh and Lillee, Chappell walked off into retirement. His legacy still seemed defined by the underarm incident. As time passed, his influence was more varied. Greg continued as an activist on the ACB's cricket committee, working as a selector, and a year after his retirement becoming Hughes's chief cricketing confidant in a crack-up more final than Greg's own. From 1984 to 1987 he was the fourth captain, after Darling, Hill and Bradman, to take a seat on the Board, until he quit in frustration at its bureaucratic inflexibility. He worked as a commentator, but his ambitions went beyond media work. He coached Australian states, development organisations, and even the Indian national team, where the quality of his ideas was impaired by his political weaknesses. Unlike Ian, whose approach to the game remained instinctive and anecdotal, Greg was a theoretician. His direct mode of expression, in the Chappell tradition, led him into conflict.

Greg would always suffer by comparison with Ian as a captain, just as Ian would suffer by comparison with Greg as a batsman. Both comparisons were a little unjust, but there is no doubting Greg's qualities as a batsman. In most selections of all-time Australian teams, Greg has been the second batsman picked.

His 7,110 Test runs are elevated by the quality of his opponents. Pakistan and England had excellent bowling attacks, and he faced the greatest pace battery ever assembled. In his time, Australia hosted the West Indies five times in nine summers and toured the Caribbean twice. When he became captain, Australia thrashed the West Indies. When he left, the West Indies were dismantling nearly every Australian cricketer's game piece by working piece. In Greg Chappell's era, Australia–West Indies games were true contests. From 1972–73, including Supertests, he scored 2,816 Test runs against them at 56.32. No other batsman came anywhere near him. His importance as the onfield leader of Australian cricket, the model of the captain-as-champion, would be emphasised by the size of the hole he left behind.

32

SOUTH TOWARDS BORDER

IF Pakistan in 1982 had been hard, two years later Hughes was taking a team to the West Indies without Lillee, Chappell, Marsh or Thomson. He had Col Egar, the sole applicant for manager. When they left home only one team member, Hogan, had signed his tour contract. Hughes, supported by Greg Chappell, opposed stringent conditions which attempted to wind back many of the benefits won after WSC. The players, showing no faith in their employer, went on the toughest tour, managed by one of the directors against whom they were in open insurrection.

If antagonism towards the Board united the players, it was the only passion that did. Hughes was too damaged by the Marsh–Lillee white-anting to be able to capitalise on their retirements. The pattern of disrespect was aggravated by the pressure of playing the most destructively effective team the game had seen.

His loss of authority was visible early. In the first innings of the First Test in Georgetown, Hughes sent an order to the last-wicket pair of Hogg and Hogan to hit out or get out. He wanted a short session at the West Indian top order. Instead, Hogg and Hogan dug in for two and a half hours, putting on 97 for the last wicket, showing that Hughes had lost not only his authority but his tactical sense.

The stand set up a lucky draw, but Hughes failed twice. At Port-of-Spain, Border batted nearly a day as Australia made 255. Holding was not playing, but Garner, Malcolm Marshall and Daniel were too much. Alderman could not hold on quite long enough for Border to get the last two runs for his century.

The West Indies scored eight for 468 on the back of Jeff Dujon's 130 before more top-order failures left Border fighting from the rear again. With nearly three hours left on the last day, Australia were eight for 196. Hogg stuck around with Border for 53 minutes, but when last man Alderman came in there were still 105 minutes to survive. Viv Richards, standing in as West Indian captain for the injured Lloyd, delayed taking the second new ball and missed his chance. When Border finally drove Garner to bring up his century, Richards called the game off.

Border said he felt 'steam ironed' by his effort, which has gone into Australian legend. His unbeaten 98 and 100 in a combined 10 and a half hours of unyielding resistance grow more astonishing with each passing year.

But defeat, after two draws, was a matter of when, not if. As the tour went on, Lawson was fined for dissent, Hogg lashed out at Hughes sparking fears – or hopes? – that the paceman would finally attack a captain physically, and tour newcomer Greg Matthews was stumbled upon smoking ganja.

Hughes himself was in bad odour after the tour match against Trinidad and Tobago at Pointe-a-Pierre. Protesting his counterpart's late declaration, Hughes made a mockery of the last overs, bunting balls softly down the wicket while his batting partner, Wayne Phillips, sat down and unbuckled his pads. Not for the first time, Hughes expressed his protest petulantly and out of proportion to the grievance. The tour disciplinary committee – Egar, Border and Lawson – fined the captain $400.

Finally Hughes's team capitulated, losing the last three Tests. In the entire series they did not take a West Indian second-innings wicket. Hughes made 215 at 21.50, with a top score of 33. The West Indians were cutting off the head, and in Hughes's case they were down to the gristle. Border's 521 at 74.43 showed that with concentration, technique and bloody-mindedness, the tide could be resisted. But Hughes lacked all three. What finally destroyed his captaincy was his lack of runs.

Australian teams have been nothing if not resilient, and in late 1984 Hughes was preparing what he believed would be a historic fightback. The West Indians were coming again. Hughes advocated the full-time appointment of physiotherapist Errol Alcott, who had been taken to the Caribbean after Hughes's observations of the West Indians' successes with their Australian conditioner Dennis 'Sluggo' Waight. To improve his team's outcricket, Hughes took them to the Australian Institute of Sport. They went to India in spring for the Ranji Trophy one-day series, and surprised all by winning three straight matches.

With his optimism, Hughes somehow generated a bullish attitude for the First Test against the West Indies in Perth. Soon after lunch, the visitors were five for 104: Greenidge, Haynes, Richards, Richie Richardson and Lloyd out. But as the afternoon wore on, Australia's energy wore out like a sugar high. Eight catches were dropped as Larry Gomes and Jeff Dujon engineered a recovery to 416. Australia's batting was traumatised in collapses for 76 (Hughes 4) and 228 (Hughes 37, another unconverted start). Not even Border could save them.

The following week in Brisbane, Hughes refused to speak to Ian Chappell after the toss, a reaction to Chappell's ongoing criticism. Treasuring the captaincy as he did, Ian was offended by what he saw as the second-rate candidacies of Yallop and Hughes. Unconstrained by team loyalty, he shared Lillee's contempt for Hughes but none of Lillee's West Australian camaraderie. Ian Chappell had not one good word to say about Hughes's captaincy.

The match was another rout. Hughes committed the pivotal blunder, dropping Richardson at 42 on his way to 138. English journalist Ian Wooldridge, having witnessed another blackwash in England in 1984, wrote that seeing Australia lose so badly was 'like finding an old mate in the next bed in intensive care'.

Hughes scored 34 and 4 as Australia went down by eight wickets. Then, on 26 November, he revealed to the world what he had been discussing privately with Greg Chappell. The man whose mental breakdown led to the underarm ball thought he had an easy time of the captaincy compared with Hughes. Greg told Christian Ryan: 'I love Kim Hughes'. Enough to counsel him to quit the captaincy.

After the Brisbane Test, Hughes sat in a press conference with team manager and ACB director Bob Merriman and only managed three and a half sentences of an intended eight-sentence statement:

> The Australian cricket captaincy is something that I've held very dear to me. However, playing the game with total enjoyment has always been of greatest importance. The constant speculation, criticism and innuendo by former players and sections of the media over the past 4–5 years have finally taken their toll. It is in the interest of the team …

Hughes paused, lip quivering. Merriman urged him to go on. Hughes, breaking into tears, asked Merriman to read the rest and made for the door. The words Hughes could not bring himself to utter were 'and myself', the too-hurtful implication that the captaincy was destroying him.

And that was that. The captaincy had overwhelmed others too, including his two immediate predecessors, but never had a man departed on terms so dramatic and personally embarrassing.

Hughes won no friends in the changing room by quitting. Lawson was angry because he would have tried to stop him. In the frankly macho world of professional sport, Hughes had fulfilled the knockers' warnings: he was a crybaby.

He did have his supporters, even in the Channel Nine mafia. Bill Lawry, who knew a thing or two about these matters, said to a Rotary Club function: 'What happened to Kim Hughes in Brisbane was like being dragged down like a dingo in the pack and devoured by your own from within and without.' Border supported Hughes with the shocked loyalty Ian Chappell had shown Lawry in 1971. When Hughes appeared at a cricket function in Adelaide a few days after his resignation, he received a standing ovation.

Of all the problems affecting Hughes the biggest, as ever, was runs, or their lack. Never was this more poignantly demonstrated than in his last 12 balls as a Test batsman, dragged out over four innings in Adelaide and Melbourne: 0, 2, 0 and 0. By the Fifth Test, he was not even a member of the team he had led three Tests earlier.

33

CAPTAINCY AS PARTNERSHIP

B Y the time he became captain in 1984, Border had scored 12 Test centuries, only one in a winning effort, against England in Perth in 1979–80. Four had come in losses, and seven in draws.

This was his qualification to be Australian captain.

Border was one of the few to know about Hughes's plan to quit in Brisbane. When Hughes showed him his resignation speech, Border felt 'gut-wrenching pain' and begged Hughes to reconsider. It wouldn't take much calculation for him to see that he, as vice-captain, was the alternative. For Border it felt like being next man up for the firing squad.

A week later, while Border was playing for Queensland against Tasmania, Greg Chappell told him he was captain. Chappell, the king become kingmaker, was as much a mentor to Border as to Hughes. In 1980–81, Border had gone to Queensland under Chappell's persuasion.

But Border feared that he was no captain. As Hughes's deputy in Pakistan in 1982, he did not envy his captain. Commenting on Chappell's and Hughes's crises, Border had admired their diplomacy, a quality he did not believe he possessed. If he were captain, he said, disputes 'might end up in a free-for-all'. And besides, in November 1984 his recent form was as poor as anyone's, with 15, 6, 17 and 24 in the first two Tests. He was feeling, quite reasonably, that the pressure of captaincy might see him out of the side.

But Chappell told him he had no choice. For his country, Border accepted the job. In Adelaide, his first move as captain – starting out the way he meant to go on – was to delegate. Bradman gave the pre-Test 'captain's' speech. Merriman ran the outfield catching practice. At his first press conference, looking like a Trojan presented with a suspicious-looking horse, Border confessed to being 'a little bit disappointed with the circumstances surrounding my appointment'.

The West Indies won easily, Border scoring 21 and 18. What followed in the series might have been a dead-cat bounce, but in the Fourth Test in Melbourne, Hilditch's six-hour 113 helped save a draw with two wickets in hand. Then, in Sydney, Border marshalled NSW spinners Bob 'Dutchy' Holland and Murray Bennett to a heartening win, Australia's first against this opponent since Christmas 1981, Kim Hughes's Test.

It would seem, over the next 12 months, that the Sydney victory owed more to West Indian complacency than Australian renewal. No corners had been turned. Things were not getting better. In fact, they were about to get worse.

During the 1983 World Cup, Graham Yallop had first met Ali Bacher. Bacher, the South African captain who had slaughtered Bill Lawry's team in 1969–70, was now the lead organiser for unofficial tours. In Leeds, Yallop, Bacher and Kepler Wessels discussed an Australian tour. Yallop, who felt he had given his all to the establishment and received little thanks, visited South Africa the next year and was flattered by Bacher's attention.

By 1985, Yallop's Australian career was over. His annus mirabilis in 1983–84 had come to a crunching halt when, in a one-day international at the MCG, he slid into the fence and injured his knee badly enough to miss the Caribbean tour. He was recalled for the Perth Test of 1984–85, scored 2 and 1, and was dropped for the fifth and last time.

Yallop had more reason than most to bear a grudge. He was the conformist who turned into a rebel. He was not alone. By 1985, he was assembling the first rebel Australian team to go to South Africa.

Yallop was to be captain, but he stood aside when Hughes, a more potent headliner, came across as well. Hughes, Yallop and other players got it into their heads that not being able to play in South Africa was infringing their freedom. Hughes, after assuring Border that he would not go on any rebel tour, signed with Bacher in a fit of pique at his exclusion from Border's 1985 Ashes tour.

Hughes would lead the ersatz Australians on two tours, averaging 43.7. Yallop averaged 27.20 on the first tour and 61.33 on the second, finishing his first-class cricket career with 14 and 69 against Northern Transvaal at Centurion Park in January 1987.

Later, Yallop, Hughes and several teammates fought bans to resume their cricket careers in Australia. Yallop played club cricket and won $12,500 in compensation for having been sacked from his job as manager of the Australian National Watersports Centre, his crime having been to play cricket on the weekends.

For an Australian batsman who averaged 41.13 in 39 Tests, Yallop ended his career in what might be called conspicuous obscurity. Unreconciled, he remained an outsider after a cricket career when he felt he received a great deal less than he gave. Many captains, as we have seen, were selected for their country on potential and given ample time to realise it. With others, such as Yallop, selectors seemed constantly looking for an excuse to leave them out. Yallop's captaincy was brief and unsuccessful, yet he showed in later years that given a proper chance he might have become a prolific top-order batsman. That he did not left him embittered, on the outside of a game he had served, when it needed him, with the best of his efforts.

Hughes also degraded his reputation in his final playing years. He won a legal challenge against a club-cricket ban and tried to make a comeback for WA for two seasons. After a bright start his batting, paralysed by a constant shuffle and compulsion to hook, let him down again. He returned to South Africa to lead Natal for a short, acrimonious stint in which 25 innings produced an average of 18.41. Thus a man who deserved great sympathy, more sinned against than sinning, became his own worst enemy.

For the 1985 Ashes tour, Border lost Hughes, Yallop, quality batsmen such as Dyson, Mike Haysman and Steve Smith, plus a bowling battery of Hogg, Alderman and Queenslanders John Maguire and Carl Rackemann to the South African rebel venture. The team he took to England was described as a Second XI. His bowling stocks comprised Craig McDermott, Geoff Lawson and a geriatric Thomson. His batting support included three men – Dirk Wellham, Wayne Phillips and Graeme Wood – who had remained with the Test team only after Kerry Packer paid them not to go to South Africa.

Perfect balance; Allan Border plays to leg

Border's batting stood above his teammates as Bradman's had. For the fourth time in six tours, he topped the aggregates. The 1985 team was popular, as all losing Australian teams in England have been, and Border led them in great spirit against his friends Gower and Botham. More than most, the 1985 squad attracted big crowds because of their friendly attitude.

Australia won the one-day series but at Headingley England racked up 533 and won by five wickets. Border played a lone hand at Lord's, his 196 the highest score there by an Australian captain since Woodfull's 155 in 1934. Chasing just 127 in the fourth innings, Australia choked before Border's unbeaten 41 saved the day.

Lord's was a momentary sunray. Two draws followed, with another century to Border at Old Trafford, before Gower took command of the Edgbaston and Oval Tests, both of which England won by an innings, for a series result of 3–1.

There were some gems to dig out of the mullock. Border's eight centuries on tour, and 66 average for the Tests, ensconced his authority. McDermott took 30 Test wickets and Lawson 22, while Andrew Hilditch and Greg Ritchie passed 400 runs. But, as in the West Indies in 1984, Australia's capitulation in the second half of the series indicated a team that lacked collective stamina. It wasn't often that an Australian team ran out of fight.

Border kept looking for light at the end of the tunnel, but there was a lot of tunnel to endure first. He brought his team home to suffer Australia's only home loss to New Zealand. Richard Hadlee took 9/52 and 6/71 in Brisbane as every batsman, save Kepler Wessels, Border and the surprising Greg Matthews, showed an absence of technique and concentration. Holland took 10 wickets on a Sydney turner, but New Zealand won the Third Test in Perth. Hadlee took 33 wickets at 12.15 and confirmed himself as the best swing-and-seam exponent since Lillee.

After Perth, Border appeared to have had enough. 'You start to wonder,' he said, 'if you're the right man for the job. If there was an obvious choice who I thought could do a better job, I'd be more than happy to stand down … I find it increasingly difficult to lift. My own enjoyment of the game is suffering. You start to wonder what you're going to do.'

Many thought he would quit. In a year, he had led Australia in 12 Tests for three wins, six losses and three draws. He felt betrayed by the rebels. He did not think of himself as a captain, and was often criticised for his 'negativity', even though 'positive cricket', in the face of another Gower century or Hadlee assault, would have been delusional.

Border did not quit, but led Australia in a series against India that was billed as Test cricket's battle for the wooden spoon. In a dreary affair which both teams were content to draw, India piled up massive totals but could not finish Australia off. Lawson succumbed to stress fractures, but Border, Matthews and David Boon occupied the crease long enough to ensure a stalemate in front of low crowds.

Border didn't know it – nobody knew it – but the turnaround was already underway. Talented but flighty cricketers were being weeded out for players of 'substance'. What did that mean? It meant players more in Border's image, cricketers of limitless limits. In came Geoff Marsh, a tough opener from WA, to partner the doughty Boon. In came Bruce Reid and Merv Hughes, bowlers of physical and mental stature. In came 19-year-old Stephen Waugh, a concession to natural talent, but seemingly a hard-bitten character as well.

Growing up in Panania, in Sydney's south-western suburbs, Waugh had honed his skills against his twin brother Mark. The first two of four sons of a bank worker father and schoolteacher mother, the Waughs, both educated at East Hills Boys' High School, excelled at soccer and tennis until junior representative honours pushed them cricket's way. While Border had been the first captain to list 'professional cricketer' as his occupation, Steve Waugh would be the first who neither studied for nor held a job outside cricket. By the time he matured in the mid-1980s, full professionalism had arrived for the elite.

Waugh, having been recognised and cultivated by under-age selectors, made his NSW debut at 19 as a bowling all-rounder. Overseen by an expression crinkled by the sun into permanent scepticism, a face never to be kidded with, his style had its idiosyncrasies. Batting, he stood in a hunched, slightly tilted stance with low wrists and punched the ball off the back foot, only moving forward to drive the most over-pitched deliveries. His bowling action was whippy and effortful, sometimes surprising batsmen with its pace. He developed both arts in the Bolton League in Lancashire in 1985, watching Border's team play at Lord's as an excited spectator.

More than his gifts, Waugh impressed with his dedication to the game, his manifest hatred of failure, and his all-round cricket smarts. But when picked for Australia against India at Christmas 1985, the 20-year-old would say he felt 'alone and isolated' in a 'very unsure' team. Border did little, personally, to ease his entry. Waugh expected to be 12th man until Ritchie injured his foot gardening, then scored a scratchy 13 and 5 and took two wickets.

Waugh's uncertainty over whether he was good enough to be a Test cricketer would last several years. He would wait until 1989 for his first century, then be dropped again in 1990. He functioned more consistently in the one-day format than in Tests. Throughout, his most influential guide was not the team captain, but the hands-on supremo of Australian cricket. That they were not one and the same person shows how profoundly the job of Australian captain changed in the mid-1980s.

Bob Simpson's 1977–78 comeback had shown him that, like Bradman, his leadership was at its best as a mentor to younger players. In 1984–85 he was made coach of NSW, a new role that he would pioneer. Entering his third career in the Australian team in 1985–86, Simpson was exactly the man Border needed by his side. Simpson could bear the grudges and work the media and run the practices. Border could play the Test matches. Simpson could absorb, even enjoy, the politics. Border, for whom politics was poison, could bat and field and make the bowling changes. It would prove an ideal combination for lifting a team off the floor. Several years would pass before the downside of such a pairing would need contemplation.

Results were slow in coming. Australia drew the first two Tests in New Zealand in early 1986, Border making twin centuries in Christchurch, but collapsed for a pitiful 103 in Auckland against the off-spin of John Bracewell to lose the series. Topping the aggregates yet again gave Border no solace. None of his bowlers had taken 10 wickets, and a captain without penetrative bowlers is no captain at all.

After a one-day loss in Dunedin, Border let loose. His team, he said, would have 'to show me whether they really want me to play for Australia and whether they want to play under me. I'll find out over the next three games and my decision will be made as to my future as a captain and a player after that. I don't think it's my captaincy, but if we continue to lose, you have to start saying, "Right, someone else has to come in."'

Clearly he was venting, but Captain Grumpy, as journalist Adrian McGregor dubbed him, was wondering if he was more hindrance than help.

The team did improve mildly, and Border led them to India the following spring. For once, in the First Test in Madras, he risked losing to get a win. It was a huge gamble, given the sacrifices that had earnt Austalia a 177-run lead. Boon and Border made centuries in 45-degree heat, and Dean Jones's 210, a Via Dolorosa of 562 minutes, was for the ages. The young Victorian right-hander was physically ill, collapsing and vomiting and putting up with his captain's taunts – 'Do you want to go off so I can put a real Australian in?' Border asked. Jones knew the next man was the

Queenslander Ritchie. Jones ended up on a drip. By the marathon's end, Simpson said he had never seen a more courageous innings.

Daringly for him, Border set India 348 on the last day. A strong batting team took up the challenge and would have sent Border into a spiral of regret but for the persistence of left-armer Ray Bright and his five second-innings wickets, and off-spinner Matthews. The last of Matthews's 10 victims in the match, Maninder Singh, was lbw, delivering the second Tied Test in 109 years.

The drama of the tie lifted the clouds from Border. Querulous with the umpires in Madras, he praised them by the end of the series. When the Second Test in Delhi was virtually washed out, Border did something unprecedented for an Australian captain in India – he offered to play an extra Test. Something, beneath the surface, was changing.

But not quickly. The following summer brought another Ashes defeat, the fifth in six series going back to 1977. Simpson was improving the team's fitness and outcricket, and Border trowelled on another load of runs including two centuries, but a resolution to play enterprising, confident cricket was based too much on hope and too little on ability. In Melbourne, Australia's over-aggression cost them their first three-day Ashes loss at home since 1901–02. A consolation win in Sydney, thanks to leg-spinner Peter Sleep and tweaker 'Peter Who?' Taylor, was no consolation at all. That it broke a 15-Test winless sequence only highlighted the problem. Australian cricket was in such disarray that Taylor's selection triggered the rumour that the ACB had erred, meaning to choose the NSW opening batsman Mark Taylor.

Border also seemed not to be in control of his team. Wellham, the experienced NSW captain, had been overruled as vice-captain by the Board. Geoff Marsh was his replacement. But neither Border nor Marsh seemed to be moving the field in Sydney – the team was listening to Wellham. It wouldn't be a problem again, as Wellham was playing his last Test.

Border packed years of insult into his bags going to India for his third World Cup. Australia had progressed further in one-day cricket than in the longer form, but their losing habits made them rank outsiders. They performed well in their group, however, and a shock win over Pakistan in the semi-final put them into the final against Mike Gatting's England. At Eden Gardens, before a crowd of de facto Australian fans (Indians cheering for the underdogs), Boon made 75 and Border 31 before their promising start petered out to a competitive but not forbidding five for 253.

England were cruising at two for 135 when Gatting took Border's finger-spinners too lightly. Mangling a reverse sweep, Gatting set off a collapse that eventually saw Australia 7 runs to the good.

Two steps forward, one step back. The World Cup vindicated Border's persistence with the captaincy. Having had such a bad time, he appeared nonplussed by the trophy. Still on friendly terms with the English, he took the cup to the changing rooms where players detached the ball from its mounting and played an indoor game.

The World Cup looks like a turnaround from here, but it was no such thing, or not immediately. Border's team beat New Zealand at home, thanks to a fast pitch in Perth, a draw in Adelaide and face-saving batting by Mike Whitney and McDermott to survive the last 29 balls in Melbourne. National celebrations ensued: Australia had saved a match against New Zealand!

A poorly attended, rain-ruined and boring Bicentennial Test in Sydney followed, then a Test against Sri Lanka in Perth that was watched by only 10,607. Border had engineered something marvellous in India, but home crowds were losing hope.

His good run on the subcontinent came to a screeching halt in Pakistan the next spring, when Border, Simpson and Egar succumbed to decades of frustration. After poor umpiring in the lead-up matches and, expecting a doctored pitch in the First Test in Karachi, Border presented the unusual spectacle of an Australian captain giving up on a Pakistan series before, rather than after, it was played. He, Simpson and Egar threatened to abandon the tour for the noble purpose of 'showing the world what's happening here'. The younger members of the team, including debutant wicket-keeper Ian Healy, were let down by the leadership's group-think of paranoia and intolerance. Border had said, after he made 150 not out and 153 in Lahore in 1980, that he would prefer never to come back. Egar was a thunderhead of incivility looking for a parade to rain on. More than the losses in 1985, the Pakistan tour of 1988 was the nadir of Border's captaincy, because this was a defeat wrought from the top down. Australia duly lost the First Test, collapsing for 165 and 116 in response to Pakistan's nine for 469, the uncanny Miandad choosing this moment to pile up 211. That Australia nearly squared the series in Lahore showed just how costly it was that Border, Simpson and Egar had let their negative thinking get the better of them.

Primed for defeat, Border's team found it in abundance with the West Indies. The Holding–Garner generation had gone, replaced by the accurate Courtney Walsh, an Antiguan lapsed basketballer named Curtly Ambrose and the Jamaican thunderbolt-thrower Patrick Patterson. Marshall, arguably the best of all the Caribbean speedmen for his swing and cut at high pace, was at his peak. The first three Tests were brutal. Steve Waugh flashed 90s in Perth and Brisbane and bounced Viv Richards, while Merv Hughes took a hat-trick over two innings to avenge Lawson's broken jaw in Perth. But those were rare highlights and the difference in class was embarrassing by the Third Test in Melbourne.

This match, Border's 100th, was one of his least enjoyable. On a wicket recalling the dark MCG days of a decade earlier, Patterson made the Australians feel like ducks in a shooting gallery. The Australians were trying to execute a new combative ethos, but coming from such juniors as Waugh and Healy, it offended West Indians as a cheekiness that asked to be put in its place. Which they did. Border's 100th Test was a heavy loss played in a bitter temper. He said: 'I get absolutely no joy from Test cricket as it has been played in this match.'

But he wasn't threatening, again, to retire. The respite he had found in the tie in Madras, the World Cup win in Calcutta, and the saved New Zealand series had renewed Border's appetite. Less tunnel, more light. In Sydney, a week after his least enjoyable Test, he gave himself an uncustomarily long bowl. By the end of the first day he had taken seven West Indian wickets for 46. Australian cricket fans, who had been urging him to bowl more, said they told him so.

Rather than lose their advantage amid the surprise of gaining it, Australia capitalised, Boon's 149 and Border's vigil – a 262-ball half-century of epic dreariness – building a lead of 177. Border squeezed out another few overs and took four more wickets. Australia won easily, and a draw in Adelaide, on a flat deck that helped Jones score his second double-century, ensured that Melbourne had been the bottoming-out that Border had been waiting for.

The national selection panel, headed by West Australian Lawrie Sawle – proof that Test experience was no substitute for an astute eye – had spent three years assembling a team that might be able to redeem Border's long, bleak decade. In Adelaide, an academy was started where some of the lessons from top cricket could be systematised and imparted to a younger generation.

The payoff, glimpses of which were seen against the West Indies in Sydney and Adelaide, arrived in England in 1989. Accustomed to winning, the English media proclaimed Border's tourists the worst in memory, though how they could be worse than the previous three tours hints at how complacent the English had become. Border had the team he wanted. Mark Taylor, Marsh and Boon were a stable tripod at the top. Then came Border, Jones and Steve Waugh, Healy, and a pace attack of Hughes, Alderman and Lawson. On a hunch, Sawle and Border had got Trevor Hohns, a tidy Queensland leg-spinner, into the squad to balance the bowling.

While England chewed through 29 players in the six-Test series, Australia used 12. Taylor scored more runs than anyone in an Ashes series other than Bradman and Hammond. Waugh batted for three Tests before losing his wicket. Healy was flawless. Jones, Boon and Marsh were reliable. Alderman, forgiven for the rebel tours, picked up where he had left off in 1981, but this time he had the whole-hearted back-up of Hughes and the canny Lawson. Hohns also played his part as Border became the first captain since Woodfull in 1934 to go to England and regain the Ashes.

Border made no Test centuries, but his batting at Headingley was reminiscent of Ian Chappell. After winning the toss, Australia

LEFT: Early in his career, Steve Waugh was a bowling all-rounder for Australia.

THE CAPTAINS 391

were two for 57. Border came out blasting, hoisting a Phil DeFreitas long hop for six over point. It was stunning first-morning batting. He made 66 runs of incalculable symbolic value, setting up Waugh's first Test century, a massive win, and the momentum for the series.

Taylor also made a maiden century, 136 in his third Test. The modest Border rated Taylor's century as 'the critical innings'. Taylor's background was middle-class but peripatetic. His father Tony was a valuer for the Rural Bank of NSW and a grade cricketer who couldn't stay in one place long enough to build a career. Mark, born in Leeton, attended schools in Mildura and West Wyalong before the family settled in Wagga Wagga. A useful back-pocket Australian Rules player, Taylor was educated in cricket by his father in an enclosed concrete garage, then by the Lake Albert Cricket Club in Wagga, home of Geoff Lawson, a club notable for rewarding 'clubmanship' ahead of individual achievement.

When Taylor was a young teen the family moved again, to Lindfield on Sydney's north shore, where, while attending Chatswood High School, he came to the attention of the former NSW batsman Neil 'Harpo' Marks. Stocky and crease-faced, Marks was a maker and breaker of young cricketers as a selector in under-age teams. He took Taylor under his wing at the Northern Districts club and in junior representative sides alongside the Waugh twins from Panania.

While the Waughs, from a religiously sporting family in the heartland of suburban Sydney, were committed to professional cricket, Taylor went to the University of NSW to study surveying, not quite trusting his cricket talent. But when NSW's openers John Dyson and Steve Smith went to South Africa in 1985, the new state opening combination was Taylor and Mark Waugh. Taylor scored 12 and 56 not out on debut against Tasmania, and four games later notched a maiden 118 against South Australia at the SCG. As he would show throughout his career, he had an Arthur Morris-like knack for adapting to the unfamiliar: his first state season yielded 937 at 49.31.

Graduating from UNSW in 1987, he put in a season with Greenmount in the Bolton League and overcame a lean run in 1987–88 to pile on 1,241 at 49.64 during the next season. He would never generate the excitement of the Waughs, but Taylor was an orthodox left-hander, nicknamed 'Stodge' but underrated aesthetically, a balanced all-round-the-wicket batsman and, like Border, a superb leaver. He was uncommonly calm. When he played and missed, or had trouble middling the ball, his response was never to try to lash boundaries to heal a wounded ego. He was also emerging, under Marks's encouragement, as a first-slip fieldsman in the class of the Chappells and Simpson, with soft hands, uncanny anticipation and a bottomless well of concentration.

Mr Perfect: Mark Taylor

The national call-up came during the despair of 1988–89. Taylor was immediately part of a winning team, scoring 25 and 3 in Sydney, then being run out both innings, for 3 and 36, during the draw in Adelaide.

It would be two years before Taylor experienced losing a Test match. From the beginning he had the sheen of a winner, and approached his cricket with the open, happy face of the unwounded. As Australia steamrolled a factionalised England team in 1989, Taylor followed his century at Headingley with 60, 62, 27, 43, 51, 85 and 37 not out, by which time the Ashes were regained. His partnership with Marsh served two purposes, giving Australia a left-right combination to unsettle the bowling and freeing Boon to plug the hole at three. Taylor and Marsh gave England agony at Trent Bridge, becoming the first pair to bat through an uninterrupted first day's play in England, reaching 301 at stumps. Seeking inspiration, Gower drank champagne during lunch. Taylor ended up batting for 552 minutes for 219, which would stand as his highest Test score for nine years.

Border's captaincy, in victory, had a harder edge. Under Simpson, there would be no more mister nice guy.

Gower, taken aback by Border's change, said later: 'He was mean to the opposition, the press and indeed his own players. He sledged pretty fiercely too … It was hyper-unfriendly.'

Gower was right – Border was unfriendly – but his players loved him to a man, and when Boon hit the Ashes-winning runs in Manchester their joy was magnified by their knowledge of what Border had been through. He was typically matter-of-fact, as he remained throughout the tickertape parade on his return to Sydney, but Lawson, along with Boon his most experienced teammate, observed Border's growth in the top job: 'AB has learned to be a good captain; Gower does not appear to be too interested in learning.'

It is one of the simplest but most insightful appraisals of Border that after five years he still saw himself as a student of captaincy. Few who did not know him could appreciate how genuinely humble Border was. He had an integrity that could not be shaken by the position he held. He was the most 'normal' individual to be a captain, and it was that very unpretentiousness that won him the kind of love, from his players, that Ian Chappell and Benaud had won for their charisma.

Border averaged 73.66 in the 1989 series, but he was outscored by Taylor, Jones and Waugh. The days of Border carrying his team were past. In his first game back, for Queensland against SA, he scored an unbeaten 144. Yet it would be two years and 25 first-class games before he scored his next century, 196, again against SA. In Test cricket, Border had scored 113 not out in Faisalabad in the spring of 1988, but his next century, 37 appearances later, would be in the spring of 1992.

There was, of course, a connection between his loss of form and the rise of his team's. A few years earlier, Mike Coward had written: 'Allan Border is Australian cricket.' He was. By 1989, he was a vital part in a team of rising champions but no longer the cornerstone.

His team scrambled through a post-Ashes let-down in 1989–90, then put the English away again in 1990–91. Steve Waugh, having lost form after his 1989 Ashes tour, was dropped in Adelaide and replaced by Mark, who introduced himself to Test cricket with a sumptuous 138. Taylor also came to earth after two marvellous years in Test cricket, failing when the English cramped him from around the wicket.

Border took his team to the final frontier in 1991 to find hostilities intensified. The old dogs of the West Indies – Richards, Greenidge,

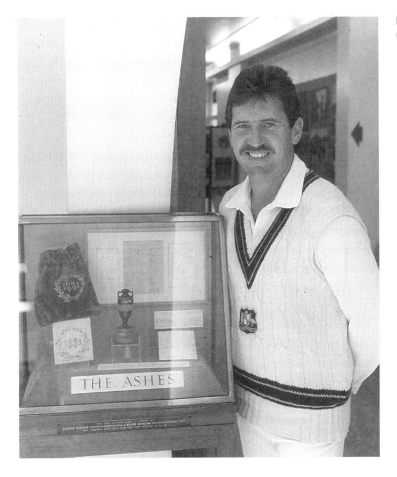

Border with the Ashes he never thought he'd win

Haynes and Marshall, all nearing the end – were prepared to engage the young Australians' aggression and turn it back at them. In the Second Test, in Georgetown, Jones was run out when he mistakenly walked after being out off a no-ball. Border was the non-striker as Carl Hooper ran Jones out, and umpire Clyde Cumberbatch, not knowing that such a run-out contravened the laws, sent Jones on his way. There was open conflict between two provocateurs in Healy and Haynes. Richards and Simpson renewed old vows. Simpson was revelling in the antagonisms stirred up in the Caribbean in 1965 and 1978, and Richards described Simpson as 'a moaner, a bad loser and a very sour sort of guy'. The WSC years would die hard.

Richards was speaking from a position of strength, because Border's team had not been able to translate their attitude into runs and wickets. After a First Test draw in Kingston, Australia were massacred in Georgetown by a brutal Richardson and Haynes in a partnership of 297, although Border took 5/68 from 30 overs. Trinidad was drawn before Greenidge, staring down calls for his sacking, scored 226 on the eve of his 40th birthday at home in Bridgetown. With Marshall, Patterson, Ambrose and Walsh taking wickets, no Australian batting effort came together until the dead rubber at St John's, where Taylor and Mark Waugh made hundreds.

Amid the mayhem of that tour Taylor was a still centre, never mentioned in either onfield squabbles or off-field shenanigans. He scored three half-centuries in the first four Tests and then, in Australia's rebound in Antigua, 59 and 144 to become the highest-scoring tourist. He and Mark Waugh were the only Australian batsmen to enhance their reputations in a nasty, unfulfilled venture.

Border's influence on his team was raising questions about whether the rock on which the team was built might be turning into the obstacle in the path of their development. At Bridgetown he took a session to score 29 with a broken thumb. It was classic Border, but Australia needed runs, not defiance. They needed runs again in the second innings when he strode bravely to bat and made a duck.

Yet Border was more determined to hold onto the captaincy in his eighth year of the job than he had been in his first or second. Having taken so many beatings, he wasn't going to give up now that things were looking smoother.

Border being Border, these years of improvement were personally difficult. His batting lost its punch, almost as if his rising team had left him without enough corners to be backed into. Rather than a triumphal march, the final two years of his captaincy became a tussle between Border and his dispensability. Few wanted to move forward without him, but it also became obvious that with him the team could not move forward.

At home in 1991–92, they beat India 4–0. The podgy, mulleted Victorian leg-spinner Shane Warne had his initiation in Sydney, and a child named Sachin Tendulkar peeled off centuries in Sydney and Perth. Border averaged 55 without a century, but the series win mattered little to him when he was told, after the Fourth Test, that his ally Marsh was being dropped.

Marsh had averaged 26 against India and much the same in the West Indies. When he heard the news in Adelaide, Border refused to take the field with his team, spending 20 minutes haranguing Sawle over the phone. Then Border, throwing a tantrum, did not fly with his men to Perth. He had a point but, as in Pakistan in 1988, lost control of the proportionality of his response. As highly as he valued Marsh, he was sending a converse message to the hapless Victorian, Wayne Phillips, who replaced Marsh for his first and only Test match.

The violence of the ups and downs increased in Border's last three seasons. At home, the 1992 World Cup was a dreadful disappointment. Unbackable favourites, Border's team was outsmarted by New Zealand and bundled out by eventual winners Pakistan. His captaincy looked formulaic next to the adventure of the New Zealanders and the quicksilver of the Pakistanis. In Colombo the next spring Australia came within a few lusty blows of losing their first Test to Sri Lanka, but Aravinda de Silva, attempting one of those blows, skied McDermott and Border ran half a lap to take a wonderful catch, then Matthews and Warne combined to pull off a great escape.

The drama and pain of the 1992–93 Frank Worrell Trophy captured Border's captaincy in microcosm. In Brisbane, a combination of rain, bad umpiring and the omission of Warne left Australia dangling on the brink of victory. Border was booked for dissent and did not turn up to his disciplinary hearing. Only the mercy of referee Raman Subba Row dealt Border a $2,000 fine rather than his first missed Test since 1979. Then Warne, reinstated in Melbourne, took 7/52, giving Australia a grand win and a dizzying vision of destruction. If history had delivered Warne into Border's hands three years earlier, he would surely have won the Worrell. But after a sodden draw in Sydney, an excruciatingly tense Fourth Test in Adelaide ended with the narrowest winning margin in Test history. In a match of nervous batting and ferocious fast bowling, Australia needed 186 on the fourth day for Border to hold that last trophy. Border himself, in a defensive rut, was bowled shouldering arms. Boon was heavied out of the match. Justin Langer, battered on debut, made a half-century but McDermott and Tim May were left to bat for a miracle which looked like it might just transpire until Walsh's bouncer brushed enough of McDermott's gear to convince umpire Darrell Hair that he was out. The image of Border pounding his worry ball into the ceiling of the Adelaide changing room, via the floor and wall, showed how this diminutive man could encapsulate a nation's feelings.

Yet Border's interviews after that soul-destroying loss show a man whose soul is intact. Border was Kipling's man in 'If'. Of course he blew up – a few months later he was abusing McDermott on the field in England – but that too was a passing storm. To have gone through what Border went through, to have survived it and eventually prospered, a man must be in possession of some of life's mysteries, whether he knows it or not: another reason why Australians loved him unreservedly.

On he went from Adelaide, not crushed but simply more Border-like. Quite un-Border-like was his first Test pair in Perth the next week as Ambrose routed the Australians.

For Taylor, dropped for Perth, it was a good Test to miss. He had been Border's vice-captain, a position which had been a graveyard for Wellham, Boon and Marsh. But although it took seven years of first-class cricket before he led his state, there was always something of the leader in Taylor. He would say that the Waugh twins 'chose' the youth representative teams of the early 1980s, but Taylor was the level-headed citizen with an uncanny ability to read the rhythms and flows of a cricket game and the personalities of teammates and opponents.

As Lawson's vice-captain for NSW, Taylor had shown an innate sense of leadership. In the 1989–90 Shield final, Lawson came down with a late injury. Not only did Taylor win the toss and the match, but he scored centuries in both innings. Captaincy obviously agreed with him.

The ACB groomed him with a B team tour to Zimbabwe, in charge of contemporaries such as Shane Warne, Steve Waugh, Paul Reiffel, Tom Moody and Michael Bevan. It was Taylor's luck that his only serious potential rival for the leadership, Waugh, lost form in those crucial years when the succession was being planned.

Taylor always seemed lucky. In Perth the selectors had wanted to spare him, not lose him. Restored for the short 1993 tour of New Zealand, he made 82 in his comeback and in England formed a partnership with another kid from Wagga, Michael Slater. Taylor's adaptable style and personality suited him well to partnerships, where he could complement either the gritty Marsh or the flamboyant Slater. For NSW he had paired with the swashbuckling Steve Small. Now, in Slater, opposites attracted again. They scored centuries in the first two Ashes Tests, and cemented a top-order partnership that would last for all but two of Taylor's remaining years.

Border's pair against the West Indies in Perth, piled onto the disappointment of falling 2 runs short of winning the Worrell, did not usher him towards the exit. His team split the New Zealand series, then beat England. In Hamilton, he passed Gavaskar's world record in front of 10 men and a brown dog with a swipe off Dipak Patel. Slightly embarrassed, he had to tell his batting parter, Healy, why everyone on the balcony was clapping.

By the end of 1993 Border wanted to keep playing, despite growing agitation among the ACB. He was Australia's first completely professional cricketer. The post-WSC settlement had given him a salary beyond $100,000, climbing through the 1990s. He was no stirrer, no unionist, no agitator. He left that kind of thing to Simpson. But by 1993, a sentiment was growing amid the ACB that it was time for Border to stand aside for the fresh, ebullient Taylor.

His last summer was a difficult one. South Africa returned from exile with a strength that surprised everyone except those who had been on the rebel tours. The First Test was a wash-out, then Border's pessimism infected his team during a small chase in Sydney. His tendency was always to worry about what might go wrong, and so, catching his drift, did his teammates. Pursuing 117, they made 111. Border recorded 84 in the redemptive win in Adelaide, but the series was scarred by squabbles over umpiring and merciless sledging.

If there was a suspicion that Border was losing control over his young team, it was confirmed in the return bout in South Africa. In Johannesburg he kept Warne on the boundary, not bowling him, through the second morning. Border was already in a funk, having run out Mark Waugh and himself on the first day. His neglect of Warne was a miscalculation. Warne was suffering from more private problems than Border knew of, and none of the Australians had experienced how vile the Wanderers crowd could be. When Border finally gave Warne the ball, and Warne dismissed Andrew Hudson, the leg-spinner lost his bearings with a show of frustration directed at the mildest of men. Hughes was also involved in dissent and a clash with spectators – not unwarranted, but ugly when repeated on televison back in Australia.

Border and Simpson, misjudging again, dealt Warne and Hughes minor punishments. The ACB, mindful of wider public reaction, overruled them, levying heavier fines. Border was angry. The incident was not really about Warne and Hughes. It was about Border. The ACB had decided that his time was up.

He knew it, too. Australia squared the series in Cape Town, but the deciding Test, in Durban, was a case study in how scar tissue can immobilise. Wessels and Border executed tactics that nullified the deciding Test, a throwback to the 1960s. Too much at stake? Too much for men who took defeat so hard. Border's last innings, on a muggy Durban afternoon, was a four-hour undefeated 42. He told his partner Mark Waugh, who was scoring a century, that he wasn't going to get out 'because this could be my last Test innings'.

Back in Australia, Border asked the ACB for time to consider his availability for another Ashes series, then the irresistible temptation of a last Caribbean tour. But the ACB invited Taylor and other senior team members to sit for what Border could only have construed as interviews for his job. In another tantrum, he retired from Test cricket on a golf course.

Nobody has ever thrown as many forgivable tantrums as Allan Border. No more admirable person has taken on so much suffering, and borne it so modestly. But without Simpson to draw criticism away, Border could not have achieved what he did. Border could not have been so loved if Simpson had not taken on being hated. For nine years they were a duumvirate of unparalleled influence and importance.

Ian Chappell believed that, by delegating so much, Border had harmed the captaincy. But Border was acting from a survival instinct. If he couldn't job-share the captaincy, it would destroy him as it had destroyed Hughes. It took a humble man to make this admission, and the wisdom of Border's humility bore fruit when his team changed in character and progressed towards confidence and competence.

His appetite for cricket still alive, Border played two more seasons for Queensland. Under Stuart Law, he scored 911 at 65 as they won their first Sheffield Shield. Border scored 48 in the final and averaged more than 40 the next season. He played his last first-class match at a near-empty MCG in March 1996, two decades after his debut.

While so many were complaining about over-scheduling, Border played 153 consecutive Tests and went on 29 tours. He scored more runs and took more catches, led more Tests and more one-day internationals than anyone. There is his stupendous performance outside Australia, where his batting average was 10 runs higher than at home. There is his one-day career, in which he invented the now-essential attacking short midwicket. He was Australian of the Year, and the medal recognising the nation's top player was named after him. He worked for the ACB before opting for a simpler life in pay-television. That he never joined the glitzier 'mafia' of Channel Nine commentary also seemed to count in his favour. Beyond the runs and the captaincy, it was the character of the man that Australians loved most. He was not our best captain, but he survived unprecedented challenges and eventually prospered. When he retired, Border enjoyed a status only approached by Bradman.

It was a different kind of admiration, for Border was a people's hero, in the sense that people can only really love what they understand.

A last assessment need only compare the Australian captaincy in 1984 with a decade later. In November 1984, it was one of the least envied positions in sport. By the end of Border's tenure, it was Australian royalty. Not that there was anything royal about Allan Robert Border. It's hard to think of any captain who has left the role in such an improved state.

34

CONCLUSIONS: THE CURRENT ERA

THE post-WSC explosion in cricket accelerates time in the same manner as a technological revolution. Just as artists responded to modernity by no longer trying to paint their subjects sitting still, but rather capturing movement through shape-shifts, the story of the Australian captaincy becomes more impressionistic after the 1980s.

Playing for the same period as Bradman, Border appeared in three times as many Tests. He led Australia 93 times, a figure that still defies belief. Many captains were miniatures; the odd long-serving one, such as Darling or Woodfull or Bradman or Benaud or Simpson, are large oil canvases. Border is an epic mural.

So gigantic was his achievement that we have to stand back and gather him in from a distance, only possible now that he has been retired for more than 15 years. This distance is not possible with the four captains who followed him: Mark Taylor, Steve Waugh, Adam Gilchrist and Ricky Ponting. As this book has used one priceless looking-glass – historical perspective – to reassess the captains and what they left the game, it would be a denial of natural justice to make such assessments of the captains since Border. Too recent, they loom too large. Instead, a few speculations will have to suffice.

One reason the administrators were so hasty to bustle Border out of his job was because they had finally, after 117 years, found the perfect captain. Expectation is a terrible burden, as Taylor had found when, after scoring 839 in his first Ashes series, he was compared with Bradman. But as a captain, it is impossible to find an Australian who so combined cricketing skill, the respect of his players, a peaceful disposition towards his Board, a diplomat's political sense, and, perhaps most importantly, the fortune to be taking over a team on the verge of greatness. Perhaps Woodfull was the only other to bring all this to the captaincy. Benaud had some of those qualities but a team that could only sporadically emerge from the dullness of its time. Bradman, the Chappells, Hassett, Border, Simpson, Murdoch, Darling, Noble and Armstrong had some but not all of the qualities Taylor brought to the job in 1994.

Most captains were strung between two poles: authority as a captain and ability as a player; a creature of the Board and a creature of the game. Even for Bradman, his teammates' trust was elusive until after the war.

Pressure? Perhaps Taylor felt it. In his first Test as captain, in Karachi, he batted for 11 balls in two innings and scored no runs. His team lost by one wicket and two of his players were offered massive bribes by Pakistan's captain. Over the next five years of Taylor's captaincy, the tag of perfection would, inevitably, look a little tatty. In the full context of Australian cricket, Taylor would not be as significant as either his predecessor Border or his successor Waugh, let alone some of the giants of the past. But a captain cannot be judged on challenges he was never asked to face, and if there were a textbook of what makes an ideal captain, Taylor would be the exemplar.

While Border had still been fighting the trench warfare of the 1980s, Taylor stood ready to order the air strikes of the 1990s. Taylor's influence on the captaincy would be both conservative and progressive. He discouraged personal headphones, card games and books in the changing room, urging his players to watch their teammates and learn more about the game. For the cricket glutton that Taylor was, this was easy. More difficult would be winding back the relationship with Simpson, who had become coach, mentor, spokesman, organiser and selector. When it came to the coach's position, Taylor was old-fashioned. In Pakistan in 1994, he ran fielding sessions himself. For the pre-match pep talk, which Border often delegated to Simpson, Taylor took the Test XI into the changing room and left Simpson outside to hit balls with the 'benchies' and tidy up the gear. Taylor, whose earnest openness engendered a friendly relationship with the media, resumed the captain's role as spin doctor.

After the peak of his power alongside Border, Simpson would be steadily marginalised and finally, in 1996, dumped.

Not that this shift in responsibilities was foreseeable on Taylor's first tour. In fact, after his pair in Karachi, he wrote grimly, 'I have at least captained Australia in one Test.' It was a match Australia controlled until the last morning, when Inzamam-ul-Haq and Mushtaq Ahmed staged a mighty stand of 57 for the last wicket to hunt down a record 314. More than that, it was the Test during which Salim Malik offered hundreds of thousands of dollars in bribes to Shane Warne and Tim May.

Taylor's attitude to the offers – also made, during the tour, to Mark Waugh – was that of a man still running for office. He did not want to be implicated, so his instinctive response was to pass the matter to Simpson and the ACB. It's easy to imagine Border, or Steve Waugh, marching to Malik's room and having it out face-to-face. Taylor did not exactly dodge the issue, but kept himself clean. He could see that he had nothing, personally, to gain by confronting Malik or making the offers public.

Taylor's captaincy was Teflon-coated. When Mark Waugh and Warne were secretly fined for having accepted money from a book-maker, Taylor skated above the murkiness, guiding his team to a fabled victory in the West Indies in 1995. His captaincy was lauded, if only for the impression of cricketing nous he exuded from first slip. The public was used to Border worrying his way through Tests. Taylor's ever-rotating jaw, either chewing gum or issuing commentary, radiated calm. His pleasant, well-fed face, with boyish teeth, never seemed less than thoughtful or more than content. Unlike

Border, he had a knack for making the bowling change that broke the partnership. Unlike Border, he seemed happy, and lucky.

The 1995 West Indies tour had echoes of Ian Chappell's in 1973. Taylor lost his opening bowlers, McDermott and Damien Fleming, to injury, and won with an unproven pace attack of Glenn McGrath, Brendon Julian and Paul Reiffel, so inexperienced that Richie Richardson would call them the worst Australian team he had faced. Perhaps, but they were still better than the West Indies. Taylor was one of many batsmen to have a skinny series, scoring only 153 in the four Tests. Steve Waugh dominated, particularly with his 200 in the decider in Kingston, during which at least 150 of the 425 balls he faced were aimed at his throat, but the lasting images were of Taylor taking the final catch and holding up the Frank Worrell Trophy, Australia's for the first time since 1978.

Simpson, who was laid up in a Jamaican hospital during that victory, would be the first structural casualty of Taylor's traditional approach. In 1996, after a fractious home series against Pakistan and Sri Lanka and a World Cup campaign that fell at the final hurdle, Simpson's re-application for his job was turned down.

So much can be, and has been, said of Simpson. Nobody has had as many different careers in cricket. First he was the child prodigy who was not quite sound enough to entrench himself at Test level. Then he came back as a merciless run machine and a pragmatic leader, the captaincy bringing out his best and worst. After a decade in retirement, he returned as the éminence grise of a below-strength team, pitched back into Test cricket by the great schism. And finally, for nearly a decade he was the coach and Svengali, feared and respected as he reinvented the way Australia played.

As coach, Simpson had a genius for tutoring eager, young, hard-working players. He was biased against those who did not conform to the characteristics he embodied and admired. He was at his worst on overseas tours when his team was beset by bad umpiring. He achieved mighty success; then, as they matured, many of those around him stopped listening.

Countless players and leaders have been more popular than Simpson. Nobody swooned at his feet as they did for Benaud or

Harvey, nobody laughed with him as they did with Hassett, few would shed blood for him as they would for Ian Chappell. There was something plain about him that rebuffed romance, and nobody in Australian cricket made more enemies. But that should not obscure the truth. Bradman aside, Simpson was the most significant Australian cricketer of the 20th century. Not even Benaud and Chappell can contest the influence Simpson wielded or the imprint he left. Because he sought to divide his opponents, views on his legacy will forever remain divided. But there is a mass of numbers that conveys more than words or opinions. Simpson was involved with the Australian team for 155 Test matches: 23 as a player, 29 as a captain the first time, 10 as a captain the second time, and 93 as a coach and sometime selector. What he lacked in charisma he made up for with unbreakable determination. If Bradman was cricket's Robert Menzies, Benaud a dashing blend of Harold Holt, Andrew Peacock and Paul Keating, and Ian Chappell its Bob Hawke, then Simpson was assuredly the game's John Howard.

The second half of Taylor's captaincy reprised an old story. As his batting subsided, the tension between his two roles tightened. Between 1996 and 1999, his team flatlined with a succession of narrow wins, over the West Indies at home and South Africa away, over England away, over New Zealand and South Africa at home, before being crushed by India away in 1998. They defeated Pakistan away later that year, then retained the Ashes against a woeful England led by Alec Stewart.

For Taylor, this period was not always happy. In a sequence in which he averaged 18 from 18 innings, he did not score a Test half-century between early 1996 and his famous comeback hundred at Edgbaston in mid-1997. Behind the scenes Steve Waugh and the vice-captain, Healy, coveted the captaincy, not so much because they wanted to undermine Taylor as to reassert the Australian principle that a captain must justify his position as a player. Taylor did not do that for more than a year, and only survived because his Board loved him and his team saved him. Nowhere was that more apparent than in Port Elizabeth in 1997, when Australia collapsed twice, burdened by Taylor's slump, yet still managed to chase down 282 in the fourth innings thanks to Mark Waugh's century. At different times both Waughs, Warne and McGrath would step forward to buy their captain another Test.

Taylor's slump also caused a bifurcation of the captaincy. Between 1977 and 1997 the Test and one-day captaincy was held concurrently. In 1997, when Taylor and Healy were dropped from the one-day team, Steve Waugh became captain and Gilchrist wicketkeeper, and the captaincy became a job-share. Taylor never believed this was healthy, and said so. Waugh thought it was healthy when he became one-day captain, even more so when he held both jobs between 1999 and 2002, but thought it was unhealthy when Ponting took over the one-day role in 2002–03. Regardless of whether splitting the jobs was good for the teams, the prestige of the position was diminished. The 'Australian captaincy' is no longer the one indivisible office. Now, with three forms of the game at the elite level, Australia can conceivably have three different captains.

A greater challenge for Taylor, when he lost the one-day captaincy, was a revival of player power. During 1997, Test and senior domestic players grew unhappy with their share of cricket's revenues. The elite internationals were well paid, but Shield regulars were earning less than the average wage. What had been a low-level irritant made the front pages in late 1997 when Graham Halbish, the sacked former chief executive of the ACB, teamed with management entrepreneur James Erskine and the Australian Cricketers' Association leader Tim May to launch a campaign for a better deal.

In a time warp to the 19th century, the elite players argued that they were responsible for a steep rise in income, while administrators countered that this income should go back into the 'grassroots'. The argument grew personal, but the big difference with 1912 was that the captain was not now a leader of the players' movement. Teflon Taylor stood to the side. Among the Test men, Steve Waugh and Healy were active advocates for players' rights. When a resolution came, the captain, Taylor, was something of a go-between. Indeed, the senior players saw him as too close to the Board, and rejected his initial proposals for compromise. It was only when a strike was threatened, and the commercial interests of Kerry Packer's Nine Network became involved, that peace was achieved. The players received better state-based contracts and the administrators retained control. The Australian Cricketers' Association became a stabilising force. The captain was almost a peripheral figure, a far cry from Dave Gregory and Billy Murdoch.

Taylor's batting never regained the heights of the late 1980s and early 1990s. He made a staunch unbeaten century in Adelaide to stave off South Africa in January 1998, and 334 not out in Peshawar later that year. But they were sparse peaks in a wasteland of inconsistency. Unhappy with the separation of the captaincy, he played through the 1998–99 Ashes series and retired as the most successful captain since Ian Chappell.

Having long desired the captaincy, Steve Waugh entered the job with little leadership experience. He had played under Lawson and Taylor at NSW, under Border and Taylor for Australia. His two seasons as one-day captain had raised questions about his leadership, and he had a determined rival in Shane Warne.

Waugh, a self-contained cricketer, spent his first eight years as a Test player battling the fear of being dropped. That was his formation, and he never cast it off. Even though he had certified himself as Australia's, and one of the world's, best batsmen since 1993–94, he continued to bat as if an assassin lurked around the next corner. The question asked about Waugh, as captain, was whether he could contain his anxieties enough to take responsibility for others'. Could he, like Taylor, truly lead, or would he be a Border-like captain who led by weight of runs?

The initial signs were worrying. On the tour of the West Indies and during the World Cup in 1999, Waugh's captaincy faced its great crises. Reversing the momentum of an apparently unbeatable Australia, Brian Lara single-handedly won Tests in Jamaica and Barbados. Warne, recovering from a shoulder injury, lost form and Steve Waugh took the decision to drop his vice-captain. Healy and Mark Waugh were also out of form. Down 1–2 with one Test to play, Steve Waugh went to Antigua wondering if he would lose the

trophy it had taken 17 years to win. But he was able to marshal his
lesser lights in Justin Langer, Colin Miller and Adam Dale – and rely
on his spearhead, McGrath – to tie the series 2–2.

Even so, it had been a close-run thing, and a few months later
in England Waugh faced being dumped as one-day captain. His
rift with Warne had widened and Australia would have missed the
World Cup semi-finals if Herschelle Gibbs had caught Waugh in
the qualifying match at Headingley. But Gibbs dropped the catch,
Waugh made a century, Warne thundered back in the semi-final at
Edgbaston, and Australia won the Cup for the first time since 1987.
Waugh's fledgling captaincy, due to his own individual brilliance
and to Warne's revival, was redeemed. There was a certain irony in
Warne having pulled Waugh's captaincy out of the fire, just as the
pair had done for Taylor back in 1997.

Steve Waugh leading his
team, most of whom thought
he was the best man for
the job.

From that point, Waugh was transformed into a captain who, rather than taking another man's team on loan, rebuilt the team in his own image. By the end of 1999, Simpson's successor as coach, the mild 'practice captain' Geoff Marsh, stood aside. Waugh used his influence to bring in John Buchanan, the Queensland mentor with a reputation for computer analysis and lateral thinking. Border and Simpson had made the Australian captaincy a partnership. Taylor, who liked to assert his authority, wanted an assistant, and got it in Marsh. Waugh, inheriting a team that had been on top for four years, was looking for someone who could challenge them to play cricket differently, not just repeat the formula.

The new era, starting in 1999–2000, made Taylor's successes look pale. Under Waugh and Buchanan, Australia won 15 Tests in a row (on top of another before Buchanan was coach). Waugh might not have been the complete captain in the traditional mould, as Taylor was at his height, but he faced a tougher challenge. Whereas Taylor had taken a rising team to the top and struggled to keep it there, Waugh took a team that was showing signs of staleness; he not only kept it at the top but led it to an unimaginable elaboration. He did not enjoy Warne's unquestioning support – Warne, frankly, thought he would have made a better captain – and Ian Chappell was never convinced by Waugh, believing him an instinctively selfish cricketer whose instincts, under pressure, were negative. But nothing can gainsay Waugh's achievements. Only record-shattering feats by their rivals could shake Waugh's team. India, in 2001, stopped the 16-game streak by becoming, in Calcutta, the third team in history to beat Australia after following on. The West Indies, in 2003, chased a world record 418 in Antigua to beat Australia in a dead rubber. England did not win a 'live' Test match against Australia between 1997 and 2005.

One possible cavil about Waugh's team concerns the wider environment of Test cricket. There can be little doubt that the standard of the opposition fell alarmingly. The West Indies, totally reliant on Lara, Walsh and Ambrose in the late 1990s, lost all semblance of competitiveness after the great bowlers' retirements. Pakistan, a regular contender from the early 1970s to the late 1990s, ceased to produce the individual brilliance that had been compensating for political incompetence and corruption. Zimbabwean cricket, strong in the 1990s, was vandalised by the Mugabe regime. New Zealand had depth but not the sharp-end of a Hadlee or a Martin Crowe. Bangladesh and Kenya did not come on as expected. South Africa slumped after their captain Hansie Cronje was exposed as a match-fixer in 2000, and did not rise again until 2007. England remained traumatised. In Waugh's years, only India and Sri Lanka provided stiff opposition. Test cricket globally was in a poor state, and has remained so to this day. That is the only query hanging over Waugh's captaincy record. But then, opponents can only play as well as they are allowed, and perhaps the direness of the opposition was a measure of the greatness of Waugh's team between 1999 and 2003.

Like Taylor, Waugh had to share the captaincy when Ponting took over the one-day job in 2002–03. He also handed the captaincy to Adam Gilchrist for one Test in 2000–01. Gilchrist, continuing the tradition of Australian stand-ins, was a peaceful individual who, far from seeking the captaincy, dreaded its responsibilities. He had sometimes led youth teams as he progressed through the ranks, but as a wicketkeeper-batsman Gilchrist understood that he could exercise leadership in other ways than tossing the coin and signing the team sheets. As Waugh sat out the Adelaide Test against the West Indies in 2000–01, Gilchrist led Australia to a narrow win and returned the mantle to Waugh with unbridled relief.

Gilchrist and Ponting, the most recent Australian captains, continue another trend we have seen through the evolution of the game, which is that players have less and less biography outside cricket. Dave Gregory was a senior public servant. Hugh Massie headed one of the country's biggest banks. Joe Darling was a farmer and parliamentarian. Monty Noble was a dentist. Even Bradman was a stockbroker and company director, Benaud and Simpson were full-time journalists and public relations operatives, Craig was a business executive and countless other Australian cricketers led careers. The last captain to attempt a career outside cricket was

Taylor, whose three years studying surveying were as far as he got. Steve Waugh was a cricketer from high school. Gilchrist worked momentarily in banks to support himself through the transition to a professional cricketer's life. Ponting, identified from his early teens at the Mowbray club in Launceston, nurtured through the academy into the national team, might have hit some rough patches in the

Adam Gilchrist stood in as captain when needed; Shane Warne pointed the way.

1990s as he grew up in public view but he was never anything but a cricketer. His likely successor, Michael Clarke, follows this theme.

Likewise, the running of Australian cricket became fully corporatised from the late 1990s. In the dark days of the Board, its secretariat was a Dickensian pair of rooms musty with filing cabinets. In the Ponting era, Cricket Australia, as it is now called, is heavily staffed and run by professional managers. The Test team has had a full-time manager, Steve Bernard, since 1997, and also full-time physiotherapists, skills coaches, dieticians, masseuses and other support crew. It is not a cricket team so much as a small corporation. The captain's role in this model is complex. Ponting is something of a divisional product manager within the Cricket Australia scheme. Just as the corporate world increasingly borrows sport's 'team' terminology, so do sporting structures emulate those of corporations. Ponting is a 'team leader' in both senses, responsible for much more than guiding his team to onfield successes. He is also the custodian of a brand, responsible to sponsors, broadcasters, corporate partners and many other 'stakeholders' in the game. The results this corporatised model produces, in finances and on the cricket field, are considerable, but will take more time to fully assess. Due to the change in the nature of the captaincy, Ponting may well end up with multiple legacies: a team which established an overall winning record yet slipped behind India, South Africa, Sri Lanka and England; a team which lost the Ashes but generated more income for Australian cricket than any other. Is Ponting a good captain? Not only is judgement premature, but the criteria for judging his captaincy are without precedent. Ponting has been captain of the Australian Test and one-day teams since 2004. Until 2009, he was also captain of the Twenty20 team. That role is, at the time of writing, held by Clarke, but may fragment again in 2010–11. Ponting's captaincy is still a work in progress. As is often the case with contemporaneous judgements, public opinion of Ponting's performance varies widely. When his teams have created controversy, as in the rancorous 2008 Sydney Test with India, snobbery about Ponting's working-class upbringing tends to surface. On the other hand, he is held in high esteem, particularly among younger cricket fans, precisely because of his competitive ways and rough edges. But in 2010, it is far too early to gain the kind of focal length on Ponting and even Steve Waugh that we have when we look at earlier captains.

Ponting's Australia lost the Ashes in 2005, regained them in 2006–07, but lost them again in 2009, when he joined Murdoch as the only captains to lose the Ashes in England twice. Ponting's team also lost at home to South Africa in 2008–09, breaking a 15-year streak in Australia. He had the misfortune to inherit a team that was shedding matchwinners: Warne, McGrath, Gilchrist, Hayden, Langer, Gillespie and Martyn. That aside, his team began rebuilding without the disintegration of the mid-1980s or mid-1950s. They defeated Pakistan at home and away, Sri Lanka at home and away, the West Indies at home and away, New Zealand at home and away, and South Africa away. They also won the 2003 and 2007 World Cups. Under Gilchrist, they defeated India in India in 2004, the first time an Australian team had won there since Bill Lawry's riot-torn but successful venture of 1969. A more considered study of the last

Ricky Ponting, throwing everything at the job

decade and a half can be found in my book *The Greatest: the players, the moments, the matches 1993–2008.*

By dodging the debate over Ponting, I am happy to accuse myself of copping out. But as I write, an Ashes series looms that will, I suspect, decide the issue of Ponting's abilities as captain. For a writer in this predicament, it's better to be a coward than a fool.

But it's fair to say, in 2010, that Ponting's captaincy has suffered the fate of all those who followed giants. He seems to lack the instinctiveness of a Taylor and the indomitability of a Waugh, and will never attain the popular affection of a Border, which is ironic considering their respective socio-economic backgrounds.

In 133 years of Test cricket, reduced by war to 117, Australia has had 42 captains, or one every three years. England, in the same period, has had 79, or one every 17 months. In the past two years alone, England has been led in Test cricket by Andrew Flintoff, Kevin Pietersen, Andrew Strauss and Alastair Cook, as well as by Paul Collingwood in the game's abbreviated versions. Every other country has had a higher turnover of captains than Australia.

This is a point worth considering, as the Australian way of finding a captain, since the 19th century, has seemed the least stable. Whereas other countries might appoint a captain for the strength of his character and retain him irrespective of his form, Australia has chosen the captain on the most contingent basis: only while he has been good enough to play Test cricket. It is remarkable that Australia, on the least predictable foundation, has built such a stable lineage.

This remarkable story has been carried on the shoulders of men who were more than just cricket captains. The most significant ones were Dave Gregory, Billy Murdoch, Jack Blackham, Harry Trott, Joe Darling, Monty Noble, Warwick Armstrong, Herbie Collins, Bill Woodfull, Don Bradman, Lindsay Hassett, Ian Johnson, Richie Benaud, Bob Simpson, Bill Lawry, Ian Chappell, Greg Chappell, Allan Border, Mark Taylor, Steve Waugh and Ricky Ponting. Of the 42 captains, these 21 led Australia in more than 90 per cent of their Tests and all but four of their Ashes tours. The others, while interesting and appealing, were subsitutes, short-termers or paradoxical figures like Kim Hughes and Ian Craig.

At this point of a book, the author is expected to make a judgment, in his humble opinion, of the best. It is too hard. Were I a player, I imagine I would have most enjoyed touring under Billy Murdoch, Lindsay Hassett or Victor Richardson. Were I a journalist, few personalities appeal as much as Richie Benaud. Were I in trouble, I would like to have Ian Chappell in my corner. Were I a parent sending my son on a long overseas tour, I can't imagine a more trustworthy steward than Bill Woodfull or Monty Noble. If I wanted to lay a bet, I'd go to Herbie Collins. If I needed a diplomat, no man could do better than Ian Johnson or Joe Darling. If I needed a captain to bat for my life, of course it would be Bradman, but I'd as gladly take Border, Greg Chappell or Steve Waugh. Or if I wanted someone to bat for a draw, I'd send out Bob Simpson and Bill Lawry. That's the trouble: when you are asked who is the best captain, you must ask in reply, best for what purpose?

Nevertheless I would maintain that there is a group that stand above all others for their achievement and their legacies. They are Murdoch, Darling, Woodfull, Bradman, Hassett, Benaud, Simpson (in his three incarnations), Ian Chappell, Border, Taylor and Waugh. These add up to 11, a nice number that I am not inclined to divide further.

STATISTICS

Australian captains

Captain	M	W	L	D	T	Span (days)	Start	End	%W/P	%L/P	%DT/P	Toss	%Toss
Armstrong, WW	10	8	0	2	0	243	17 Dec 1920	16 Aug 1921	80.00	0.00	20.00	4	40.00
Bardsley, W	2	0	0	2	0	18	10 Jul 1926	27 Jul 1926	0.00	0.00	100.00	1	50.00
Benaud, R	28	12	4	11	1	1833	05 Dec 1958	11 Dec 1963	42.86	14.29	42.86	11	39.29
Blackham, JM	8	3	3	2	0	3569	14 Mar 1885	20 Dec 1894	37.50	37.50	25.00	4	50.00
Booth, BC	2	0	1	1	0	33	10 Dec 1965	11 Jan 1966	0.00	50.00	50.00	1	50.00
Border, AR	93	32	22	38	1	3400	07 Dec 1984	29 Mar 1994	34.41	23.66	41.94	46	49.46
Bradman, DG	24	15	3	6	0	4276	04 Dec 1936	18 Aug 1948	62.50	12.50	25.00	10	41.67
Brown, WA	1	1	0	0	0	2	29 Mar 1946	30 Mar 1946	100.00	0.00	0.00	0	0.00
Chappell, GS	48	21	13	14	0	2707	28 Nov 1975	26 Apr 1983	43.75	27.08	29.17	29	60.42
Chappell, IM	30	15	5	10	0	1665	12 Feb 1971	03 Sep 1975	50.00	16.67	33.33	17	56.67
Collins, HL	11	5	2	4	0	1748	05 Nov 1921	18 Aug 1926	45.45	18.18	36.36	7	63.64
Craig, ID	5	3	0	2	0	72	23 Dec 1957	04 Mar 1958	60.00	0.00	40.00	3	60.00
Darling, J	21	7	4	10	0	2268	01 Jun 1899	16 Aug 1905	33.33	19.05	47.62	7	33.33
Giffen, G	4	2	2	0	0	68	29 Dec 1894	06 Mar 1895	50.00	50.00	0.00	3	75.00
Gilchrist, AC	6	4	1	1	0	1415	15 Dec 2000	29 Oct 2004	66.67	16.67	16.67	4	66.67
Gregory, DW	3	2	1	0	0	661	15 Mar 1877	04 Jan 1879	66.67	33.33	0.00	2	66.67
Gregory, SE	6	2	1	3	0	88	27 May 1912	22 Aug 1912	33.33	16.67	50.00	1	16.67
Harvey, RN	1	1	0	0	0	5	22 Jun 1961	26 Jun 1961	100.00	0.00	0.00	0	0.00
Hassett, AL	24	14	4	6	0	1335	24 Dec 1949	19 Aug 1953	58.33	16.67	25.00	18	75.00
Hill, C	10	5	5	0	0	449	09 Dec 1910	01 Mar 1912	50.00	50.00	0.00	5	50.00
Horan, TP	2	0	2	0	0	84	01 Jan 1885	25 Mar 1885	0.00	100.00	0.00	1	50.00
Hughes, KJ	28	4	13	11	0	2075	24 Mar 1979	26 Nov 1984	14.29	46.43	39.29	13	46.43

Jarman, BN	1	0	0	1	0	6	25 Jul 1968	30 Jul 1968	0.00	0.00	100.00	100.00	1	100.00
Johnson, IWG	17	7	5	5	0	712	26 Nov 1954	06 Nov 1956	41.18	29.41	29.41	29.41	6	35.29
Lawry, WM	25	9	8	8	0	1112	19 Jan 1968	03 Feb 1971	36.00	32.00	32.00	32.00	8	32.00
Lindwall, RR	1	0	0	1	0	6	26 Oct 1956	31 Oct 1956	0.00	0.00	100.00	100.00	0	0.00
Massie, HH	1	1	0	0	0	5	20 Feb 1885	24 Feb 1885	100.00	100.00	0.00	0.00	1	100.00
McDonnell, PS	6	1	5	0	0	582	28 Jan 1887	31 Aug 1888	16.67	83.33	0.00	0.00	4	66.67
Morris, AR	2	0	2	0	0	1097	22 Dec 1951	22 Dec 1954	0.00	100.00	0.00	0.00	2	100.00
Murdoch, WL	16	5	7	4	0	3628	06 Sep 1880	12 Aug 1890	31.25	43.75	25.00	43.75	7	43.75
Noble, MA	15	8	5	2	0	2071	11 Dec 1903	11 Aug 1909	53.33	33.33	13.33	13.33	11	73.33
Ponting, RT	71	47	12	12	0	2330	08 Mar 2004	24 Jul 2010	66.20	16.90	16.90	16.90	34	47.89
Richardson, VY	5	4	0	1	0	81	14 Dec 1935	03 Mar 1936	80.00	0.00	20.00	20.00	1	20.00
Ryder, J	5	1	4	0	0	107	30 Nov 1928	16 Mar 1929	20.00	80.00	0.00	0.00	2	40.00
Scott, HJH	3	0	3	0	0	41	05 Jul 1886	14 Aug 1886	0.00	100.00	0.00	0.00	1	33.33
Simpson, RB	39	12	12	15	0	5237	01 Jan 1964	03 May 1978	30.77	30.77	38.46	48.72	19	48.72
Taylor, MA	50	26	13	11	0	1561	28 Sep 1994	05 Jan 1999	52.00	26.00	22.00	52.00	26	52.00
Trott, GHS	8	5	3	0	0	619	22 Jun 1896	02 Mar 1898	62.50	37.50	0.00	62.50	5	62.50
Trumble, H	2	2	0	0	0	19	14 Feb 1902	04 Mar 1902	100.00	0.00	0.00	50.00	1	50.00
Waugh, SR	57	41	9	7	0	1769	05 Mar 1999	06 Jan 2004	71.93	15.79	12.28	54.39	31	54.39
Woodfull, WM	25	14	7	4	0	1532	13 Jun 1930	22 Aug 1934	56.00	28.00	16.00	48.00	12	48.00
Yallop, GN	7	1	6	0	0	105	01 Dec 1978	15 Mar 1979	14.29	85.71	0.00	85.71	6	85.71

All-time world records

The greatest number of Test victories by a captain is 47 (Ricky Ponting, Australia).
The greatest number of Test matches played by a captain is 93 (Allan Border, Australia).

BATTING (as captain)

Player	M	Inn	NO	Runs	HS	Avrge	100s	50s	0s	Ct	St
Armstrong, WW	10	13	2	616	158	56.00	3	1	2	8	0
Bardsley, W	2	2	0	15	15	7.50	0	0	1	1	0
Benaud, R	28	40	4	816	77	22.67	0	5	4	32	0
Blackham, JM	8	14	7	154	74	22.00	0	1	2	11	4
Booth, BC	2	3	0	51	27	17.00	0	0	0	1	0
Border, AR	93	154	24	6623	205	50.95	15	36	7	89	0
Bradman, DG	24	38	7	3147	270	101.52	14	7	5	18	0
Brown, WA	1	1	0	67	67	67.00	0	1	0	0	0
Chappell, GS	48	86	10	4209	235	55.38	13	19	7	59	0
Chappell, IM	30	54	3	2550	196	50.00	7	14	4	46	0
Collins, HL	11	19	1	724	203	40.22	2	3	0	6	0
Craig, ID	5	7	0	103	52	14.71	0	1	2	1	0
Darling, J	21	37	2	750	73	21.43	0	5	5	15	0
Giffen, G	4	7	0	273	58	39.00	0	3	0	4	0
Gilchrist, AC	6	11	2	305	104	33.89	1	1	1	30	0
Gregory, DW	3	5	2	60	43	20.00	0	0	0	0	0
Gregory, SE	6	6	0	72	37	12.00	0	0	0	0	0
Harvey, RN	1	2	0	31	27	15.50	0	0	0	1	0
Hassett, AL	24	41	1	1881	167	47.03	7	8	0	13	0
Hill, C	10	18	0	699	191	38.83	2	3	3	11	0
Horan, TP	2	4	0	99	63	24.75	0	1	1	2	0
Hughes, KJ	28	51	2	1726	106	35.22	2	10	2	18	0
Jarman, BN	1	2	0	14	10	7.00	0	0	0	3	0
Johnson, IWG	17	26	8	460	73	25.56	0	3	4	9	0
Lawry, WM	25	47	6	1920	205	46.83	4	11	2	17	0
Lindwall, RR	1	1	1	48	48*	-	0	0	0	1	0
Massie, HH	1	2	0	23	21	11.50	0	0	0	0	0
McDonnell, PS	6	12	0	138	35	11.50	0	0	3	1	0
Morris, AR	2	4	0	68	45	17.00	0	0	0	0	0
Murdoch, WL	16	29	4	877	211	35.08	2	1	3	13	0
Noble, MA	15	29	3	992	133	38.15	1	7	1	12	0
Ponting, RT	71	128	12	6205	209	53.49	19	31	6	84	0
Richardson, VY	5	5	0	84	45	16.80	0	0	0	9	0
Ryder, J	5	10	1	492	112	54.67	1	4	0	8	0
Scott, HJH	3	6	0	110	47	18.33	0	0	0	2	0
Simpson, RB	39	71	4	3623	311	54.07	10	16	3	62	0
Taylor, MA	50	89	7	3250	334*	39.63	7	16	4	84	0
Trott, GHS	8	12	0	350	143	29.17	1	2	1	11	0
Trumble, H	2	3	0	31	22	10.33	0	0	0	4	0
Waugh, SR	57	83	12	3714	199	52.31	15	10	6	34	0
Woodfull, WM	25	38	3	1503	161	42.94	2	12	3	2	0
Yallop, GN	7	14	0	424	121	30.29	2	0	1	3	0

BATTING (as player)

Player	M	Inn	NO	Runs	HS	Avrge	100s	50s	0s
Armstrong, WW	40	71	8	2247	159*	35.67	3	7	4
Benaud, R	35	57	3	1385	122	25.65	3	4	4
Blackham, JM	27	48	4	646	66	14.68	0	3	4
Booth, BC	27	45	6	1722	169	44.15	5	10	5
Border, AR	63	111	20	4551	162	50.01	12	27	4
Bradman, DG	28	42	3	3849	334	98.69	15	6	2
Brown, WA	21	34	1	1525	206*	46.21	4	8	1
Chappell, GS	39	65	9	2901	247*	51.80	11	12	5
Chappell, IM	45	82	7	2795	165	37.27	7	12	7
Collins, HL	8	12	0	628	162	52.33	2	3	0
Craig, ID	6	11	0	255	53	23.18	0	1	1
Darling, J	13	23	0	907	178	39.43	3	3	3
Giffen, G	27	46	0	965	161	20.98	1	3	5
Gilchrist, AC	90	126	18	5265	204*	48.75	16	25	13
Gregory, SE	52	94	7	2210	201	25.40	4	8	12
Harvey, RN	78	135	10	6118	205	48.94	21	24	7
Hassett, AL	19	28	2	1192	198*	45.85	3	3	1
Hill, C	39	71	2	2713	188	39.32	5	16	6
Horan, TP	13	23	2	372	124	17.71	1	0	2
Hughes, KJ	42	73	4	2689	213	38.97	7	12	8
Johnson, IWG	28	40	4	540	77	15.00	0	3	6
Lawry, WM	42	76	6	3314	210	47.34	9	16	4
Lindwall, RR	60	83	12	1454	118	20.48	2	5	9
McDonnell, PS	13	22	1	817	147	38.90	3	2	3
Morris, AR	44	75	3	3465	206	48.13	12	12	4
Murdoch, WL	2	4	1	19	8	6.33	0	0	0
Noble, MA	27	44	4	1005	89	25.13	0	9	3
Ponting, RT	75	119	15	5821	257	55.97	20	21	7
Richardson, VY	14	25	0	622	138	24.88	1	1	5
Ryder, J	15	22	4	902	201*	50.11	2	5	1
Scott, HJH	5	8	1	249	102	35.57	1	1	0
Simpson, RB	23	40	3	1246	92	33.68	0	11	5
Taylor, MA	54	97	6	4275	219	46.98	12	24	1
Trott, GHS	16	30	0	571	95	19.03	0	2	6
Trumble, H	30	54	14	820	70	20.50	0	4	7
Waugh, SR	111	177	34	7213	200	50.44	17	40	16
Wessels, KC	24	42	1	1761	179	42.95	4	9	3
Woodfull, WM	10	16	1	797	141	53.13	5	1	3
Yallop, GN	32	56	3	2332	268	44.00	6	9	2

MOST CONSECUTIVE VICTORIES BY CAPTAINS

Player	Number	From Test	Date	To Test #	Date	World rank
Ponting, RT	16	1779	26 Dec 2005	1857	06 Jan 2008	1
Waugh, SR	15	1463	14 Oct 1999	1531	01 Mar 2001	2
Armstrong, WW	8	135	17 Dec 1920	142	05 Jul 1921	6

OPPORTUNITIES TO ENFORCE A FOLLOW-ON (5 or more)

Captain	Opportunities	Number enforced	Wins when the follow-on was enforced	% Wins of times the follow-on was enforced
Ponting, RT	13	4	3	75.00
Waugh, SR	10	8	7	87.50
Border, AR	8	8	7	87.50
Woodfull, WM	5	4	3	75.00
Bradman, DG	5	5	5	100.00
Taylor, MA	5	3	2	66.67

DECLARATIONS MADE IN MATCHES BY CAPTAINS (10 or more)

Captain	Number of declarations	Matches with a declaration	Wins after declaration	% Wins after declaration
Ponting, RT	35	29	23	79.31
Border, AR	30	26	12	46.15
Waugh, SR	21	19	16	84.21
Taylor, MA	20	19	13	68.42
Chappell, GS	16	14	7	50.00
Chappell, IM	13	11	5	45.45

HIGHEST INDIVIDUAL SCORES (of 200 or more)
BY AUSTRALIAN CAPTAINS

Captain	Score	V	Inn	Test	Series	Venue
Taylor, MA	334*	Pak	1st	2nd	1998–99	Peshawar (AN)
Simpson, RB	311	Eng	1st	4th	1964	Old Trafford
Bradman, DG	270	Eng	2nd	3rd	1936–37	Melbourne
Chappell, GS	235	Pak	1st	2nd	1979–80	Faisalabad
Bradman, DG	234	Eng	1st	2nd	1946–47	Sydney
Simpson, RB	225	Eng	1st	4th	1965–66	Adelaide
Bradman, DG	212	Eng	2nd	4th	1936–37	Adelaide
Murdoch, WL	211	Eng	1st	3rd	1884	The Oval
Ponting, RT	209	Pak	1st	3rd	2009–10	Hobart
Ponting, RT	207	Pak	1st	3rd	2004–05	Sydney
Lawry, WM	205	WI	1st	2nd	1968–69	Melbourne
Border, AR	205	NZ	1st	2nd	1987–88	Adelaide
Chappell, GS	204	Ind	1st	1st	1980–81	Sydney
Collins, HL	203	RSA	1st	2nd	1921–22	Old Wanderers
Simpson, RB	201	WI	1st	4th	1964–65	Bridgetown
Chappell, GS	201	Pak	1st	2nd	1981–82	Brisbane
Bradman, DG	201	Ind	1st	4th	1947–48	Adelaide
Border, AR	200*	Eng	1st	4th	1993	Headingley

BOWLING (as captain)

Player	M	Balls	Mdns	Runs	Wkts	Avrge	Best	5wi	10wm
Armstrong, WW	10	1379	77	416	17	24.47	4-26	0	0
Benaud, R	28	10720	506	3559	138	25.79	6-70	9	0
Border, AR	93	2517	130	961	24	40.04	7-46	2	1
Bradman, DG	24	22	1	10	0	-	0-4	0	0
Chappell, GS	48	2131	96	683	23	29.70	3-49	0	0
Chappell, IM	30	716	27	298	6	49.67	1-4	0	0
Collins, HL	11	456	26	129	2	64.50	1-9	0	0
Giffen, G	4	1418	69	581	26	22.35	6-155	3	0
Gregory, DW	3	20	1	9	0	-	0-9	0	0
Hassett, AL	24	33	0	26	0	-	0-1	0	0
Horan, TP	2	16	1	5	0	-	0-0	0	0
Hughes, KJ	28	1	0	6	0	-	0-6	0	0
Johnson, IWG	17	2980	148	1096	39	28.10	7-44	1	0
Lawry, WM	25	6	0	6	0	-	0-6	0	0
Lindwall, RR	1	270	16	100	2	50.00	1-40	0	0
Noble, MA	15	2055	101	745	31	24.03	7-100	1	0
Ponting, RT	71	102	5	52	1	52.00	1-9	0	0
Ryder, J	5	413	16	180	5	36.00	2-29	0	0
Simpson, RB	39	4520	168	2037	41	49.68	4-45	0	0
Taylor, MA	50	18	1	11	1	11.00	1-11	0	0
Trott, GHS	8	786	18	396	11	36.00	2-13	0	0
Trumble, H	2	561	29	191	11	17.36	5-62	1	0
Waugh, SR	57	756	25	340	3	113.33	1-2	0	0

BOWLING (as player)

Player	M	Balls	Mdns	Runs	Wkts	Avrge	Best	5wi	10wm
Armstrong, WW	40	6643	330	2507	70	35.81	6-35	3	0
Benaud, R	35	8388	299	3145	110	28.59	7-72	7	1
Booth, BC	27	436	27	146	3	48.67	2-33	0	0
Border, AR	63	1492	69	564	15	37.60	3-20	0	0
Bradman, DG	28	138	2	62	2	31.00	1-8	0	0
Chappell, GS	39	3196	112	1230	24	51.25	5-61	1	0
Chappell, IM	45	2157	60	1018	14	72.71	2-21	0	0
Collins, HL	8	198	5	123	2	61.50	2-47	0	0
Giffen, G	27	4973	365	2210	77	28.70	7-117	4	1
Gregory, SE	52	30	0	33	0	-	0-4	0	0
Harvey, RN	78	414	23	120	3	40.00	1-8	0	0
Hassett, AL	19	78	2	52	0	-	0-52	0	0
Horan, TP	13	357	44	138	11	12.55	6-40	1	0
Hughes, KJ	42	84	4	22	0	-	0-0	0	0
Johnson, IWG	28	5800	182	2086	70	29.80	6-42	2	0
Lawry, WM	42	8	1	0	0	-	0-0	0	0
Lindwall, RR	60	13380	403	5151	226	22.79	7-38	12	0
McDonnell, PS	13	52	1	53	0	-	0-11	0	0
Morris, AR	44	111	1	50	2	25.00	1-5	0	0
Noble, MA	27	5104	260	2280	90	25.33	7-17	8	2
Ponting, RT	75	437	18	190	4	47.50	1-0	0	0
Ryder, J	15	1484	55	563	12	46.92	2-20	0	0
Scott, HJH	5	28	1	26	0	-	0-9	0	0
Simpson, RB	23	2361	85	964	30	32.13	5-57	2	0
Taylor, MA	54	24	2	15	0	-	0-15	0	0
Trott, GHS	16	1105	29	623	18	34.61	4-71	0	0
Trumble, H	30	7538	423	2881	130	22.16	8-65	8	3
Waugh, SR	111	7049	307	3105	89	34.89	5-28	3	0
Wessels, KC	24	90	3	42	0	-	0-2	0	0
Yallop, GN	32	192	5	116	1	116.00	1-21	0	0

BIBLIOGRAPHY

Baum G, *The Waugh Era: The Making of a Cricket Empire 1999–2004* (ABC Books, 2004)

Beecher E, *The Cricket Revolution* (Newspress, 1978)

Benaud R, *Anything But ... An Autobiography* (Hodder & Stoughton, 1998)

Border A, *Beyond Ten Thousand: My Life Story* (Swan Publishing, 1993)

Bradman D et al, *Bradman to Chappell* (Australian Broadcasting Commission, 1974)

Bradman D, *Farewell to Cricket* (Hodder & Stoughton, 1950)

Cashman R et al (eds), *The Oxford Companion to Australian Cricket* (Oxford University Press, 1996)

Chappell I, *A Golden Age: Australian Cricket's Two Decades at the Top* (Pan Macmillan, 2006)

Chappell I, *Chappelli* (Hutchinson, 1976)

Crowley B, *A Cavalcade of International Cricketers* (Macmillan, 1988)

Gibson A, *The Cricket Captains of England* (Cassell, 1979)

Giffen G, *With Bat and Ball* (Ward Lock & Co, 1898)

Gilchrist A, *True Colours: My Life* (Pan Macmillan, 2008)

Guha R (ed), *The Picador Book of Cricket* (Picador, 2001)

Haigh G, *The Big Ship: Warwick Armstrong and the Making of Modern Cricket* (Text Publishing, 2001)

Haigh G, *The Border Years* (Text Publishing, 1994)

Haigh G, *The Summer Game* (Text Publishing, 1997)

Haigh G (ed), *Endless Summer: 140 Years of Australian Cricket in Wisden* (Hardie Grant Books, 2002)

Haigh G and Frith D, *Inside Story: Unlocking Australian Cricket's Archives* (News Custom Publishing, 2007)

Harte C, *A History of Australian Cricket* (Andre Deutsch, 1993)

Hutchinson G and Ross J (eds), *200 Seasons of Australian Cricket* (Macmillan, 1997)

Knox M, *Taylor & Beyond* (ABC Books, 2000)

Knox M, *The Greatest: The Players, The Moments, The Matches 1993–2008* (Hardie Grant, 2009)

Martin-Jenkins C, *The Complete Who's Who of Test Cricketers* (Rigby, 1980)

Miller A (ed), *Allan's Cricket Annual* (Allan Miller, 1996–99)

Moyes J, *Australian Cricket: A History* (Angus & Robertson, 1959)

Noble MA, *The Game's the Thing* (Cassell, 1926)

Perry R, *Captain Australia* (Random House, 2000)

Piesse K, *The Taylor Years* (Viking, 1999)

Pollard J, *Australian Cricket: The Game and the Players* (Hodder & Stoughton, 1982)

Ray M, *Border & Beyond* (ABC Books, 1995)

Robinson R and Haigh G, *On Top Down Under* (revised edition) (Wakefield Press, 1996)

Ryan C, *Golden Boy: Kim Hughes and the Bad Old Days of Australian Cricket* (Allen & Unwin, 2009)

Simpson B, *The Reasons Why: A Decade of Coaching, A Lifetime of Cricket* (HarperSports, 1996)

Taylor M, *Mark Taylor: A Captain's Year* (Ironbark Press, 1997)

Taylor M, *Time to Declare: An Autobiography* (Ironbark Press, 1999)

Waugh S, *Out of My Comfort Zone: The Autobiography* (Viking, 2005)

Webster R, *First Class Cricket in Australia Vol 1* (the author, 1991)

Webster R, *First Class Cricket in Australia Vol 2* (the author, 1997)

Whitington RS, *The Courage Book of Australian Test Cricket 1877–1974* (Wren Publishing, 1974)

Wisden Cricketer, *Story of the Ashes: Cricket's Greatest Rivalry by the Writers Who Were There* (Wisden Cricketer Publishing, 2009)

Wisden Cricketers' Almanack (John Wisden & Sons, 1992–2008)

Wisden Cricketers' Almanack Australia (Hardie Grant Books, 1998–2005)

INDEX